THE
LEARNING PARADIGM
COLLEGE

THE
LEARNING PARADIGM
COLLEGE

JOHN TAGG

Palomar College

Foreword by Peter T. Ewell

ANKER PUBLISHING COMPANY, INC.
Bolton, Massachusetts

The Learning Paradigm College

ISBN 1-882982-58-4

Composition by Deerfoot Studios
Cover design by Frederick Schneider/Grafis

Anker Publishing Company, Inc.
176 Ballville Road
P. O. Box 249
Bolton, MA 01740-0249 USA

www.ankerpub.com

This book is dedicated to

Marilee,

who made it possible,

and

Dylan,

who makes it necessary.

About the Author

John Tagg is Associate Professor of English at Palomar College in San Marcos, California. He is coauthor, with Robert B. Barr, of "From Teaching to Learning: A New Paradigm for Undergraduate Education" (*Change*, 1995). For the past several years, he has conducted workshops and made presentations at many colleges and universities on organizational transformation and the Learning Paradigm.

Table of Contents

Foreword

Some two years ago, I received a manuscript from John Tagg in my capacity as an Executive Editor of *Change* magazine. Entitled "Building the Learning Paradigm College... From the Ground Up," it was intended to build on an article coauthored with Robert Barr called "From Teaching to Learning: A New Paradigm for Undergraduate Education" that had appeared in November 1995—arguably the most widely cited piece that *Change* has ever published. The 60-page manuscript in front of me was dense, delightful, and serpentine. I knew immediately I could not use it. I wrote John saying that the piece was too long for us and that we could perhaps think about running something dedicated to just one of the many themes he addressed. Ironically, I also told him that I thought the piece was not long enough; inside it was a book struggling to get out. I have no idea how John felt when he got my reply. Letters of rejection, however politely worded, are never easy to write or receive. But I like to believe that he experienced a moment not unlike one he describes in this volume when Michael Bassis, president of Olivet College, broke through a faculty impasse about which of many particular strands of curricular reform to pursue by saying "why not do it all?"

The Learning Paradigm College is, quite simply, a remarkable book. Since the mid-1980s with the publication of such reports as *Involvement in Learning* and *Integrity in the College Curriculum,* we have seen enormous ferment around the edges of the American undergraduate experience. Myriad movements—collaborative learning, learning communities, service learning, learning assessment, and technology-mediated learning (to name only a few)—have graced our landscape. Each now boasts a cadre of dedicated followers, a distinctive language, a network of conferences and consultants, and a deeply felt sense of manifest destiny. We have learned a lot from these experiences. But transformation of the kind envisioned by the groundbreaking reports of more than 20 years ago have yet to occur. John tells us why the organizational structures and cultures of our institutions—what he calls our dominant paradigm for teaching and learning—won't let us go there. So long as we are centered on instructional delivery, instead of the central act of students making meaning from their encounters with problems and new knowledge, well-intentioned reforms will never take.

Though simple, this observation is both revolutionary and subtle. For one thing, it helps explain the sometimes-maddening reaction of many faculty when they first encounter what John calls the Learning Paradigm—"don't we already do that?" I believe that the vast majority of faculty *do* care deeply about student learning and are committed personally to trying to improve it. But they can't get outside their own experience and, unable to, are apt to resent critiques of current instructional practice as attacks on their own competence and commitment. In this volume, John does a particularly good job unpacking why we have such a hard time getting beyond our current frames of reference. From the architecture of our classrooms, through the ways we handle instructional time and dissect content by subject, to the forms we use to account student academic achievement, they quietly institutionalize everything we do. And lacking a new conceptual starting point that's outside the world we now inhabit, we simply don't see it.

In helping us to see, John doesn't argue with us. His language remains compellingly that of the veteran classroom teacher—encountering every day pedagogical problems of a very personal nature to come to very personal insights about how we might see differently. But his parables are systematic, passionate, and relentless. They are backed by the best of cognitive science and educational research, and are illustrated by an array of examples of best practice drawn from many kinds of institutions. John is the first to say that he cannot present a finished blueprint for the Learning Paradigm College. Instead, once taught to see, he relies on *us* to work through his many examples from our own perspectives—and to build our own blueprint. Once we start doing this, he has us hooked. We are making meaning of this material for ourselves, to inform our own practice, just as we'd hoped our students might do.

Indeed, an important premise of this work is that we have to begin it from inside our students' heads. As a foundation for his argument, John presents a compelling research-based picture of how most students experience the act of schooling. They quickly learn the rules of classroom instruction and how to play by them. They pass tests and amass credentials. And they appear listless and dull in classrooms, while animated and inquiry-oriented once they leave them. Understanding how students view themselves as learners and how they construct the task of learning may be especially important for us as card-carrying academics because, as good kids who liked school, most of us probably did not experience classrooms in this way. Yet when asked about our own most powerful personal learning experiences, most of us would likely quote examples drawn not from school but from family, friends, and real-life situations.

This work also means that we need to take assessment seriously, not as the kind of accountability-based external mandate that many faculty think of first when they hear the "A-word," but as rich and meaningful feedback about our own performances. I have always maintained that the essence of assessment is nothing more than the act of turning the basic principles of scholarship, in which we all were trained, back onto our own practice of the arts of teaching and learning. As John emphasizes, we need to recapture this meaning for assessment and engage in reflective practice about our work in the same spirit of inquiry that we pursue our scholarship—no matter what the outside world may ask for.

But most of all, this work is about integrity—about each of us walking the talk that we say we believe. As John reminds us, students are better observers than we give them credit for. If we set low expectations and hurry to the next appointment, they will react accordingly. But if we take each opportunity to confront a question or solve a problem as a new personal challenge—and aren't afraid to say we don't always know the answer—they will start seeing what learning really looks like. One of the most powerful moments for me personally in reviewing this book was John's point about the need to create good beginners—students aware that they will never finish their learning and will always be starting over the task of acquiring new knowledge and skills. We are all perpetual beginners in this business, even though each time we begin we may know more and be able to do more. In this spirit, after I wrote him two years ago, I am profoundly glad that John began again.

Peter T. Ewell
Vice President
National Center for Higher Education Management Systems
October 2002

Preface

BACKGROUND AND PURPOSE

This book grew out of a sense of the incongruity between the goals of my work and the means available to achieve those goals. It seemed that the more seriously I took the task of teaching, the more difficult it became, and many of the difficulties seemed to be a product of the overall design of the system in which I worked. I suspect that many who work in colleges and universities have similar experiences. When my colleague Robert Barr first explained to me his formative theory of the Learning Paradigm, it clarified a great deal that had to that point been obscure. He provided me, to use a metaphor I shall return to often, a new lens through which to see my work and its institutional setting. He and I embarked upon a joint project of refining and clarifying that theory that resulted in our article "From Teaching to Learning: A New Paradigm for Higher Education," published in *Change* magazine in 1995. I was surprised by the reception that our article received. It was widely read, widely duplicated, and widely distributed. It clearly struck a responsive chord with many in the higher education community. It also sparked vociferous criticism in some quarters. I was surprised by both the positive and the negative reactions, both by their quantity and their vehemence.

I have been fortunate to have had the opportunity over the past several years to present workshops and make presentations at a number of colleges and universities and to work with some organizations trying to shape the changes coming to higher education. In discussions with many colleagues in the United States and Canada, it has grown increasingly clear to me that there is a strong and increasingly coherent movement for purposeful change, change guided by principles and tested with evidence. Most conspicuously, many in (and outside of) higher education recognize that our institutions are not consistently achieving their fundamental purposes well, are not serving their students as they might. At the same time, people seem daunted by the barriers to initiating purposeful reform within institutional structures as they currently exist. Complicating the task is the fact, widely acknowledged, that while some institutional structures have become more rigid, students have changed. Many of today's students seem to call for educational tools that just aren't available to the conventional college.

So interest in different approaches is on the rise, as is frustration at the unanticipated difficulties posed by attempting to implement such approaches. And part of this frustration arises from the growing multiplicity of innovations available. The growth of technology has both reinforced and been reinforced by the growth of nonconventional providers of higher education. Polarizing debates have arisen concerning many of these alternatives. How shall we sort them out, pick and choose? With so much available, how can we tell what is promising and what threatening? These are important questions, but my impression is that much of the most rancorous argument is about subsidiary or even trivial questions. Many of the innovations that are most popular are merely tinkering with peripheral functions, leaving the flaws of core structures untouched.

It strikes me again and again that much of the difficulty we have in sorting out what to do derives from differences in perception. I have had the privilege of listening as an outsider to the conversations of faculty, administrators, and staff at a number of colleges about their own processes. In many of those conversations, people use certain key terms or concepts as placesavers or markers, without ever really exploring their underlying meaning. And often when someone tries to get to those underlying meanings, certain predictable things happen that result in changing the subject and deflecting the conversation. The root problem is how people see their own institutions and their own work. If they could agree on what they see when they look at the college, they could agree on what to do about it. But frequently two people, looking at the same institution, see very different things.

We need to see higher education through a new lens. And that is a process that I hope to facilitate with this book. By providing an interpretive framework for many of the familiar aspects of college work and college life, I hope to help readers see higher education in terms of the underlying functional relationship of core processes. If we can see how the structures of our institutions relate to the goals and purposes we are trying to achieve, we can see as well how we need to change them in order to better realize those purposes.

ORGANIZATION

So this book is an effort to organize the discussion of higher education reform and to propose a set of categories that lead that discussion in productive directions.

Introducing the Learning Paradigm

In Part I, I briefly summarize some of the evidence that the problems of higher education over the past 20 to 30 years have been remarkably persistent and impervious to large-scale reform (Chapter 1). I then address the phenomenon of widespread innovation that fails to achieve fundamental improvement (Chapter 2). The explanation for this pattern of difficulties lies in the implicit theory, the institutional paradigm, that governs most colleges and universities today: the Instruction Paradigm (Chapter 3). And the solution is to make a fundamental paradigm shift to the Learning Paradigm (Chapter 4). The material in Part I is similar to that presented, more briefly, in our 1995 article and is based on the foundational thinking of Robert Barr, which provided the framework for that article.

Understanding Our Learners

If we are to flesh out the idea of the Learning Paradigm, we need to begin by making a realistic assessment of the learners and deciding what kind of learning we aim to achieve. In Part II, I first offer an assessment of today's undergraduate learners (Chapter 5) and offer a framework for understanding their academic motivation and degree of involvement with learning (Chapter 6). This leads to an analysis of approaches to learning and a description of what student attitudes and practices colleges and universities should seek to promote (Chapter 7).

A Framework for Producing Learning

If we have an idea of who the learners are and what kind of learning we want them to achieve, we next need to determine how to produce that type of learning. To do so, we need to develop a framework for discussing what colleges do that is not derived from the formal properties of current institutional practice but that encompasses all of the factors that affect learning. In Part III, I suggest such a framework, a metaphor that encompasses flexibly the whole learning environment of the college, and a set of six analytical categories that we can use to examine and test a learning environment (Chapter 8). I then examine the Instruction Paradigm college using these categories and suggest in some detail why its failures are inherent to its governing paradigm and not merely the result of incompetence or accident (Chapter 9).

The Learning Paradigm: Six Essential Features

In Part IV, I offer a description of the essential features of the Learning Paradigm college. After an initial overview (Chapter 10), each chapter in this section explains one of the principles that should guide the Learning Paradigm college and then provides several institutional examples of colleges and universities that are implementing the principle or making very credible attempts to implement it (Chapters 11–16). The reason for presenting multiple examples of institutions is twofold. First, I want to point out that these principles can be applied by different kinds of colleges and universities, that they are not dependent on the Carnegie classification of the institution. Second, I want to suggest that different institutions can implement these principles in different ways, that the Learning Paradigm is not a rigid blueprint for specific changes but a flexible guide to ongoing experimentation and testing of institutional processes.

Becoming a Learning Paradigm College

Having described what the Learning Paradigm college should attempt to do, it remains to return to the practical question suggested in Part I of how colleges can change in fundamental ways. In Part V, I discuss the possibility of transformative change, first, by addressing some of the practical barriers that the Instruction Paradigm poses to reform in core processes (Chapter 17). Then I describe some of the scaffolding that institutions need to build in order to overcome these barriers and create leverage for long-term reform (Chapter 18). I conclude by suggesting that most, if not all, of what we need to do will emerge from an honest engagement with our work and our students, if we can see both through the new lens that the Learning Paradigm offers (Chapter 19).

CONCLUSION

I wrote this book to describe an alternative to the model of education in place in many institutions of higher education. I wrote this book to suggest that we are not forever bound to existing structures and their resultant strictures; changing the academy is indeed possible. I have seen such changes in action in the programs presented in this book. And I have seen the success and satisfaction—among administrators, faculty, and students—that accompanies these changes. I wrote this book to present a vision through a new lens, a vision that I believe more closely represents the experience we all yearn for in our colleges and universities.

John Tagg
October 2002

Acknowledgments

The ideas developed in this book are the product of conversations, exchanges, and collaborations with more people than I can count. I am grateful to all of them, even though I have space here to name only a few.

I owe a special debt of gratitude to my colleague and sometime coauthor Dr. Robert B. Barr. I am grateful to him, first, for creating and introducing to me the idea of the Learning Paradigm and much of the foundational theory on which this argument is based. Second, and equally important, I appreciate the many hours of conversation and collaboration, over a period of several years, through which my own thinking was tested and refined.

Robert McHenry reviewed the text in the first draft and provided careful and thoughtful advice that is reflected throughout the final product.

Several colleagues who have worked with me at Palomar College over the last decade have assisted in the development of these ideas. William Flynn, director for five years of the North American Conference on the Learning Paradigm, has been a frequent collaborator over the last several years who has also helped to put me in touch with a number colleagues at colleges and universities across the country. Dr. George Boggs, former president of Palomar College, continues as president of the American Association of Community Colleges to promote and advance many of the principles advocated here. Patrick Schwerdtfeger and Christine Barkley have been collaborators on many projects over the years and also provided useful feedback on several chapters as the text developed.

My colleagues in the Assessment of Learning Project (ALP) at Palomar constituted a real and purposeful community of practice focused on student learning for several years. Working with them refined and tested my own thinking about many of the issues discussed here. I am grateful for the hard work, dedication, and thoughtful engagement of Teresa Laughlin, Fari Towfiq, Robert Sterken, the late Cynthia Watson, Barbara Schnelker, Lee Kerckhove, Jose Esteban, Michael Arguello, Lise Telson, Gene Jackson, and Michelle Barton.

I appreciate the assistance of the many people in colleges and universities across the country who have assisted me in the research for this book.

Many are acknowledged in the text, but others are not. The following list is incomplete, but includes many of those who have been especially helpful: Louis Albert, Karen Anderson, Paul Anjeski, Julia Barchitta, Lois Bartholomew, Joan Bennett, Aaron Berman, Barbara Cummings, Amy Driscoll, Diane Doberneck, Barbara Duch, Thomas Ehrlich, Zohreh Emami, Donna Engleman, Scott Evenbeck, Frank Fear, Kathy Fear, Sandra Gregerman, Maria Hesse, Jeffrey Howard, Ann Leffler, Josina Makau, Christine Maslach, Marybeth Mason, Robin McCoy, Jean McGregor, Peggy Moe, Patrick Nellis, Jean O'Brien, Terrel Rhodes, Gail Robinson, Michael Rodriguez, Beth Ryan, Carol Geary Schneider, Robert Shoenberg, Jayne Rowe, Daniel Seanor, Barbara Leigh Smith, James Wallace, Jane Wellman, Catherine Wilson, Cynthia Wilson, Ralph Wolff, and Swarup Wood

Finally, my thanks to Susan Anker for her seemingly infinite patience and thoughtful editorial guidance throughout.

PART I

A NEW PARADIGM?

....

It was not an unusual experience, in the great scheme of things. Something like it has probably happened to you. But it was a defining moment for me. When I was in seventh grade—I think it was seventh grade—the school nurse came to our class one day and administered a standard vision test. You know, the one where you cover one eye and try to read the chart with rows of letters in decreasing size. That was the day I discovered I was nearsighted. I had had no idea until that day. My vision had probably been gradually deteriorating for a year or more, so gradually that I never perceived a difference. I thought that what I saw was what everybody saw. I thought that what I saw was just what was there to see.

My parents, of course, took me directly to an optometrist, who prescribed corrective lenses, which were ordered forthwith. A couple of weeks later, we went to pick them up. During both visits to the optometrist, I was able to view the eye charts with the new lenses, and that was interesting. But an eye chart is not in itself very interesting, and it was something I had seldom seen before. Seeing the eye chart was not much like seeing normal things. The optometrist's office was a long, narrow room with blank walls, equipment, and the eye charts. The eye chart was the only object at any distance. There wasn't much to see. So when I picked up my new glasses and put them on for the first time I was pleased, but in a sort of abstract way.

The long, skinny optometrist's office was in a department store; it was actually situated at the back of the department store, so you had to walk the whole length of the store to reach it, and the whole length of the store again to reach the door. The department that immediately adjoined the optometrist's office sold small kitchen appliances: mixers, blenders, toasters, that sort of thing. When we opened the door and stepped out of the optometrist's office the first thing I saw—it was on a shelf perhaps 15 feet away—was a blender: a bright white base with a tall glass beaker on top of it capped with a white lid. I remember it vividly even though I saw it for just a few seconds over 40 years ago. I have no recollection—none whatso-ever—of the optometrist himself. I know it was a man, but I couldn't tell you whether he was tall or short or what color hair he had or what he was wearing. But the blender shines like the Morning Star in my memory.

The optometrist and my parents were close to me. They didn't look much different after I put on my glasses than they had before. But the world at a distance, the world I had walked through to get to the op-tometrist's office, was completely different when I left the office than it had been when I entered it. And the first harbinger of that difference was the blender. Seeing it, a common and familiar household object, at a dis-tance, I was shocked, amazed. I experienced, for one of the first times in my life, awe.

My eyes did not, of course, rest on the blender. I looked up, and around, at the mixers and the toasters, then down the isle to the pots and pans and farther to the televisions, and all around at the people. *Every-thing* was different. Everything, I knew, was the same. I had just walked past the same shelves, many of the same people. But it was all completely different. The lines of objects were so clear, so fine. The old blurry world I had passed on the way in had been resculpted in 20 minutes time, and now everything bore clean, sharp edges and carried a burden of detail that seemed impossible. We passed sofas and chairs with fabric bearing clearly discernable patterns and varied but precisely delineated textures. We saw lawn mowers with clear, metal handles and small knobs, etched with a pre-cision that seemed to approach the absolute. We passed paint cans with utterly precise lettering covering their labels and hammers with distinct claws and saws with fine, sharp teeth so clear that they were frightening. As we walked through the store I gasped in amazement. *Everything* was different. There was more of everything, yet in the same space.

And then we reached the door and stepped outside. And I saw the most remarkable thing that I had ever seen in my life. Those of you who wear glasses perhaps know what I'm talking about. I saw trees. It probably wasn't really the first time. I must have seen them when I was younger, but I had forgotten. To me it seemed like the first time. I *saw* trees. Trees, as it turned out, were not large masses of fuzzy green. No, trees had leaves, so many leaves! More than you could ever count. There must have been millions. Because each individual tree bore such an abundance of leaves on each branch, and so many branches—it was, in the literal and substantial sense of that much-abused word—overwhelming. I think I physically stepped back from the force of it. Of course, I knew trees had leaves. I had seen leaves up close. What I was denied was the experience of abundance, of pattern, of complexity, of—well, you know. You've seen trees, haven't you? I have rarely been overwhelmed, I mean really overwhelmed, but I was then. My eyes were filled so full with sight that I didn't know if I could bear it.

I got used to it. Within a week or so the world seemed more or less normal again. But for a long time I reveled in the pleasure of all that detail, all the world there was to see. I never forgot. I began to learn on the day I got my first pair of glasses that the way you see the world depends on you as much as it depends on the world. I say I began to learn that because it took many years for the lesson to take firm shape—and I don't think I am quite finished learning it yet. I had been seeing everything thorough defective lenses for so long that I was deceived about what was right in front of me. And the worst deception was that I did not even know I had been deceived. New lenses changed everything. And that was not a metaphor or a hyperbole. They really did change everything.

I share this experience, right at the beginning, in part to explain my affection for the lens metaphor, which I will use repeatedly in the following argument. Beyond that, there is no particular point to it, except perhaps this: When we see through a new lens, it is impossible ever to go back to thinking of the world the way we did before. I will be urging you, over the upcoming pages, to see your work and the places where you work through a new lens.

1 The Challenge

THE PROBLEM OF PURPOSE

What are colleges for? Like many such questions, this one is often ignored because it is so important. And it is most likely to be ignored by those of us who work in colleges. It is to you—the teachers and administrators, the librarians and registrars, the deans and counselors who do the daily work of higher education—that this book is chiefly addressed. I am addressing you about the nature of your work and the places where you work because I believe—contrary to much you may hear elsewhere—that the future of higher education is in your hands. I think that we—for I am one of you—have lost sight of some things that are essential in our work, and I hope to call those things to mind. The places where we work are so familiar to us, the schedules and rules so constant, the routine so natural that we can easily come to assume that they have always been that way. In a way, we—or anyone who works in the same environment for a long time—become a bit myopic about our environment just as a function of having been in it for a long time. We cease to notice what our environment implies about the purposes and goals of our institutions. "The things we see every day," G. K. Chesterton wrote, "are the things we never see at all." The ubiquitous features of the organizations for which we work become invisible to us, and we cease to notice how powerfully they affect our lives, and our students' lives.

The fact that we do not notice the structures of our organizations does not mean that we like them. Indeed, in my experience, most colleges are beset by an underlying dissatisfaction, a sense that things don't fit quite right. This shows itself often in complaints and conflicts that recur in slightly modified form over the years. One feature of this dissatisfaction is a pattern of blame. Frequently, groups or individuals within the college see themselves as victims, an innocent and well-intentioned us besieged by the ignorant or venal them. I want to suggest that at most colleges the visible enemy—the them that is blighting our lives and impeding our work—is not the enemy at all. The real root of our most persistent and pernicious problems is the invisible enemy, the one we don't see because we see it every day: the organizational paradigm governing our institutions. Our organizational paradigm is like a lens: We don't see it; we see through it, but it determines how we see everything else. Like a lens, we can test it, we can look at it and discern its properties. We can even learn to correct for its deficiencies. If we can make the invisible visible, we can begin to see the way out of our most persistent problems.

One place to start in thinking through that way out is to recognize that our problems, the challenges that we meet every day, are indeed persistent. Today we hear a good deal about "accountability," variously defined. Higher education systems and institutions seem to be a focus of critical attention from several directions. But the key criticisms of what colleges are doing have recurred for at least a quarter of a century—much longer in some cases—and have been expressed first within the academy.

When I speak of *colleges* I mean undergraduate colleges, both within and independent of universities, the institutions that prepare students for the baccalaureate degree. Colleges, in this sense, were the core institutions that gave birth to the modern research university, the sprawling state university, and the multitasked community college. Whether one thinks that the undergraduate college should be the core of the modern university in the sense of the heart, the functional center, may depend on where one stands. But when most people hear the word "college," their first thought is of the places where undergraduates go to get a college education. Certainly research, scholarship, graduate and professional education, and community service are important and valuable roles for universities and colleges to perform. But here I want to focus on the original and still important purpose of undergraduate education.

So, how well are undergraduate colleges doing? How well do they work? That brings us back to the prior question: What are they for? Or to put it a little differently, what should a college education mean? Perhaps, to get our bearings, we might ask, what *does* it mean? The people who hold the answer to that question are the students. What is their answer? Consider this reflection by a University of Michigan senior:

> So you get here and they start asking you, "What do you
> think you want to major in?" "Have you thought about what
> courses you want to take?" And you get the impression that's
> what it's all about—courses, majors. So you take the courses.
> You get your card punched. You try a little this and a little

that. Then comes GRADUATION. And you wake up and
you look at this bunch of courses and then it hits you: They
don't add up to anything. It's just a bunch of courses. It
doesn't mean a thing. (Willimon & Naylor, 1995, pp. 57–58)

HOW ARE WE DOING?

I begin every semester—I teach writing at a community college—by asking all of my students to describe their goals for the course, inviting them
to be as expansive and personal as they wish. The predominant goal is a
grade—sometimes an "A," sometimes just a good grade. One student, as
honest as he was outspoken, wrote what many others were thinking but
were afraid to publicly state: "I want to get this class out of the way, and
get all the others out of the way, and get that diploma so I can get out of
this place and get a job."

Is college, for many of our students, a barrier rather than a path? Is it
something to be gotten out of the way, over, past? Is college mainly a hoop
for jumping through? Certainly not for all, but probably for many.

What are these students missing? What can we who know better point
out to them, other than higher salaries for those who jump through the
hoops? What does college accomplish for students?

That question has been addressed with increasing persistence within
the academic community for the past two decades. And it has been addressed most often on the assumption that colleges exist to bring about
some significant outcomes for and in the students who attend them. In
1984 the Study Group on the Conditions of Excellence in American
Higher Education, a blue-ribbon panel assembled under the auspices of
the National Institute of Education, published its report, *Involvement in
Learning: Reclaiming the Potential of American Higher Education*. The
Study Group expressed serious concerns about many aspects of higher education, including the lack of clear standards and the increasing size of institutions. They pointed out that the measures conventionally used to assess institutional performance—"endowments and expenditures, the
breadth and depth of curricular offerings, the intellectual attainments of
faculty, the test scores of entering students"—were merely inputs to institutions that served as "proxies for educational excellence": "None of them
tells us what students actually learn and how much they grow as a result of
higher education. As a result, we have no way of knowing how academic

institutions actually perform" (p. 15). The report made a series of recommendations for fundamental change in colleges and universities that still bear up well, nearly 20 years later.

In 1985, the Association of American Colleges (AAC, now the Association of American Colleges and Universities, AAC&U) assembled a select committee under the leadership of Mark H. Curtis, then president of the AAC, to address "the loss of integrity in the bachelor's degree." Their statement, *Integrity in the College Curriculum: A Report to the Academic Community*, asserted that "evidence of decline and devaluation is everywhere" (p. 1). Examining the curriculum, the group concluded that "What is now going on is almost anything, and it goes on in the name of the bachelor's degree" (p. 4). These two reports triggered widespread discussion and may have helped to provoke more research into the question of just what colleges were accomplishing.

In 1991, Ernest T. Pascarella of the University of Illinois, Chicago, and Patrick T. Terenzini of the Center for the Study of Higher Education at The Pennsylvania State University published their massive volume *How College Affects Students: Findings and Insights from Twenty Years of Research*. They reviewed most of the research on the impact of higher education for the previous 20 years. Their findings were detailed, nuanced, and not easy to summarize. But after weighing the evidence from a variety of sources on the cognitive and emotional development of students they concluded that

> There is little consistent evidence to indicate that college selectivity, prestige, or educational resources have any important net impact on students in such areas as learning, cognitive and intellectual development, other psychosocial changes, the development of principled moral reasoning, or shifts in other attitudes and values. Nearly all of the variance in learning and cognitive outcomes is attributable to individual aptitude differences among students attending different colleges. Only a small and perhaps trivial part is uniquely due to the quality of the college attended. (p. 592)

Alexander Astin, a leading member of the study group and director of the Higher Education Research Institute at the University of California at Los Angeles (UCLA), began to study the effects of college in the 1960s, gathering longitudinal evidence on students as they progressed through college and beyond it. He reported the conclusions of this initial

research in his 1975 book, *Four Critical Years.* In 1993, he updated the
results in a new study, *What Matters in College:* Four Critical Years *Revisited.* Astin drew his data from the Cooperative Institutional Research
Program (CIRP), administered by the Higher Education Research Institute at UCLA, "the largest ongoing study of the American higher education system, with longitudinal data covering some 500,000 students and
a national sample of more than 1,300 institutions of all types" (Astin,
1993, p. 4). Using the input-environment-outcomes (I-E-O) model,
Astin tried to find out how colleges changed their students, what value
they added beyond what students brought with them to the college environment. The results were distressing. And the trends that Astin observed were disturbing. He noted that research on higher education had
identified a number of characteristics that seemed to have a positive impact on student learning; for example, small institutions were more effective than large ones, residential colleges more effective than commuter
colleges, full-time programs more effective than part-time. Yet the
growth of higher education ignored these findings:

> [M]any of the policies that seemed to govern the expansion of
> public higher education during the years following the Second
> World War were really at variance with what was suggested by
> the research.... My conclusion ... was that these contradic-
> tions existed because policy makers had been guided more by
> *economic* than by *educational* considerations.... (1993, p. 434)

This led to a tension, if not a direct contradiction, between what institutional leaders said and what institutions did:

> Institutions espouse high-sounding values, of course, in their
> mission statements, college catalogues, and public pro-
> nouncements by institutional leaders. The problem is that the
> explicitly stated values—which always include a strong com-
> mitment to undergraduate education—are often at variance
> with the actual values that drive our decisions and policies.
> (1993, p. 235)

Using research of this kind, in 1993, nine years after *Involvement in
Learning,* the Wingspread Group on Higher Education, chaired by former
Labor Secretary William Brock and including several prominent college
presidents, surveyed the collegiate prospect. They cited the Department of

Education's National Adult Literacy Survey (NALS), which found that "surprisingly large numbers of two- and four-year graduates are unable, in everyday situations, to use basic skills involving reading, writing, computation, and elementary problem-solving" (p. 5). The Wingspread Group concluded:

> A disturbing and dangerous mismatch exists between what American society needs of higher education and what it is receiving. Nowhere is the mismatch more dangerous than in the quality of undergraduate preparation provided on many campuses. The American imperative for the 21st century is that society must hold higher education to much higher expectations or risk national decline. (p. 16)

THE URGE TO INNOVATE

The critique of higher education is ongoing, and it has not been ignored. The growing evidence that undergraduate education is not adding value for students as it should has inspired many efforts at reform. Colleges and universities have reexamined assessment, pedagogy, course design, advisement, and the entire architecture of undergraduate education. Accrediting agencies, professional organizations, government agencies, and private foundations have provided a variety of incentives and opportunities for colleges to innovate. If we look at the lists of the major publishers in higher education over the last decade of the century recently concluded, we could easily come to see the 1990s as the Decade of Innovation in higher education.

But it is hard to resist the conclusion that, in terms of significant innovation for student learning, the whole amounts to less than the sum of the parts. Gary Quehl, William Bergquist, and Joseph Subbiondo (1999) of the Center for the Study of Innovations in Higher Education, reflecting on the last half of the 20th century—the "'Golden Age of Innovation' in American higher education"—conclude that "many educational innovations were relatively short-lived because they were unable to compete for scarce resources with vested practices or were unseated by the force of conventional wisdom" (p. 2).

Consider the centerpiece of efforts to improve learning outcomes at colleges: assessment of student learning. It should go without saying that unless institutions have reliable information on the actual outcomes of educational programs for students, they are in no position to improve those outcomes. Hence an obvious step toward adding value for students is to measure their learning. On this principle, the North Central Association of Colleges and Schools, the accrediting organization for over a thousand institutions in 19 states, in 1989 embarked on an initiative to require significant student learning assessment at all colleges. A decade later, in 1999, Cecelia Lopez, associate director of the association's Commission on Institutions of Higher Education, reviewed the progress of this effort. She concluded, "After ten years of steady effort, the major lesson the commission has learned from its assessment initiative is that it is not easy to gain universal acceptance of the efficacy of assessing student learning" (p. 5). A national survey conducted by the National Center for Postsecondary Improvement (NCPI, 1999) in the same year found "fairly substantial institutional activity in collecting student-assessment data" (p. 53). At the same time, "Perhaps the most disappointing finding was that institutions reported they are not using student-assessment data very extensively in academic decision-making, and they believe this information has little or no impact on institutional performance..." (p. 56). As Ted Marchese, executive editor of *Change* magazine and a longtime leader in reform efforts, concluded, the assessment movement "has produced widely observed rituals of compliance on campus, but these have had only minor impacts on the aims of the practice—to improve student learning and public understanding of our contributions to it. To say the least, this is a disappointment" (p. 4).

As with assessment, so it is with pedagogy and changes in faculty roles to emphasize student learning outcomes. Marvin Lazerson, Ursula Wagener, and Nichole Shumanis (2000) of the Institution for Research on Higher Education at the University of Pennsylvania reviewed the substantive progress of reform efforts in colleges and universities at the end of the last century. They concluded, "a genuine teaching-learning revolution seems far away" (p. 19). They found that "While the repertoire of innovative teaching practices grows, we are uncertain that institutional leaders are connecting incremental changes to *systemic* strategies for making teaching and learning a central, highly rewarded activity on their campuses" (p. 19).

INNOVATION IS NOT TRANSFORMATION

Kay M. McClenney (1998), vice president of the Education Commission of the States, was speaking about community colleges, but her summary of the state of higher education reform at the end of the century applies to the whole of undergraduate education:

> The reality is that innovation does not equal transformation, and multiple innovations do not add up to fundamental change. Effective innovations are seldom effectively replicated. Even when replicated, innovations seldom change institutions or systems. Evidence of this fact is widely available and equally widely ignored. It is convenient to ignore because otherwise we might have to disrupt the status quo. In fact, the willingness to allow innovation on the margins is a way of containing it, preventing it from contaminating "core functions." Innovation on the margins relieves pressure on the institution to create more essential change. (p. 1)

Reform of higher education faces a problem of scale. Exciting experiments abound but have only slight impact on business as usual. Successful innovations seem to have no longer a shelf life than unsuccessful ones. Public avowals of institutional leaders are often radically at odds with the actual conduct of institutions. The rhetorical "students" who are the subject of much concerned commentary and commitment in speeches and vision statements often have no relevance at all to the way institutions treat the flesh-and-blood students who actually attend classes, drop classes, and receive grades and diplomas. As Terry O'Banion (1997), founding president of the League for Innovation in the Community College, puts it, innovations that fail to change the fundamental processes of institutions amount to little more than "trimming the branches of a dying tree" (p. 1).

Many who have engaged in discussions of these issues at their own campuses have wobbled away from those conversations with an unnerving sense of vertigo. The ground seems to shift even as they speak. There often seems no solid foundation, no clear common purpose that they can call upon to stabilize perceptions and arguments. The reason is that, even as we gather more evidence and marshal more arguments about educational performance, most institutions cannot claim with any plausibility to have reached a clear and consistent answer to the question that began this chapter: What are colleges for?

The Problem of Scale: Why Innovations Don't Transform Colleges

SAYING AND DOING

Why is it so difficult to get colleges to do what they say they want to do? If we read the pronouncements of college presidents, the statements of mission or purpose in college catalogs, and the expressed standards of accrediting agencies, we get the clear impression that colleges are primarily dedicated to providing an education of the highest quality to all of their students. But we find that innovations intended to achieve that very result are often mired in bureaucracy, buried in regulations, hampered by apathy, or limited by inadequate resources. And when such innovations are successful by educational standards, they often do not expand; other institutions do not imitate them, and they are seldom provided with the infrastructure of institutional support that leads to permanent status. Educational innovations suffer from a problem of scale. Widespread experimentation does not lead to large-scale improvement. We can almost say that, in the realm of innovations for learning in higher education, nothing fails like success. Institutions, offered the chance to affirm their own espoused values, won't take yes for an answer. There are, of course, exceptions. Indeed, this book is largely devoted to highlighting those exceptions. They are growing in number, but they remain exceptions. The Wingspread Group (1993) concluded:

> There is a growing body of knowledge about learning and the implications of that knowledge for teaching. What is known, however, is rarely applied by individual teachers, much less in concert by entire faculties. We know that teaching is more than lecturing. We know that active engagement in learning is more productive than passive listening. We know that experiential learning can be even more so. We know we should

12

evaluate institutional performance against student outcomes. We know all of this, but appear unable to act on it. It is time to explore the reasons for our failure to act. (p. 14)

Organizational theorists Chris Argyris of Harvard University and Donald Schön, late of the Massachusetts Institute of Technology (Argyris, 1982, 1992, 1993; Argyris, Putnam, & Smith, 1985; Argyris & Schön,1974, 1978, 1996), explored the question of saying one thing and doing another in an organizational setting. They concluded that individuals and organizations often hold two kinds of theories of action: one that governs what they say and a quite separate theory that governs what they do. They called these two kinds of theories espoused theory and theory-in-use.

Espoused Theories and Theories-in-Use

"Espoused theories are those that an individual claims to follow. Theories-in-use are those that can be inferred from action" (Argyris, Putnam, & Smith, 1985, pp. 81–82). The important insight here, confirmed through considerable research (Argyris, 1992), is that when individuals diverge from their espoused theories, they do not do so randomly or opportunistically, but according to an organized and patterned set of assumptions and rules, a theory:

> It is true that what people do often differs from the theories they espouse. We are saying, however, that there is a theory that is consistent with what they do, and this we call their theory-in-use. Our distinction is not between theory and action but between two different theories of action: those that people espouse and those that they use. One reason for insisting that what people do is consistent with the theory (in-use) that they hold, even though it may be inconsistent with their espoused theories, is to emphasize that what people do is not accidental. They do not "just happen" to act in a particular way. Rather, their action is designed; and, as agents, they are responsible for the design. (Argyris, Putnam, & Smith, 1985, p. 82)

The existence of these two parallel theories of action often leads to paradoxical and confusing consequences. While individuals are, by definition, aware of their espoused theories, they are often unaware of their theories-in-use. At the same time, their theories-in-use govern their behavior, while their espoused theories do not. "Although people [often] do not behave congruently with their espoused theories . . . , they do behave congruently with their theories-in-use, *and* they are unaware of this fact" (Argyris, 1982, p. 85). If I am acting on the basis of a tacit theory of which I am unaware (my theory-in-use), the consequences of my actions will often seem perplexing in light of the espoused theory of which I am aware, and which I therefore use as an assumed framework for thinking about my actions. Paradoxical consequences require an explanation, and if I am unaware of the contradictory theories at work in my own mind, I will tend to seek that explanation in the external environment, often in the behavior of others. This could explain much of the conflict and miscommunication that goes on in organizations.

Organizations as well as individuals hold espoused theories and theories-in-use. We can discover an organization's espoused theory by looking at the official pronouncements of leaders and spokesmen and examining its vision or mission statements. We can discover its theory-in-use by observing its organizational behavior: "In order to discover an organization's theory-in-use, we must examine its practice, that is, the continuing performance of its task system as exhibited in the rule-governed behavior of its members" (Argyris & Schön, 1978, p. 16).

PARADIGMS

Institutions of higher education, like other organizations, often espouse theories that differ from their theories-in-use. Furthermore, complex organizations frequently employ several separate or overlapping theories-in-use. At a certain level of generalization, the multiple theories of action that govern an organization converge in a consistent, rule-generating and boundary-defining framework: an organizational paradigm. The term "paradigm" refers to an example that serves as a model. The philosopher and historian of science Thomas Kuhn (1970) applied the term to the whole construct of assumptions and rules that create the framework in which a scientific community operates. Thus, astronomers who worked in the framework of Ptolemy's cosmology adopted one paradigm, which Copernicus replaced with another. Aristotelian dynamics likewise gave way to Newtonian. Scientific paradigms are thus built around examples of theory or experiment that provide models for further scientific work, and they give rise to the rules of science, both limiting and generating rules for the conduct of working scientists.

Organizational Paradigm

An "organizational paradigm," as I will use the term here, consists of the framework of examples, models, and rules that define the boundaries of the organization's proper activities and that generates new rules governing those activities. Thus an organizational paradigm is the overall theory-in-use of the organization. The people working in the organization are often unaware of major elements of the paradigm that governs their behavior. Much of what we know about organizational paradigms we know only tacitly. We learn it only by living through examples of organizational behavior that reflect the paradigm. Why is it that new members of an organization, even after reading all of the manuals and going through the official training, often have no sense of what the organization is really like? For the same reason that old hands know all the unwritten rules and can correct the newcomers instantly in concrete cases. The paradigm that governs an organization often cannot be—or never is—explicitly stated. But through living and working in an organization, one learns the paradigm through experiencing examples that define it in practice.

The answer to the question with which we began this chapter—why don't colleges do what they say they want to do?—lies in the nature of the organizational paradigm that governs most colleges.

Instruction Paradigm

Robert B. Barr (1995) first identified the overall theory-in-use of most colleges and universities as the Instruction Paradigm. In the Instruction Paradigm, the mission of colleges and universities is to provide instruction, to offer classes. The successful college, by Instruction Paradigm standards, is the one that fills classes with students and thus grows in enrollment.

The Instruction Paradigm has taken hold of higher education since the Second World War (Tagg, 1998). In its present form, the Instruction Paradigm incorporates many organizational characteristics that have developed during this period. It took root at a time when colleges, especially public institutions, experienced rapid growth and developed a standardized national framework for the transfer of credit, similar course requirements, and nearly identical course design. The student credit hour or "Carnegie unit"—the standard of an hour per week in class as the metric for educational activity—emerged late in the 19th century as a tool to achieve both quality control and increased efficiency for colleges, at about the same time Frederick J. Taylor was improving the productivity of factories by segmenting work into measurable units and maximizing their efficiency through time-and-motion studies (Drucker, 1968, 1993). Both developments were useful at the time, and both came to be misapplied as contexts changed. With the growth of college enrollment after the Second World War, the student credit hour became the means for transforming colleges into factories for the production of transferable credits for a burgeoning and mobile population. As Peter Ewell (n.d.) points out, "degree levels in this country have become almost exclusively defined in terms of the hours of classroom time required to complete them." This implies, of course, a correspondence between classroom time and educational value. "The system of student transfer is built on the assumption that courses with equivalent titles and credits represent the same learning experience— of content and developed competence—at all institutions" (Schneider & Shoenberg, 1998, p. 18). This has always been an assumption; no institutions have ever tested the assumption empirically in more than a trivial way. But given this assumption, along with the pressure to provide access to increasingly large numbers of students, the standardized national system of transferable course credit provided the soil in which the Instruction Paradigm could germinate and grow. Today, "transfer has become so pervasive that at many public institutions, both two- and four-year, the transfer process controls the academic program" (Schneider & Shoenberg, 1998, p. 17).

Alexander Astin was largely right when he explained the counterintuitive course taken by higher education since the war. He was correct, of course, in noting that colleges had not merely ignored the advice of research on educational effectiveness but had moved resolutely in the opposite direction. And we can hardly doubt his view that "policy makers had been guided more by *economic* than by *educational* considerations..." (1993, p. 434). But this is a bit too simple. For many policy makers, the meaning of "education" had changed. Formal processes had become the purpose of the institutions. Courses, which the funding mechanisms of public colleges had made the economic backbone of the institutions, had come to define the educational mission in the Instruction Paradigm. The mission of colleges became putting more students in more classes. For most colleges in a highly standardized and interdependent system of transferable credit, a means—offering courses—had become the end, if not the definition, of higher education. Experiments around the edges rarely touched this central theory-in-use. As Barr (1998) notes, "Without a vision and design for the whole of the system, incremental changes do not add up to anything significant" (p. 23). Innovations that explored other means, alternative processes of doing what colleges claimed to be doing, could survive on the periphery, but such experiments could not gain purchase on the core of the institutions—not because they were good or bad but because they were simply irrelevant to what colleges had come to be: factories for the production of full-time-equivalent students (FTES), transcript-generating machines.

An organizational paradigm conditions the way we see the organization we work in, and a paradigm that is widely, but tacitly, held by many organizations and that generates the tools and standards of organizational commerce and communication powerfully shapes perceptions. The Instruction Paradigm has become not only the rules of the game in higher education but the lens through which many who work in colleges see their own institutions and their roles in those institutions.

3 The Instruction Paradigm: Process Before Purpose

MEANS AND ENDS

The fundamental flaw of the Instruction Paradigm is precisely that it substitutes a means for an end. It raises formal organizational processes (courses, transcripts) to the level of institutional mission. In the Instruction Paradigm college, maintaining and expanding the paradigmatic process of delivering instruction is what makes the college a college, what defines it as an institution of higher education. Instruction, of course, is generally a good thing. But it is an instrumental good. Teaching is valuable if and when it leads to learning, but not otherwise. Instruction in three-unit college classes often leads to learning, and when it does, to the extent it does, it adds value for students and for society. It can be a useful tool. But it is only a tool. When we make the production of tools the objective and ignore what the tools were meant to achieve we produce warped priorities and incoherent plans. To say that the mission of a college is instruction is like saying that the mission of General Motors is to produce assembly lines or that the mission of a hospital is to keep its beds filled (Barr & Tagg, 1995).

When we confuse the means and the end we freeze the means. If colleges exist to produce instruction, then activities that aren't instruction, however the paradigm defines it, are simply excluded. And if instruction produces diminishing value, if it becomes a less effective tool, this fact is concealed from us.

It is not necessary here to examine the Instruction Paradigm in detail or to provide an abundance of examples of its manifestations. If, as I am suggesting, the Instruction Paradigm is the global theory-in-use of most colleges, then readers who work at colleges need only look around their own institutions to find examples of it in abundance. But a brief outline will help to clarify where to look.

THE CORE: A MODEL OF TEACHING

The mission of a college in the Instruction Paradigm is to provide instruction, conceived mainly as offering three-unit lecture classes and modest variations. As Carol Geary Schneider, president, and Robert Shoenberg, senior fellow at the AAC&U (1998), point out, "The modal course, as all know, is three credit hours, which is defined as a set number of periods in the classroom. All sorts of modifications or equivalents are possible, but the three-credit course is the standard coin of the realm" (p. 17). At the core of the Instruction Paradigm is a conception of teaching as the transmission of information from teachers to students. The paradigm thus emerges from a model of pedagogy that defines and gives value to everything else in the institution.

John Biggs (1999), a scholar of teaching who has taught in schools of education in Canada and Hong Kong as well as his native Australia, describes three levels of thinking about teaching. In the first, the focus is on what the student *is:* "learning is a function of individual differences between students"; in the second, the focus is on what the teacher *does:* "learning is a function of teaching" (p. 21). His description of these two levels of thinking vividly characterizes the central assumptions of the Instruction Paradigm, beginning with level one:

> The view of university teaching as transmitting information is so widely accepted that delivery and assessment systems the world over are based on it. Teaching rooms and media are specifically designed for one-way delivery. A teacher is the knowledgeable expert, the sage-on-the-stage, who expounds the information the students are to absorb and report back accurately, according to their ability, their motivation, even their ethnicity.... The curriculum is a list of items of content that, once expounded from the podium, have been "covered." How the students receive that content, and what their depth of understanding of it might be, are not specifically addressed. The language is about what the teacher does, not what the student does. Level One is founded on a *quantitative* way of thinking about learning and teaching...which manifests itself most obviously in assessment practices. Learning outcomes are quantified into units of knowledge of equivalent value: a word, an idea, a point. These are either correct or incorrect, and

> converted by a common currency, usually a percentage, to
> make them interchangeable. The number of units accrued
> becomes an index of learning ability. (pp. 21–22)

Level one is a *"blame-the-student* theory of teaching, based on student deficit. When students don't learn . . . , it is due to something the students are lacking . . ." (p. 22).

Level two, in which learning is a function of teaching, "is still based on transmission, but of concepts and understandings, not just of information" (p. 22). Thinking about teaching in this model places the responsibility for effective transmission on the teacher, rather than the student. Hence, it "is also a deficit model, the blame this time being on the teacher" (p. 23).

Both level one and level two thinking about teaching fall within the Instruction Paradigm. The basic model is of the teacher delivering instruction to students. The paradigmatic example of instruction is the single teacher lecturing to listening students. (Level 3 is described in the next chapter.)

There are options within the Instruction Paradigm. But they are restricted. If we are left with the options of level one or level two within a closed system, the result is inevitably a zero-sum game, and we are ultimately condemned to declining levels of performance and increasingly rancorous disputes over who will get the blame for the decline. Both level one and level two thinking imply a zero-sum model of responsibility: "a win-lose or zero-sum notion of responsibility . . . is useful for assigning blame. If one party is responsible, then another is not" (Barr, 1998, p. 24). Evidence from outside the system that could point the way to improvement tends at once to reinforce the existing structure of the system and incapacitate efforts for significant improvement. All evidence of decline in student performance (lower test scores, employer complaints, grade inflation) rebounds upon the party responsible for the decline.

In such a system, since the basic process model is fixed, it is in the self-interest of the participants to deflect blame. Thus, organizational defensive routines come to govern much interaction. Argyris (1992) defines defensive routines as "any action or policy that prevents human beings from experiencing negative surprises, embarrassment, or threat, and simultaneously prevents the organization from reducing or eliminating the causes of the surprises, embarrassment, and threat" (pp. 102–103).

The Instruction Paradigm college generates many such defensive routines. And the polarity of either level one or level two thinking about instruction creates a framework of ready-made defensive routines. When problems arise under level one, the organization has only three choices: 1) increase resources (more money for smaller classes, more books, better support facilities), 2) raise the level of incoming students (selective admissions) or 3), when those approaches aren't available or don't work, move to level two: teach harder. If students aren't doing their job, the only thing we can do about it is to improve teaching. But when pressures arise under level two, the only defense faculty members see in this framework is to retreat to level one again: We've invested in professional development and honed our instructional skills, and the students still aren't learning; it must be the students' fault!

On the playing field of the Instruction Paradigm, this cycle of blaming the students and blaming the teachers tends to be reenacted, frequently enlivened by the auxiliary defensive routine of blaming the administration. One result is that the players tend to repeat the same moves over and over again over a period of years and even decades. Faculty members and administrators who have watched this dynamic play itself out over many years often come to believe that there really is nothing new under the sun, at least in the self-contained world of colleges and universities. The only thing more predictable than the repeated debates is their lack of consequence. It is in the nature of organizational defensive routines to allow free exercise of blame and self-righteousness while insulating the system from fundamental improvement. It was perhaps observing this process at work that led Daniel Patrick Moynihan to observe that "The reason people get so emotional about academic politics is that so little is at stake."

STRUCTURE

An organizational paradigm both determines and is determined by organizational structure. Peter Senge (1990) of M.I.T. points out that "systemic structure" does not just refer to

> ... structure outside the individual. The nature of structure in
> human systems is subtle because *we* are part of the structure.
> This means that we often have the power to alter structures
> within which we are operating.

> However, more often than not, we do not perceive that
> power. In fact, we usually don't see the structures at play
> much at all. Rather, *we just find ourselves feeling compelled to*
> *act in certain ways.* (p. 44)

By "structure" I mean "those features of an organization that are stable over time and that form the framework within which activities and processes occur and through which the purposes of the organization are achieved" (Barr & Tagg, 1995, p. 18). As Senge points out, the people in the system are part of its structure and their behavior can alter and shape that structure. But because systemic structure is, like other aspects of the organizational paradigm, invisible to us, we are much more likely to be shaped by it than to consciously shape it. Structure in this sense places some tools for some tasks ready to hand and removes or obscures others. As Abraham Maslow famously observed, "if you only have a hammer then you treat everything like a nail." If you only have a lecture, you treat everything like a three-unit class.

The Instruction Paradigm imposes an atomistic structure on most colleges. That is to say, the parts are prior to the whole, and both limit and determine the character of the whole. Because it is rooted in an example of a single process, it facilitates the duplication of that example with some variations but resists radical reshaping of the process. "In its universe, the 'atom' is the 50-minute lecture, and the 'molecule' is the one-teacher, one-classroom, three-credit-hour course. From these basic units the physical architecture, the administrative structure, and the daily schedules of faculty and students are built" (Barr & Tagg, 1995, p. 19). The college is a collection of classes, and the classes are, or at least seem, prior to the college; they are what the college is made of. As Barr (1998) points out, "All manner of problems are solved in the Instruction Paradigm by offering another three-unit course. If students are failing to learn to think critically, then offer a course in critical thinking. If students think that ethics is irrelevant to business, then offer a course in business ethics" (p. 24).

We can see the basic atomistic structure of the Instruction Paradigm college in virtually every aspect of its organization and functioning. We will consider how this structure affects five subsystems of colleges: faculty and administration, curriculum, calendar, assessment and pedagogy, and criteria for success and accountability.

FACULTY AND ADMINISTRATION

Harking back to an older conception of the university, we might well think that the faculty is the core of the institution, and that was certainly the case for the first universities and for American colleges for a long time. But it is no longer true of undergraduate colleges. To the extent that their work is relevant to the education of undergraduates, "the faculty" can be defined at most colleges as the people who teach the classes. Or, to put the same thing a little differently, they are the academic employees of the institution who are not administrators. Beyond that it is hard to find much that all faculty members have in common. The faculty as a collegial community of scholars involved in a shared project survives in the rhetoric of education but is hard to find at most institutions. Members of the faculty are, of course, important people in the life of a college, people with great influence; however that influence *at the institutional level as it affects undergraduate students* is largely exercised through the academic departments. At most colleges, academic departments hire faculty members, and academic departments in the Instruction Paradigm college derive their power from their role as depositories for classes. Administrations, to the extent they are involved in undergraduate education, are largely structures for organizing and channeling the activities of departments. Departments may have once derived their integrity from some reasonable consensus about bodies of knowledge or the approaches they took to scholarship, their academic disciplines. But it is hard to defend the view that in today's college academic disciplines have much coherence except as the rhetorical window-dressing of departments. William Schaefer (1990), professor of English and formerly executive vice-chancellor at UCLA, points out:

> The way disciplines presently are and long have been divided into departments is arbitrary. Why, for instance, should the study of literature be spread across ten or more departments while the study of history is generally encompassed in one? In foreign language departments, why is the literature of a particular country but not its history or philosophy or art normally taught? Why, if we choose to divide the cake geographically, do we not have a department of "France" or of "China"? Why not study the past in comprehensive chronological units with departments of "The Nineteenth Century" or "Nineteenth Century Europe" or "Nineteenth Century

America" rather than separating scholars (and courses) concerned with those periods into a dozen or more departments? Or are such chronological-geographical divisions still viable at all? (p. 47)

While the disciplines that form the traditional basis of many academic departments are grounded in history, the scholarship of the very faculty members who make up those departments increasingly calls into question the arbitrary dividing lines between them. Schneider and Shoenberg (1998) observe:

> If "department" and "discipline" ever were synonymous in the ways the model implies, they certainly are no longer so. The degree to which a discipline represents a paradigmatic structure of knowledge that provides, in and of itself, a viable organizational principle for undergraduate learning is called into question by the increasing interdisciplinarity of both student interests and faculty behaviors, not only in their teaching but in their research as well. The scholarly concerns of individual faculty members within almost any academic department encompass a wide diversity of topics and methodologies, often those primarily associated with other disciplines. One anthropologist may be studying evidence derived from analysis of tooth enamel in different cultures; another working in the same department may be producing a history of ideas about race and biology. One economist may be studying principles of supply and demand as they affect all markets even as a colleague pursues a comparative cultural analysis of family economic decision-making. (pp. 13–14)

Yet departments thrive as the chief organizing framework for the instructional work of colleges. In Schaefer's (1990) words, "departments have a life of their own—insular, defensive, self-governing, compelled to protect their interests because the faculty positions as well as the courses that justify funding those positions are located therein" (p. 43). If the bricks that make up the college are courses, departments serve as the frames, the lumber that aligns and supports the bricks as they are stacked higher and higher.

CURRICULUM

The word that Instruction Paradigm colleges use to designate the total range of classes available to students is "curriculum." Over 90% of undergraduate colleges offer students a "distributional" curriculum (Astin, 1993). This means that students confront lists of courses subdivided in various ways and select from the lists, much like selecting various dishes from the options laid out on a given day in the cafeteria. Some classes or groups of classes in the distribution are required for some or all students, but wherever possible students are given multiple options to meet a given requirement. With few exceptions, the grouping of courses taken at a given time and the sequence of courses in the student's college career are left up to the student.

In Latin, the word "curriculum" means "a race or racecourse," implying a purposeful movement toward a goal. In the Instruction Paradigm college, "curriculum" means a list of classes, a basket of instructional bricks to be stacked, in any order. "To express its perceived incoherent, hodgepodge character, this distribution system has been variously and irreverently dubbed a supermarket, cafeteria, grab bag, or green-stamp endeavor (accumulate credits, paste 'em in, and redeem 'em for a diploma)" (Gardiner, 1994, p. 34). Because separate departments, each competing for its own share of enrollment, produce the curriculum, we should expect them to produce a basket of classes that have no very clear relation to one another, that are selected more for their difference than for their similarity. And that is what we find. We might well see when we look at today's college curriculum what Alfred North Whitehead (1929) found when reviewing the English school curriculum of 1917: "The best that can be said of it is that it is a rapid table of contents which a deity might run over in his mind while he was thinking of creating a world and has not yet determined how to put it together" (p. 7).

As Biggs (1999) suggested in the previously quoted passage, "The curriculum is a list of items of content that, once expounded from the podium, have been 'covered'" (p. 21). The metaphor of "coverage" is intrinsic to the Instruction Paradigm and seems to bring with it a set of assumptions that are widely accepted, and rarely if ever tested, about the relationship between class coverage and student development. It would, of course, be an easy matter to test these assumptions, especially as they relate to the curriculum taken as a whole. We might, for example, pose this question to all seniors, to be answered in a short essay: "What core common questions were the educational experiences you have had at this college designed to address, and how and how well did they address those questions?" The reason such a "test" is never given is that it would primarily test, not the students, but the curriculum. It would therefore address one of the underlying assumptions of the Instruction Paradigm that there is a coherent relationship between "coverage" and learning, that the curriculum gets students somewhere in particular (rather than any place more or less at random). If we are honest, we will have to say that the highest marks for clarity, accuracy, and honesty at most colleges today would have to go to the student who responded "They haven't; they didn't." We would also have to rate very high the response of that senior we heard from in the first chapter, "It's just a bunch of courses. It doesn't mean a thing."

CALENDAR

The academic calendar is determined by what the college does. What the Instruction Paradigm college does is offer classes. All classes are alike, so all classes are of the same length: a semester or a quarter. I have conducted an informal poll of faculty and staff from a number of colleges over the past few years—about 25 colleges ranging from small, private liberal arts colleges to research universities to community colleges. While I have not kept precise count, the total number of respondents now certainly exceeds 5,000. I pose this question: "How many of you would say this yourselves, 'I learn all subjects at the same rate'?" Then I ask for a show of hands. So far, the count is something in excess of 5,000 *no*, and 0 *yes* votes. Not even as a joke or an act of protest has anyone ever said yes to that question. Yet all of these people, without exception, work at institutions designed on the premise that all students could answer yes to that question. The theory-in-use of colleges, as enacted in the calendar, is that all students learn all subjects at exactly the same rate, and that all students learn at the same rate as all other students. (The theory, which some may hold, that the density of learning is maintained in different classes by adjusting the content in light of the difficulty is never in fact tested with students. And there are no common standards shared by the faculty members who design classes in different disciplines to maintain equal content. It is all guesswork, and no matter how accurate the tuning of content may be, it always assumes that all students learn at the same rate.) The National Education Commission on Time and Learning (1994) addressed the premise of a standardized length for all courses:

> If experience, research, and common sense teach nothing else, they confirm the truism that people learn at different rates and in different ways with different subjects. But we have put the cart before the horse: Our schools...are captives of clock and calendar. The boundaries of student growth are defined by schedules...instead of standards for students and learning.

The number of weeks in a semester, like the courses in a student's schedule, is for all practical purposes randomly determined. While it has historical roots, there are no persuasive grounds for believing that the semester is a framework that works well for most students. Indeed, some research indicates that a much shorter term leads to better results for conventional courses (Logan & Geltner, 2000). Results in many courses would lead us to suspect that many students would profit from a longer time to complete their work. The root problem that the commission identified, that boundaries are set by schedules rather than standards, flows directly from the Instruction Paradigm. The conventional schedules are aspects of conventional classes, and conventional classes define the Instruction Paradigm college.

ASSESSMENT AND PEDAGOGY

The nearly ubiquitous product of a college education is a transcript. And a transcript almost always consists of a collection of discrete end-of-term grades in discrete classes. The summary of the student's performance in the Instruction Paradigm college is the numerical average of all end-of-term grades, the grade-point average. The GPA is emblematic of the atomistic nature of the Instruction Paradigm college. The whole here is the numerical average of the parts, each part given equal weight, the sequence or pattern of the parts irrelevant in the computation of the average. The trajectory of the student through the curriculum, as well as the consistency or lack thereof in the student's work, is invisible in the GPA. Of course, the whole transcript tells a bit more than the GPA, but not much. Colleges preserve student transcripts and devote considerable resources to protecting their

integrity. The theory-in-use of colleges clearly includes the value that transcripts are permanently important documents.

The only artifact of student performance that the college preserves is
the record of end-of-term grades from discrete courses; students and
teachers alike get the message. Assessment of student work in courses
tends to be powerfully biased toward the simply quantifiable. As Biggs
(1999) described it earlier, "Learning outcomes are quantified into units of
knowledge of equivalent value: a word, an idea, a point. These are either
correct or incorrect, and converted by a common currency, usually a percentage, to make them interchangeable" (p. 22). I am not suggesting here
that college teachers by and large believe that such an approach is wise or
effective. But in the Instruction Paradigm college, to recall Senge's (1990)
characterization of the impact of organizational structure, "we just find
ourselves feeling compelled to act in certain ways" (p. 44). Indeed, the actual conduct of pedagogy, conditioned by the atomistic structure of Instruction Paradigm colleges, is probably an area where the espoused theories and theories-in-use of faculty members diverge most clearly. Lion F.
Gardiner (1994), associate professor of zoology at Rutgers University, concluded a survey of the research on classroom assessment in this way:

> Experience in colleges and universities and many published
> studies consistently suggest that faculty in this country care
> deeply about their students' developing higher-order cogni-
> tive skills. It is equally clear from the studies reviewed here
> that our tests do not generally assess such skills. Our tests are
> thus in all too many cases unable to produce evidence relevant
> to our students' reasoning. (p. 63)

As to the actual conduct of teaching, the contrast is similar. Research on
the efficacy of lecture as a means of instruction is clear and consistent. As
Wilbert McKeachie (1999) of the University of Michigan summarizes it,

> A large number of studies have compared the effectiveness of
> lectures with other teaching methods. When measures of
> knowledge are used, the lecture proves to be as efficient as
> other methods. However, in those experiments involving
> measures of retention of information after the end of a
> course, measures of transfer of knowledge to new situations,
> or measures of problem solving, thinking, or attitude change,

or motivation for further learning, the results show differences favoring discussion methods over lecture. (pp. 66–67)

At the same time, "studies have repeatedly confirmed the pervasiveness of the lecture" (Gardiner, 1994, p. 38). The Instruction Paradigm college was designed, so to speak, for lecture. To do otherwise is like swimming upstream.

CRITERIA FOR SUCCESS AND ACCOUNTABILITY

The great frustration in some quarters over accountability flows directly from the fact that Instruction Paradigm categories are not translatable into meaningful statements about what those outside the academy care about. The Instruction Paradigm imposes upon colleges a formal definition of required tasks or processes, and the meaning of those tasks or processes can be expressed only in terms of other formal tasks or processes. It is easy to quantify the work of the Instruction Paradigm college because we can count repetitions of parallel forms with no regard for their meaning by any functional standard. Thus the numbers that most colleges report are largely self-referential: Enrollments and GPAs can be compared to equivalent figures from other colleges but not to any meaningful referents in the world outside the academy. Viewed from a functional perspective, however, these processes all turn out to be instrumental; the instructional forms are the means to ends, but the functional outcomes, the ends of educational processes, are shrouded in mystery—the college has nothing of substance to report about these outcomes. That was the critique that the *Involvement in Learning* report made in 1984, and it is still largely valid today.

The criteria by which most people must evaluate most colleges are simply irrelevant to any consequential outcomes. The available criteria are quantitative and determined by inputs. *U.S. News & World Report* has made these kinds of criteria famous in its rankings of colleges, and several other widely read magazines have followed suit. They assume, essentially, that colleges that have and expend more resources—that attract "better" students and more highly educated faculty, amass larger endowments, and build more labs and bigger libraries—are better. Russell Edgerton (1997), for 19 years president of the AAHE, wrote a thoughtful and influential white paper on higher education when he assumed the directorship of education programs at the Pew Charitable Trusts. He notes therein:

As nonprofit organizations, colleges and universities strive not to make annual profits but to achieve the more elusive goal of institutional excellence: to be "the best," whatever that may mean. The problem is, excellence is defined as having the best resources, including the most talented students and the most widely recognized faculty. Thus, the higher the SAT scores of the entering freshman class and the more renowned the faculty, the higher the "quality" of an institution is presumed to be. Few people ask whether the institution's resources are being used to produce gains in student learning.

To see the work of colleges in terms that have meaningful referents, we must change the system we use to think about the college. We must adopt a new paradigm, one that makes the purpose, rather than formal processes, of colleges as institutions the organizing principle of our thinking and acting.

The features of the Instruction Paradigm are so familiar to most of us that we have ceased to be aware of them as institutional choices, as options that were chosen at some point by institutional leaders. Our vision of the essential purpose of our institutions has gradually deteriorated to the point that, without ever realizing it, we are functionally blind to the educational implications of the world we work in every day. We can see what is before us only if we look through a new lens.

The Route to Transformation: The Learning Paradigm, Old and New

A CLEARER VIEW

To transform colleges will require changing the governing organizational paradigm to one that places the end before the means. Barr has described this alternative paradigm as the Learning Paradigm (Barr, 1995, 1998; Barr & Tagg, 1995). What the Learning Paradigm proposes is simply to take hold of the horse and lead it to its proper position in the front of the cart, to put purposes before processes. "The key," as Edgerton (1997) points out, "is to think first in terms of student learning, and then reengineer the way academic work gets done from this perspective."

Where the Instruction Paradigm highlights formal processes, the Learning Paradigm emphasizes results or outcomes. Where the Instruction Paradigm creates atomistic structures, the Learning Paradigm creates holistic ones. Where the Instruction Paradigm attends to classes, the Learning Paradigm attends to students.

In the Learning Paradigm, the mission of colleges and universities is to produce student learning. This end is primary; the means are secondary and are to be judged by how well they achieve the end.

At the core of the Learning Paradigm is a model of the teaching-learning process that focuses on the learner learning. John Biggs (1999) calls this level three thinking about teaching. The focus in level three is on "what the student does":

> Level three sees teaching as supporting learning. No longer is it possible to say: "I taught them, but they didn't learn." Expert teaching includes mastery over a variety of teaching techniques, but unless learning takes place, they are irrelevant; the focus is on what the student does, on what learning is or is

not going on. . . . Getting students to understand at the level required is a matter of getting them to undertake the appropriate learning activities. This is where a level three, student-centered theory of teaching departs from the other models. It's not what *we* do, it's what *students* do that is the important thing. (p. 24)

In order to completely embrace level three thinking, we—faculty members, administrators, and staff—must ourselves take responsibility for student learning as the goal and product of our work. But to do so, we must free ourselves from the zero-sum mental model of responsibility. In the Learning Paradigm,

> When one takes responsibility, one sets goals and then acts to achieve them, continuously modifying one's behavior to better achieve the goals. To take responsibility for achieving an outcome is not to guarantee the outcome, nor does it entail the complete control of all relevant variables; it is to make the achievement of the outcome the criterion by which one measures one's own efforts. In this sense, it is no contradiction to say that students, faculty, and the college as an institution can all take responsibility for student learning. (Barr & Tagg, 1995, p. 15)

Where the Instruction Paradigm is atomistic, the Learning Paradigm is holistic. That is to say, where the Instruction Paradigm sees the parts, the formal instructional processes, as prior to the whole, the Learning Paradigm sees the whole as prior to the parts. And the whole in question here is, of course, the whole experience of the students. Thus the Learning Paradigm is rooted in a view of students as integral beings, not merely functions of instructional processes. What counts in college is the value added for students, the growth in their knowledge, capacities, and abilities as a result of their college experience. Astin (1985) has described the purpose and function of college as talent development. His I-E-O model captures the concept of holistic growth:

> *Inputs* refer to the characteristics of the student at the time of initial entry to the institution; *environment* refers to the various programs, policies, faculty, peers, and educational experiences to which the student is exposed; and *outcomes*

refers to the student's characteristics *after* exposure to the environment. Change or growth in the student during college is determined by comparing outcome characteristics with input characteristics. (1993, p. 7)

Note that the effort here is to consider the impact of the whole college environment on the student, and to look at the overall impact of college as a learning environment, not the isolated impacts of the parts. In other words, we are concerned with how college changes students, how they are different for having been immersed in a given college as learning environment.

TRYING NEW APPROACHES

What difference will the holistic view of students as learners make to the way we would design the learning environment? A large part of the remainder of this book is devoted to answering that question in a reasonably specific way. But we can certainly say this initially: If we do not take the parts for granted as the inherent structures of college, we will take a much more expansive and experimental view of how the many and varied processes involved in a college education interact. If we start with the assumption that any learning environment we design will be constructed of three-unit semester classes terminating in letter grades, and that if it is not constructed of these parts it is irrelevant to our project because it isn't really a college, then we are bound to produce a minor variation on what we already have, with all of its limitations and inadequacies. But if we look at three-unit classes, semesters, grades, and the rest as options to be viewed alongside the whole range of student experiences, we may find that activities on the periphery of the Instruction Paradigm college are actually closer to the core of students' learning experience than those we have thought were more central.

If we begin by asking students what *they* think has been important in their own education, we may find ourselves examining options that we were unaware even existed. And if we then construct research designs that allow us to test the learning efficacy of various environmental experiences in a sophisticated way, we may discover that student experiences interact in ways that are completely unaccounted for by the Instruction Paradigm college. In fact, I will suggest that we have already done these things, at least enough to make a preliminary design of the Learning Paradigm college that we can use as a basis for further development. That is what I will outline in Part IV.

I will not attempt here to parallel the discussion of the Instruction Paradigm with a corresponding outline of the Learning Paradigm because that would be misleading in several ways. We can describe many of the characteristics of the Instruction Paradigm college fairly specifically because we have a large set of examples and a large body of research about them. But we have a small group of colleges that have more than a few years experience with serious transformation in the direction of the Learning Paradigm, and a larger group that have embarked recently on promising reforms. We would be ill advised to make the processes of any institution or group of institutions the touchstone for all of our thinking about transformation. The Learning Paradigm college needs to be a learning organization in the double sense that it is an organization that produces learning and an organization that learns. To take responsibility for student learning ultimately means not just to promote learning for students but to model it by becoming a learning organization (Senge, 1990).

Because they are rooted in and ultimately defined by standardized processes, Instruction Paradigm colleges are remarkably similar to one another. The various branches of the knowledge factory all use interchangeable parts. Learning Paradigm colleges will be much more different from one another. Colleges that are rooted in a vision of learning for real students will realize different visions for different students. While instruction is a unitary concept, learning is not. There is no single learning, fitting for all people at all times. Learning is fundamentally a process of changing to adapt to a changing environment, so we cannot prescribe in advance what everybody will need to learn.

SOME OBJECTIONS TO THE LEARNING PARADIGM

Indeed, this is one of the objections that has been made to the whole concept of the Learning Paradigm, that it is content-free. That is not quite accurate. It is not content-free; it is field-dependent. That is to say, the formulation of the Learning Paradigm for any given time and place is dependent on the environment, the learners, and the goals. The challenges that the environment poses, the capacities and attitudes the learners bring to the process of meeting those challenges, and the goals that emerge from the need to support the learners in meeting the challenges will be different in various times and places. What I propose to outline in the remainder of this book is not a definitive Learning Paradigm college for all times and places, but a set of principles appropriate to today's learners.

Before doing so, it will be helpful to consider some other objections that have been made to the basic idea of the Learning Paradigm.

It Reinforces Corporatization

One such objection is that the Learning Paradigm, with its emphasis on outcomes, reinforces the commercialization or corporatization of higher education. I think this is nearly the opposite of the truth. To the extent that these terms have any meaning in terms of the experience of students and are not just being used as counters to advance the speaker's political views, the commercialization of higher education has been the work of the Instruction Paradigm. It is the Instruction Paradigm knowledge factory that has turned students into widgets and education into an assembly line of interchangeable parts. The Instruction Paradigm drive to quantify has reduced assessment to standardized tests and GPAs.

Economic behavior is a source of rich and instructive metaphors that we can use to discuss educational processes, and I will use such metaphors extensively later on. Such metaphors can be useful when they clarify relationships by helping us to see them in a new light. They do not necessarily imply a kind of economic reductionism. The reductionism that we should fear has already taken place: Colleges have literally sold out educational values for increased revenue from increased enrollments, and they have been doing so for years. There is no way of addressing this decay of educational quality in the framework of the Instruction Paradigm because educational quality is not one of the quantifiable formal processes that the Instruction Paradigm counts as relevant. The natural trajectory of development in the Instruction Paradigm is that grades will get higher while learning declines. As we shall see, that has happened, and it will continue to happen until the theory-in-use of colleges changes.

The question of what learning is for and what learning is valued, whether students attend college to become liberally educated persons or to prepare for careers, is an important one, but one that I shall not attempt to address fully here. However, the Learning Paradigm does have some important implications for this issue. Those implications will become clear when we discuss the type of learning that we seek. But there is also a great deal of freedom for individual institutions to shape their own answers to these questions.

It Is a Straw Man

Some have suggested that the whole attack on the Instruction Paradigm is a straw-man argument because the Instruction Paradigm doesn't really exist. One critic suggested that "No one has ever defended the notion that the lecture is the ideal educational form or that the best scheduling and delivery option is the one-hour class.... There are no advocates for [the] instructional paradigm because there is no such thing" (Traverso, 1996, p. 2). I hope it will be clear by now that I am not at all suggesting that college faculty and administrators advocate the Instruction Paradigm. For the most part educators do not "believe in" the Instruction Paradigm; they merely follow it. That is because it is the theory-in-use of colleges as institutions. The espoused theories of educators are, by and large, more congruent with the Learning Paradigm. So even though faculty members do not defend "the notion that the lecture is the ideal educational form" we continue to lecture substantially more than we do anything else (Gardiner, 1994; Grubb, 1999). Though neither faculty nor administrators defend the notion "that the best scheduling and delivery option is the one-hour class," the one-hour class remains the dominant option that we do in fact schedule. And though, as Astin pointed out, leaders in higher education espouse the value of quality undergraduate education at every opportunity, the conduct of their institutions undermines that quality in a number of ways. Something fishy is going on here. Should not the fact that nobody will defend the Instruction Paradigm raise questions about why we are all enacting it? It appears very much as if there is a theory-in-use at work that we are unaware of, but because of which, as Senge (1990) suggests, "we just find ourselves being compelled to act in certain ways" (p. 44). The Instruction Paradigm is not a straw man; it is the animating spirit of the knowledge factory.

It Is Not a New Idea

Another criticism is that the Learning Paradigm is not a new idea. And, of course, it is not. The idea that colleges exist to help students to learn is as old as colleges themselves. It can be traced through the history of higher education. And, as we have already seen, it is explicit in the work of those theorists and researchers who have helped us for the past several decades to discover what was really happening at colleges and think through the consequences. Indeed, I suspect that the Learning Paradigm has been the espoused theory of most educators for a long time. I hope it is the theory that we would all, on reflection, believe and espouse. And we believe it, not because it is surprising or new, but because we recognize in it the essence of what we have already believed and embraced. Ultimately, most educators will see in the Learning Paradigm a reflection of themselves as they want to be and a vision of their institutions as they want to make them.

But it is worth making these two paradigms explicit in order to explain why we so often do not do what we believe we should. Contrasting the vision that so often drives our actions with the vision that inspires us and speaks to our hearts and minds helps us to see a way out. If we recognize that the Learning Paradigm is a real option, but not—for most of our colleges—a reality, then we are empowered to define how we want to be different, to articulate the change that we want to achieve, that we want to become.

Finally, let me acknowledge that it is tricky to compare paradigms, and it is easy to create confusion. When comparing alternatives, it is easy to fall into the assumption that the alternatives are polarized and mutually exclusive. But this is not the case. If we think of organizational paradigms as something like the rules of a game, including the description of the playing field, the relationship of the Instruction Paradigm and the Learning Paradigm is something like that displayed in Figure 4.1. The Learning Paradigm expands the playing field and allows us to move in areas that

Figure 4.1

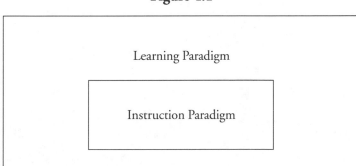

would be out of bounds in the Instruction Paradigm game. But we can still cover the same area we could in the old game. Anything you can do in the Instruction Paradigm you can still do in the Learning Paradigm: lecture, give multiple-choice tests, schedule three-unit classes. All of these moves will be legal in the new game, just as they were in the old one. The difference, and it is a vital difference, is that the object is different. The goalposts have been moved, so to speak. So we are headed for a different place, aiming for a different outcome. This diagram also reveals something else: the Learning Paradigm game is bigger. We have farther to travel to make a goal or score a point. That might look daunting. Indeed, it might be daunting. We will not be willing to play this larger game unless the goal is worth it. So we need to spell out that goal, and the moves and plays that it will take to reach it.

PART II

THE FOUNDATION:

THE LEARNERS AND THE LEARNING

Before we can define with any clarity how the Learning Paradigm college will be different from existing colleges, we must ask who the learners will be and how we propose that they learn. It is the essential task of the Learning Paradigm college to change people, to make them different from what they were, because learning is always change. So the foundation for clear thinking about this task is to ask whom we propose to change and how we propose to change them: who shall learn what and how shall they learn it? The first question, then, must be who are the learners? That is a question that cannot be answered fully in the aggregate. One of the first tasks of the Learning Paradigm college will be to answer that question more specifically for the particular body of learners who present themselves to a particular college. But I believe that there are certain generalizations we can productively make about the students who are entering colleges today. The most important characteristics of incoming students *as learners* are their attitudes and beliefs about colleges as learning environments and about themselves as learners. So we begin with a consideration of those questions (Chapters 5 and 6).

The question of what and how students should learn will obviously have many different answers for different students and different institutions. But here again, especially in considering how students should learn, we can make some useful generalizations that will provide guidance for designing effective learning environments (Chapter 7).

5 The Learners

WHAT DO THE LEARNERS BELIEVE ABOUT COLLEGE?

"Everyone seems to bemoan the fact that students just aren't what they used to be—that they are not as prepared or as motivated as they were in the 'good old days' of teaching" (Silverman & Casazza, 2000, p. 3). I am not in a position to comment on the "good old days," which I can't claim to recall with much clarity, but there is ample evidence that college students have changed over the years and that the students most likely to attend college today pose distinctive challenges. We cannot even begin to think productively about designing a learning environment appropriate to our time without attending first to the learners. And the place to begin is with the mental models of learning in an institutional setting—schooling—that today's students bring to today's colleges.

What, we will be asking here, are students' theories about the question that we encountered in the first chapter: What is college for? For students certainly have theories. And those theories are not based on a reading of the college catalog or mission statement. Students come to colleges with well formulated theories-in-use about schooling, about academic institutions in general, that are based on their own previous experience with schools. Robert Leamnson (1999), a biologist at the University of Massachusetts, Dartmouth, previews what we will discover about many incoming students:

> But certainly these young people must have learned something during those 19 years. They must be better prepared for college than a five-year-old. This is true. They have indeed learned a lot. Some of what they have learned, however, is counterproductive. Many will have habits, of mind and body, quite inappropriate for the task they are about to undertake. In the case of first-year students, a prominent element of teaching might be thought of as a reconstructing of the student mind. Making the difficult but necessary conceptual

changes might involve something like demolition before construction can begin. (p. 35)

American colleges and universities today probably have a wider and more varied mix of students than any system of higher education in the world. Nonetheless, a large majority of college students are under 25, so if we want to get an approximate idea of the capacities and limitations of today's college students, we will look to secondary schools.

While students have been learning all their lives, the assumptions and attitudes they bring to college will be based on their mental model of school learning. The default model for engagement with academic work that the vast majority of students bring to college is the one they formed in high school. Today, those students closest to their high school experience seem to pose the most serious challenge to colleges. A very high percentage of them fail to make the transition successfully, at least at first. Three-quarters of the students who receive a high school diploma enter some form of postsecondary education within two years after graduating (Education Trust, 2000). But "More than one quarter of the freshmen at 4-year colleges and nearly half of those at 2-year colleges do not even make it to their sophomore year" (Education Trust, 2000, p. 6). Returning students who have spent time in the world of work tend to be better students, by and large, than recent high school graduates. Yet even those often revert to mental models of schooling that they formed in K–12 when they reenter an academic setting.

So what can we say about the students who emerge from high school? Laurence Steinberg of Temple University reported on a ten-year study of more than 20,000 high school students in his 1996 book *Beyond the Classroom*. He paints a disheartening picture of the high school experience:

> [W]hen they are in school, a large proportion of students are physically present but psychologically absent. According to their own reports, between one-third and 40% of students say that when they are in class, they are neither trying very hard nor paying attention. Two-thirds say they have cheated on a test in the past year. Nine out of ten report that they have copied someone else's homework. (p. 67)

Most high school students in Steinberg's study spent no more than four hours a *week* on homework—in contrast with students in other industrialized countries, who spend four hours each *day* (p. 19). Only 20% of American high school students devote ten or more hours a week to homework (p. 68). Over a third report that they simply do not do the homework they are given (p. 68). Half say their classes are boring (p. 71). Peer pressure tends to work against academic achievement, a goal that does not inspire most high school students (p. 19).

Why is this? Is it that students don't realize the value of school? Quite to the contrary, most students recognize precisely the value of school. What they systematically fail to recognize is the value of learning. Here we come to a fairly explicit statement of students' theories about what schooling is for. "Do students believe in the benefits of schooling?" Steinberg asks.

> Students believe in the benefits associated with getting a diploma or a degree, but they are skeptical about the benefits associated with either learning or doing well in class. In other words, students believe that their success in the labor force will depend on the number of years of school they complete—they correctly believe that college graduates stand a better chance of getting good jobs than high school graduates...At the same time, however, they do not associate later success either with *doing well* in school...or with *learning* what schools have to teach. (p. 75)

THE SECONDARY SCHOOL FOUNDATION

In part, students are disengaged from school because the desired payoff—the diploma—requires no real engagement. Students correctly perceive that if they just "hang out" for four years and avoid incarceration, they will probably graduate. As the National Commission on the High School Senior Year (2001) concluded,

> American secondary schools appear to have been largely impervious to the reform energy of recent decades. Despite the efforts of many, the organization and structure of most comprehensive high schools look very similar to those of high schools of generations ago. High schools have stood still amidst a maelstrom of educational and economic change swirling around them. (p. 20)

This helps to explain why American students make less progress in high school than students in other industrialized countries do, than they themselves did in elementary and middle school, and than their predecessors in earlier generations did (Education Trust, 2000). These patterns should give us pause, because "the quality and intensity of high school coursework is the single most important determinant of who succeeds in college—more important than class rank or scores on college admissions tests" (Education Trust, 2000, p. 12). It should also give us pause because the pattern of disarray we see in high schools mirrors to a considerable degree the situation of the Instruction Paradigm college, as described earlier. The Education Trust (2000), in its report to the National Commission on the High School Senior Year, cautioned,

> For, in truth, most of the problems that characterize secondary education in this country—unclear and differential standards, uneven teaching, little curricular coherence—can be found in spades in higher education as well. Indeed, these two systems are intertwined in so many places that neither can solve its own problems without the other's cooperation. (p. 16)

I raise this point here merely to caution against two easy errors: the tendency to blame the high schools for the problems of higher education and the suggestion that we can solve those problems by closer contacts between high schools and colleges. While I think that closer contacts between high schools and colleges would be good, today both systems are largely locked in the Instruction Paradigm. (We will see an example later on of promising cooperation involving a university with an innovative curriculum.) We will not quickly find our way out of the wilderness with the nearsighted leading the myopic.

High school students today define the payoff of schooling almost exclusively in terms of external rewards. Steinberg found that "intrinsic motivation plays a relatively small role in motivating student performance in adolescence and beyond. . . . [T]he most common reason students gave for trying hard in school was not genuine interest in the material, but getting good grades in order to get into college" (1996, p. 74).

It is worth noting that this tendency seems to carry on into college. The 1993 survey conducted by the Carnegie Council on Policy Studies in Higher Education indicates that college students are in it largely for the money, and more so than in previous years: "Fifty-seven percent of undergraduates believe that the chief benefit of a college education is increasing one's earning power, an 11-percentage-point increase since 1976" (Levine & Cureton, 1998, p. 115). Perhaps even more arresting, "More than one-third (37 percent) admit that, if they thought attending college wasn't helping their job chances, they would drop out" (Levine & Cureton, 1998, p. 116).

WHY ARE BETTER STUDENTS BETTER?

To this point, we have been considering the whole range of high school students. How similar or different is the average student compared to the excellent student? University of Chicago psychologist Mihaly Csikszentmihalyi and his colleagues Kevin Rathunde and Samuel Whalen studied 200 talented students at two highly regarded high schools in the Chicago area and reported the study in their 1993 book *Talented Teenagers: The Roots of Success and Failure.* They selected the students for the study on the basis of teacher recommendations, confirmed by test results and other performance indicators. These students had already distinguished themselves as exceptionally talented in at least one of five domains: mathematics, science, music, athletics, or art. The researchers used the Experience Sampling Method (ESM), a technique in which subjects trained to fill out a questionnaire reporting their subjective states are given electronic pagers and instructed to report their experience when the pager beeps. The questionnaire, in this case, was designed to elicit information about the students' attention level, mood, and attitudes.

The researchers were able to examine students' attitudes in different circumstances. For example, they compared students in terms of volition (were they doing what they wanted to do?) and attention (what were they thinking about?) while in the corridors of the school, in the cafeteria, in classrooms, and while engaged in extracurricular activities. They found considerable variations in both volition and attention:

> In the classroom . . . attention is quite focused—an outcome that distinguishes talented from average adolescents. Yet motivation is quite low. Three fourths of the time when these talented teens reported from the classroom they did not want to do what they were doing. (p. 180)

Extracurricular activities pose a dramatic contrast with the classroom: "In fact, extracurricular activities evoke levels of concentration that rival the intensity of classroom examinations. Yet they do so in a way that sustains voluntary involvement" (p. 180).

The researchers compared student experiences in terms of the students' subjective sense of potency, esteem, challenge, skill, and involvement:

> The one fourth of the time when classes were experienced as voluntary, students did not have such strong feelings of potency, skill, and involvement as they did when involved in extracurriculars, but they reported equally strong feelings of success, satisfaction, and meeting one's expectations (self-esteem). Moreover, the level of challenge was typically higher than in extracurricular activities. When classwork was experienced as obligatory, on the other hand, students reported feeling worse at a statistically significant level than how they felt when involved in either voluntary classwork or extracurricular activities, on all measures except challenge. (p. 180)

Indeed, obligatory classwork uniquely had a negative effect on the students' sense of potency, esteem, skill, and involvement. The authors conclude:

> Obligatory classes appear to pose challenges that outstrip and depress a student's sense of skill and most other indicators of psychological well-being. Faced with such experiences, it is no mystery that teenagers typically do not want to be in class, even teenagers whose academic success might lead us to expect otherwise. (p. 180)

Good students and average students resemble one another in some ways and differ in others. Nearly all high school students are essentially disengaged from their mandatory academic work at an emotional level. If even the best students experience negative feelings of potency, skill, involvement, success, and self-esteem during mandatory classwork, we can assume that those negative experiences affect average students even more powerfully.

THE CHALLENGE: A DESTRUCTIVE THEORY
OF ACADEMIC ENGAGEMENT

Academic success or learning for its own sake in a classroom setting does not offer most students any significant personal rewards. If we separate learning and cognitive development in the classroom from the external rewards tied to it—grades, graduation, college admission—we discover that most high school students find learning in the classroom setting neither motivating nor rewarding and find failure to learn neither unpleasant nor threatening. Most of those students who thrive academically in high school do so through an exercise of will, managing to devote a high level of attention to matters they find intrinsically unrewarding.

The paradoxical truth seems to be that even students who demonstrate very high skills in a particular domain and thrive in extracurricular activities that test those skills often find classwork in the same domain uninspiring and unrewarding. Students who excel in the math club are often bored in math class. Superb student journalists often find their English classes tedious. And if this is true of excellent students, *a fortiori,* average students, for whom the level of challenge in standard course work is relatively higher and the sense of personal competence relatively lower, will find their classes even less rewarding.

And as we consider the state of incoming students, we need to make an effort of will to free ourselves from our own perspective and assume the student's. From the perspective of faculty and administrators, the chief characteristic of incoming students is that they are different from the students we have already come to know: They are new. And for many of these students, the college itself is new, and this newness is one of the most important tools we have, while it survives in the student mind. But while this college may be new, schooling is not. Indeed, incoming students are as familiar with schooling as with their own homes and as firmly entrenched in their attitudes toward it as toward any aspect of life. The groove of schooling is deeply etched in their psyches when they get to us. Leamnson (1999) puts it this way: "[C]ollege freshmen are, by and large, sick to death of school. Thirteen years is a long time by any standards, but for typical first-year college students it's 70% of their lives. Far too many see college simply as the last of the hurdles" (p. 35).

We must constantly remind ourselves when considering these issues that all students are individuals and that these generalizations apply with varying degrees of accuracy to most and not at all to some. General evidence about the nature of most students can guide us to formulate better policies, but they will guide us best if we do not exaggerate their significance. What we can say with fair confidence at this point is that most students who leave high school and enter college bring with them a set of attitudes and beliefs about schooling and their interaction with educational institutions that tend to insulate them against learning rather than to prepare them for it.

We need to explore more deeply the reasons why nonfunctional mental models of schooling take hold with many students, and we will do so in the next chapter. But we can say even at this point what is fairly clear, I suspect, to nearly everyone who teaches freshmen: One of the fundamental challenges that colleges face today is to change the way incoming students think about the school setting, about academic work, and about their own relationship to academic institutions. Unless colleges can change the attitudes and beliefs that disable many students as learners, most of their efforts to create effective learning environments will be ineffective.

6 Self-Theories and Academic Motivation

PERFORMANCE AND LEARNING GOALS

Students' beliefs and attitudes about schooling are intimately connected to their beliefs and attitudes about themselves. From the perspective of students, the purpose of college depends upon how they believe they can use college to achieve meaningful personal goals. And that in turn depends in large measure upon students' beliefs about themselves, their self-theories.

Research into student motivation and self-regulation has resolved many questions over the past few decades and has produced an increasingly vivid and nuanced description of the way students think about themselves and their learning (Covington, 1992, 2000; Silverman & Casaza, 2000.) Researchers have asked how students set goals and how their beliefs about themselves and their goals affect their behavior. Martin Covington, a psychologist at UC, Berkeley, and one of the premier researchers in the field of motivation, reports that there is broad agreement among many researchers that students tend to adopt one of two kinds of achievement goals: learning goals or performance goals.

> Although researchers have favored different designations for learning goals, such as task goals or mastery goals, there is general agreement that...learning goals refer to increasing one's competency, understanding, and appreciation for what is being learned. Likewise, there is general agreement that performance goals, whether referred to as ego goals or self-enhancing goals, involve outperforming others as a means to aggrandize one's ability status at the expense of peers. (Covington, 2000, p. 174)

Carol Dweck (2000), a psychologist at Columbia University, explains the distinction in this way. Performance goals are "about winning positive judgments of your competence and avoiding negative ones" (p. 15). With learning goals, on the other hand, your purpose is "increasing your competence" (p. 15). Performance goals aim at short-term effect and value appearances over substance; learning goals seek to increase long-term abilities.

Learning goals and performance goals are not mutually exclusive; one can value both the task itself and the outcome of the task. And both kinds of goals can be motivating. Indeed, they can complement one another (Hagen & Weinstein, 1995). However, many people tend to value one kind of goal over the other, though which kind of goals they set may be different in different domains of activity (Dweck, 2000). The evidence we reviewed in the last chapter indicates that students' implicit theories of schooling assume performance goals in academic contexts.

In general, a pattern of performance goals that excludes or minimizes learning goals inhibits learning. In the 1980s, Ohmer Milton, Howard Pollio, and James Eison (1986) developed an instrument to survey students and place them on what they called the LOGO (Learning Orientation/Grade Orientation) scale. The LOGO surveys attempted to identify students who set learning goals and students who set a specific type of performance goal: good grades. Along with the LOGO survey, the researchers had students complete five other survey instruments to evaluate their personality traits, study habits, levels of anxiety, and locus of control, among other factors. They found:

> When considering students [with high learning orientation and low grade orientation], one finds the following distinguishing personality traits: greater abstract reasoning ability; higher levels of sensitivity, self-motivation, and inner directedness; and a greater interest in new ideas and intellectual matters. These students also report lower tension and frustration levels. They are more inclined to trust personal hunches, preferring to look for possibilities and relationships rather than to work only with known facts. These students acknowledge the highest level of responsibility for personal actions (that is, high internal locus of control) and pay least attention to the importance of luck or fate (low chance locus of control scores) in determining their successes or failures. Academically, they employ the most effective study methods, hold the most positive educational attitudes, and report both

the highest levels of facilitating anxiety and the lowest levels of debilitating test anxiety. In short, they can be expected to impress instructors as intellectually and emotionally able, willing, and interested—and they are. (pp. 134–135)

In contrast, the researchers found that students with low learning orientation and high grade orientation

> ...are distinguishable by personality traits that include a strong desire to do the right things and to act in conventional ways.... [T]hey also report the highest levels of tension or anxiety.... They report the lowest degree of internal locus of control. These students reported the lowest levels of facilitating test anxiety and a consistent pattern of low scores on the study habits and academic attitude dimensions. Although these learners are anxious to do well in established and traditional sorts of ways—for example, they have a high level of concern for the grades they receive—they have poor study skills, high levels of debilitating anxiety, and a generally concrete manner of approaching tasks. (p. 135)

Benjamin Dykman (1998) of Washington State University has studied the relationship between goal choices and depression. He developed a Goal Orientation Inventory that would divide college students into validation-seeking individuals (performance goals) and growth-seeking individuals (learning goals). "Validation-seeking individuals" he writes,

> are those having a strong motivational need to establish or prove their basic worth, competence, or likability.... [They] show an accompanying tendency to appraise difficult or challenging situations as major tests or measures of their basic worth, competence or likability. In other words, validation-seeking individuals see their basic worth, competence, or likability as being "on the line" when faced with challenging or difficult situations. (p. 143)

In contrast, Dykman finds,

> Growth-seeking individuals are those who have a strong motivational need to improve or grow as people, develop their capacities, and realize their potential.... Thus, growth-seeking

individuals are willing to confront challenge or adversity in order to grow, improve, and reach their fullest potential. Stemming from these growth needs, growth-seeking individuals show an accompanying tendency to appraise difficult or stressful situations as opportunities for learning, growth, and self-improvement. (p. 143)

Correlating goal orientation with a number of other indices of academic and personal well-being, Dykman found a strong positive correlation between validation-seeking behavior and depression, and a strong negative correlation between growth-seeking behavior and depression.

The kinds of goals students set in an academic context are an important indicator of the students' self-theories. Learning goals, as the above research indirectly confirms, are a sign of what Albert Bandura (1997) refers to as "self-efficacy," the belief in a given context that one has the capacity to meet the challenges likely to be presented. One manifestation of self-efficacy is that "the extent to which students believe they will be successful in a particular course plays an important role in the types of goals they set for themselves as well as in the amount of effort they invest in working toward these goals" (Hagen & Weinstein, 1995, p. 45). Anastasia Hagen and Claire Weinstein (1995) describe the research findings concerning the results of high and low self-efficacy in a way that echoes the above description of students who set learning and performance goals:

> In achievement situations, students with high self-efficacy have been shown to actively participate in learning activities, show greater effort and persistence, and achieve higher levels of academic performance than students with low self-efficacy.... Even when experiencing difficulty, students with high self-efficacy tend to work longer and harder than students with low self-efficacy. Conversely, students with low self-efficacy frequently show less persistence and may attempt to avoid the learning situation altogether. (p. 45)

But while students' self-theories may to some extent determine their goal choices, those self-theories in academic settings also seem to be shaped by the experience of schooling. High school students, as we have seen, tend to see performance goals as implicit in the design of schooling. Students' choice of goals is an intersection where their theories of themselves meet their theories of schooling. Milton, Pollio, and Eison (1986), writing about college students, suggest that LO or GO orientation reflects the student's classroom experience:

> We feel that a student may be grade-oriented not because he
> or she necessarily wants to be, but because such an orientation
> is a plausible and situationally effective way of dealing with
> the traditional classroom environment as well as with early
> postcollege endeavors. In many instances, an instructor's
> classroom policies and procedures make such an orientation
> seem both logical and reasonable for the student. (p. 142)

I question placing the responsibility here primarily on the classroom instructor when the whole design of the classroom in most institutions places performance goals to the forefront. But the point that the students' experience of school conditions the goals they tend to frame in academic settings is beyond dispute. Students will adapt their own goals to the situational context. And students who see school as calling for more positive goal choices will make them. As Covington (1992) points out, "students who see schools as agents for promoting learning for its own sake get better grades, are more satisfied with school, and are less likely to drop out" (p. 157).

ENTITY AND INCREMENTAL THEORIES

What causes students to adopt learning goals or performance goals? Carol Dweck (2000) has explored this question in some detail and in a way that I find especially useful in examining the core elements of students' self-theories as they affect education policy. She summarizes her ideas and their implications for educators in her book *Self-theories: Their Role in Motivation, Personality, and Development.* Dweck suggests that people tend to hold one of two fundamental theories about their own and other people's abilities in a given domain.

Entity Theory

Some people are entity theorists. An entity theorist views intelligence and ability as fundamentally fixed and unchangeable—solid, like a rock, not subject to manipulation. Thus entity theorists will make global judgments about their own or other people's abilities. In application to learning, entity theory emerges in the views that you either get it or you don't, that you're good in some subjects but poor in others, that you're either smart or dumb. It is the predominant perspective that Steinberg (1996) finds among high school students and Covington (1992) finds among college students. For the entity theorist, an experience of failure or frustration becomes direct evidence for a diagnosis of fundamental incompetence and a rationale for avoiding or withdrawing from future challenges. According to Dweck, the student entity theorist seeks affirmation through "[e]asy, low-effort successes, and outperforming other students. Effort, difficulty, setbacks, or higher-performing peers call their intelligence into question—even for those who have high confidence in their intelligence" (p. 3).

Incremental Theory

In contrast to entity theorists are incremental theorists, who believe that intelligence and ability are changeable and contingent rather than fixed and fundamental—malleable like clay, subject to manipulation, addition, and subtraction. Incremental theorists will tend to look at the local circumstances rather than make global generalizations. Faced with failure or frustration, the incremental theorist will try again and consider strategies for change. Dweck

> found a clear and significant relation between the students'
> theories of intelligence and their goal choices: The more students held an entity theory of intelligence, the more likely
> they were to choose a performance goal, whereas the more
> they held an incremental theory, the more likely they were to
> choose the learning goal. (p. 21)

Dweck and her colleagues have studied students of all ages, from preschool through adulthood. And they have been careful to match students of similar abilities in comparing the effect of self-theories on academic performance. They have demonstrated that self-theories are much more influential than simple self-confidence when approaching challenging tasks. In one study of students making the transition from elementary to junior high school, they found that "students with an entity theory showed a marked decline in their class standing" (p. 31). The most surprising result, however, was that "many students who showed this decline from high to low academic standing were entity theorists who had *high* confidence in their intelligence" (p. 31). Incremental theory students, on the other hand, "showed a clear improvement in their class standing" (p. 31). Dweck's conclusion applies immediately and directly to the transition from high school to college: "Entering a challenging scholastic setting with a belief in fixed intelligence seems to set students up for self-doubt, anxiety, and drops in achievement. The entity theory puts a premium on immediate demonstrations of intellectual ability rather than on mastery over time" (p. 32).

The entity/incremental theory framework for considering self-theories is especially useful because it highlights what is probably the central issue in determining student goal choices: their attitude toward failure. Martin Covington (1992) quotes Max Beerbohm's remark that "There is much to be said for failure. It is more interesting than success" (p. 231). Covington then points out that "Failure is interesting partly for the fact that successful thinkers actually make more mistakes than those who give up easily and therefore preserve their unblemished record of mediocrity, and also for the fact that mistakes can usually be set right by trying again" (p. 231).

Learning, from its very beginnings, entails a process of courting failure and learning to play with it. None of us would be walking or talking—and certainly not reading, writing, and calculating—had we not embarked at an early age on the systematic project of doing things that were definitively impossible for us and repeatedly failing at them for an extended period of time. Those of us who have observed young children learning to walk or talk have noticed that toddlers are so called because they do not fear falling down and often seem to positively enjoy it. Toddlers are all incremental theorists and embrace learning goals with gusto. And this principle that trying the currently unachievable is an intrinsically interesting endeavor drives successful enterprise at every stage of life. The text you are reading now began as a magazine article and failed itself into a book.

As we grow older, we learn not to learn by learning to fear and hide from failure. And this approach to failure, if pervasive, has dramatic implications not only for school performance but also for life performance in general. Dykman's research, discussed earlier, hints at the kind of damage that pervasive fear of failure can do to people's lives. Dweck's research, too, repeatedly shows that an orientation that sees failure as an enemy to be avoided produces a response of helplessness in potential learning situations and thus repeatedly and systematically inhibits learning.

An individual is not solely an entity theorist or an incremental theorist. I may be an incremental theorist in one domain (math or video games) but an entity theorist in others (athletics or music). And self-theory, even in a given domain, is not necessarily stable over time. It can change.

CAN WE MODIFY SELF-THEORIES AND GOALS?

Dweck and her colleagues tested the hypothesis that self-theories are not merely correlated with goal choices but cause those choices. To do so, they presented randomly selected groups of students with written passages that argued for entity or for incremental theory and then posed those students tasks at which they were not likely to succeed initially. In one study, two groups of fifth-grade students were presented with the contrasting passages to read and were then given a choice of tasks to perform, one a task designed to satisfy performance goals, the other designed to satisfy learning goals.

> Students who read the entity theory passage were significantly more likely than the others to select a performance goal task to pursue—they wanted to look smart. ... [T]hose who read the incremental theory passage were more likely to select the learning goal task to pursue—they wanted to become smarter. (p. 24)

Dweck drew two important conclusions from this study. The first was that "students' theories of intelligence can have a direct effect on their goals and concerns. Theories of intelligence *cause* students to focus on performance goals or learning goals" (p. 24). The second conclusion was that "we can influence students' theories. Although students came to our study with their own theories, what we told them had a clear impact. This means that people's theories of intelligence are malleable" (p. 24).

Both Dweck and Randall Bergen studied college students. Bergen wrote two *Psychology Today* type articles: One made a strong case that intelligence is a fixed quality, genetically determined (entity theory); the other argued equally persuasively that intelligence is malleable and can be developed by individual effort (incremental theory). Using these articles, Bergen "found that the articles had a clear impact on student's theories of intelligence and on their persistence in the face of failure . . ." (Dweck, 2000, p. 25).

Dweck and three colleagues conducted a similar study focusing on the question of whether the prior persuasion would influence students' persistence. Students were again randomly selected to read the articles advocating entity theory or incremental theory. Students were then asked to work a set of problems, given feedback on their results, and then asked to work another set. After receiving feedback on their performance on the first set, however, they were given an opportunity to take a tutorial, introduced as one that had been effective in the past in improving performance. Most of the students who had done well on the first set of problems chose the tutorial before doing the second set (73.3% of those who had read the incremental theory article and 60% of those who had read the entity theory article). But of those who had performed relatively poorly on the initial task, 73.3% of the students who had read the incremental theory article chose to take the tutorial. Of the students who read the entity theory article, 13.3 percent did. Dweck concludes:

> [W]e have shown that it is possible to influence students' theories about their intelligence, and that when we do so we influence their goals and concerns. Those who are led to believe their intelligence is fixed begin to have overriding concerns about looking smart and begin to sacrifice learning opportunities when there is a threat of exposing their deficiencies. Those who are led to believe their intelligence is a malleable quality begin to take on challenging learning tasks and begin to take advantage of skill improvement opportunities that come their way. (p. 26)

SELF-THEORIES AS INFORMATION FILTERS

This research seems to indicate that students receive and attend to information about their own performance differently depending on their self-theories. My own observations of and conversations with students persuade me that entity and incremental theories predispose students to see information that comes to them in response to their efforts in radically different ways. Entity theorists tend to see the information that comes to them in response to their efforts as *evaluation* or *summative assessment*.

Incremental theorists tend to see the same information as *feedback* or *formative assessment.*

I will use the terms "evaluation" and "feedback" to distinguish between these ways of thinking about information. By "evaluation" I mean information that states or confirms a judgment on a performance or a person. By "feedback" I mean information that illustrates the effect of a performance in light of some standard or goal and that the performer can use to improve future performances (Wiggins, 1996). Some assessment activities are more likely to produce evaluation, some feedback. For example, the SAT and other such tests are nearly pure evaluation; the only information the test-taker receives is a global score, and the specific questions as well as the defects of the answers given are kept secret. The individual receives no specific information about his or her performance that could be used to modify future performances. On the other hand, clear suggestions for revision on an ungraded draft of an essay or report that must be rewritten are nearly pure feedback. The individual receives only information that can be used to modify the performance, but no global judgment of it. Grading tends to be an evaluation-heavy mode of conveying information about student performances; good tutoring, on the other hand, tends to be feedback-heavy.

The mode of delivering information about a performance can condition the way students receive that information, but to some extent evaluation or feedback is in the eye of the beholder. Entity or incremental theory serves as an information filter, a kind of selective lens, allowing the student to perceive some data in the environment as relevant and important and other data as meaningless noise. I have increasingly structured my own classes over the past several years to be feedback-intensive. Yet many students seem to systematically deflect feedback or to convert it into implicit evaluation. Indeed, some students appear to see evaluation as the only meaningful response to activities in a school setting. Confirmed entity theorists have no interest in feedback. It is invisible to them. I once tried to explain to an intelligent young woman that I would respond to her essay with suggestions for revision but would not assign it a letter grade. (This is now my standard procedure.) She clearly made an effort to process what I was saying, and clearly could not do so easily. After several minutes of conversation, my explanation came back to me, reprocessed through her framework of understanding: "Oh, so this version doesn't really count." To many students, only evaluation counts. On the other hand, the student who comes in after the test genuinely seeking the reasons why she missed certain problems is acting as an incremental theorist: She wants to translate the evaluation she received into feedback she can use to improve performance. Very detailed comments on student work are often likely to be ignored. Entity theory highlights the grade and filters out the comments. The grade has ontological weight for these students; the feedback is idle chit-chat.

When self-theories function as information filters, they lock students into a particular mode of goal setting. Feedback sustains learning goals; they cannot survive without it. Conversely, performance goals can be defined as the quest to receive positive evaluations and avoid negative ones. The student who is trying to get better at something must have feedback. The student who is trying to get praised must have evaluation. In the previously described research, mediated changes in self-theories change the kinds of information students recognize as relevant and important. Tutoring, when done well, is an almost pure feedback activity; in a tutorial session the student only receives information for the purpose of improving performance, and the student is seldom evaluated on the basis of this performance. The students who chose the tutorial in Dweck's study were seeking out feedback. The students who rejected it were implicitly classifying feedback as irrelevant noise. If a brief intervention can alter student behavior so significantly, how great must be the impact of the student's ongoing role in the total environment of the school?

SELF-THEORIES AND THE AMERICAN CULTURE

There is considerable evidence that entity theory is the predominant pattern in American schools and that schooling does much to reinforce it. Indeed, this distinction may well apply to a degree to Western industrial nations in general. Other cultures that perform consistently better in terms of educational outcomes often seem to inculcate incremental theory. Steinberg (1996) found that "Compared with individuals from other cultures, Americans are far more likely to believe that success in school is dependent on native intelligence, that intelligence is fixed—either by genes or early experience—and that factors in the emotional and social realms play only an insignificant role in students' academic success" (pp. 92–93).

This conclusion is strikingly affirmed by Harold Stevenson of the University of Michigan and James Stigler of UCLA (1992) in their detailed study of elementary schools in the United States, Japan, and China. The chief difference they find that accounts for the superior performance of the Asian over the American schools is the attitude toward the relationship between effort and ability: what self-theories the larger culture and the schools tend to reinforce in students. They find that "American children, teachers, and parents emphasize innate abilities as a component of success more strongly than their Chinese and Japanese counterparts do" (pp. 94–95). Closely paralleling Dweck's analysis of students who embrace an entity theory of intelligence, they note that

> An overemphasis on innate abilities has insidious implications for children's development and education. Children who believe that their high ability is sufficient to ensure success find little reason to work hard. Alternatively, children who perceive themselves as having low ability and doubt that they can master their lessons through continued effort also have little reason to work hard. (p. 95)

And, of course, their findings about the difference between American and Asian elementary school students are precisely same as Steinberg's findings about high schools: that the American students do *not* work hard compared to their Asian counterparts. They pose a warning that surely must resonate even more strongly for higher education—where the teachers who teach these elementary school students are formed—than it does for those their study directly addressed:

> An emphasis on innate ability makes Americans preoccupied with categorizing children as a basis for deciding who can benefit from particular kinds of education. Expectations of "low ability" children are reduced, and they finish their education with inadequate skills and insufficient knowledge for finding jobs and adapting successfully to contemporary society. We suggest that the American emphasis on innate abilities is harmful and is undermining the pursuit of public education—indeed, of democracy itself. (p. 95)

I am not suggesting that students do not differ in native abilities. Of course they do. We each come into the world with a certain genetically determined potential, with tendencies toward strength and weakness that can reasonably be called innate. And our potential is further shaped by environmental factors—such as diet, exposure to toxins and contaminants, and the behavior of caregivers—that influence our physical and psychological development before and after birth. All of this is beyond dispute. However, there is impressive and growing evidence that these biological potentials are only a small portion of our full potential, and that that potential is complex and not easily estimated (Perkins, 1995; Gardner, 1983, 1999). This is not the place to explore this issue in detail, but we can say that the international comparisons just referred to and the evidence recounted earlier in this chapter support beyond reasonable doubt the view that, as a practical matter, intelligence is never fixed at birth. People differ in potential even at a very young age. But people realize the complex possibilities they are born with only through growing and learning. Not everything is possible, but much is. If I believe that my IQ is my destiny, it will be—but only because I believe it.

DEVELOPMENTAL STAGES AND SELF-THEORIES

Stevenson and Stigler's (1992) study and much of Dweck's (2000) research focused on elementary-age children. But Covington (1992) suggests that young children are natural incremental theorists and that the transition to entity theory accelerates considerably around the age of 13:

> Children believe that high effort rather than low effort is indicative of ability. In time, however, through a combination of social comparisons, competition, and the advent of adult-like reasoning, ability status emerges as the dominant value over effort. And with this change comes a reversal in the cue value of effort. It is now high effort, not low effort, that leads to suspicions about one's ability. (p. 83)

Whatever the point or process of transition, by the time they reach college most students have been systematically drilled in entity theory as it applies to academic work. Research by Covington and Omelich and others with college students has attempted to directly discover what the students value most in the academic setting. "College students estimated how much ability others would attribute to them given various test successes, including those for which they had studied very hard or barely at all" (Covington, 1992, p. 78). While students preferred high effort to low effort as an explanation of success, "when a choice between high-effort and high-ability explanations was given—and push came to shove—students preferred being perceived as able. . . . In fact, for some students ability status is so important that they go to great lengths to disguise the role of effort in their successes" (Covington, 1992, p. 79).

K. Patricia Cross (2001) summarizes the situation aptly: "One of the oddities of the traditional American culture, especially the youth culture, is that it is better to be thought lazy than stupid. Thus, in the competition of the classroom, students prefer to be seen by others as succeeding through ability rather than through effort" (p. 9).

The students entering our colleges today come with a variety of disadvantages. What they believe about themselves and what they believe about academic institutions tend both to disable them for doing their best work and to frustrate our best efforts to help them become active, autonomous, lifelong learners. Students did not invent these defective beliefs; they were produced in large measure by the educational environment in which students have lived for 12 or more years (see Table 6.1 for a summary). But these beliefs can be changed. And it should be the primary mission of colleges and universities to change them.

Table 6.1

Self-theories

Entity Theory	Incremental Theory
Fixed, global judgments about intelligence and ability: You're smart or you're dumb.	Local, malleable judgments about intelligence and ability: If you work harder you'll do better.
Effort is a sign of low ability: If you have to try hard, you must not be smart.	Effort is the way of accomplishing goals: If you want to succeed, you'll try hard.
Attuned to evaluation; filters out feedback.	Attuned to feedback; filters out evaluation.
Performance goals: seeks to win positive evaluations and avoid negative ones.	Learning goals: seeks to increase competence.
Response to failure: withdrawal, excuses, avoidance; failure is a sign of low ability.	Response to failure: increased effort; failure requires modified strategy, redoubled effort.

7

Approaches to Learning

WHAT IS LEARNING?

To this point we have somewhat misleadingly used the term "learning" as if it were a unitary concept. But, of course, there are many kinds of learning and many different processes to which that term applies. As the discussion of student motivation in the last chapter suggests, students' goals in approaching a given task will powerfully condition the kind of learning they do.

So what is learning? Robert Leamnson (1999), a biologist, defines it as "stabilizing, through repeated use, certain appropriate and desirable synapses in the brain" (p. 5). Ference Marton and Shirley Booth (1997) suggest, "Learning is mostly a matter of reconstituting the already constituted world" (p. 139). And John Biggs (1999) says

> Learning is . . . a way of interacting with the world. As we learn, our conceptions of phenomena change, and we see the world differently. The acquisition of information in itself does not bring about such a change, but the way we structure that information and think with it does. Thus, education is about conceptual change, not just the acquisition of information. (p. 13)

I think that all of these statements are consistent and all of them are accurate. If we look a bit more closely, we see that they suggest that all learning activities are not the same, that some are more valuable than others.

At the physical level, learning almost certainly does involve changes in the brain. Research with animals has confirmed that learning processes change the brain in ways that other forms of activity do not. The Committee on Developments in the Science of Learning of the National Research Council (1999) gives the example of experiments with rats in which one group was put on a treadmill to exercise vigorously while another group ("acrobats") learned how to pass through an elevated obstacle course. The exercising rats increased the density of blood vessels in their brains compared with both the acrobats and a control group of "cage potatoes" that didn't exercise at all. "But when the number of synapses per nerve cell was measured, the acrobats were the standout group. Learning adds synapses; exercise does not" (National Research Council, 1999, p. 108). The report concludes, "learning imposes new patterns of organization on the brain, and this phenomenon has been confirmed by electrophysiological recordings of the activity of nerve cells" (p. 109).

When we learn we change. We become physically different than we were before the learning experience. The duration and scope of the difference, and how it will affect our future choices and behavior, depend on a number of factors.

LEARNING AND REMEMBERING

Learning is closely connected with memory. If I heard you say something but can't remember what it was the next day, it will be obvious that I have not learned it. The student who reads the text but can't remember the material for the test never argues, "But it's not fair, I learned the material, but then I forgot it." Forgetting, in the commonsense view, vitiates learning. We can distinguish between short-term and long-term memory, factual and procedural memory (Sylwester, 1995). While scholars still dispute the precise taxonomy of memory, most agree that we remember in stages and retain deeper memories longer. A plausible distinction that has clear implications for education is between episodic and semantic memory. Five psychologists from three universities in the United Kingdom—Martin Conway, Timothy Perfect, Stephen Anderson, John Gardiner, and Gillian Cohen (1997)—have attempted to distinguish learning outcomes in an academic setting using this framework.

Drawing on the work of pioneering cognitive psychologist Endel Tulving, Conway and his colleagues posit a distinction between remembering and knowing. We remember through the system of episodic memory. Episodic memory is memory that depends on the concrete recollection of the episode of learning; "episodic memory is autobiographical and preserves the spatiotemporal properties of original experiences" (p. 394). For example, when I try to recall the name of someone I have met only recently, I will seek to replay in my mind the event of our meeting. When I try to recall the name of an organ or a bone for my anatomy test, I will replay in my mind the diagram I studied in the textbook or perhaps a mnemonic rhyme I memorized as an easy-to-recall context for the previously unfamiliar name. Remembering, in this sense, is "defined as having recollective experience, a state in which images, feelings, and other context-specific details relating to a past event come to mind, such that the experience is that of mentally reliving a particular episode" (p. 394).

Semantic memory (also referred to as schematic or conceptual memory) operates quite differently. "Semantic memory does not preserve such [contextual] information but is a kind of mental thesaurus that retains conceptual representations including the meanings of words, numbers, rules, and societal constructs. It is organized and accessed in terms of meaning" (p. 394). The contents of semantic memory do not need to be recalled through replaying the episode of learning; I just know them. I have no recollection of the context in which I learned that Thomas Jefferson was the chief author of the Declaration of Independence, that Abraham Lincoln was president during the Civil War, or the names and order of the days of the week, months of the year, or planets of the solar system, or most of the words in my vocabulary. I just know these things. (I might, in some cases, remember the context in which I learned some of this information, but my access to the information does not depend on my being able to replay the episode of learning in memory.) The contents of semantic memory are embedded in the context of meaning I carry around with me all the time; they are linked to my fundamental framework of understanding, the mental models or schemas that structure my mind.

We do not just remember facts, as in these simple examples, but also rules, algorithms, and procedures, and the distinction between episodic and semantic memory applies here as well. (Contrast the mathematics professor's access to problem solving algorithms with that of the beginning student in Algebra 1.) The two memory systems operate independently but are closely related, and "the episodic system is embedded in the semantic system" (p. 394). We usually recall new information initially through episodic memory until it has been linked to preexisting mental schemas and has entered semantic memory. In all applications, the contents of semantic memory are obviously much more quickly and efficiently accessible than the contents of episodic memory.

In their study, Conway et al. explored the question of how students experience memory when learning new information in college classes. They studied four first-year psychology lecture courses and three sections of interdisciplinary research methods classes. They modified the multiple-choice final examinations in all sections by asking students to indicate, for each answer, a memory-awareness category: remember, know, familiar, or guess. In other words, they asked students to indicate not only what they thought the correct answer was, but also how they thought they were re-trieving that answer from memory. In order to receive credit for a correct answer, students were required to also answer the memory-awareness cate-gory question. The researchers then retested the students in one of the lec-ture classes at the end of the summer term, using the same procedure.

They found that "when knowledge acquisition is tested immediately after a lecture course has been completed, students with higher marks out-perform their colleagues because they remember more" (p. 408). On the other hand, "when students were retested after a filled retention interval during which additional learning took place, the dominant response cate-gory shifted from remembering to knowing" (p. 408). This reflects an R-to-K (remember-to-know) shift; if information initially retained in episodic memory is not to be permanently lost to memory, it needs to be shifted into semantic memory within a fairly brief window of time. So

> the relative preponderance of remember responses in an ini-tial test, and know responses in a later retest, reflects a de-crease in the accessibility of episodic memories. At the same time as this occurs there may, however, be a corresponding development of schematized knowledge representations [se-mantic memory] to which access becomes increasingly auto-matic. (p. 408)

Conway et al. analogize the contents of memory to the books in a li-brary and the schemas that provide the framework for semantic memory to the indexing system:

> At some point in the process of acquisition a learner reaches a point where the requirement for schematic organization is pressing. Just as a library beyond a certain number of volumes becomes unusable without an effective indexing system, so does unorganized semantic knowledge; the students taking the lecture course are, we suggest, at this point. They have ac-quired knowledge of a number of different subdomains of psychology. Much of this knowledge is in the form of episodic

memories (hence the dominance of remember responses in the tests on these courses), but as these memories increase, they rapidly become inaccessible and now some type of organization is required if the already acquired knowledge is to support problem solving and further learning. At the close of a lecture course then, the student has the opportunity to begin the process of schematizing their knowledge: They have sufficient knowledge to make schematization a benefit, and this knowledge, because of frequency of exposure, is in the process of shifting into a semantic form. (p. 409)

The implications of this process in terms of the kinds of lecture course studied are clear: "if there had been no summer examinations... and if the class test and course work had been the sole means of assessing and determining level of learning, then for many students..., learning could cease shortly after completion of the lectures" (p. 411). And for learning to cease before the R-to-K shift is complete, while "knowledge is still in the process of shifting from an episodic to a conceptual form and, therefore, subject to rapid forgetting" (p. 411), would mean that most of the newly acquired knowledge would be permanently lost to memory.

In contrasting the memory awareness of students in the lecture classes to that of students in the research methods classes, the researchers found something interesting: Successful students in the research methods classes resembled successful students on the retest more than successful students on the initial examinations in the lecture classes. Students at the end of the research methods classes were more likely to rely on semantic rather than episodic memory for right answers, like the students who did well on the retest of the lecture classes but unlike the students who did well on the final examinations in the lecture classes. They found that even students who received lower grades in the research methods classes tended to rely more on semantic than episodic memory. They found that this was true even though teachers and students uniformly agreed that the research methods courses were more difficult than the lecture courses. They found that "on these courses the students encountered the to-be-acquired knowledge repeatedly across classes, often paired with different concepts across contexts, and in different problems" (p. 410). Thus, "because of the repetition of material across multiple contexts and the interactive problem-solving orientation of the learning, the schematization process is facilitated and an R-to-K shift occurs during, rather than after, the course" (p. 410).

This study also confirmed what is entirely predictable and has been widely observed in other research: "The inescapable conclusion is that the just know state is a generally more reliable indicator of an accurate answer than is the recollective state" (pp. 410–411).

Some of the things we learn we remember for a while and then forget. Some things we learn we integrate into our permanent conceptual scheme and simply know. Fully integrated knowledge is more reliable than the knowledge that has not been so integrated. And the way we learn things appears to have an effect on the speed and efficiency with which we integrate learned material. None of this is surprising, I hope, but it is important if we are to think clearly about how to design effective learning environments.

STUDENT APPROACHES TO LEARNING

As research on memory indicates, the way students learn, the approach they take to learning largely determines the kind of learning they engage in. Paul Ramsden (1992), professor at the Institute of Higher Education at Griffith University in Brisbane, Australia, puts it this way:

> Many research studies have shown that the outcomes of students' learning are associated with the approaches they use. *What* students learn is indeed closely associated with *how* they go about learning it. It does not seem to matter whether the approaches are measured by means of questionnaires or interviews, whether the subject area is engineering or history or medicine, or whether the outcomes are defined in terms of grades or in terms of some qualitative measure of learning... (p. 53)

John Bowden, director of Educational Program Improvement at RMIT University (formerly the Royal Melbourne Institute of Technology) in Australia and Ference Marton, professor of education at the University of Göteborg, Sweden, in their book *The University of Learning* (1998) state the case so that every college teacher will recognize it: "One of the greatest problems in institutional forms of learning is that students study for the tests and exams, instead of studying to grasp the object of learning

and instead of studying for life" (p. 13). We saw one example of this difference in the variation between performance in the research methods classes
and the lecture classes. But how can we characterize more clearly the difference in the way individual students approach the learning task?

Marton and Roger Säljö (1976), also of the University of Göteborg,
embarked upon research in the 1970s based on the premise that "for the
understanding of 'what it takes to learn,' a description of *what* the students learn is preferable to the description of *how much* they learn" (p. 4).
In other words, they sought to differentiate qualitatively, rather than
quantitatively, between effective and ineffective learners. In their initial research they gave a group of students a learning task—an essay to read, a
problem to solve—and then asked the students questions about what they
had done. They found a significant qualitative distinction in the students'
responses, which appeared to be linked to the students' approaches to processing the information. For example, when students were given an essay
of several paragraphs to read, some responded by listing the information
presented in the essay more or less in the order it appeared. Other students
extracted the major point or points of the essay and related supporting information hierarchically to the point or thesis. When asked how they approached the task, the students gave responses that corresponded to their
summaries of the essays. Students who took the linear recall approach to
summarizing essay content described their approach with comments like
these:

> "Well, I just concentrated on trying to remember as much as
> possible."

> "I remembered . . . but, I'd sort of memorized everything I'd
> read . . . no, not everything, but more or less."

> "It would have been more interesting if I'd known that I
> wasn't going to be tested on it afterwards, 'cos in that case
> I'd've more, you know, thought about what it said instead of
> all the time trying to think now I must remember this and
> now I must remember that."

> "There were a lot of different lines of thought to follow and
> to try and memorize." (Marton & Säljö, 1976, p. 9)

Marton and Säljö characterized this approach as "surface-level processing." These students, when they viewed the object of learning, were focusing on the *signs,* in this case the words of the essay.

In contrast, students who reported a more coherent and integrated understanding of the essay made comments like this about their way of processing the material:

"...I tried to look for...you know, the principal ideas..."

...and what you think about then, well it's you know, what was the point of the article, you know."

Interviewer. ["]But when you were going to start, you tried to think: what came at the beginning of the article?["]

Subject. ["]No, I...I tried to think what it was all about..."

"I thought about how he had built up the whole thing."

This approach they called "deep-level processing" because these students were focusing not on the signs but on what was signified, the meaning of the essay.

In Marton and Säljö's initial research, "qualitative differences in approaches to learning were associated with discernible differences in the outcome of learning: Deep approaches were related to grasping the author's message, and surface approaches were related to miscomprehending or missing the message altogether" (Marton & Booth, 1997, p. 22). These connections have been amply confirmed in subsequent research (Bowden & Marton, 1998; Marton & Booth, 1997; Ramsden, 1992).

"An approach," Paul Ramsden (1992) points out, "is not about learning facts versus learning concepts: It is about learning *just* the unrelated facts (or procedures) versus learning the facts *in relation to* the concepts. Surface is, at best, about quantity without quality; deep is about quality and quantity" (p. 45). Surface learning is learning for the sake of reproducing the signs; it is by definition *superficial,* in every sense of that word, both literal and figurative. Deep learning is learning for the sake of understanding meaning. This is not to say, of course, that students who take a deep approach to learning always understand correctly or productively. It is, however, to say that if they do not take a deep approach, they have no hope of understanding at all. As Ramsden (1992) puts it, "Surface approaches can never lead to understanding: They are both a necessary and a

sufficient condition for poor quality learning. Deep approaches are a necessary, but not a sufficient condition, for high quality outcomes" (p. 59).

   The distinction between deep and surface approaches to learning will
not, of course, be surprising to teachers. We see the distinction enacted before us every day. And we know that deep learning is more valuable than
surface learning. Learning facts, lists of terms, dates, rules, or concepts is
learning. And in some circumstances it is useful learning. But the knowledge that students use in practical problem solving and thinking is the
knowledge framed in the context of what they really believe and find
meaningful. Deep learning is learning that takes root in our apparatus of
understanding, in the embedded meanings that define us and that we use
to define the world. Surface learning floats lightly on a matrix of repetition
and reinforcement, abstracted from who we are and what we deeply know.

CHARACTERISTICS OF DEEP AND SURFACE LEARNING

Alfred North Whitehead (1929), in his justly famous essay *The Aims of
Education,* warns us that "above all things we must beware of what I will
call 'inert ideas'—that is to say, ideas that are merely received into the
mind without being utilised, or tested, or thrown into fresh combina-
tions" (p. 1). Whitehead, I think, was referring to the same distinction
that Marton and Säljö later explored in some detail when he distinguished
between ideas that are "inert" and those that are "utilised": "By utilising an
idea, I mean relating it to that stream, compounded of sense perceptions,
feelings, hopes, desires, and of mental activities adjusting thought to
thought, which forms our life" (p. 3). To utilize an idea, in other words, is
to engage it at the level of meaning—connected to the larger framework of
meaning that forms our life.

Deep Learning Is Active; Surface Learning Is Inert

We have internalized Whitehead's distinction as a commonplace, though
worded rather differently. Active learning, we will probably say, is to be
preferred to rote or passive learning. This is true enough, if we mean by it
that learning takes place by the action of the learner, and that the learner
who is seeking to connect new knowledge to his or her existing body of
ideas is approaching learning at a different level than the learner who is
simply picking up bits of information for the test. In a deep approach to
learning, the learner is the agent, an agent in motion, moving through,

using, and shaping the object of learning. I think we misspeak when we refer to passive learning because that is an oxymoron. The learner can never be entirely passive and still learn anything. Learning can't be done to you. I would prefer Whitehead's term "inert" to characterize the nature of a surface approach to learning. In a surface approach, the learner regards the object of learning as stationary, inert, a set piece to be observed from just one angle and not to be handled.

Scholars have developed diagnostic questionnaires based largely on extensive interviews with students about their own approaches to learning. The best known and most widely used are the Approaches to Learning questionnaire developed by Noel Entwistle and his colleagues at the University of Lancaster in the UK and the Study Process Questionnaire developed by John Biggs in Australia. These questionnaires present the kinds of statements indicative of surface or deep approaches. Surface approaches are indicated by statements such as these: "I usually don't have time to think about the implications of what I have read"; "I find it best to accept the statements and ideas of my lecturers and question them only under special circumstances"; and "I find I tend to remember things best if I concentrate on the order in which the lecturer presented them." The following statements, on the other hand, indicate deep approaches: "In reading new material I often find that I'm continually reminded of material I already know and see the latter in a new light" and "When I'm tackling a new topic, I often ask myself questions about it which the new information should answer" (Ramsden, 1992, p. 52). Students who take a deep approach are active movers in the design of their own learning; students who take a surface approach are afraid to disturb the dust on the inert and unconnected objects of their fleeting attention.

Deep Learning Is Holistic; Surface Learning Is Atomistic

Swedish scholar Lennart Svensson suggests the alternative terminology "holistic" and "atomistic" to characterize the distinction (Marton & Booth, 1997). His point is that the learner taking a surface approach sees information as discrete bits, separate and isolated atoms. The learner taking a deep approach, on the other hand, seeks to integrate information. She seeks to integrate the separate bits of information, say in an essay, into a coherent whole. She also seeks to integrate this message into her preexisting framework of thought. Thus students taking a deep approach report continually connecting new learning with prior knowledge. They report questioning new ideas and comparing them with old ones. They frequently emphasize the central role of seeking the main point or key message to be extracted from new learning. Students taking a surface approach, on the other hand, say things like "Although I generally remember facts and details, I find it difficult to fit them together into an overall picture" (Ramsden, 1992, p. 52).

A holistic approach is connected; an atomistic approach is isolated. One implication of the atomistic nature of a surface approach is that it tends to sever the objects of learning from their connections with the world at large. A holistic approach is a connected approach, and thus a practical one in the sense that it relates to decisions and beliefs that make a difference to our lives. An atomistic approach is an isolated approach, impractical in the sense that its products don't help us to live our lives. As Ramsden puts it, "A student may focus on passing a course or completing a particular learning assignment, such as a laboratory report or examination, as an end in itself, or alternatively on the meaning the course or assignment has in relation to the subject matter and the world that the subject matter tries to explain" (pp. 46–47). "Cognitive growth," John Biggs (1999) says, "lies not just in knowing more, but in the restructuring that occurs when new knowledge becomes connected with what is already known" (p. 73).

A surface approach generally stops with episodic memory; a deep approach seeks to integrate information into semantic memory. Semantic memory is holistic in precisely the sense that it is integrated into a large and personal framework of meaning, while episodic memory is atomistic in the sense that it relies not on a connection with a coherent, meaningful framework but on discrete, concrete experiences. Looking back at the research of Conway and his colleagues from the perspective of the distinction between deep and surface learning, it does appear that students in the research methods classes were more likely to take deep approaches than those in the lecture courses. And students in the research methods classes tended to know information rather than just remember it at the end of the semester at a much higher rate than students in the lecture classes. A deep approach to learning appears to accelerate the R-to-K shift.

A Deep Approach Reinforces Incremental Theory; A Surface Approach Reinforces Entity Theory

We might seem to have come full circle here. I began the last chapter by discussing learning goals and performance goals, and it could easily appear on a quick survey that the distinction between deep and surface approaches is merely a paraphrase for the distinction between learning and performance goals. The situation is somewhat complicated by the fact that the bulk of the research on motivation and goal setting seems to come from North America while the bulk of the research on deep and surface learning seems to come from Europe, the UK, and Australasia. While the major conclusions of these two bodies of research are entirely consistent, they are not merely redundant. The concept of approaches to learning is in one sense broader than the concept of achievement goals, in another sense narrower. I will mention the sense in which it is broader here and discuss the sense in which it is narrower later in this chapter. Deep or surface approaches to a learning task are different ways of *seeing* the object of learning (Marton & Booth, 1997; Bowden & Marton, 1998). The student who takes a surface approach does not see past the sign to what the sign means and then sets the meaning aside as being irrelevant to his purpose. He doesn't see past the sign. The surface learner suffers from a form of cognitive near-sightedness. For the student taking a surface approach, the sign *is* the meaning; the first appearance is all there is. The student who takes a deep approach, of course, also sees the sign—reads the words of the essay or story or poem, follows the statement of the problem, looks at the diagram. But for the student who sees through the lenses of a deep approach, the signs are cues for analysis and interpretation. They are part, but not all, of what he seeks to understand. It is perhaps most accurate to say that deep and surface approaches are different levels of awareness of the learning object.

We can go a step further and recognize that, for a given learner, the object of learning is what she is aware of. Or, to put it a little differently, she constitutes the object of learning through her act of experiencing it. As Ference Marton and Shirley Booth (1997) put it, "the object of learning is constituted in the course of learning. . . . [L]earning is the constitution of the object of learning" (p. 161). This idea of the constitutive function of learning led them to the global claim, presented at the beginning of this chapter, that "Learning is mostly a matter of reconstituting the already constituted world" (p. 139). The implications of this view, of course, go far beyond the present discussion. The point I am making here is that deep and surface approaches to learning involve a fundamental mode of awareness of, or means of constituting, the learning object. Thus approaches to learning are certainly influenced by achievement goals, but are not reducible to them. That means that the research on motivation and approaches to learning are important to one another and relevant to each other, but not redundant.

But it will be clear, I hope, that just as students' self-theories strongly condition their choice of achievement goals, and these goals strongly condition their approaches to learning, so their approaches to learning reinforce or undermine their self-theories in various ways. We saw in Chapter 6 that incremental theorists, those who believe that effort can increase ability, are more likely to form learning goals rather than performance goals while entity theorists, those who believe ability is fixed, are more likely to form performance goals rather than learning goals. Through performance goals, of course, we seek to look smart, through learning goals to get smarter.

The incremental theorist is more likely to take a deep approach to learning. If I believe that I can get further by trying harder, can clarify misunderstandings by rereading, can develop a solution by trying a different approach, I will be much more likely to do all those things than if I think they are a waste of time. But likewise, the experience of a deep approach to learning will increase the chances that I will believe that effort will pay off. Incremental theorists tend to seek feedback on the consequences of their actions; feedback is the fuel of a deep approach to learning. So incremental theory and a deep approach to learning reinforce one another.

Likewise, if I believe that my abilities are set and that the consequences of my actions provide evaluation of my abilities, then I will tend to assume that what I see is what I get. If effort is evidence of low ability, then the very act of seeking out feedback would imply a negative evaluation. Entity theory and a surface approach to learning reinforce one another.

A Deep Approach Reinforces Mindfulness; A Surface Approach Reinforces Mindlessness

In 1976, coincidentally the same year in which Marton and Säljö were describing their interviews with university students in Sweden, psychologists Ellen Langer of Harvard and Judith Rodin of Yale were studying geriatric residents of a nursing home in Connecticut. They divided the residents into a control group and an experimental group. The purpose of the study was to find out what would happen if the nursing home residents were given more control over their own lives. So the rules governing the experimental group were altered to increase their level of control in what would seem to most of us trivial ways.

> For example, these residents were asked to choose where to receive visitors: inside the home or outdoors, in their rooms, in the dining room, in the lounge, and so on. They were also told that a movie would be shown the next week on Thursday and Friday and that they should decide whether they wanted to see it and, if so, when. In addition to choices of this sort, residents in the experimental group were each given a houseplant to care for. They were to choose when and how much to water the plants, whether to put them in the window or to shield them from too much sun, and so forth. (Langer, 1989, p. 82)

Members of the control group were also given a plant but were told that the nurses would care for it. The daily schedules of the two groups were largely the same except that the staff made most of the decisions for the control group while the experimental group was required to make a variety of choices for themselves.

Three weeks after the study concluded, the researchers assessed its effects on the participants. Behavior, subjective reports of the participants, and ratings by the staff indicated that the experimental group had improved dramatically in comparison with the control group. Then 18 months later, they returned:

> At that time we also measured the residents' physical health. While, before our study began, the health evaluation ratings of the two groups (based on their medical records) had been the same, eighteen months later the health of the experimental group had improved while that of the comparison group had worsened. The most striking discovery, however, was that the changed attitudes we had initiated in these nursing home residents resulted in a lower mortality rate. Only seven of the 47 subjects in the experimental group had died during the 18-month period, whereas 13 of the 44 subjects in the

comparison group had died (15% versus 30%). (Langer,
1989, pp. 83–84)

This startling outcome from such an apparently modest experiment
set Langer, working over the years with several colleagues, on a search for
an explanatory apparatus. A review of the interesting and varied studies
that shaped her thinking would take us too far afield here, but she describes many of them in her books *Mindfulness* (1989) and *The Power of
Mindful Learning* (1997). She studied a broad range of subjects from
young children to old people in schools, residential institutions, and the
workplace. The thesis she developed outlines two broad approaches to
learning, using a very expansive sense of the term "learning": mindfulness
and mindlessness.

> A *mindful* approach to any activity has three characteristics:
> the continuous creation of new categories; openness to new
> information; and an implicit awareness of more than one
> perspective. *Mindlessness*, in contrast, is characterized by an
> entrapment in old categories; by automatic behavior that
> precludes attending to new signals; and by action that oper-
> ates from a single perspective. (1997, p. 4)

To oversimplify slightly, when the researchers changed the environment for the nursing home residents so that those men and women became conscious agents of their own lives—agents and not merely patients—the patients adopted a more mindful approach to their own lives.
And as a result, they lived longer and better lives. They came to see information not as inert, fossilized circumstance, but as living feedback about
their own choices, opening up the growing power of choice.

A deep approach to learning is mindful and a surface approach mindless, and this alternate set of categories helps to highlight a characteristic of
approaches to learning that deserves to be emphasized. The three characteristics of mindfulness are the continuous creation of new categories,
openness to new information, and an implicit awareness of more than one
perspective. These characteristics are approaches to introducing variation
and variety into the objects of thought, of triangulating reality by looking
at it from different angles. This quality of variation is a key element of a
deep approach to learning. And it is at the core of what educational insti-

tutions need most urgently to do. Bowden and Marton (1998) put it quite explicitly:

> The most important thing about institutional forms of learn-
> ing, such as studying at university, is that they are supposed
> to prepare students for handling situations in the future, sit-
> uations which are often very much unlike the situations in
> which students are being prepared. These future situations are
> more or less unknown. The more rapidly the world changes,
> the less can be said about them and the more unknown they
> become. And the world is changing more and more rapidly,
> many would say. The instrument we have for preparing stu-
> dents for an increasingly unknown future is our current
> knowledge. We have to prepare them for the unknown, by
> means of the known and we have to work out how that can
> be done. (p. 6)

The student leaving college today is bound to segué into a new episode. The world inexorably addresses us with the deathless transition line of the immortal Monty Python: And now for something completely different! How can we prepare students not for this or that, but for the different? How enable students not to follow this or that algorithm, but for the genuine mystery of the future? Bowden and Marton point out that "the capability of dealing with varying situations in the future, through discerning their critical features and focusing on them simultaneously, originates from experiencing variation in the past. The variation has to be experienced" (p. 51). And while this sounds daunting, brief reflection will show that most of us have been doing it all of our lives. By "variation" we can simply mean

> exploring something by more or less systematically looking
> at it from various perspectives. Children explore objects by
> turning them around, by throwing them, sometimes by
> tasting them, and usually by feeling them. Researchers do
> something similar, metaphorically speaking, when they ex-
> plore their objects of research. We become familiar with
> objects in our world in this way, and with the abstract phe-
> nomena of scholarship. It is in this way that . . . we become

capable of experiencing the whole when only a part of it is given. (Bowden & Marton, 1998, pp. 51–52)

A deep approach to learning, fully realized, makes us mindful in precisely this sense of seeing things from more than one angle, turning them over and taking in what is new about them, coming to see them in a new light and in new categories. A surface approach, on the other hand, is explicitly mindless in that, standing in one place, we take the surface revealed at a particular angle of light as all there is, and so we make the world two-dimensional, static, and dead. We might say that to see what we perceive through the lenses of a surface approach is to see them as flat, two-dimensional. To see these same objects through the lenses of a deep approach, to see them mindfully, is to see them in all three dimensions, with depth, from varying perspectives. To see the world through the lenses of a deep approach is to see the variety even in the familiar, to experience the continuing newness in what we have already seen.

To see the world mindfully is to see it with imagination, the faculty that permits us to see the unseen, to create wholes for mere surfaces. "Imagination" is the word that Whitehead (1929) used in his essay on "Universities and Their Function." As he anticipated the distinction between deep and surface learning, I think he anticipated as well the role of mindfulness in education when he wrote:

> So far as the mere imparting of information is concerned, no university has had any justification for existence since the popularization of printing in the 15th century.... The justification for a university is that it preserves the connection between knowledge and the zest of life, by uniting the young and the old in the imaginative consideration of learning. The university imparts information, but it imparts it imaginatively. At least, this is the function that it should perform for society. A university which fails in this respect has no reason for existence. This atmosphere of excitement, arising from imaginative consideration, transforms knowledge. A fact is no longer a bare fact: it is invested with all its possibilities. It is no longer a burden on the memory: It is energising as the poet of our dreams, and as the architect of our purposes. (pp. 92–93)

A Deep Approach to Learning Is Enjoyable; A Surface Approach Is Unpleasant

For all of the reasons recounted above, students who take a deep approach to learning enjoy the process, look forward to studying, and spend more time in study. Paul Ramsden (1992) summarizes his conclusions from reviewing many interviews with students about their own approaches to learning in this way:

> No one reading the interview material...could fail to be struck by the regularity with which students obliged to use a surface approach to a task, or to an entire course, describe their feelings of resentment, depression, and anxiety. In contrast, deep approaches are almost universally associated with a sense of involvement, challenge, and achievement, together with feelings of personal fulfillment and pleasure. (p. 58)

The kind of involvement and enjoyment that deep learning involves will be familiar to most readers from personal experience. Mihaly Csikszentmihalyi (1990), whose study of talented teenagers we discussed in Chapter 5, has for some years studied the phenomenology of enjoyment in contexts like deep learning. He calls the experience "flow" and defines it in terms of eight characteristics:

> First, the experience usually occurs when we confront tasks we have a chance of completing. Second, we must be able to concentrate on what we are doing. Third and fourth, the concentration is usually possible because the task undertaken has clear goals and provides immediate feedback. Fifth, one acts with a deep but effortless involvement that removes from awareness the worries and frustrations of everyday life. Sixth, enjoyable experiences allow people to exercise a sense of control over their actions. Seventh, concern for the self disappears, yet paradoxically the sense of self emerges stronger after the flow experience is over. Finally, the sense of the duration of time is altered; hours pass by in minutes, and minutes can stretch out to seem like hours. The combination of all these elements causes a sense of deep enjoyment that is so rewarding people feel that expending a great deal of energy is worthwhile simply to be able to feel it. (p. 49)

The flow experience is autotelic; that is, we pursue the experience for its own sake. And the balance of capability and challenge, the level of concentration, the goal-directedness, and the dependence on feedback in flow activities are all distinctive features of a deep approach to learning. I am not suggesting that deep learning and flow are the same thing. But I doubt that anyone has ever achieved flow while cramming for a final exam. Most, if not all students seek out flow experiences outside of school contexts, in sports, music, video games, even in work. But if they are to have the experience in an academic setting, they will have to come to it through the route of a deep approach to learning, or not at all.

Whatever else a college education may do, if it does not teach students to enjoy substantive and challenging learning, it will be largely pointless in the long run. If lifelong learning is to be more than a hollow cliché, students must discover the joy of learning.

> The most critical task in human development is to learn to create flow in productive, prosocial activities, thereby making it possible to maximize the quality of both personal and social life. This is what Plato meant when he said that the most important task of education is to teach young people to find pleasure in the right things. (Csikszentmihalyi, Rathunde, & Whalen, 1993, p. 15)

The characteristics of deep and surface approaches to learning are summarized in Table 7.1.

HOW THE LEARNING ENVIRONMENT AFFECTS APPROACHES TO LEARNING

In Chapter 6, we saw that self-theories can be modified by changing the learning environment. The same is true of approaches to learning, but more clearly and powerfully so. This is because in large measure the defective approach to learning, the surface approach, is not a natural development but an artifact of a particular kind of learning environment: school. Surface approaches to learning develop in response to the institutional environment of Instruction Paradigm schooling. I am not suggesting at all that teachers at any level desire or intend to promote surface approaches to learning. Indeed, in my experience quite the opposite is the case. No one knowingly advocates surface approaches. However, the characteristics of

Table 7.1

Approaches to Learning

Deep	Surface
Focuses on the signified: meaning of the text, problem, etc.	Focuses on the sign: the surface appearance of the text, problem, etc.
Active: learner is the conscious agent of understanding	Inert: learner receives what is given, remains static
Holistic: learner sees how object of learning fits together and how it relates to prior learning	Atomistic: learner sees object of learning as discrete bits of data
Seeks to integrate information into semantic memory	Generally stops with episodic memory
Reinforces and is reinforced by incremental theory	Reinforces and is reinforced by entity theory
Reinforces and is reinforced by mindfulness	Reinforces and is reinforced by mindlessness
Experienced as enjoyable, open to flow experience	Experienced as unpleasant, closed to flow experience

the Instruction Paradigm already discussed impose surface approaches as a theory-in-use for many students. As Bowden and Marton (1998) put it, "It is in situations set up with the explicit purpose of learning... that the very distinction between surface and deep approaches can be observed" (p. 58). Not to put too fine a point on it, students learn a surface approach to learning in school.

How does this happen? I noted in Chapter 3 that the fundamental error of the Instruction Paradigm is to supplant the end (learning) with the means (instruction) for the whole institution. The same thing happens with students on another level. Bowden and Marton trace the origins of a surface approach:

> So why do learners under certain circumstances focus on the sign instead of what it signifies, on the words rather than on the meaning and on the surface rather than on what the surface is the surface of? Paradoxically enough, the surface approach

seems to originate from experienced demands to learn. This is a kind of means-ends reversal. A text, a problem formulation, which is supposed to be a means to learn what the text or the problem is about, becomes the primary focus of the learner, an end in itself. Learning, which is the aim of the whole exercise, is experienced as a demand, and living up to the demand of proving that one has learned (for instance, by recalling the text read) becomes dominant in the learner's awareness. (p. 57)

In other words, students learn a surface approach when they come to view the various tasks of schooling—taking tests, writing essays, solving set problems, getting good grades—not as means to a larger end but as ends in themselves. In a very significant sense, the problems of schooling derive from the simple fact that students do not do as we say; they do as we do. I suggested earlier in this chapter that the concept of approaches to learning was both broader and narrower than the concept of self-theories. It is broader in that it addresses a student's mode of awareness, his way of seeing the object of learning. But it is narrower in the sense that the opposition of deep versus surface approach to learning is limited to contexts of schooling. (Obviously, people learn in a superficial and insignificant way in social settings other than schooling, and in some of those settings there may even be incentives for superficiality parallel to those that promote surface learning in school settings. But it is fairly clear that surface learning as defined by Marton and Säljö and explored in the substantial research project that they began is an artifact of schooling.)

Approaches to learning can vary, of course, in application to different subjects and tasks. A student is more likely to take a deep approach, for example, in a subject that she comes to with a prior interest, more likely to take a surface approach in a subject that she views as irrelevant to her personal concerns and welfare. However, there is a tendency for students to adopt global mindsets to academic tasks, to studying and school work. Ramsden (1992) has distinguished between approaches and orientations to learning. An orientation is an approach to academic work in general, at either deep or surface level. The questionnaires mentioned earlier measure these global orientations. I hope it is already clear that the characteristics identified earlier as being associated with Instruction Paradigm colleges are precisely those that train students in a surface orientation to academic learning. We will explore that issue more fully in the next section.

If formal schooling creates the habits of a surface orientation to learning, we would expect that more schooling would reinforce those habits and separation from an academic environment would decrease them. I found myself formulating a personal and anecdotal version of precisely that expectation several years ago. It came to my attention one semester as I took attendance on the first day of class. Acutely aware of the danger that teachers can impose their expectations on their students, and having seen ample evidence that my first-day expectations bore no reasonable relationship to actual student potential, I made an effort to monitor those expectations. I discovered, somewhat to my surprise, that the students I was happiest to see in class were students who had been away from schooling for a considerable time. Certainly, I had formed a bias of sorts in favor of older students, but I found that I had a more positive expectation for older students who were just returning to college, as opposed to those who had been around for a while. I discussed these perceptions with colleagues, many of whom confirmed similar patterns of expectation. I even joked that perhaps if we wanted to raise the quality of our students we should require high school graduates to work for a few years before returning to college.

I was both pleased and disturbed to discover that this phenomenon was not just in my head. Furthermore, it seems to be confirmed not just in the United States but internationally. One of the more interesting studies is that of Lyn Gow and David Kember (1990) at the Hong Kong Polytechnic. The subjects of this study were all bilingual in English and Cantonese, and their native language was Cantonese. The students in this study were very different in a number of ways from the average North American college student. Thus we can probably not ascribe the results to cultural factors. The researchers used Biggs' Study Process Questionnaire to determine the orientations to learning of students and compare those orientations with other information about the students, such as how long they had been away from school and how long they had attended college. They found that students were more likely to adopt deep approaches and less likely to adopt surface approaches the longer they had been away from school. "As they become older, and presumably more mature, their intrinsic interest in study tasks grows. With the passage of time, there seems to be a general tendency away from a surface orientation towards a deeper approach" (p. 312). There appears to be one disturbing exception to this encouraging tendency, however: college. "The likelihood of a student adopting a deep orientation seems to decline as a student progresses through a course of study" (p. 313). Overall, "it is possible to visualize an image of the population employing a surface orientation less as the influence of their schooling declines" (p. 312). The title of this article is "Does Higher Education Promote Independent Learning?" Gow and Kember conclude:

> In neither the research reported in this article nor in the literature cited is it possible to discover any evidence that higher education was promoting the qualities of independent learning toward which they aspire. Indeed there is some evidence that students may become less likely to employ a deep approach as they progress through their course of . . . study. It is, therefore, questionable whether typical higher education is succeeding in meeting the cited goals that are espoused by both government and lecturers. (pp. 314–315)

This was, of course, a single study in a distinctive cultural environment. But John Biggs (1999), surveying international research on the question, concludes that "the longer most undergraduate students . . . stay in [college], the less deep and the more surface-oriented they tend to become, and the more their understanding is assessment related. The tendency is almost universal. . . . Learning tends to become institutionalized" (pp. 34–35).

The point here is that the learning environment does in fact have a powerful effect on student orientations to learning. The question of how to shape that environment for more positive results we will address in the next section. But we cannot say that student approaches to learning are beyond the control of colleges. Quite to the contrary, those qualities of the learners that we in higher education most bemoan and most ardently wish to change appear to be largely a product of the learning environment of Instruction Paradigm schools and colleges.

We saw in Chapter 5 that one of the chief barriers to better learning was the body of beliefs students hold about college and schooling in general. Initially, those beliefs seem strange and inexplicable; we can see vividly that what students believe about college and what we who do the work of colleges believe are diametrically opposed. We saw in Chapter 6 that many of the warped and mistaken beliefs that students hold about schooling flow from dysfunctional beliefs they hold about themselves and their own abilities. We saw there and in this chapter that students hold many of these dysfunctional beliefs about schooling because they learned them in school. Indeed, we have seen that the most fundamental failure of learning is largely a product of the school environment. In putting the means before the end and hence freezing the means—rigidly abstracted from life as we live it—our students are doing as we do rather than as we say they should. They are following the model that colleges as institutions set for them. So we have come full circle. Our students are wrong in what they believe about learning, but they may perhaps be wiser than we know in what they believe about schooling. They have, after all, been there.

Paul Ramsden quotes Whitehead on the contrast between surface and deep approaches to learning:

> In my own work at universities, I have been much struck by the paralysis of thought induced in pupils by the aimless accumulation of precise knowledge, inert and unutilised.... The details of knowledge which are important will be picked up ad hoc in each avocation of life, but the habit of the active utilisation of well-understood principles is the final possession of wisdom. (Whitehead, 1929, p. 37)

Ramsden then observes:

> Surface approaches have nothing to do with wisdom and everything to do with aimless accumulation. They belong to an artificial world of learning, where faithfully reproducing fragments of torpid knowledge to please teachers and pass examinations has replaced understanding. Paralysis of thought leads inevitably to misunderstandings of important principles, weak long-term recall of detail, and inability to apply academic knowledge to the real world. A surface approach shows itself in different ways in different subject areas, but it leads down the same desolate road in every field, from mathematics to fine arts. Once the material learned in this way is reproduced as required, it is soon forgotten, and it never becomes part of the student's way of interpreting the universe. (p. 60)

We have seen enough in this brief summary of what students believe about schooling and about themselves and how different student approaches to learning affect the process to begin to put some flesh on the bones of our outline of the Learning Paradigm college. At a minimum, we can say that colleges should promote a deep orientation to learning and discourage a surface orientation. Of course, I have no doubt that readers of this book would probably have said that without being prompted. But it would have been a casual observation for many, not a declaration of our essential mission. It should now be clear that the quality of learning an institution promotes is what gives that institution meaning and value. Underlying everything the institution does and overriding every other consideration, a college must promote a deep orientation to learning and discourage a surface one or it actively undermines its very rationale for being. Whatever our perspective on higher education, if it is a perspective based in reality, we must accede to the primacy of quality learning.

Without quality, we have nothing of value left to count in the calculation of quantity. If students do not learn well, it matters really not at all how many tests they pass, how high their grades, how much data they cover. It will all be lost and meaningless if it is not rooted in understanding. It is among the cruelest hoaxes of incoherent thought to hold that we must invest in policies that promote surface learning because they are financially affordable. We must come to see that we do not save money when we waste money. No system will sustain the interminable perpetuation of rampant waste, investment in educational structures and processes that not only fail to add value but actually diminish the values we claim to be dedicated to. We will buy cheap only until we recognize that what we are buying is worthless. Policies and environments that promote surface learning do not save money; they tax us with failure and burden us with loss.

Now that we have filled out the concept of learning and the learners, we are in a position to address the design of learning environments that will produce the learning we want for the learners we have.

PART III

THE LEARNING ENVIRONMENT

OF THE COLLEGE

....

The design of learning environments can substantially shape the kinds of learning students do. Some learning environments promote incremental theory while others promote entity theory. Certain qualities of learning environments facilitate a surface orientation to learning while others facilitate a deep orientation. But before we can plan effectively to design effective learning environments, we need to get a clear idea of what we ought to mean by "learning environment." After all, there is almost no imaginable situation or context in life that is not, at least potentially, a learning environment. So what kinds of things are we referring to here?

In my experience, the response of most educators to discussion of the problems of colleges as learning environments is to seek remedies, to ask for solutions, but to do so in a certain way. The most usual formulation is something like "How can we change the classroom experience to address these problems?" Or perhaps "What are some solutions we can take into our classrooms?" Likewise, the default tendency in education research is to accept the assumption that the fundamental organizational module of the Instruction Paradigm, the classroom, must be the fundamental learning environment of colleges. Thus even some of the most enlightened scholars of education consistently speak of how to innovate in the classroom, how to reform the classroom, how to raise the quality of the classroom experience. This seems to me a grave—though unconscious and inadvertent—error. It assumes in advance an answer to a question that we should be asking: Is the classroom itself the right learning environment for all purposes?

Or are there other and different models of learning environments that we should consider?

And, of course, students, with very few part-time exceptions, do not encounter the college in the classroom or even a classroom but in several different classrooms, with different subjects and different teachers. So if we want to picture the whole experience of the student, we need a larger canvas than the classroom. In the next two chapters I will suggest an approach to this problem.

The Whole That Determines the Parts

THE LEARNING ENVIRONMENT IS LARGER THAN THE CLASSROOM

In the atomized world of the Instruction Paradigm, the parts precede the whole. A college is a collection of classes. But for students, the parts of their educational experience are given meaning in terms of their conception of the whole. The learning environment of the student certainly includes the classes the student takes. But it includes all of those classes, and it includes the sequence of those classes, the relationships between them, and their relationship to the rest of the student's experience. And, as we have already seen and will see again, the experiences that most deeply affect students in school or college are more often than not outside the classroom.

Students' orientations to learning—their general tendency to take a deep or surface approach to studying and learning—are not the product of a single course or teacher but of their overall experience over many years of schooling and of the expectations founded on that experience. And just as the entering student's orientation has been shaped by the totality of his previous schooling, so everything he sees, hears, thinks, feels, and does at college will further shape that orientation. As one who has for several years taught courses that fail in a variety of ways to fit the conventional classroom mold, I have found that students have usually developed a tacit and unconscious, but standardized, set of expectations for college classes based on the totality of their previous experience. And it is often a set of expectations that insulate the students' preexisting assumptions from change in the classroom. I tested this hypothesis directly for a few years by asking students to respond at the very beginning of the semester to the question "What is a college class?" Even though I provided a rationale for the question, the overwhelming sense of the responses was that it was a silly, if not downright stupid, question because everybody knows what a college class is. (The most interesting responses came from students new to college, who could still imagine different possibilities.) Most of the students in my classes entered them with a fairly standardized Instruction Paradigm model of a college class firmly in mind. It's something you take from a teacher to get units so you can get a degree. It meets so many hours a week in a classroom. Within these limits, what a class amounts to is largely up to the teacher—it is something that students expect to find out, not decide. Most students had trouble saying much about it, precisely because it was so obvious. But as we moved through the semester, we found that in fact their model of a college class had a good deal more detail under the surface. For example, when we came to do serious collaboration and peer review, many students found that irrelevant to our mission. It's inherent to a college class that the teacher gives grades. And then when the teacher wouldn't give them letter grades on their work, many thought it was outright heresy. It turns out to be implicit in many students' idea of a college class that the teacher should tell them fairly specifically what to do. But there also seem to be limitations on what kinds of things the teacher has a right to request. So I heard the recurrent question or expression of doubt (frequently following what seemed to me a splendidly clear and vivid description of a task or assignment): "What exactly do you want?" "I'm not sure just what you want." The feeling of power and importance I experienced from so many young people expressing concern for my personal desires was, however, always short-lived. Answers like "I want you to write about something that you really care about" or "I want you to tell the person sitting next to you why you believe this so that he can explain it accurately to someone else" didn't generally cut it. Certain kinds of teacherly desires are out of bounds. And if your answer to "What do you want?" doesn't follow the rules, well, it's not fair. And you're expected to know the rules because it is, after all, a college class, and everybody knows what that means. A teacher who pretends not to must be lying because nobody can really be that dumb and hold down a steady job.

Many students have internalized a separation of school from life, and that virtually assures a surface orientation to learning. That is, they have adopted as their own the Instruction Paradigm model of academic processes as entirely self-referential, having meaning only in terms of other academic processes, and not in terms of anything outside the academy. So when told that what I want is for them to say, in writing, something that they really believe and think is important, many students find themselves confused. Some, in class, will even—I do not have the imagination to make this up; it really happened—say that they don't think anything is important. (Most are more artful about it.) When you get the student who denies holding opinions and abjures personal desires one-on-one, how-ever, you hear a different story. Yes, she does care about some things. Yes, he does hope for a certain kind of future and not for another kind. But many students can't easily think about these deeply held hopes and beliefs in the context of school. As Robert Leamnson (1999) puts it, "One of the most obstinate notions that needs dislodging from the minds of new stu-dents is their conviction that school, including college, does not deal with real things. . . . For many, school has come to represent a totally contrived and artificial system" (p. 39). Another way of putting it would be that for many students school is about the signs, abstracted from what they might signify. To bring in meaning is cheating. As a student, I want to know whether this will be on the test. When I ask the teacher "What do you want?" I mean what signs do you want me to produce, in what order, what do you want me to say? I know in advance that we are in the business of producing lists of parts here; you don't have the option of telling me, out of the blue, that you want me to integrate them into wholes. If you tell me you want me to reflect on what I really believe, to put myself on the line about what really counts, you're cheating. Though that's not quite accu-rate. I accept and expect that you will *tell* me these things. I've heard them all my life. But a dozen or more years of schooling have shown me that in-tegrating school with my real life is neither demanded nor expected of me, that signs are what really count in school and meaning is something that teachers and administrators like to talk about but don't consistently ex-pect. The teacher or the institution that suddenly begins to "walk the talk" is breaking the unwritten rules. They really are cheating. The incidence of student cheating has been much noted. I suspect that most of it is merely self-defense, fighting fire with fire. Students cheat because their teachers cheat, tit for tat. For teachers to bring reality into the classroom, to the student who has adopted a thoroughgoing surface orientation, is cheating, breaking the unwritten rules that "everybody knows." They're asking for it. (I do not, of course, approve of student cheating; indeed, I think that we should do everything in our power to eliminate it. This begins with shaping a learning environment that deters rather than inspires it.)

In the Instruction Paradigm, the basic template for dealing with challenges is to create a class. So one Instruction Paradigm response to the deficiencies of students as learners is to create how-to-learn classes: Becoming a Master Student, College Success Skills, or something of the like. Some such classes (though, I fear, not most) are even designed to emphasize a deep approach to learning. Paul Ramsden, D. G. Beswick, and John Bowden (1986) conducted an interesting study at the University of Melbourne in Australia, using a very sophisticated form of learning skills intervention. The learning skills groups consisted of students in the same departments, meeting weekly with faculty from the department and other staff. They evaluated students' approaches to learning before and after the term. The results were, at first glance, perverse. They found that "attendance at learning skills groups increased the reported incidence of surface approaches" (p. 161). With understatement that, to my ear, approaches irony, they note:

> It is perhaps a little sad that staff who were genuinely concerned to improve the quality of undergraduate learning appear to have produced effects which, while they might have helped students to reach short-term goals, are certainly not in accordance with the declared academic values of the individuals or of the institution. (p. 162)

The problem, they concluded, was that even when a specific class was designed to shape the student's approach to learning, the individual class or program could not overcome the meta-lessons of the student's overall experience:

> Whether based on concepts from cognitive psychology or on commonsense notions of "good study habits," such experiments may have limited relevance to the problem of improving student learning because they do not take account of the interaction between students' intentions and the context of learning. Students actively and critically extract from skills programmes what is useful to them; "what is useful" is a function of their perceptions of the requirements of assessment and teaching. (p. 162)

Students do not absorb a fundamental orientation to school learning as a result of a single experience—even an experience designed to affect their orientation—but as a product of their total experience. So if we are to get at how to change that orientation, we need a framework that encompasses that total experience. To focus initially or, worse, exclusively on the class-room is to accept in advance the atomism of the Instruction Paradigm as a foundation for our thinking. It is this atomistic way of thinking about what we do that models and begets the atomism of a surface approach to learning. We should not import this fundamental error into our thinking about learning environments at the very beginning.

It remains true that one can, for some students and in the course of one semester, work a certain level of transformation. You can get quite a few students to swim up stream, against the flow of most of their school experience, and engage some ideas at a deep level. And classes that do this often stay with the students, become models of a kind of learning experience that opens up new possibilities to them. We examined evidence in Chapters 6 and 7 that shows that even brief interventions can affect a student's approach to learning in a given situation. It should be the goal of every teacher to create a transformative learning environment in his or her classroom. Good teaching counts, and it counts for a lot. We can and should exert every effort to create classrooms that help students to experience a deep approach to learning. But we need to keep in mind the distinction between an approach and an orientation to learning. An individual's approach to learning in a given situation is field-dependent, a specific approach appropriate to a specific task in a specific context. The same individual's orientation to learning in academic settings is field-independent, the default setting for academic learning no matter what the subject or context. Local circumstances—a distinctive assignment, authentic assessment, a background in the subject, personal goals—may well inspire a student to adopt a deep approach at some times in some classes. But the same student may revert to a surface orientation in the absence of these special factors, where "it's just another class." I suspect that it is rare for students to encounter such fortunate experiences two or three semesters in a row, from different instructors in different courses. And it must be even more unusual for students to encounter deep approaches to learning in a consistent enough form, with a consistent enough support structure, to come to expect them on a regular basis and to thus see them as inherent in the operations of the college. Try this thought experiment—or if you think you can somehow get your students to reveal themselves, try the actual experiment. What if we could ask students the following questions and get honest answers, what would they say? Just two questions: Do you believe that you will have to reflect seriously on your own beliefs and make thoughtful decisions about the course of your life to get a college degree? Do you believe that you will have to get high scores on multiple-choice tests to get a college degree? Even great classes that inspire students to take a deep approach to learning cannot change students' fundamental expectations of schooling unless they are part of a change in the overall learning environment. Indeed, even the language students use to describe their most powerful learning experiences testifies to the rule that these exceptions prove. Listen to students as they tell you about their engagements with a deep approach to learning in the classroom: "It was completely different from my other classes"; "I've never had a class like it"; "It was the first time in my life I'd been so involved in a class." The extraordinary class stands out in bold relief from the overall learning environment. But in the Instruction Paradigm we have no construct, no language to describe this "overall learning environment" that includes, but is not limited to, the curriculum and the courses.

A FRAMEWORK FOR REFLECTING ON THE LEARNING ENVIRONMENT

David Perkins (1992) of the Harvard Graduate School of Education and Project Zero has coined the metaphor of the "cognitive economy" of schools to bring to light "the metaphorical economy of gains and costs that students encounter" (p. 156). I find the analogy helpful because it allows us to look at the institution as a system, as an integrated whole, but also to treat students as individuals with different interests and backgrounds. Perkins points out that students, even when they behave in ways we deplore, are often acting as rational agents, responding to the costs and gains available to them within the institutional setting of schools. Characterizing most public schools, he says,

> One might call the cognitive economy of the typical classroom a cool rather than a hot cognitive economy—one that does not motivate the energy needed for complex cognition of students but runs at an altogether lower level of cognitive demand. (p. 159)

Complex cognition involves the active engagement with ideas required for deep learning. For students, a deep approach to learning is a high-cost activity. It requires more time and effort and entails a greater risk of failure than more superficial strategies. Yet the benefit provided in the context of school is not commensurate to this cost because

> very commonly, so far as grades and teacher approval go, complex cognition buys students no more than the simpler path of getting the facts straight and the algorithms right. No wonder, then, that students perfectly reasonably do not automatically gravitate toward complex cognition. (p. 160)

I propose to use this analogy a little differently than Perkins does. He refers to the cognitive economy of the classroom. For the reasons given above, I would prefer to think in terms of the cognitive economy of the whole institution, the cognitive economy of the college. To speak of the cognitive economy of the classroom makes a good deal more sense when speaking about elementary school, which is Perkins's major focus, because most elementary school students spend the bulk of the day in one classroom with one teacher. In such an arrangement, the classroom does encompass much, if not all, of the student's experience at the school. But that formulation works much less well in the context of higher education, where most students take a variety of different classes and have much more discretionary time.

An analogy taken from economic activity, of course, is likely to spark a certain amount of negative reaction from some in higher education, so let me clarify what I mean by the analogy and what I do not mean. There has been much discussion in recent years of the commercialization or corporatization of higher education. Some have argued that pressures to manage colleges like private businesses endanger the quality of education. Referring to students as customers will reliably raise some hackles at a faculty meeting. I sympathize with much of this critique. I have already criticized the tendency of colleges to respond to revenue incentives in the money economy to the detriment of educational values. This approach has helped to establish and maintain the Instruction Paradigm. By the way, this is in no sense a new issue. Whitehead (1929) had occasion to caution the college leaders of his day, "universities cannot be dealt with according to the rules and policies which apply to the familiar business corporations" (p. 100). But I think that this whole conversation runs the risk of distracting us from what is really important. To oversimplify only slightly, the reason some are attracted to the business model for running a college is that there simply is no college model that makes sense and inspires consensus. We have lost sight of what a college should be by mistaking the means we have long adopted for autonomous ends.

What I am proposing here has nothing to do with treating students as customers or running the college like a business. I am proposing to compare the framework of personal constraints and choices that we find in a college with that which we find in the money economy because by doing so we can see more clearly the incentives, disincentives, and constraints on choice that act on students in college. The incentives and disincentives I will refer to, however, relate to student approaches to learning and investments of their time and energy, not to money. (Of course, money is sometimes a relevant incentive even in the cognitive economy, as when a student decides to work longer hours, thus limiting study time. But money incentives are not predominant in the cognitive economy.) Indeed, the term "cognitive economy" should not be seen as a full-fledged metaphor. Rather, it harks back to the older, but not obsolete, sense of the word "economy," which is derived from a Greek term referring to household management. To speak of the economy of a place or a people is to view it as a household or family, an integral system. The term highlights the role of husbanding and managing resources, as a family must. But those resources need not be monetary. So when we speak of the cognitive economy we are simply speaking of the system for managing and allocating cognitive resources, wherein lies the true value of the educational enterprise.

The analogy to what we conventionally think of as the economy is a loose one, as Perkins points out:

> But there is a liberating advantage to the loose fit. In particular, lacking an equivalent of money, the cognitive economy of schools and classrooms does not press us to reduce all costs and benefits to some standard cognitive currency. While the common yardstick of the dollar in Keynesian economics yields mathematical rigor, it also generates unsettling equivalences: How many dollars is health worth? How many dollars is a life worth? In the cognitive economy of schools and classrooms, we can frame costs and benefits more loosely but flexibly in terms of the diverse qualities that count—effort invested, confusions encountered, experiences cherished, understandings gained, skills attained. Most of all, rewards in a

cognitive economy need not be selfish in character. Altruism counts as well. (p. 158)

Indeed, the cognitive economy provides us with a framework for reflecting on the activities of colleges and universities that can help us to develop a countervailing model to the model of college as corporation. It therefore allows us to marshal a coherent rationale, grounded in sound evidence and academic values, for resisting financial pressures to maximize the efficiency of instruction at the cost of devaluing learning.

AN ANALYSIS OF THE COGNITIVE ECONOMY

I will follow Perkins in making the distinction between a hot and a cool cognitive economy. As I will use the terms here, a "hot" cognitive economy is one that promotes a deep orientation to learning, hence encourages risk-taking, learning goals, and incremental self-theories. A "cool" cognitive economy, on the other hand, promotes a surface orientation to learning, hence discourages risk-taking and encourages performance goals and entity self-theories. Complex cognition is an entrepreneurial activity in the cognitive economy, and incremental theorists are the entrepreneurs, taking risks for the sake of growth.

If we are to examine the cognitive economy of the college, we need to decide what questions to ask about it, what categories to consider in analyzing it. I propose the following with no claim that they are comprehensive, perfectly logical, or scientifically verifiable. Indeed, the categories of analysis I propose here are specifically designed to reveal ways in which colleges could be changed to achieve a hotter cognitive economy; they can help us to differentiate between the cognitive economy of an Instruction Paradigm college and a Learning Paradigm college. They can help us to see the different aspects of the college in terms of how they affect the whole picture in light of the core mission of making student learning happen. The first five categories present characteristics of the way the institution interacts with students. To these I have added a sixth, alignment, that refers to the interrelation of the first five. I offer, then, the following categories for our analysis: goals, activity, information, time, community, and alignment. These categories are not neatly separate; they are all highly interdependent upon one another. They are not presented in order of priority or importance; they are so closely connected that it would be pointless to try to order them in any sequential way. I will briefly explain each before applying them.

Goals

How does the cognitive economy value and respond to students' goals— or we might say values, beliefs, priorities. Students as persons have considerable integrity when they enter college; they have ideas about what they want and what they don't. How does the cognitive economy react to and act upon the individual student's sense of what is important and what is not? In the money economy, at least in a relatively free market, prices rise with demand. (I am not defending public taste here, just pointing out that the economy tends to serve it.) What people value more highly is identified by the economy so that resources are channeled to support its production. But if prices are arbitrarily set, the result is often surpluses of what people value less and shortages of what people value more. In terms of the cognitive economy, perhaps the central question is whether the institution tries to impose goals on students, extrinsic goals that ignore the students' own inclinations, or creates a process by which the students can pursue their own goals. A hot cognitive economy will tap into intrinsic goals; a cool one will impose extrinsic goals on students.

Activity

How does the cognitive economy value and respond to what students do? A hot economy, cognitive or otherwise, is one that elicits a high level of activity. Does the cognitive economy promote a high level of activity? Are some kinds of activities more valued and rewarded than others? Are they public and visible or private and secret? In the money economy, more productive activities tend to be rewarded with higher pay or prestige than less productive ones. What level of cognitive activity and what kinds of activities does the college encourage, promote, and reward, and how often? A hot cognitive economy, one that taps into the productive power of intrinsic goals, will generate a high level of cognitive activity. A cool cognitive economy will maintain a much lower level of activity.

Information

What channels of information does the cognitive economy create? What kinds of information does it capture and report back to students? What does it filter out and discard? We know that in the money economy, inadequate information will skew decisions and lead to irrational choices. The pricing system, for example, should generally reflect the cost of production; if prices are manipulated, say by monopoly power, to misrepresent the true cost of production, then consumer decisions will lead in the long run to improper distribution of goods and services. We have already distinguished two modes of information that are available and have an effect in the cognitive economy of the college: feedback and evaluation. What ratio does the institution achieve? A hot cognitive economy will maintain a high ratio of feedback to evaluation; repressing feedback to achieve a high degree of evaluation will cool the cognitive economy. Feedback fuels a high level of activity and reinforces intrinsic goals.

Time

We can look at an activity in term of the time horizon it affords. By the time horizon I mean basically the response to the question "How long will I have to live with the consequences of this decision?" In the money economy, a variety of factors determine the time horizon for various choices and actions, some self-determined, some imposed by the environment. Our lives are given shape and stability by key decisions made for the long term: choice of a career, a marriage partner, a house. When we invest money, we usually make at least an implicit judgment that we hope to reap the consequences in the short, middle, or long term. How does the cognitive economy shape students' time horizon for their learning choices? In a hot cognitive economy, a long time horizon for core learning activities will shape significant, ongoing efforts. Ongoing feedback on intrinsic goals supports students in maintaining a long time horizon and a high level of cognitive activity. A short time horizon will tend to cool the cognitive economy and bias students' choices toward immediate rewards that can be gained by surface approaches; it will promote cognitive speculation rather than long-term investment.

Community

In the money economy, we rely on the community of friends and family to advise us and, sometimes, to protect us. We are more likely to take a risky job if we have a stable family to fall back on; we are more likely to take risks on the job if we have trusting and supportive coworkers. Where such support systems are lacking in the money economy, the government often steps in through systems such as Social Security, unemployment insurance, and public assistance to provide community support in an impersonal but financially effective way. How does the cognitive economy affect the social support system of students, and how does that affect their willingness to take risks, try new things, and persist in their efforts in the face of short-term difficulties? A hot cognitive economy depends on continuous risk taking. Pursuing intrinsic goals for the long term requires feedback, but it also requires the safety net of reliable community support. The lack of a supportive community will cool the cognitive economy by raising the risk of long-term investments.

Alignment

In any system, the degree to which activities are aligned will determine to a considerable extent the power of the system to achieve desired outcomes. In any organization, if the divisions are working for different objectives, if the right hand doesn't know what the left hand is doing, activities will tend to cancel one another out. If the system lacks integrity, it will be less effective. In the money economy, if fiscal and monetary policy push in different directions, neither one will have its desired effect. We can already see, I hope, that the effect of the five categories listed above will be synergistic. A long time horizon creates more opportunities for feedback, as does an increased level of activities. Keeping key performances private, on the other hand, tends to discourage the collaboration that builds community support. The cognitive economy of a college can be aligned to achieve a cool or a hot learning environment. But misalignment, mixed messages, apparent contradictions, will tend to cool the cognitive economy. John Biggs (1999) views the system a bit more narrowly than I am doing here, but I think his caution applies: "To work properly, all components are aligned to each other. Imbalance in the system will lead to a breakdown, in this case to poor teaching and surface learning" (p. 25).

Table 8.1 summarizes the essential distinctions between a hot and a cool cognitive economy. In the next chapter, we will examine the Instruction Paradigm college under these six headings. In Part IV, we will consider how the cognitive economy might be better designed to create the Learning Paradigm college.

Table 8.1

The Cognitive Economy of Colleges

Hot	Cool
Goals	
Emphasizes intrinsic goals	Emphasizes extrinsic goals
Activity	
High level of cognitive activity; highest rewards for high cost activities: deep approaches, complex cognition	Low level of cognitive activity; high rewards for low-cost activities: surface approaches, retention
Information	
High ratio of feedback to evaluation	Low ratio of feedback to evaluation
Time Horizon	
Long time horizon; decisions bear consequences in the long term	Short time horizon; decisions bear consequences in the short term
Community	
Strong support community	Weak support community
Alignment	
Institutional behavior consistent, aligned with learning mission	Institutional behavior aligned with instruction mission or misaligned

9 The Cognitive Economy of the Instruction Paradigm College

A DESIGN FOR A COOL COGNITIVE ECONOMY

The cognitive economy of the Instruction Paradigm college today reinforces many of the destructive attitudes that students bring from high school. The academic calendar, cafeteria-style general education, and the grading process most powerfully shape the cognitive economy that students experience. For most entering students, their time and effort is the cost to be weighed against the benefit of as high a grade as may reasonably be bought with the available resources. The student, as a rational agent in this cognitive economy, seeks the cheapest possible success. From the students' perspective, the highest value class is one that produces the highest grade for the least effort. Different students respond to this system of incentives differently. Some students will seek to maximize profit and, confident of success in some areas, may choose those courses—and to a lesser degree the activities within courses—that will generate predictable success. Some students will seek to limit costs: Doubting their capacities, they may withdraw from effortful challenges quickly if rewards do not appear readily accessible. The conventional classroom is more conducive to risk avoidance than to risk seeking and hence encourages students to set performance goals rather than learning goals. In a system driven by the student credit hour and the GPA, students rationally choose to win positive judgments where they can and to reduce their investment of effort where they cannot.

As teachers, we want our students to be incremental theorists and to take a deep approach. We repeatedly tell students that effort makes a difference, that they will learn through failure, and that they can succeed if they try. These are good and important lessons, and as classroom teachers we should convey them with as much clarity, charity, and vigor as we can. I am certainly not saying that individual teachers cannot make a difference. We can and do. But whatever teachers say, the whole pattern of rewards and penalties officially sanctioned by the college or university tends to create a system that models and reinforces a very different lesson. In a college governed by the Instruction Paradigm, the parts limit the whole. Good teaching can do a lot. But when teachers are isolated in the separate cells of our classrooms, our individual efforts are divided and fragmented and, as we shall see below, can seldom be aligned with a coherent institutional mission. The cognitive economy of the college as an institution is often beyond the control of the faculty in many significant ways. The whole of the college curriculum, as experienced by many students, is less than the sum of the parts. Let us consider the six analytical categories of the cognitive economy and see how the Instruction Paradigm college performs, what kind of cognitive economy it produces.

GOALS: THE INSTRUCTION PARADIGM COLLEGE ENCOURAGES STUDENTS TO PURSUE EXTRINSIC GOALS

The Instruction Paradigm college, like most secondary schools, establishes and devotes substantial resources to preserving a system of external rewards based on faculty evaluations of student work. The almost universally sanctioned machine designed for this purpose is the system of letter grades in individual classes, averaged out to a global evaluation, the grade-point average or GPA. The importance that students place on grades in many cases simply mirrors the importance that colleges place on them: The transcript of grades is the only artifact of a student's stay at a college that the college preserves in perpetuity. The theory-in-use of most colleges as institutions is that grades are the most important thing that students bring away from the college. As we have seen, most students come from high school motivated primarily to get the diploma, secondarily to get good grades. That reward, in the cognitive economy of the college, becomes an autonomous artifact, linked only vaguely to the course from which it emerged.

The ultimate reward—the only language the college has to speak about students—the GPA, is entirely autonomous, severed from all links to specific student performances. What does a 2.5 or a 3.2 mean? What does it say about the student? No one has the slightest idea. Or everyone has a different idea, which amounts to the same thing. Milton, Pollio, and Eison (1986), in their careful and comprehensive analysis of the effect of grades in college discussed in Chapter 6, point out an inherent characteristic of grades as presently configured in most colleges:

> A grade is a unidimensional symbol into which multidimensional phenomena have been incorporated, a true salmagundi. Translated, this means a given grade can reflect the level of information, attitudes, procrastination, errors or misconceptions, cheating, and mixtures of all of these plus other ingredients; all of this was noted in the literature over 50 years ago as well as today and is well known but ignored. The lone letter symbol is a conglomerate which specifies none of its contents. (p. 212)

Whatever a GPA means, it means less than it used to. The role of grades in the cognitive economy of the college assures grade inflation. If the major motivator for student performance is the grade (and it is) and students bargain strongly and consistently for the highest grade for the least effort (and they do), then over time the significance of grades will diminish (and it has). Too many grade points chasing too little effort, to paraphrase a definition of monetary inflation. George Kuh (1999), of the Center for Postsecondary Research and Planning at Indiana University Bloomington, has examined student survey data for the four decades from the 1960s through the 1990s to find out what is behind the rising grades. We should hardly be surprised at his finding that increasing GPAs actually reflect less student effort. He concludes: "That students are getting higher grades for lower levels of effort suggests that a tacit agreement has been struck between faculty and students in the form of a disengagement compact: 'You leave me alone, and I'll leave you alone'" (pp. 112–113).

Grades, seen as personal goals for students, are performance goals. When grades become the primary motivator of student performance, they obscure and diminish other motivators. The student must weigh her own learning goals against the short-term performance goal sanctioned by the college. When there is a conflict, the cognitive economy gives precedence to the short-term goal of the grade. So the reward system of the classroom not only does not provide or tap into intrinsic goals, it tends to repress those goals, rewarding the student for setting them aside to jump through the required academic hoops. If students believe that they can achieve acceptable grades by employing a surface approach to learning, they will generally do so because a surface approach is "cheaper" in terms of time and effort than a deep approach. And most students come from high school well trained in the surface approach. If they do not, their peers will tutor them. As Kuh (1999) points out, "Student culture is surely a mediating factor in the amount of effort students put forth, as always; that is, returning students 'teach' new students how much academic effort is required to get by" (p. 112).

It is true that a deep approach offers great personal rewards for students in terms of satisfaction and long-term pleasure. But two factors make this option largely inoperative for most students. First, they don't know this and aren't likely to find out as a result of trying for a better GPA. Students can discover the intrinsic rewards of a deep approach to learning only by using a deep approach. If they have not done so often in an academic setting, they will not know what the intrinsic rewards can be. Even where students have been exposed to the pleasures of deep learning in an academic setting, they often believe that the experience was an anomaly, dependent on an extraordinary teacher or other special circumstances. They don't think to try it on their own in an environment that does not encourage such an approach. Second, many of the rewards of a deep approach are realized most fully in the long term. As we shall see, the short time horizon that the Instruction Paradigm college imposes on the learning process makes investments for the long term unlikely for many students.

We shall have occasion to reflect on the effects of grades and the grading system several times in describing the cognitive economy of the Instruction Paradigm college. This is because, as we shall see in more detail below, assessment systems have a disproportionate effect on other aspects of the whole system and powerfully shape student perceptions and expectations.

ACTIVITY: THE INSTRUCTION PARADIGM COLLEGE DEVALUES STUDENT PERFORMANCE

Students do things in the classroom, of course. And student activities may even be the major emphasis and organizing principle in some classrooms. However, that emphasis is optional for the teacher, not structured into the nature of the activity. Furthermore, no matter how great the emphasis on student performance in a particular classroom, the actual performance is usually visible only to a small cohort of students and the faculty members involved in a particular class; it is private rather than public. What the institution reifies and preserves as a permanent record of the class is the teacher's evaluation of the student, the grade, not the student performance. Many classes are designed primarily so that the teacher may cover a body of material. Whenever this is the case, student performances will be secondary, derivative, and artificial.

There is an important qualifier here. Even when they are not linked directly to outside activities, skills classes like drawing, choral singing, volleyball, and welding come closer to requiring continuous student performance than more academic classes like sociology, history, and biology. That means that the cognitive core of the curriculum, the common body of essential knowledge and skills that all students should have in common, is most likely to be encountered by students as inert knowledge, easily accessible to surface approaches.

There are two issues here. One is how active students are, how much time they spend doing the work of learning. The other is what kind of work they are doing. On the first question, we have already seen the results of George Kuh's study covering four decades of higher education experience that concluded that the level of effort that college students exert has been declining right along with increasing grades. Karen Maitland Schilling, professor of psychology at Miami University, and Karl L. Schilling (1999), deputy director of policy for the Virginia State Council of Higher Education, recently conducted a study of faculty and student expectations at several universities and colleges. They compared the amount of time students expected to devote to study at admission to college with parallel expectations after the first year. Their surprising finding: "Students report working even less than they expected!" Such a condition nearly defines a cool cognitive economy. Perhaps even better evidence, because drawing on a larger sample, has been produced by the National Survey of Student Engagement (NSSE) (2002). Directed by Kuh, the NSSE (pronounced "nessie" by its friends) surveyed in its first two years over 155,000 first-year and senior students at 470 four-year colleges and universities. Students were asked how much time they spent preparing for class: "studying, reading, writing, rehearsing, and other activities related to your academic program" (NSSE, 2001). As the NSSE 2001 report concludes, "Many students spend only about half as much time preparing for class as faculty members claim is necessary, about one hour for each class hour instead of two hours" (NSSE, 2001, p. 13). Of first-year students, 44.5% reported spending ten hours per week or less on study; 78.8% reported spending less than 20 hours. The corresponding figures for seniors were 44.5 and 78.3 (NSSE, 2002). This tends to support Schilling and Schilling's view that "Students appear to determine in their first months on campus how much time they will devote to academic pursuits, and this pattern of time allocation is durable over the rest of their college experience."

On the question of what kinds of activities students engage in, we can say that a system designed to promote extrinsic goals will tend to promote a surface approach, and we have already seen ample evidence that most colleges, overall, do that. Schilling and Schilling specifically addressed the question of what sort of activities students engage in. They conclude:

> Actual work fell short of expectations not only in the amount of time invested but also in the kinds of activities in which students engaged. For example, texts were emphasized rather than primary source materials; in science, students reported memorizing formulas and definitions and rarely using the scientific method; studying relied on the most passive of study strategies rather than higher-level thinking skills....The reported lived experience of students in the first year is apparently less demanding of student time than either faculty or students themselves had expected.

The NSSE shows a considerable range of student reports, both between and within various types of colleges, on questions relating to level of academic challenge, so we should be careful not to overgeneralize from the statistics. But we should also expect a certain number of students to come to college as involved and interested young scholars motivated by personal goals. What the statistical evidence seems to show is that many colleges do not create an environment that encourages and rewards a high level of student activity. Students appear to calculate quite reasonably early in their college experience the cost of passage, so to speak. And the students appear to be right, as indicated by the fact that the level of investment in time and effort by freshmen maintains relatively stable for seniors.

INFORMATION: INSTRUCTION PARADIGM COLLEGES MAXIMIZE EVALUATION AND MINIMIZE FEEDBACK

In individual classrooms, individual teachers can provide an environment rich in feedback for the period of the course. But at most colleges, as at most high schools, it is the very definition of a course that it ends with the term and that it ends with a final and permanent evaluation. In today's world, even taxes are sometimes avoidable. The only truly implacable realities are death and the transcript. End-of-term grades are pure evaluation, with no element of feedback, because end-of-term grades are final and offer no opportunity for reevaluation. Conventional courses reify and concretize evaluation at the expense of feedback.

Students get information about their performance and others' expectations from a variety of sources. We use the term "assessment" in a somewhat confusing way to refer to both feedback and evaluation (formative and summative assessment). In the cognitive economy of the Instruction Paradigm college, however, the institution reifies and highlights assessment as evaluation. The result is that, from the point of view of student learning, bad information drives out good in a kind of Gresham's law of assessment. This is often true even for courses and learning experiences that seem to have the potential to promote a deep approach to learning. Noel and Abigail Entwistle (1991) of the University of Edinburgh in the UK have studied the relationship between testing procedures and approaches to learning. They acknowledge that teachers often intend to promote deep approaches to learning and a focus on meaning. However, assessment actions speak louder than lecture words:

> While lecturers may espouse these high level objectives, the teaching which students experience and the examination questions set seem often to encourage much more limited goals—the accurate reproduction of course content. Students are strongly influenced by the form of assessment they expect: Multiple-choice formats, or an emphasis on detailed factual answers, push students towards a surface approach, while open, essay-type questions encourage a deep approach. (p. 208)

Milton, Pollio, and Eison (1986) reported a study that confirmed what will probably be obvious to most teachers: that the preponderance of students prefer multiple-choice tests. (About 70% tend to prefer multiple-choice tests as opposed to 30% who prefer essay tests.) Of even greater interest is the reason why students prefer such tests. The authors conclude:

> From the student's perspective, there is a definite preference
> for multiple-choice over essay examinations, and this is largely
> unrelated to a desire to learn course material: The preference
> reflects a common belief that such tests are easier to take and
> to get good grades on. (p. 172)

So students tend to prefer multiple-choice tests because they believe
they will be able to get better grades on them, and multiple-choice tests
tend to reinforce a surface approach to learning. Recall our discussion of
the role of self-theories as information filters in Chapter 6. We saw that entity theorists, who set performance goals, tend to see information about the
consequences of their actions as evaluation, while incremental theorists,
who are more likely to set learning goals, see such information as feedback.
The preference of most students for multiple-choice tests is based explicitly
on the view that such tests are likely to produce better evaluations. (Multiple-choice tests are capable of producing feedback to students, of course,
but that is not what most students are looking for.) Students' preference for
multiple-choice tests merely reflects the fact that they see classroom assessment as primarily evaluation, not feedback. They are filtering out the feedback and focusing on the evaluation. But they do this, to paraphrase Entwistle and Entwistle, because the assessment system they have been exposed to has pushed them toward a surface approach. As Ramsden (1992)
puts it, "Unsuitable assessment methods impose irresistible pressures on a
student to take the wrong approaches to learning tasks. It is our assessment,
not the student, that is the cause of the problem" (p. 68).

The Instruction Paradigm college generates a cognitive economy that
accentuates the role of assessment as evaluation and diminishes the role of
assessment as feedback. For many students assessment is, pure and simple,
grading. And grading is defined and used by the institution as evaluation.
We can see, of course, that student perceptions of the information they receive are strongly influenced by other factors as well. Students who are intrinsically motivated to understand a subject or master a process will be
much more likely to set learning goals, to aim at improvement of their
skills or knowledge, and will therefore seek out feedback before evaluation.
Students who are more active will see many more opportunities for finding and responding to feedback. Likewise, students for whom the learning
task has a long time horizon will be more likely to seek out feedback because they will have more opportunities to respond to it.

TIME: INSTRUCTION PARADIGM COLLEGES IMPOSE A SHORT TIME HORIZON ON LEARNING

When we discuss the time horizon for learning, recall, we are considering the answer to the question "How long will I have to live with the consequences of this decision?" And the decisions we are considering, of course, are the decisions students make about spending time and energy on study and learning. A short time horizon will create an inherent, almost irresistible, incentive to adopt a surface orientation to learning. If I don't need to hold on to this knowledge very long, why expend the energy it takes to learn it deeply? Why clutter up my head with all those synaptic patterns if I won't be using them in a couple of months? The students' perception of the time horizon for learning is thus one of the most crucial aspects of the cognitive economy.

In the Instruction Paradigm college, time is held constant while learning varies. For the core parts of the Instruction Paradigm, three-unit classes, time is parceled out into identical segments called quarters or semesters. In this connection, we might reflect on the meaning of one nearly ubiquitous artifact of the Instruction Paradigm structure, so common that most colleges designate a specific space for it in the academic calendar: the final examination. The final examinations that many institutions require teachers to administer during final examination week tend to become paradigmatic models of college assessment in the student mind, assessment par excellence. *The American Heritage College Dictionary*, 3rd edition, defines "final" in this way: "Forming or occurring at the end, last, ultimate." Indeed, it is that characteristic of being last that gives final exams their particular emotional salience for students. The final exam in Algebra I is the last exam in Algebra I. After it is over, Algebra I is finished. I don't need it any more. We do not want students to believe this, but this is what we tell them. After finals, it's over, done, finished. Finals are, well, final.

The problem is that students take this message with a devastating literalness that often undermines the value of all the work done in the semester. Conway and his colleagues (1997), in the study discussed in Chapter 6, specifically examined the resilience of the knowledge students marshaled for the final exam by reexamining the same students after the summer session. They concluded:

> For the courses sampled in this study, if there had been no
> summer examinations of the four lecture courses and if the

class test and course work had been the sole means of assessing and determining level of learning, then for many students... learning could cease shortly after completion of the lectures. Our findings suggest that at this point knowledge is still in the process of shifting from an episodic to a conceptual form and, therefore, subject to rapid forgetting. It is not until some time later, following many further exposures to the course material and protracted independent study, that knowledge fully shifts to a schematic and more stable and durable form. Thus, assessments that occur close in time to the presentation of the new material and that once taken eliminate the requirement for further study virtually ensure that knowledge is not primarily represented conceptually and in durable form. Quite clearly an undesirable outcome for any course in higher education. (p. 411)

Quite clearly. To paraphrase, courses designed with final exams that the student really believes are final exams virtually ensure that students will quickly forget most of what they learned.

The point here is not that the semester is too short. (Though it is certainly true that 16 to 18 weeks is not long enough for some students to master what they need to in some courses.) Indeed, a strong case can be made that for many classes and many students, the semester is too long. But ultimately squabbles between advocates of semesters and quarters and short-term classes simply miss the point. The key point in the preceding quotation is that final examinations, in the student's mind, "*eliminate the requirement for further study.*" It doesn't matter how long the term is. What matters is that the term—semester, quarter, whatever—contains the learning rather than being contained by it. If students experience semesters as stopping places on a continuous journey, they are harmless administrative conveniences. If they experience them as autonomous time-capsules of learning, in which the institutionalized assessment of knowledge that concludes them is the last application for the learning they will encounter, then this system condemns most students to a surface orientation to learning. If the end of the semester marks the time horizon for the learning, we irretrievably trivialize that learning. The self-contained, one-term class, the molecule from which the curricular matter of the Instruction Paradigm college is built, creates in the student's mind a short time horizon that inevitably chills the cognitive economy.

COMMUNITY: INSTRUCTION PARADIGM COLLEGES ISOLATE STUDENTS FROM SUPPORTIVE COMMUNITIES

Students who know, spend time with, and seek support from other students and from faculty and other staff members persist and succeed in college at a much higher rate than students who do not. Alexander Astin (1993) concluded that "the student's peer group is the single most potent source of influence on growth and development during the undergraduate years" (p. 398). Many colleges have recognized the importance of peer support and have devised programs for both residential and nonresidential students that seek to make use of this principle. The conventional pattern of separate courses, each with a separate cohort of strangers, is radically dysfunctional. It denies students peer support by, for all practical purposes, denying them peers. And while communities do develop, sometimes, around majors or vocational programs, they are almost completely lacking for the students who need them the most.

We know that students are most likely to drop out of college in the first year. And we know as well that students in the first year of college have just entered a new environment that is peopled largely by strangers. The obvious causal connection between these two facts can hardly escape us. Other aspects of the cognitive economy of the Instruction Paradigm college tend to undermine efforts to build community. The emphasis on evaluation creates a competitive climate in which students see one another as potential opponents rather than partners. Privacy and secrecy reinforce this ethos of individuality. Distributional general education requirements place the selection of classes in the hands of the student but make it virtually impossible for the student to use this power in such a way as to construct a meaningful community. The short time horizon through which students experience the fragmented curriculum makes it difficult for them to build relationships with other students in the classroom. In spite of all of these barriers, students do establish communities of support—the students who remain in college do, that is.

Our anecdotal impressions of college performance are skewed by the fact that the students for whom our institutions fail most damagingly simply disappear. We see them only in their absence from the following year's statistics. We don't hear their stories. They don't come back and ask us for recommendations to graduate school. They don't return alumni surveys, because they have never graduated. They simply fall off the radar. A cognitive economy that leaves students without a meaningful support community is one of the chief reasons why they disappear.

In this respect, college is worse than high school for many students, which is one reason why many successful high school students drop out of college. In high school, most students have a stable peer group for four years. When they come to college they lose this vital support system, and if they cannot replace it fairly quickly, they are at grave risk for returning to an established peer group that excludes college success. This risk is obviously greater for commuting students and commuter colleges.

ALIGNMENT: AT INSTRUCTION PARADIGM COLLEGES, ELEMENTS OF THE COGNITIVE ECONOMY ARE USUALLY MISALIGNED

While colleges vary in the extent to which the elements of the cognitive economy are aligned, I know of no college that is systematically aligned in consistent pursuit of the Instruction Paradigm. The reason is simple. Nobody believes in the Instruction Paradigm. Nobody defends it. Nobody thinks running institutions for the purpose of keeping the classes full is really a good idea. Administrators and faculty members enforce the Instruction Paradigm rules because they believe they have to, and often do so with deep resentment and distaste. At many colleges, many of the best teachers consider it their personal mission to subvert and undermine the administrative rules and procedures that the Instruction Paradigm imposes, and often to help students subvert them. That is certainly my approach. Faculty members who are active learners themselves, as researchers, not only understand a deep approach to learning but often embrace it as a major life project. When they enter the classroom, these teachers want to share the best kind of learning with their students, want to open up the possibilities for the truly transformative learning that has shaped them as scholars as well as teachers. (Indeed, one of the reasons many faculty members prefer their research activities to their teaching activities is that they find it possible to take a deep approach to learning in the lab or in the study, whereas they find that the classroom constrains them to superficial and redundant activities. Not to put too fine a point on it, some faculty find the classroom problematic for many of the same reasons students do.)

Even by Instruction Paradigm standards, the curriculum is seldom aligned from the point of view of students simply because of the enormous variation in standards, criteria, and assessment methods from course to course. Even assuming the highest standards for individual faculty members, it is impossible for a faculty of a hundred or more to just spontaneously adopt a consistent approach to pedagogy and assessment without careful collaborative planning. Where such faculty planning is absent, even good classes may be so different from one another as to produce no recognizable patterns for students to hold on to. The result was summarized as well as could be hoped for by that senior quoted in Chapter 1: "It didn't add up to anything. It was just a bunch of courses." That is an excellent definition of misalignment.

I am convinced that most teachers do their best to be honest with students, and that means that teachers, especially the best teachers, undermine the Instruction Paradigm system at every turn. They tell students that learning is more important than grades, that they should plan for the long term, that they should follow their dreams, that they can do great things. While many teachers, torn about their paradoxical role in their institutions, try to rationalize the GPA and the semester system as somehow being able to serve students' long-term interests, many make no effort to conceal their disdain for the bureaucratic baggage of the college as knowledge factory. Students who get a good education at college inevitably get radically mixed messages about what college is for and what matters in education: The institutional paradigm tells them one thing; the people who carry it out, especially those who model learning at its best, tell them—explicitly or implicitly—quite a different thing.

Today many—if not most—institutions are trying to change, hence the spate of innovations that we discussed in Chapters 1 and 2. As I pointed out there, such innovation, even where it has reached the level of permanent change, often fails to transform fundamental institutional practices. The result is that some institutional policies seem to go against the overall trend, without reversing that trend: mixed messages, misalignment in the big picture. In fact, the most dramatic and effective innovations in institutional practice can often result in the most severely mixed messages. An excellent example of such a phenomenon is the widespread response to the problem of lack of community support for new students discussed above. Because this problem directly affects enrollment, it rises to a level of concern even in the Instruction Paradigm college. The Instruction Paradigm college, after all, is in the business of enrollment. Vincent Tinto (1998), professor of education at Syracuse University, notes that research over the past 20 years has produced "a growing consensus among researchers and theorists alike about the major forces shaping student persistence" (p. 167):

> Perhaps as a reflection of this consensus, administrators and policy planners have increasingly turned to this body of work to provide empirical justification for the institutional policies they develop to promote student persistence. The result has been the proliferation of a wide variety of "retention" programs (e.g. freshman year seminars, mentoring programs) designed to enhance the likelihood that students will persist to degree completion. But while we have witnessed changes in programming for students, in particular in the domain of student affairs, we have not seen comparable changes in the academic side of the house or in the organization of higher education. In this regard, the educational experiences of students have remained largely unchanged, their education relatively unaffected by the research on student persistence. (pp. 167–168)

At some institutions, student services programs have adapted to student needs in dramatic ways, while the curriculum has remained unforgiving. In discussions with student services people at a few of these colleges, I have found that some of them have come to, perhaps unconsciously but nonetheless clearly, regard the conventional curriculum as the enemy and view themselves as guides who help students to pass through the minefield of institutional requirements without serious injury. The misalignment of institutional processes becomes vividly clear when counselors or mentors come to view their jobs in large measure as circumventing the built-in design of the instructional program. Other institutions have comprehensively revised their curriculum for some cohorts of at-risk students, say for developmental or first-year students, providing learning communities, developmental sequencing of learning activities, and offering integrated support services. But in the second year, all of this goes away and the student is cast back onto the assembly line of the knowledge factory. The extended time horizon that such first-year programs consciously seek to create can be suddenly collapsed for students when they are thrown into the free-for-all registration process as sophomores. The student in such a misaligned cognitive economy faces the same kind of confusion as does an investor for whom the government's fiscal policy seems to indicate one course of action and its monetary policy another.

I do not mean in these comments any negative criticism of such innovations, which in my view are almost always seeking to do the right thing and often succeed for many students. The point is simply that such reforms, while they may be good in themselves, inevitably contribute to the misalignment of the total educational environment unless and until the rest of the environment is realigned to match them. They warm up the cognitive economy for many students, but the misalignment of processes and purposes in the whole institution can have a chilling effect.

If we are concerned with the student's whole experience at the college, with the orientation to learning that the institution produces, then we need to pay attention to alignment. If we are concerned with the overall cognitive economy of the institution, then we need to pay attention to alignment. If we are concerned about the long-term trend of institutional change, the survivability of positive reforms, then we need to pay attention to alignment.

THE NEED FOR TRANSFORMATION

The Instruction Paradigm college produces a cool cognitive economy, and the causal factors are not incidental. Rather, the factors that can most effectively deter a deep orientation to learning and promote a surface orientation are inherent to the Instruction Paradigm and derive from the basic architecture of the college structured on that paradigm. This does not mean, of course, that college students don't learn or that there are not enclaves of excellence in most colleges. It does mean that institutions maintain a cognitive economy that fails to promote the fullest development of all students and that actively impedes the development of many. It does not mean that colleges do not innovate effectively to promote student learning. It does mean that such innovations will fall short of their potential until the fundamental structures of the institution are aligned with them. It most emphatically does not mean that there is some cookie-cutter model of what a Learning Paradigm college is like that can correct all of the errors of the old paradigm. As we shall see in the next section, the Learning Paradigm is unlike the Instruction Paradigm in that it is not a unitary model that dictates a single set of structures or patterns that all must follow. Indeed, it is better to think of the Learning Paradigm as a journey rather than a destination. It is more like the scientific method, or a spiritual quest, than it is like a recipe or a blueprint. A hot cognitive economy will be, first and foremost, an environment open to exploration, one that rewards experiment and discovery. It will be, to say the same thing a little differently—and as accurately as possible—a rich learning environment.

Today we know more about students and how they learn than we ever have before. This knowledge has empowered us to see that we can do better. Today, as never before, the argument for a paradigm shift in the way we think about, organize, and carry out undergraduate education is supported by evidence that all but compels consent among those who approach the issue with good will and open minds. As that consent to certain key insights reaches the level of consensus, it empowers us. As Carol Geary Schneider and Robert Shoenberg (1998) of the AAC&U observe:

> The groundwork for success has already been laid in the form of an emerging consensus about what matters in undergraduate education and some promising pedagogical strategies for getting there. We need to seize the opportunity for building a more purposeful, powerful and integrative structure and practice for undergraduate education that the consensus can make possible. (p. 25)

In Part IV, we will consider a functional outline for this new structure from the perspective of the student's experience: the cognitive economy of the Learning Paradigm college.

PART IV

A DESIGN FOR LEARNING

If we begin our thinking about how to design college and university programs with the assumptions and structures of the Instruction Paradigm, then we will tend to reproduce with relatively minor variations the same flaws and limitations we seek to correct. Just as deep and surface approaches to learning involve different ways of seeing the object of learning, so a shift from the Instruction Paradigm to the Learning Paradigm means a different way of seeing what colleges do. Rather than being bound by the

119

atomistic categories of the Instruction Paradigm, we need to learn to see the work of colleges as they affect the whole experience of the learners. We need first to envision the cognitive economy of the college, then to reconstruct the mechanism of the college around it. It is not easy to see the familiar with new eyes. But it is the only way to change the world.

Parker Palmer (1998) relates an experience that exemplifies the rethinking and reseeing we need to do:

> I once led a faculty workshop where the conversation had turned toward students, and many participants were complaining about how silent and indifferent they are. The workshop was being held in a glass-walled conference room at the core of a new classroom building, and the curtains that might have shut off our view of the surrounding hallways had been left open. In the midst of the student-bashing, a bell rang and the classrooms surrounding the conference room began to empty out. The halls quickly filled with young people, talking to each other with great energy and animation.
>
> I asked the faculty to observe the evidence before us and then asked them to explain the difference between the students they had been describing and the ones we were now seeing: "Is it possible that your students are not brain-dead? Is it possible that their classroom coma is induced by classroom conditions and that once they cross the threshold into another world, they return to life?" (p. 42)

In the following chapters we will turn away from the exclusive focus on the classroom that tends to dominate thinking about college in the Instruction Paradigm and look both beyond and within the classroom for that other world, where our students can return to life.

10

The Cognitive Economy of the Learning Paradigm College

THE COGNITIVE ECONOMY BEYOND THE CLASSROOM

In their detailed study of talented high school students, Csikszentmihalyi, Rathunde, and Whalen (1993) found that Parker Palmer's observation was no anomaly. Recall that the researchers in this study (described in Chapter 5) used electronic pagers to trigger responses from over 200 high school students at random times during the day. The questionnaire that students filled out indicated, among other things, whether students were doing what they wanted to be doing (volition) and whether they were thinking about what they were doing (attention). These were students who had been identified in advance as talented, so not surprisingly they exhibited a high level of attention in the classroom, but this high level of attention was accompanied by a very low level of volition. Volition, as Palmer and the members of his faculty workshop observed, was much higher in the corridors than in the classroom. Not surprisingly, volition was highest in the cafeteria. But these settings provided almost the reverse picture from the classroom (though with less extreme variation): High volition accompanied markedly lower attention. There was one setting in the school environment where both volition and attention were high: extracurricular activities.

I began my teaching career, some years ago, as a forensics coach and speech teacher at a large state university. I coached a group of students, of vastly varying skill levels, in various competitive speaking events while at the same time teaching basic speech and argumentation courses in the general education curriculum. I observed that the students involved in extracurricular forensics were, by orders of magnitude, more engaged, interested, and motivated than those in the regular classes. Furthermore, it seemed to me that they learned a great deal more. While coaching I had

121

the experience of real teaching, of providing feedback that students used to improve. And all of them, perhaps the novices even more dramatically than the more accomplished, did improve. In the classroom, by contrast, I seemed to be engaged in a perpetual accounting and rule-enforcing exercise in which the students systematically did the minimum. Only rarely could I see any significant improvement in a student in the course of the semester. Looking back on the experience now, I would say that the cognitive economy of the forensics program was dramatically hotter than the cool cognitive economy of the classroom. In talking with colleagues working with students in journalism, theater, music, and athletics I came to the conclusion that nothing distinctive about me or my subject explained this difference. Students who were involved in extracurricular activities were generally better students than students in class. I even had several opportunities to make a direct comparison of the same students inside and outside the classroom. They seemed to be smarter, more serious, more effective students outside the classroom. The challenge of effective teaching, for me, came to be framed by this formative experience: How can I get the students in the classroom to learn like the students on the debate team? I'm still working on that project, some 25 years later, with a little, but not much, success. Why is it so hard? Because the Instruction Paradigm structure limits what happens in the classroom in certain ways that curtail student motivation and inhibit learning.

When I first read Csikszentmihalyi's research on talented high school students, it struck me as clearly and intuitively true and entirely consistent with my own experience. And as I began to examine how the cognitive economy of the school interacts with students as the agents of learning, I realized that we have not far to seek for examples of a hot cognitive economy: excellent, well-designed extracurricular activities. And as I have pursued the question, my definition of "activities" has broadened to include many learning environments that do not fit the conventional mode. By the way, I have chosen to use the term "extracurricular" as opposed to the currently popular "cocurricular" because I think it is a more accurate description of the relationship between the two kinds of activities in most colleges. The term "cocurriculum" implies that the activities it encompasses are in some way coordinated with the academic program. At most colleges, this is simply not the case. The most involving student activities are outside the academic curriculum. That, as we shall see, is a source of their strength.

The idea that the curriculum should be more like extracurriculars is hardly a new one. And the objections to this idea are legion and familiar: Students in extracurriculars are self-selected; they are an elite few; they get more time and resources; they tend to have higher native abilities, and so forth. There is some truth to these claims. However, there is more truth to the claim that well-designed extracurricular activities not only attract good learners, they create them. Richard Light (2001), developer and director of the Harvard Assessment Seminars, summarizes his conclusions from over a decade of interviews with seniors at Harvard and several other institutions in his book *Making the Most of College: Students Speak Their Minds*:

> I assumed that most important and memorable academic learning goes on inside the classroom, while outside activities provide a useful but modest supplement. The evidence shows that the opposite is true: Learning outside of classes, especially in residential settings and extracurricular activities such as the arts, is vital. When we asked students to think of a specific, critical incident or moment that had changed them profoundly, four-fifths of them chose a situation or event outside of the classroom. (p. 8)

When activities outside the classroom do create good learners, they do so because of certain characteristics of such programs that differ from our academic programs in ways that are directly relevant to promoting a deep orientation to learning and incremental theory among students.

ALIGNMENT MAKES THE WHOLE

In the following chapters, we will consider the characteristics of a hot cognitive economy, a cognitive economy that promotes a deep orientation to learning and discourages a surface orientation, that nurtures incremental self-theories and transforms entity self-theories, that makes students lifelong learners by initiating the life of learning while they are in college. Let me begin, however, with a reminder of the end. As we move through the first five characteristics of a hot cognitive economy, we can do so coherently only if we keep one eye at all times on the sixth: alignment. Any of these characteristics severed from the rest will produce less than we hope for.

Aligning the Five Characteristics of a Learning Paradigm College

1) *A Learning Paradigm college should support students in pursuing their own goals.* But if we simply take the personal goals that most late adolescents or young adults bring with them to college, we will be raising up a generation of video-game mavens—or even worse, a generation committed to the narrow and shallow pursuit of material wealth.

2) *A Learning Paradigm college should require frequent student performances.* But student performances done for their own sake will quickly deteriorate into a dismal and uninspiring ritual of pointless display.

3) *A Learning Paradigm college should provide frequent and ongoing feedback.* But feedback that is not understood by the performer in a larger context of intrinsic goals and publicly accessible standards often degenerates into trivial grading.

4) *A Learning Paradigm college should assure a long time horizon for learning.* But a long time horizon without intrinsic motivation and effective feedback will discourage students and lead to lower persistence.

5) *A Learning Paradigm college should provide for stable communities of practice.* But communities that do not incorporate intrinsic motivation and continual feedback over a long period of time usually provide cover for declining standards rather than scaffolding for raising standards.

I do not mean to suggest that the Learning Paradigm college will need to have every jot and tittle in place in order to create a hot cognitive economy. But I do mean to suggest that it is the cognitive economy, and the alignment of different activities to produce a coherent whole, that ultimately matters. With that in mind, we can proceed to examine what it takes to produce the hot cognitive economy of the Learning Paradigm college.

A Challenge, not a Blueprint

In what follows, I am not proposing a detailed blueprint for the Learning Paradigm college. Indeed, in this section I am not directly addressing the organization of the college at all. I am attempting to describe the kinds of experiences that will constitute a hot cognitive economy for students. Peter Vaill (1996), professor of human systems in the School of Business and Public Management at George Washington University, in his book *Learning as a Way of Being* introduces the concept of a process frontier: "A *process frontier* is a new area of activity for the organization or a substantial modification in the way something has been done heretofore" (p. 135). I offer below several process frontiers for colleges and universities. But Vaill points out that organizations facing process frontiers cannot avoid the work of creatively reformulating institutional practice to meet the new challenges. Indeed, the magic of the process frontier is that it offers the organization the opportunity to learn! A process frontier, understood as a challenge to meet, offers a learning experience. So what follows will be neither a blueprint nor a cookbook. Vaill warns:

> Institutional learning philosophy and practice have bred into many of us an obsession with "how to do it." This obsession amounts to a desire *not* to have a learning experience! We do not want to go through the creative learning that process frontiers require. Rather, we want a protocol that takes the messiness and the anxiety out of the process frontier. We want our learning to be targeted and efficient. (p. 136)

I will provide examples under each characteristic of a hot cognitive economy that illustrate how some institutions are formulating a response to the process frontier in question. I make no claim that these examples represent the best practices or the best institutions; they illustrate the principles. Many other institutions not mentioned here are doing similar things. My purpose is not to provide a list of the best colleges or programs; it is to clarify through a few concrete illustrations how some institutions are approaching the process frontier in each case, to show that the thing can be done. Some of the examples present colleges that have been pursuing a given approach for years or decades, some are more clearly works in progress. Some examples will be more detailed than others.

I will intermingle examples of research universities, state colleges and universities, liberal arts colleges, and community colleges. This goes a bit against the grain of much recent literature in higher education and the inclinations of many institutions. There is a tendency for institutions to group themselves by Carnegie classification and to assume that they can learn productive lessons only from institutions that are similar. I have lost count of the number of times I have heard educators discount powerful examples of transformative change with the comment, "Well, of course, they're an X and we're a Y." As if Carnegie classification were destiny. It seems to me too that educators at every type of institution seem to think that their institutional type is the most beset by problems and impervious to change. "Well, of course, *they* can do it; they're a small liberal arts college/large research university/state-supported/private. But we could never do it here because we're a . . . ."

I think this is a mistake. My own conversations with educators from all institutional types have shown me how similar their problems and complaints are. Many of the complaints that research universities receive from the employers of their baccalaureate graduates are strikingly similar to those that technical colleges receive concerning students who have received their vocational certificates. Faculty in upper-division majors and programs and even graduate programs often report the same problems and challenges as those in general education programs and even developmental courses, though at different levels. And this is just what we should expect. If students come to college with a surface orientation to learning, and that orientation persists through the lower division, it will still be there when the student advances to upper division work. This is not to deny the important differences between different types of institutions. It is, however, to suggest that a cool cognitive economy is the enemy of all who are interested in learning, at every level and form of education. Educators have a tendency to want to see their own institutions as distinctive, different. And this is an entirely healthy desire if acted on in a healthy way. As I have suggested before and will suggest again, the Learning Paradigm opens up many opportunities to pursue a distinctive institutional path in ways that reward students with distinctive and valuable learning experiences. In the Instruction Paradigm framework of standardized processes, however, the chief hope of distinctiveness resides in institutional type within a geographical region. So institutions take what pride they may in falling in a particular Carnegie classification, since their curriculum and educational programs are for all practical purposes interchangeable with any other. If institutions want to become truly distinctive, to add special value to their students' experience, they can best find the way to do so by looking at a variety of other institutions and at the variety of ways institutions have sought to create a hot cognitive economy. In this process of discovery, community colleges and liberal arts colleges have much to learn from research universities, and research universities in turn from community colleges and liberal arts colleges. I will not ignore the differences between institutional types here, but neither will I exaggerate them, as I think we often do.

These examples, then, are case studies of institutional learning that illustrate how some institutions are learning; they are not recipes to be followed mechanically. Why? Precisely because the whole governs the parts, and the alignment of the elements of the cognitive economy is more important than any of them taken separately. Several of the institutions we will consider could be used as examples of multiple principles. These will often be examples of institutions that are moving toward better alignment around learning goals. But as I hope those examples will make clear, alignment must be earned through the labor of learning; it can neither be bought nor borrowed. So the purpose of the following chapters is not so much to lay out conclusions or models that educators can follow as to define the lessons that we as educators need to learn.

11 A Learning Paradigm College Promotes Intrinsically Rewarding Goals

THE IMPORTANCE OF INTRINSIC MOTIVATION

A hot cognitive economy can survive only if people can use it to achieve real and important goals. We will devote ourselves for a short time, to gain money or grade points, to tasks that are designed by others and serve purposes we care little about. But for the long term, for tasks that require a genuine investment of self, we need to care about both the process and the outcome. We invest ourselves in what really matters to us.

Students who can link their college work to their intrinsic interests consistently enjoy college more. The conclusions of social science research on the role of goals in motivation are straightforward. Albert Bandura (1997) summarizes them this way:

> Goals are unlikely to have much effect if there is little personal commitment to them. Goal commitment can be affected by the degree to which they are personally determined. When people select their own goals, they are likely to have greater self-involvement in achieving them. If goals are prescribed by others, however, individuals do not necessarily accept them or feel obligated to meet them. (p. 218)

Richard Light (2001) points out that students spend most of their time outside of the classroom, and that most of that time for college students is discretionary:

> That leads to a simple but enormously powerful finding that shines through interview after interview with graduating seniors. Those students who make connections between what goes on inside and outside the classroom report a more

128

> satisfying college experience. The students who find some
> way to connect their interest in music, for example, either
> with coursework or with an extracurricular volunteer activ-
> ity or both, report a qualitatively different overall experience.
> (p. 14)

Perhaps even more relevant in the educational context, we grow only when we invest ourselves in this way. As Csikszentmihalyi (1990) puts it, "Paradoxically, it is when we act freely, for the sake of the action itself rather than for ulterior motives, that we learn to become more than what we were" (p. 42). Kris Gerulski, a 2000 graduate of Michigan State University, puts it this way:

> It bothers me that we typically measure success in college by
> GPA and whether or not you make the Dean's List. These
> things are not about growing; they are about mastering the
> system. I wonder how many students know whether they are
> growing and what the word "growing" means to them? (Fear,
> Latinen, Woodward, and Gerulski, 2000)

When we speak of intrinsic goals, there is often a tendency to think of an individual's goals as fixed and stationary. In fact, what we all want is movement, to get somewhere. The truly motivating (which means, of course, "moving") goals are not just external objects that we seek to own; they are ways that we seek to live. We have all known people who have worked hard at jobs that did not promote their personal growth. Most of us have experienced at one time or another the dead-end job, terminal not only in terms of chances for promotion but in terms of chances for development and excitement. Work, per se, does not seem to help us grow. Certainly the acquisition of money is no route to happiness—though the game of acquisition may be one that the player enjoys. People who don't grow aren't happy. Indeed, the concept of intrinsic goals is not a simple one. It does not mean simply chosen. Some of our choices are driven by more deeply held values and aspirations than others. And most of us don't really know what is inside us, what it is that fundamentally drives or rewards us, until after we have reflected on the question.

Csikszentmihalyi's (1990) analysis of flow provides an excellent framework for understanding how people change. In a wide range of studies of people in various walks of life and of different ages and levels of ability, he found that the flow experience changed them:

> It provided a sense of discovery, a creative feeling of trans-
> porting the person into a new reality. It pushed the person to
> higher levels of performance, and led to previously un-
> dreamed-of states of consciousness. In short, it transformed
> the self by making it more complex. (p. 74)

The essence of flow is the experience of balance between the demands of the task and the capacity of the person:

> In all the activities people in our study reported engaging in,
> enjoyment comes at a very specific point: Whenever the op-
> portunities for action perceived by the individual are equal to
> his or her capabilities. Playing tennis, for instance, is not en-
> joyable if the two opponents are mismatched, the less skilled
> player will feel anxious, and the better player will feel bored.
> The same is true of every other activity: A piece of music that
> is too simple relative to one's listening skills will be boring,
> while music that is too complex will be frustrating. Enjoy-
> ment appears at the boundary between boredom and anxiety,
> when the challenges are just balanced with the person's ca-
> pacity to act. (p. 52)

Goals, in this framework, become intrinsically rewarding not because of some inherent qualities they possess, but because their pursuit falls within the range of potential enjoyment. We work hard and long to achieve a goal only when we have the experience of approaching it. We seek a goal when we think we can have that experience. We give up when we don't. This concept will suggest to many readers Lev Vygotsky's (1978) idea of the zone of proximal development (ZPD). Children learn, Vygot-sky suggested, when new tasks fall in the range that is a little more chal-lenging than they can handle by themselves, but still possible for them to master with the support of adults or peers: "The zone of proximal devel-opment defines those functions that have not yet matured but are in the process of maturation, functions that will mature tomorrow but are cur-rently in an embryonic state" (p. 86). Learning happens when challenge and support are in balance, and embryonic functions can mature into realized abilities. We can hardly doubt the link between learning in this sense and pleasure or enjoyment.

We should keep in mind that the learner's subjective belief in the accessibility of the goal is crucial here. Hence, it seems reasonable to expect that incremental theorists will tend to project a larger ZPD than entity theorists simply because of their belief that effort is likely to bear results. Recall Dweck's study, described in Chapter 6, in which students who had adopted an incremental self-theory with respect to a particular learning task pursued a tutorial program aimed at improving their performance at a much higher rate than students who had adopted an entity theory.

If we try to design an environment that simply does what the students come to us wanting to do, we trivialize the whole educational process. The reason most students need to come to college, rather than simply receive vocational training, is to help clarify their long-term goals, to discover their heretofore undiscovered potential, to surprise themselves. In this sense we would serve students poorly if we treated them as customers and followed the dictum that the customer is always right. One of the most important jobs of colleges is to get students to do things they don't start out wanting to do. But it is crucial, if this process is to work, that the students come to choose those tasks, to discover that they in fact want to do and to be more than they had before.

What we often fail to recognize is the power of the learning environment to create motivation. Bandura (1997) points out:

> Most of the things people enjoy doing for their own sake originally held little or no interest for them. Children are not born innately interested in singing operatic arias, playing contrabassoons, solving mathematical equations, writing sonnets, or propelling shot-put balls through the air. But with appropriate learning experiences, almost any activity, however trifling it may appear to others, can become imbued with consuming personal significance. (pp. 218–219)

We have created environments where students are exposed to a range of subjects and content in course-sized chunks. Their response to these subject requirements is simply to get them out of the way unless they relate to prior interests. Our first aim should be to create motivating learning environments, no matter what the subject may be. If we can do that, we need not settle for second-rate goals. Not only is there no conflict between students' enjoying learning and doing it well; if they do not enjoy it, they will not do it well. But the nature of that enjoyment is all-important, and the mission of the college is to direct students onto those paths where they will find pleasure in growth and satisfaction in wisdom. What T. S. Eliot (1943) said of poetry applies to education in the Learning Paradigm college: "To understand a poem comes to the same thing as to enjoy it for the right reasons" (p. 128). To succeed in college comes to the same thing as to enjoy it for the right reasons.

OWNERSHIP, SOVEREIGNTY, AND RESPONSIBILITY

To whatever extent students see learning tasks as chosen and as relevant to their personal goals, they are more likely to embrace those tasks and learn to enjoy them. As Whitehead (1929) noted some years ago, "There can be no mental development without interest. Interest is the *sine qua non* for attention and apprehension" (p. 31). Csikszentmihalyi (1997) points out, "There is quite extensive evidence showing that even if one does not experience flow, just the fact of doing something in line with one's goals improves the state of mind" (p. 137). He suggests that

> a simple way of improving the quality of life is to take ownership of one's actions. A great deal of what we do (over two-thirds, on the average) are things we feel we have to do, or we do because there isn't anything else we feel like doing. Many people spend their entire lives feeling like puppets who move only because their strings are pulled. Under these conditions we are likely to feel that our psychic energy is wasted. So the question is, why don't we *want* to do more things? The sheer act of wanting focuses attention, establishes priority in consciousness, and thus creates a sense of inner harmony. (p. 137)

Approaching the question from the other direction, and drawing upon a different but substantial body of empirical research, Bandura (1997) concludes:

> Goals are unlikely to have much effect if there is little personal commitment to them. Goal commitment can be affected by the degree to which they are personally determined. When people select their own goals, they are likely to have greater

> self-involvement in achieving them. If goals are prescribed by
> others, however, individuals do not necessarily accept them or
> feel obligated to meet them. (p. 218)

Recall the experience of the patients in the nursing home in Langer's (1989) study for whom ownership of even simple daily tasks opened up the route to mindfulness and a fuller life. A robust learning environment is one that encourages students to take ownership of their actions by helping them to link those actions with their personal goals. The corollary to ownership of one's actions is responsibility for them. It involves a sense of controlling the consequences by determining the actions. Clearly, this sense of ownership and responsibility reinforces and is reinforced by incremental self-theories. The belief in one's ability to take responsibility and ownership, hence to influence the outcome, both constitutes and enhances the sense of self-efficacy with respect to learning. As Bandura (1997) points out, "Belief in one's learning efficacy activates and sustains the effort and thought needed for skill development. Conversely, self-inefficacious thinking retards development of the very subskills upon which more complex performances depend" (p. 61).

We found in Chapter 7 that adopting a deep approach to learning involves a different way of seeing the object of learning. One important aspect of this different way of seeing is this sense of ownership. Is what I see when I look at the object of learning mine or is it under the control of somebody else? The opposite of ownership, as I am using the term here, is something like helplessness, the sense Csikszentmihalyi identified of being a puppet whose strings are pulled by someone else. Consider the difference between watching a videotape of an event that has already taken place and seeing an event unfold in real time before you. Consider the difference between being a participant in a baseball game or the birth of a child or a conversation and watching it from the outside. We internalize goals, make them intrinsic, by taking ownership of and responsibility for them. This almost always entails reflecting on the goals themselves, learning about the meaningfulness of the task through experiment, learning to recognize the object of learning as ours, as reachable in our personal world. Vaill (1996) emphasizes the importance of creative learning as a component of learning as a way of being. He contrasts creative learning with institutional learning, which is essentially guided by what we have identified here as the Instruction Paradigm. "The essence of the institutional learning model," he writes, "is the idea that learning is the process of transferring information from one who knows to one who does not know. If there is no 'body of knowledge' to be transferred, institutional learning does not know quite what to do" (p. 62). This can lead to a pedagogy in which goals set in the classroom are "clear," but at the price of being, from the point of view of the student, "arbitrary or meaningless clear goals" (p. 62). In contrast, "In creative learning, exploration of the meaningfulness of the goal is *part of the learning itself*" (p. 62).

This exploration of the meaningfulness of the goal is the only way we can creatively adapt and develop it. And it is a way of asserting ownership or —to use a related term coined by Walker Percy—"sovereignty" over the goal and the object of learning. In a deep and damaging sense, the imposition of external goals in the Instruction Paradigm college makes students into consumers. Percy (1954), in his extraordinary essay "The Loss of the Creature," frames this issue vividly. (It is with some hesitation that I excerpt a work so perfectly realized on its own terms. I salve my conscience with the hope that readers may be inspired to seek out the whole essay. It is well worth the effort.) Percy writes:

> A young Falkland Islander walking along a beach and spying a dead dogfish and going to work on it with his jackknife has, in a fashion wholly unprovided in modern educational theory, a great advantage over the Scarsdale High School pupil who finds the dogfish on his laboratory desk. Similarly the citizen of Huxley's *Brave New World* who stumbles across a volume of Shakespeare in some vine-grown ruins and squats on a potsherd to read it is in a fairer way of getting at a sonnet than the Harvard sophomore taking English Poetry II. (p. 56)

Why? "To put it bluntly: A student who has the desire to get at a dogfish or a Shakespeare sonnet may have the greatest difficulty in salvaging the creature itself from the educational packaging in which it is presented" (p. 57).

This difficulty is acute because it presents a special case of a difficulty that pervades contemporary industrial society. It is what Percy characterizes as the loss of sovereignty over our own experience of the world. "The creature" of the title of his essay is the thing itself, the object of experience: a Shakespeare sonnet, the Grand Canyon, or the person sitting next to you. The things of our world are so embedded in symbolic apparatus and interpretation that we are like tourists, not seeing the Eiffel Tower or Half Dome but testing it against the postcard and television images that have already defined the thing for us. We are challenged daily to free the world we see from "its citadel of symbolic investiture" (p. 51). The world is so thoroughly interpreted by the various domains of expertise that we can only with difficulty get at it. And for many this loss of sovereignty "is a generalized surrender of the horizon to those experts within whose competence a particular segment of the horizon is thought to lie" (p. 55).

The challenge is especially acute for educators and students—the scholars in universities, after all, are the experts who have "staked out" for themselves "[t]he whole horizon of being" (p. 54). The Harvard student facing the Shakespeare sonnet has two strikes against him. The thing itself is concealed by its educational packaging, and he doesn't know it: "The great difficulty is that he is not aware that there is a difficulty; surely, he thinks, in such a fine classroom, with such a fine textbook, the sonnet must come across! What's wrong with me?" (p. 57). And as everyone who has attempted to teach Shakespeare to undergraduates will agree, this question besets not just the student but the teacher as well.

Hope lies in the fact that the student who discovers the object by accident still has some chance of retrieving it. What's the difference?

> One might object, pointing out that Huxley's citizen reading his sonnet in the ruins and the Falkland Islander looking at his dogfish on the beach also receive them in a certain package. Yes, but the difference lies in the fundamental placement of the student in the world, a placement which makes it possible to extract the thing from the package. The pupil at Scarsdale High sees himself placed as a consumer receiving an experience-package; but the Falkland Islander exploring his dogfish is a person exercising the sovereign right of a person in his lordship and mastery of creation. He too could use an instructor and a book and a technique, but he would use them as his subordinates, just as he uses his jackknife. (pp. 57–58)

There are two characteristics of the second sort of situation that distinguish it from the first, Percy suggests:

(1) an openness of the thing before one—instead of being an exercise to be learned according to an approved mode, it is a garden of delights which beckons to one; (2) a sovereignty of the knower—instead of being a consumer of prepared experience, I am a sovereign wayfarer, a wanderer in the neighborhood of being who stumbles into the garden. (p. 60)

It is by recognizing, indeed insisting upon, the sovereignty of the student as knower that we create the possibility that college will open before that student a world that beckons like "a garden of delights." It is through seeking for the meaningfulness of the object of learning as a part of the learning process that students may regain that sense of sovereignty that empowers them to seek learning for its own sake as "a person exercising the sovereign right of a person" rather than as a "consumer receiving an experience package."

GOALS FOR CHANGE: CREATING GOOD BEGINNERS

What is a wayfarer? The term suggests a voyager seeking discovery, a searcher for the yet unseen. A wayfarer is one who seeks out beginnings, new engagements, new sights. If we revert to the language of the cognitive economy, the wayfarer is an entrepreneur, an experimenter. If a college is to create a hot cognitive economy, it must spark a spirit of cognitive entrepreneurship in students, inspire them to take risks for the sake of building something new, rather than condition them to take orders dutifully. As Bowden and Marton (1998) noted in Chapter 7, "We have to prepare [students] for the unknown by means of the known and we have to work out how that can be done" (p. 6). Vaill (1996) characterizes the state of change in the world of work today as "permanent white water." Life today, he asserts, largely "consists of events that are surprising, novel, messy, costly, and unpreventable" (p. 14). One of the weaknesses he identifies in the institutional learning model is that it presents the purpose of learning as getting it right rather than ongoing experimentation. That model

has taught us to think of learning...in building-block terms. We have been receiving powerful messages from the dawn of our awareness that we must get out of the beginner mode and into the mode of competent performer as quickly as possible. (p. 80)

But if we are to act wisely in a rapidly changing world, the goal of ceasing to be a beginner can paradoxically diminish our effectiveness. Vaill is specifically referring to managers in business organizations, but his point applies to nearly every walk of life, and probably earns the italics (Vaill's) most clearly in higher education: "*ten years from now each of us will be even more profoundly and thoroughly settled in the state of being a perpetual beginner*" (p. 81).

I participated a couple of years ago with my colleague Bob Barr in a conversation with a group of faculty leaders from the college of pharmacy at a large research university concerning the nature of pedagogy in their program. One faculty member was persistent in defending the lecture as a necessary mainstay of his discipline:

> Research is moving so rapidly that any textbook is outdated by the time it sees print. Most of my lectures are devoted to the ten to 20% of the material in their textbooks that is supplanted by new research each semester, sometimes each month! There's no other way they are going to get that information but by lecture.

Bob turned to the faculty member and asked, "If ten to 20% of the material in the textbook is outdated each semester, how much of the material in your lecture will still be valid by the time your students graduate and become practicing pharmacists?" The faculty member took several moments to process the implications of the question. Then he said, "I guess I may have to rethink this." He was aware that his discipline was in a state of permanent white water, but he hadn't had time to work out the implications. I suspect he was too busy keeping up with the research! What he was coming to realize was that his job was no longer that of producing accomplished experts. Rather, the most important role he had was that of producing effective beginners.

Not just the world of work, but the world of civic and personal life will change the way we conceive of ourselves and others as successful learners. Vaill says, "We do not need competency skills for this life. We need *in*competency skills, the skills of being effective beginners" (p. 81).

I do not mean here to accede to the sometimes overblown rhetoric of change with which technologists, futurists, and journalists often assault us. But it is hard to see how anyone with a solid decade of adult life can doubt that things become different more often and more significantly than they used to. Change has traction in the world we live in, and it moves faster than it did twenty years ago. And just this circumstance calls for the incompetency skills that Vaill refers to—calls for them in, among others, college teachers. I conclude from conversations with dozens of other college teachers over the past few years that I'm not the only one who finds that the ground under the teacher is constantly shifting, that teaching, if it is to work by almost any definition, must become more experimental. I recognize the workers who feel "more and more like beginners"; I am one of them.

If teachers need to learn to become better beginners, all the more so do students. Becoming better beginners means setting goals in permanent white water, formulating partial and untested but coherent goals that can be shaped by experience and feedback. It is a cliché that the purpose of education is at base learning how to learn. What can that mean if not learning to be a perpetual beginner? And, as Percy (1954) suggests, it is precisely the beginner, the explorer, who can see the world best: "Every explorer names his island Formosa, beautiful. To him it is beautiful because, being first, he has access to it and can see it for what it is" (p. 46).

The worst mistake students make in their thinking about the larger process that college represents is believing that they can finish it. The worst mistake we make is believing that they can postpone starting it. Marshall A. Hill, assistant commissioner of the Texas Higher Education Coordinating Board, in commenting on ideas for addressing the incoherence of the atomized curriculum, expresses this perverse hope: "Perhaps coherence will come after they leave us and embark upon the 'lifelong learning' for which we seek to equip them" (Shoenberg, 2001, p. 11). That reading of the role of higher education, that lifelong learning starts after college, leads us to act in ways that tell students in no uncertain terms that *life* starts after, or at least outside of, college. College, in this Instruction Paradigm framework of thinking, is not about learning to be a beginner; college doesn't even count as a beginning. Beginnings, real life and real learning, happen after graduation, after you've been deinstitutionalized, gotten the instruction out of the way.

If we can convince students that the project is indeed underway, that therefore college is not an interlude but a critical phase in their progress, they can come to see it as part of something they have already begun, though perhaps inchoately and without recognizing it, that will continue beyond the degree. And that continuing project, in a world of permanent white water, will be one of countless beginnings. The magic of this way of seeing college is that it makes college not only challenging and relevant but exciting, truly that "garden of delights" that beckons us to enter and explore. What could be more exciting than the prospect of navigating continuous change, constantly adapting and growing to meet new challenges? Indeed, it is the stimulation of change that creates excitement. That is why people play games, even games that have no substantive consequences, just for the thrill of navigating the white water of change. How much more exciting can the game be if they are not just playing it but living it? That balance of challenge and capacity that defines flow can be maintained for years, for a lifetime, only if the learner grows, so that challenges are not simply repeated but expand with developing ability. That means that becoming an effective beginner is probably necessary even in a calm and stable time. In a time of permanent white water, it is what keeps us afloat.

MICHIGAN STATE UNIVERSITY: THE LIBERTY HYDE BAILEY SCHOLARS PROGRAM DESIGN FOR THE "WHOLE STUDENT"

The Liberty Hyde Bailey Scholars Program in the College of Agriculture and Natural Resources at Michigan State University was founded in 1998. Named for one of the founding fathers of modern horticulture (and a native of Michigan), the Bailey Scholars program seeks to create a learning community in which students can embark quite self-consciously on the project of lifelong learning. The Declaration of Bailey hangs in the Commons, the main meeting room in Wills House, home of the program: "The Bailey Scholars Program seeks to be a community of scholars dedicated to lifelong learning. All members of the community work toward providing a respectful, trusting environment where we acknowledge our interdependence and encourage personal growth" (*Bailey Scholars Program*, 2001). The Bailey scholars (as of this writing, about 70 undergraduates), each with an academic major from the 17 offered by the college, complete a 21-credit minor, a Specialization in Connected Learning. The Bailey program is interesting in part precisely because it is not closely integrated with the larger curriculum of the college in which it resides. It overlays the existing curriculum without changing it. Hence it is a kind of program that almost any institution could begin to implement immediately, without making major changes to the existing curriculum. However, to the extent that such a program succeeds, it will inevitably create a certain tension because of its incongruity with the larger institution.

Ron Whitmore, a faculty member, and Diane Doberneck, academic learning coordinator for the program (2000), point out that

> During the early development of the program, a fundamental intellectual shift was made away from the teaching paradigm, in which the focus is on teachers, content, and teaching products, toward the learning paradigm, in which the focus is on *learners* and their *learning process*. (p. 3)

Thus the program is collaborative to a degree that is unusual in higher education:

> Bailey faculty members do not teach courses; they serve as learning conveners. Believing that all faculty and students are on a common and lifelong voyage of discovery, we blur the distinctions between students and faculty. We are all co-learners, and Bailey courses are venues of collaborative learning. Students and faculty—jointly—decide what they want to learn. (Fear et al., 2000)

Thus the Bailey approach recognizes the status of both faculty and students as perpetual beginners, and hence participants in a common project. Of course, faculty members and students do not come to the project from the same place. But they do come to it in the spirit of beginners initiating a new experiment.

Bailey students develop a learning plan, beginning with "the five questions," which are also questions repeatedly raised in the Bailey program: "Who am I? What do I value? What is my worldview? How do I learn? How can I connect (and balance) my professional and personal worlds?" (Fear, Doberneck, McElhaney, & Burkhardt, 1998, p. 4). Through constant revision of the learning plan and through self-directed and collaborative activities, students work toward answers to those questions. Each student takes 12 elective credits as part of the program, but "they do not select from a predesigned list of courses created by the faculty. They select credit experiences with the help of the Bailey Academic Learning Coordinator that fit *their* respective learning plans" (*Bailey Scholars*, 2001). Grades are assigned; however, "[g]rading systems in Bailey are designed collaboratively by students and faculty members each time a course is offered. Learners decide how they will learn accountably and responsibly. Faculty members then assign grades using the collaboratively designed system" (*Bailey Scholars*, 2001). Participants speak of "the Bailey way of learning," which is summarized well enough, perhaps, on the wall of the Commons: "active, experiential, progressively self-directed, increasingly complex, and reflective learning" (Fear et al., 1998, p. 7).

The Bailey Scholars Program is a relatively small component of the total coursework that a student will take at MSU. However, its impact on students seems to be disproportionate to its size in the curriculum. Carole Robinson (personal communication, January 10, 2002)—a Bailey fellow and doctoral student—suggests that, for most of her students, "Being in Bailey helps them to deal with traditional classes better." Betty Atkinson, a Bailey student, puts it this way: "I incorporate Bailey into other classes. You can bring so much more to a discussion because Bailey has taught me to change my way of thinking" (Fear et al., 1998, p. 5). Michael Rodriguez (personal communication, January 24, 2002), a junior who has been involved with Bailey for only a year, had the experience of taking an economics lecture course before, and then again after, he became a Bailey scholar. Bailey made a difference, he says, in how he experiences large lecture classes:

> I find myself sitting in class a lot and actually thinking about, reflecting on, what the professor is trying to teach me. And I don't take notes rapidly and just try to get all the information. I find myself thinking about it. . . . I really relate it to my experience now more, and I don't think I would have done that before.

Robin McCoy (personal communication, January 24, 2002), a sophomore in her second year in Bailey says, "It definitely has an impact on every class that I take, because I want that extra, that something more from each class. I want to really connect with the information that I'm learning."

Consider the five questions: Who am I? What do I value? What is my worldview? How do I learn? How can I connect (and balance) my professional and personal worlds? These are good and important questions, and they remain good and important questions for you and me, not just for undergraduates. They are persistent questions that go to the heart of learning as a way of being. The answers will determine whether one is a lifelong learner, an effective beginner. The answers will change as we move through life. Though the exercise would be amusing, it is hard to see how you would present these questions on a multiple-choice test. It is hard to see how an individual could set and approach deep learning goals without asking at least some of these questions. A serious effort to answer these five questions will also provide the answer to another, crucial, question: Why and how does this object of learning, the subject or knowledge or skill that is being put before me now, matter? Or does it? Without at least a provisional answer to that question, the student has no incentive to approach learning at a deep level, and indeed it would be uneconomical to do so.

For students, these questions are relevant to the whole college experience. But they are questions that are not addressed in most college classes. One of the key strengths of the Bailey Scholars program is that it puts these questions on the blackboard, so to speak, and leaves them up there even when students are doing something else. It returns to them repeatedly. And thus it involves students in continuous reflection about connection. Of course, some college classes do ask students to address these questions. I try to get students to address some of them in my own classes. The problem with that approach is that the classroom context tends to diminish the reach of even the most powerful and important questions. The questions are contained by the class, rather than containing the class. So while addressing these questions in the context of an individual class may give students a sense of ownership within the context of that class, it probably does not give students a sense of ownership of the whole pattern of their classes and academic goals. The Bailey Scholars program steps outside of the conventional classroom and creates a space where students can stand to look at their whole academic experience. If we think of the five questions as the lever with which students can raise their academic work to the level of involvement with their intrinsic goals, the Bailey seminars and other activities serve as the fulcrum against which that lever can rest.

To change the metaphor, a program like Bailey seeks to become a lens through which students can see their whole academic experience, and more. To the extent that it succeeds, students can regain their sovereignty over their own learning by seeing that they are in fact the sovereign subjects in the learning transaction, the doers of the action. As Robin McCoy puts it: "It switches the emphasis from building a career to building a life."

Most students in a large university, like Percy's Falkland Islander and Harvard student, are doubly disabled by not knowing that they are suffering under a disability. Percy's (1954) suggestion is to shake things up:

> I propose that English poetry and biology should be taught as usual, but that at irregular intervals, poetry students should find dogfishes on their desks and biology students should find Shakespeare sonnets on their dissecting boards. I am serious in declaring that a Sarah Lawrence English major who began poking about in a dogfish with a bobby pin would learn more in 30 minutes than a biology major in a whole semester; and that the latter upon reading on her dissecting board
>
>> That time of year Thou may'st in me behold
>> When yellow leaves, or none, or few, do hang
>> Upon those boughs which shake against the cold—
>> Bare ruin'd choirs where late the sweet birds sang.
>
> Might catch fire at the beauty of it. (p. 61)

This is not the place to delve fully into the magic of this solution, but we can say that part of that magic is that it breaks the hold of expectations on aspirations. We give up to the student a fundamental authority in hopes that she will take it on. There are no guarantees in such an approach, but there are boundless possibilities. Wisdom, in this and many other things, begins in recognizing the limitations that we need to overcome. Percy asks:

> Does this mean that there is no use taking biology at Harvard and Shreveport High? No, but it means that the student should know what a fight he has on his hands to rescue the specimen from the educational package. The educator is only partly to blame. For there is nothing the educator can do to provide for this need of the student. Everything the educator does only succeeds in becoming, for the student, part of the educational package. The highest role of the educator is the maieutic role of Socrates: to help the student come to himself not as a consumer of experience but as a sovereign individual. (p. 63)

Perhaps the greatest contribution that a program like Bailey can make is to let the student know that he has a fight on his hands, and what the stakes are. Diane Doberneck describes a class discussion in one of the Bailey seminars about the issue of grading, and the conflicts between the Bailey approach and that taken in other courses. One student rather eloquently described the tension between setting your own goals and being evaluated and judged by others and concluded, "All of us, all of our lives, will live in both worlds." True enough, but not all of us know it. Perhaps, by opening the other world, Bailey helps the student to triangulate her own position with respect to the university. Junior Michael Rodriquez finds: "I guess I'm more focused on gaining knowledge that can help me grow as a person and learn more about myself and why I'm here. I guess I wasn't really learning that in any of my other classes." Bailey seeks to place a sonnet on the dissecting board, so to speak, and to empower students with the possibility of becoming sovereign individuals, even in class.

OLIVET COLLEGE: DESIGNING A CURRICULUM FOR STUDENT RESPONSIBILITY

The Bailey Scholars program is an example of a relatively small program within a large university that seeks to change the cognitive economy for some students. It also seeks to highlight the misalignment of existing programs and hence to suggest alternatives. But is it possible to realign the whole institution, for all students? It is possible to try, and many institutions are doing so. An example that provides interesting contrasts with the Bailey approach is being carried out at a small liberal arts college about 40 miles from Michigan State. Olivet College, in Olivet, Michigan, recently embarked on a transformation of its educational program through the Olivet Plan (*Olivet College*, 2002). The cornerstone of the Olivet Plan is the Olivet College Compact. Every incoming student affirms the series of commitments in the Compact, all of which begin with the words "I am responsible for." The first reads:

> I am responsible for my own learning and personal development. We recognize the critical importance of taking ownership for our learning. We seek to learn from the full range of our experience, to be open to new experiences and new ideas

and to continuously pursue excellence and fulfillment in our intellectual, social and spiritual pursuits.

Espousing the student's responsibility for his or her own learning is not terribly unusual in college catalogues and mission statements. What will change the cognitive economy is for the college to take that espousal seriously in its practice. Olivet is an example of a college that is trying to embody its espoused theory in its theory-in-use. And the core of that theory, as expressed in the Olivet College Compact, directly addresses student ownership of their own learning and their own goals.

Olivet College, founded in 1844, has a rich and proud history. Its founding charter made it the first institution of higher education in the country to admit students of all races. (Oberlin College in Ohio, which was founded before Olivet by the same man— Congregationalist missionary John J. Shipherd—was the first to admit women.) "Moreover, Olivet's egalitarian charter expressly provided for the inclusion of students who were 'not rich in this world's goods,' a bold public statement for an era when college education was typically reserved for the economic elite." (This and much other background information about Olivet comes from the excellent case study prepared by Michael K. McLendon (n.d.), assistant professor of higher education at Vanderbilt University, for the W. K. Kellogg Foundation's Forum on Institutional Transformation.)

In 1992, Olivet College experienced a nasty racial incident that revealed a campus in deep crisis. High faculty turnover and poor student recruitment and retention were among the symptoms. One faculty member described the college in this way: "We were dysfunctional, . . . just really bad. We had a demoralized faculty, a weak governance structure, and abusive relationships." The departure of a president followed a clash between white and African-American students and introduced a period of several years of soul-searching and earnest reflection. This process moved forward aggressively under a new president, Michael Bassis, who assumed office in 1993. Through studying other examples of innovative institutions and reflecting on their own values and history, the Olivet community came to a redefinition expressed in the Vision of Education for Individual and Social Responsibility, adopted in 1994. It begins:

> Olivet College is dedicated today, as it was in 1844, to the principle that the future of humanity rests in the hands, hearts, and minds of those who will accept responsibility for

themselves and others in an increasingly diverse society. (*Olivet College*, 2002)

First-year students take a two-credit course called The Olivet College Experience. It "prepares students for living and learning that is described in The Olivet College Compact and The Olivet Plan" (*Olivet College*, 2002). Taught in sections of 15 to 20 students by an instructor supported by student peer-teachers, the course guides students in exploring the elements of the Olivet College Compact and introduces them to the other distinctive features of the Olivet program: learning communities, portfolios, service learning, and the senior year experience. Students develop learning goals in the course and begin addressing those goals through the development of their portfolios. Students continue to shape and develop their goals after the first year through the continuous development of the portfolio as they move through the general education program and into the major, taking a one-hour portfolio seminar each semester. The general education program begins with the first of two linked courses called "Self and Community" that asks students to examine the concept of responsibility laid out in the compact. Students take that responsibility largely through the ongoing work on the portfolio, which culminates in the senior year experience:

> The Senior Year Experience includes: 1) A clear demonstration of the link between general education and major course of study; 2) Preparation for the transition from college . . . ; 3) Clear articulation of how the student explored the issue of individual and social responsibility during their entire college experience. (*Olivet College*, 2002)

Students take classes, but those classes are linked to the process of portfolio development. The college template for course syllabi links course content to the development of portfolio exhibits so that courses are linked to the student's developing research and goals. While classes meet on a normal schedule, only portfolio classes meet on Wednesdays, leaving this time free for off-campus and other activities. The *Portfolio Program User's Manual* (1997), which lays out the portfolio process in detail for the student, explains the rationale for the portfolio:

> The portfolio is designed to encourage you to take ownership of your educational process, to promote reflections, and to

help you make connections among your learning experiences—to bring all aspects of your college and life experience together. (section 4.1, p. 3)

Robert Petrulis (2002), director of the Portfolio Assessment Program, reports:

> One distinctive principle of the Olivet College portfolio process is that students are encouraged to incorporate learning from whatever source—coursework, employment, internships, volunteer activities, and so forth—into their portfolios. Self-reflection is a central concern of the process. Students are encouraged both to show what they know, and to discuss what it means to them in both the portfolios and in the portfolio seminars. (p. 94)

One component of the portfolio is the Student Development Transcript (SDT), which is a record of "out-of-class involvement and learning experiences" including "part-time jobs, leadership training, community service, and student organization responsibilities" (*Portfolio Program User's Manual,* 1997, section. 3, p. 5).

Kathy Fear (personal communication, January 24, 2002), professor of education and director of Educator Development, says, "The classroom walls here are not walls. We're outside, we're doing things." Part of the Olivet Plan is a service learning requirement, but student activities outside the classroom go beyond the requirement. Education classes, for example, work with children in nearby elementary schools. "When they're in real life situations," Fear reports,

> addressing the complexity of real problems and developing a desire for learning, it isn't hard, it really isn't. Students take ownership of teaching elementary students; they care about them. We go into a district that's 95% low income.... I swear you can't do it yourself as a professor in a college classroom. You have to embed students in contexts that really give them the ownership, the commitment to bigger things. Parker Palmer calls it "the grace of great things." When they're out there with these poor kids and they bring you the stories of their lives, you just step back and you let it happen, connecting the texts that they're reading to help them understand.

Criminal Justice students work in communities with proactive community policing programs. Business students calculate insurance risk and work with problems of insurability and risk for community agencies and groups. As at any college, the quality of teaching and the depth of learning probably vary from class to class. But the focus of the whole curriculum and of the cocurriculum is clear: individual and social responsibility. In the Olivet Plan that was designed in 1995, the portfolio and the curriculum both culminate in the Senior Year Experience. In 2002 the faculty voted to connect and integrate the Olivet Plan in seminars that combine the portfolio and service learning, and connect with "real life" experiences within seminars, beginning with the first year and continuing throughout four years. The faculty realized that they need to challenge students on the first day they set foot on campus to pull together the evidence and carry through the commitment they make when they become Olivet students and affirm the first sentence of the Olivet College Compact: "I am responsible for my own learning and personal development."

Olivet College presents a fairly unusual picture in American higher education: a college that has actually designed its curriculum and programs to match its espoused goals. In other words, Olivet has sought to design a program and a curriculum that explicitly and repeatedly thrusts ownership of learning and learning goals upon the student, that explicitly declares student sovereignty over their own learning at the beginning, and that calls on students to continuously reclaim that sovereignty as long as they are students. Another way of putting it might be to say that Olivet seeks to steep students in the habits of lifelong learning.

Olivet has sought to redesign the cognitive economy of the college on the explicit principle of student ownership of, and responsibility for, their own learning. The emphasis that the college places on social responsibility, on the individual's responsibility to the society beyond college, reinforces the reach and scope of the personal responsibility that it declares central. The Olivet Plan expresses the opposite of the view that lifelong learning begins after college. It declares in no uncertain terms that college is at the center of life, and that life—the life in which we will seek and learn, succeed and fail, make ourselves—is at the center of college.

VALENCIA COMMUNITY COLLEGE: ADVISEMENT FOR OWNERSHIP

The approach to encouraging student reflection on goals and integration of intrinsic goals in academic programs that is probably most accessible for most colleges is advisement. If you want students to set their own goals, tell them. Nearly all colleges have established systems of student advisement and these systems can affect student attitudes and behavior.

We can distinguish between two levels of advising, on the parallel with the levels of learning: deep and surface levels. Surface level advising deals only with the superficial aspects of education: What courses do you need to get your degree, what requirements need to be met? A deep approach to advising pushes students to formulate personal goals, to test those goals, and to use their education to develop and achieve them. A surface approach to advising deals only with the external signs: the credits and hours and classes and degrees. A deep approach deals with the meaning of educational experiences, specifically the meaning to the student. A deep approach to advising can be effective only when supported by the institution as a whole. There is no point to telling students to implement their goals if those goals can find no purchase in their classroom experience. The Bailey Scholars program and Olivet College have adopted a deep approach to advising, and have implemented, in very different ways, the curricular systems to support the mentoring and advisement programs they have created. The final example we will consider in this chapter is a very different sort of college that is seeking to begin, in effect, with advisement. It remains to be seen how deep the approach will go, but it is an example worth considering.

Valencia Community College in Orlando, Florida, is a comprehensive community college with four campuses and about 40,000 students, many of them part-time or in noncredit programs. It is similar to many other community colleges in that of the 5,000 or so first-time college students who come to Valencia each year, about 90% are mandated by placement testing into developmental reading, writing, or mathematics courses (Nellis, Clarke, DiMartino, & Hosman, 2001). Valencia has embarked upon a Strategic Learning Initiative and formulated a plan to become more learning-centered. The first goal of the plan is to "shape Valencia's culture by making learning the chief value and design principle in every College policy, procedure, plan, and initiative" (*Valencia Community College Strategic Learning*

Plan, 2001, p. 8). The plan covers a wide range of college programs and activities. Goal 4 is "Learning by Design." The vanguard program is a greatly expanded and fully articulated advisement system called LifeMap. LifeMap shows up, not just in the plan, but all over the four campuses.

When I visited the Valencia campus in the fall of 2000 I had never heard of LifeMap. But you can't be on campus long without getting the word. A student entering Valencia's West campus to register for classes, go to the library, or have lunch in the cafeteria is met at every turn by large, colorful posters and banners picturing a variety of students in a variety of activities over slogans such as "Life's a trip. You'll need directions" and "Taking life one semester at a time? Students who succeed have a plan." It is hard to imagine that a student could matriculate at Valencia without hearing about LifeMap. The college has invested considerable money and effort in calling it to the attention of students and getting them involved. At a large, public, open-access institution like Valencia, the first step is to get the students' attention.

Efforts to expand educational opportunity to underserved groups bring home a recurrent paradox: The open access college is also an open exit college. The easier it is to enter college, the easier it is to simply leave. An open gate swings both ways. This phenomenon affects retention and persistence rates at many public institutions, but nowhere more dramatically than at community colleges. There are a number of reasons for this, but certainly one of the most important is that the approach colleges have taken to preparing underprepared students for college work has often isolated them from the larger college community, denied them ownership of their own education, and made it impossible for them to recognize their intrinsic goals in the college program. Many developmental students come to college with no clear idea of what they are developing or why. And many are channeled into programs that explicitly postpone questions about intrinsic goals and personal meaning until a later date. Developmental students, almost by definition, enter college with a deficient sense of self-efficacy with respect to academic work. Often they are shunted directly into developmental courses that have no clear connection with the larger college curriculum or the larger goals of education. Sometimes such courses seem to cast the students back into the meaningless patterns of test and drill that they learned to dislike so heartily in high school. The failure rate for such courses is high, and the price of failure is usually to repeat the failed experience again with minor revisions. If developmental programs are really going to develop students' abilities, they must be designed to introduce students to college, and to do so in a way that connects with students' intrinsic goals. I don't think any of this is controversial among developmental educators, but it is not easy to do in the Instruction Paradigm college.

Valencia is attempting to address the needs of students through advisement that allows them to link their intrinsic goals to their educational program from the very beginning. One way they seek to do this is to increase the rate of success for students early on. Goal 2 of the Strategic Learning Plan is "Start Right: Ensure that students experience extraordinary learning success in their earliest encounters with the college and establish a solid foundation for success in future learning" (*Valencia Community College,* 2001, p. 9). One means to that end is to "[e]nsure that new students develop a meaningful plan for their educations as early as possible in their careers at Valencia." The outcome they seek is to have "[s]tudents successfully complete courses and programs 'at the front door' at dramatically improved rates."

Students either on or off campus can access LifeMap and get a detailed description of the program, including the introductory assessments, on the program Web page. A student who executes the full LifeMap advisement algorithm will confer with faculty members about her educational background and goals; complete online assessment surveys concerning life goals, career goals, academic interests, educational goals, and current workload; meet with peer advisors and a counselor to develop an education plan; and register for the Student Success course. The process is simplified probably as much as is possible, but it directs students repeatedly toward reflection on their own goals and the relevance of their educational plans to those goals.

With LifeMap, Valencia is attempting to implement the "developmental advising model." The team that formulated the process describes developmental advising as "a student-centered approach toward developing a relationship among students, faculty and other college professionals..." (Valencia Community College, 2000). Developmental advising, as implemented in LifeMap, is intended to be "an ongoing growth process which assists students in the exploration, clarification, communication, and implementation of realistic choices based upon self-awareness of abilities, interests, and values" (Valencia Community College, 2000). To implement developmental advising completely, of course, will require a major adjustment in many college functions.

Eventually, Valencia hopes to "fully integrate LifeMap into curricular and co-curricular learning experiences" (*Valencia Community College,* 2001, p. 11). Valencia's Strategic Learning Plan envisions the coordination of course work around core competencies across the curriculum so that "students experience Valencia as a coordinated program of learning rather than a collection of courses" (p. 11). A Cyber Portfolio, yet to be implemented, would link work in courses and provide a cumulative record of student development.

The college has made some initial assessments of the effects of the system. They have compared, for example, cohorts of students before and after the implementation of LifeMap to determine whether it seems to make a difference in the courses students take and their rates of completion. For example, comparing the cohort of students attending fall 1992 through summer 1994 with those attending fall 1997 through summer 1999 reveals some interesting differences. Completion rates for college preparatory courses (developmental courses) increased significantly between the two time periods in reading (17.4 percent increase), writing (11 percent increase), and mathematics (14.5 percent increase) (Valencia Community College, 2000). From 1994–1995 to 1999–2000 the proportion of first-time college students returning for the next semester rose from 65% to 74%. While such statistics don't show a direct causal relationship between advisement and success, they are certainly encouraging.

The key to making developmental advisement a reality is coordinating advisement with the academic program. That means not only that counselors and advisors need to change the way they do business, but teaching faculty need to change too. To support this change, Valencia has embarked upon an ambitious professional development program designed to prepare teachers to carry through on the purposes of LifeMap. Valencia has also done something highly unusual in higher education: They have begun to assess their faculty development programs on the basis of student outcomes. That is to say, rather than just asking faculty members how successful their professional development has been, they have looked at the retention rates and other indices of success in courses taught by faculty who have been through the professional development program compared with those who have not. They have also compared the outcomes achieved by the same teachers before and after professional development. The result has been some impressive evidence that investments in professional development for faculty can indeed result in changes in student behavior. In 1998, the college conducted a pilot test of 12 faculty members who participated in a professional development seminar addressing four pedagogical issues: critical thinking, diversity, developmental advisement, and assessment. The professional development program itself was performance-based; participating faculty redesigned their courses in light of the principles they discovered and developed in the seminars. The pilot courses demonstrated considerably higher retention and success rates than nonpilot courses. While 68% of students in pilot developmental courses passed with a grade of "C" or better, only 56% in nonpilot courses did. Retention in pilot courses was 78%, as opposed to 69% in nonpilot courses (Nellis et al., 2001). Furthermore, pilot courses demonstrated higher passing rates than nonpilot courses in the same class in previous semesters.

More recently, Valencia has attempted to expand the potential reach of faculty development with the support of technology. Using software developed for online faculty development courses, Valencia has piloted a problem-based Internet course. One component is to make teachers familiar with LifeMap, how it works, and how to adapt their courses to the planning and development process that students are involved in. Responses from the 32 faculty members (mostly adjuncts) who completed the course were provocative. A few, even after working through the LifeMap material, seemed to simply miss the point. One criticized LifeMap on the grounds that "Students have to take responsibility for their own actions..." (Nellis, n.d., p. 5). But most respondents were positive in their reaction, revealing both the value of the program and the need to better inform teachers about it. One wrote:

> OK, I am as guilty as some of the rest of you. I admit it. I, too, glanced through the [LifeMap] material when it was first created and thought to myself what a good idea for the students. Only now, when I have had an incentive to really look closely at it (and actually READ it) have I discovered what a valuable resource it is for instructors! (p. 4)

Several teachers integrated LifeMap materials into their course, and others expressed the intention to do so in the following semester.

Today, Valencia appears to have a very impressive advisement system that has the potential to greatly increase student ownership of their own learning goals *if the academic program can be coordinated with it.* To date, the advisement system remains largely autonomous, operated out of Student Services, coordinated only intermittently with what actually happens to most students in the classroom. However, Valencia's Strategic Learning Plan lays out the elements that would have to be in place for the advisement system to be integrated with the instruction and assessment systems. Whether or not Valencia achieves that integration, it presents a model of how it might be done. Valencia is trying to change the cognitive economy to give students early and effective ownership of their learning goals. The effort, even to this point, is instructive.

PROCESS FRONTIER: GOALS

Some students come to us already possessed of an internal sense of direction and an ability to turn their learning experiences to the service of their intrinsic goals. Some have wrested ownership of their own learning goals from the educational environment through extraordinary personal insight, fortunate mentoring, or perhaps simply good luck. Many more, however, come to their college learning experiences conditioned to respond to, and even to seek, external direction and validation. All too often, these are incapable of seeing much anything beyond the educational packaging of learning experiences and hence can hardly see the meaning because they are focusing exclusively on the signs. These students can learn to take ownership of their own learning goals and integrate learning with life, but they can learn it only if the environment supports that lesson. The first process frontier of the Learning Paradigm college is to promote intrinsic goal setting and student reflection on and ownership of their own learning goals.

All Learning Paradigm colleges will not be alike. Indeed, the standardization of external forms that we find in the Instruction Paradigm college should diminish as colleges come to experiment more freely with alternative approaches. Institutions can promote intrinsic goals in a variety of ways. The examples we have considered here suggest some approaches. At a minimum, colleges should ask undergraduates to reflect on their goals and to consider the relationship between those goals and their academic programs. Then they should give students real opportunities to shape the academic program in light of their goals. The challenge colleges face is to empower their students to take responsibility for their own learning. Unless that happens, learning won't.

A Learning Paradigm College Requires Frequent, Continual, Connected, and Authentic Student Performances

THE CENTRALITY OF PERFORMANCE

An irreducible quality of a hot cognitive economy is common to all extracurricular activities: they are *activities*. They are designed around what students do. What extracurricular sports, music, drama, speech, and journalism have in common is that they are more or less complex structures for facilitating, assessing, refining, and displaying student performances. And that, in the Learning Paradigm college, is what the curriculum should be. I have suggested five defining qualities of what a Learning Paradigm college would require in terms of the nature and amount of student activity. Let us take a moment to clarify them.

STUDENTS SHOULD COMPLETE TASKS THAT ARE VISIBLE AND MEANINGFUL TO OTHERS

By student performances I mean that students should be attempting to complete tasks that are visible and meaningful to others. A performance is in a sense autonomous, it is an accomplishment, a piece of work that stands alone to the extent of at least having value not entirely derived from its context. In this sense, studying for a test is an activity, but not a performance. A performance is not a drill or an exercise; it is in some sense a completed activity. Grant Wiggins (1993), president of the Center on Learning, Assessment, and School Structure (CLASS) and a leading scholar of assessment, suggests that performance is the product of applied understanding: "Understanding is not cued knowledge: performance is never the sum of drills; problems are not exercises; mastery is not achieved by the unthinking use of algorithms" (p. 207). Drills and tests present the student with a static choice, the only consequence of which will be the evaluation of the choice itself. But performance involves a dynamic interaction with the environment. As Marcia Mentkowski, director of the Office of Institutional Research and Evaluation at Alverno College, and associates (2000) point out, "In the domain of performance, the learner extends experience into an envisioned future. The performer envisions and acts in the face of contingency and actively revises his or her actions in the light of their consequences" (p. 185). I am not suggesting, of course, that studying is an unimportant activity. But the nature of studying is qualitatively different if it is done to prepare for performance and if it is done to prepare for drills or tests. I am not suggesting that students should never take tests or do drills or exercises. However, we should never confuse drills with actual performances. The student writing an article to be published in the student newspaper is engaged in performance. The student writing an essay exclusively for the purpose of demonstrating that she can follow the rules assigned by the teacher is engaged in an exercise. Exercises are worth doing as a means of preparing for performance. But it is the performance that gives the exercise meaning and connection with the larger world. If we want to construct a cognitive economy that encourages students to adopt a deep orientation to learning, we must construct it of student performances. A student who takes a deep approach to learning is almost by definition approaching learning as a preparation for and execution of performances, as here defined.

We should take care to avoid any confusion with the use of the word in the term "performance goals," which cognitive psychologists contrast with learning goals, as we discussed in Chapter 6. Students who embrace performance goals seek to look good rather than get better. When we speak of student performances, there is no implication that they are a product of performance goals. Indeed, requiring frequent student performances encourages students to formulate learning goals, goals for improvement.

STUDENT PERFORMANCES SHOULD BE AUTHENTIC

Authentic tasks, according to Wiggins (1998) are "the kind of work real people do . . ." (p. 21). It might be more accurate to say that they are the kind of work people do in real situations, situations where their actions will have significant consequences. If the only consequence of the action is the evaluation of the actor, we cannot say that the action has significant consequences. So authentic student performances are performances of a kind that people do for their own sake. Writing a letter to the editor or a complaint to a business, balancing your checkbook, paying your bills, designing a Web page, measuring the contaminant level in the local water supply—these are authentic performances, they are the kind of work real people do. Fred M. Newman, professor of education at the University of Wisconsin, Madison, and Doug A. Archbald, assistant professor of education at the University of Delaware (1992), expand on the point:

> The . . . most critical distinction between authentic achievements and traditional achievements in schools is that authentic achievements have aesthetic, utilitarian, or personal value apart from documenting the competence of the learner. When people write letters, news articles, insurance claims, poems; when they speak a foreign language; when they develop blueprints; when they create a painting, a piece of music, or build a stereo cabinet, they try to communicate ideas, to produce a product, or to have impact on others beyond the simple demonstration that they are competent. Achievements of this sort have special value which is missing in tasks contrived only for the purpose of assessing knowledge (such as spelling quizzes, laboratory exercises, or typical final exams). The cry for relevance is, in many cases, simply a less precise expression of this desire that the accomplishment should have value beyond being an indicator of success in school. . . .
>
> [T]his vision of authentic achievement requires students to engage in disciplined inquiry to produce knowledge that has value in their lives beyond simply proving their competence in school. Mastery of this sort is unlikely to be demonstrated in familiar testing and grading exercises. Instead, it is more often expressed in the completion of long-term projects

which result in discourse, things, and performances of interest to students, their peers and the public at large. (pp. 74–75)

In an educational context, we can ask students to perform, but in a
way that has no clear connection with the world outside and beyond the
academy. Here, even though the performance may rise above the level of
mere drill, it still lacks authenticity. Student performances should be authentic because authentic tasks are at least open to intrinsic motivation
and a deep approach to learning, while inauthentic tasks, unless they are
seen as a preparation for subsequent authentic tasks, are not.

Expertise in any field consists of the ability to perform authentic tasks
effectively. If we want students to become expert at anything, they must
eventually do the sorts of things experts do. It is precisely the quality of having a practical context and purpose that generates both the motivation and
the deep approach. The National Research Council (1999) points out, "Experts' knowledge cannot be reduced to sets of isolated facts or propositions
but, instead, reflects contexts of applicability: that is, the knowledge is 'conditionalized' on a set of circumstances" (p. 19). This means that knowledge
for the expert "includes a specification of the contexts in which it is useful"
(p. 31). Being conditionalized on a set of realistic circumstances, having a
plausible and meaningful context, makes tasks authentic.

STUDENT PERFORMANCES SHOULD BE FREQUENT

In a Learning Paradigm college, students would not have the option of in-
ertness. A high level of activity would be mandatory. Frequent performance
leads to more time on task, and that is essential for learning. As the National Research Council (1999) points out, "In all domains of learning, the
development of expertise occurs only with major investments of time, and
the amount of time it takes to learn material is roughly proportional to the
amount of material being learned" (pp. 44–46). By "time on task," of
course, we must mean student time doing the work of learning. Time spent
in a classroom is largely irrelevant to the measurement of time on learning
tasks. Indeed, for many students, time spent listening to faculty lectures is
not time spent on learning tasks in any meaningful sense. What counts, and
what we should count in calculating meaningful student time spent in effective learning, is student performance or preparation for performance.

STUDENT PERFORMANCES SHOULD BE CONTINUAL

Student performances should be continual rather than highly intermittent or concentrated in one time period. Students should not be intensely active as freshmen and then take a long break as sophomores. Students should not be passive as freshmen and then tossed into a cauldron of activity as junior or seniors. Students should not be inert for the first ten weeks of the semester, then break into a flurry of activity for the last six. Whether they have majors or not, whether they are in career or academic programs, whether developmental or advanced, full-time or part-time, all students should be active all the time. Well, perhaps not all the time. Performances should be continual rather than continuous.

STUDENT PERFORMANCES SHOULD BE CONNECTED

What students are doing at one point in the curriculum should be relevant to what they will do at other points. Another way of putting this would be to say that student activities should be integrated. We saw in Chapter 7 that one of the keys to a deep approach to learning is to see the objects of learning as connected to a larger framework and hence linked together. In the absence of this sense of connection we are memorizing fragments, not building a framework for understanding. This implies that student performances should be relevant across disciplines. Both the requirement of authenticity and the requirement of connection mandate that student performances should not all be narrowly designed as evidence of disciplinary specialization. As the late Donald Farmer (1988), academic vice president at King's College, put it: "Higher education today graduates students with discipline-based minds who will need to function in an increasingly complex and interdisciplinary environment in the 21st century. Learning to make connections should be a high priority for all students" (p. 53).

This is not to deny the importance of mastery of the knowledge and skills distinctive to a major or professional goal. It is to suggest that such knowledge and skills should be transferable and communicable, that specialists in the modern world need to be able to use their knowledge and apply their skills in coordination with specialists in other fields and in ways comprehensible and persuasive to nonspecialists. Connection, in an increasingly interconnected world, is inherent in excellence.

WHY STUDENT PERFORMANCES ARE IMPORTANT

The primacy of student performances in a well-designed learning environment suggests dramatic changes in curriculum and pedagogy at most colleges. Why are student performances so important? For three reasons.

We Learn Skills and Knowledge-in-Action Through the Practice of Skillful Performance

It is not just that performing activities that require skill is the best way to master skills; it is the only way. Skills are simply not translatable into declarative knowledge for the purposes of learning. The reason is that many of the elements of skillful action are tacit rather than explicit. As scientist and philosopher Michael Polanyi (1958) observed, "the aim of a skilful performance is achieved by the observance of a set of rules which are not known as such to the person following them" (p. 49). I have tested this principle on college and university faculty members (as well as students) for several years now by posing one of the examples that Polanyi uses to illustrate the point: riding a bicycle. How, when riding a bicycle, do you keep from falling down? The answers that I have received to that question from highly educated academics, many tenured, all claiming to be able to actually ride a bicycle, range from "practice" to "lean back and forth" with an impressive variety of creative ideas between. You might pause for a moment to formulate your own response to the question before reading on. Out of groups adding up to several hundred participants by now, I have only twice received the correct answer. (In fairness, I should point out that I usually ask physicists to refrain from answering on the principle that they have an unfair advantage.) Polanyi states the answer this way:

> The rule observed by the cyclist is this. When he starts falling to the right he turns the handlebars to the right, so that the course of the bicycle is deflected along a curve towards the right. This results in a centrifugal force pushing the cyclist to the left and offsets the gravitational force dragging him down to the right. This manoeuvre presently throws the cyclist out of balance to the left, which he counteracts by turning the handlebars to the left; and so he continues to keep himself in balance by winding along a series of appropriate curvatures. A simple analysis [!] shows that for a given angle of unbalance the curvature of each winding is inversely proportional to the

square of the speed at which the cyclist is proceeding. (pp. 49–50)

I would say that nearly all, unquestionably many, bicycle riders have no idea how they do it. But they do it nonetheless. Furthermore, understanding the principles behind maintaining balance on a bicycle would not improve the speed or agility of a cyclist. As with other physical skills, students of the bicycle do not attend lectures on cycling, nor do they read textbooks or take tests on their knowledge of the physical principles behind cycling. They ride their bikes. Likewise, people who want to play the piano or draw or jump high or sing songs or write cursive learn these skills through performing them. It cannot be done otherwise.

These examples, of course, are of largely physical skills that require little propositional knowledge for basic performance. Many skills have a more explicitly knowledge-based component, such as those exercised by an accountant or an attorney or a writer—or a teacher. But no matter how dense the knowledge base of a skilled activity, the application of that knowledge in the world involves a tacit dimension to the same degree as riding a bicycle or swimming.

Empirical research has confirmed the essential insight that skill development depends on practice. The National Research Council (2001) notes that in the evidence on learning "certain laws of skill acquisition always apply." The first of these they characterize as "the power law of practice":

> acquiring skill takes time, often requiring hundreds or thousands of instances of practice in retrieving a piece of information or executing a procedure. This law operates across a broad range of tasks, from typing on a keyboard to solving geometry problems. . . . According to the power law of practice, the speed and accuracy of performing a simple or complex cognitive operation increases in a systematic nonlinear fashion over successive attempts. (p. 85)

Through Performance, We Integrate Knowledge and Transfer It to New Applications

Recall the research of Conway et al., discussed in Chapter 7. They compared students in lecture/test courses with students in an interdisciplinary research skills course in which they were actually applying the research skills they studied: a course assessed through testing compared with a course assessed on performance. They found that students transferred what they learned into semantic memory more quickly when they were applying what they learned by doing research and writing papers. It is through performance that we learn to integrate knowledge into our general framework of understanding so that it can be transferred to new applications. Mentkowski and associates (2000) put it this way:

> Performance is the integration of knowing and doing—in class and off campus. It is a kind of learning in which a student is actively engaged and involved, whether it be in creating a painting, solving an experimental design problem, or developing a public relations strategy for a business. Students see integration of knowing and doing as an ongoing interactive process in which both knowledge and experience are repeatedly transformed, and so it encourages transfer of learning. Thus, learning as integrative is intertwined with learning as experiential. Developing as a competent performer means internalizing curricular abilities. (pp. 227–228)

The late Donald Schön (1983) of the Massachusetts Institute of Technology calls the process of developing increasing mastery as a practitioner "reflection-in-action." Certainly subject matter knowledge is important. But that knowledge is trivialized if it is merely testable, but not usable. Schön (1983) characterizes the reflective process of designers—architects, urban planners, and the like—as "a conversation with the materials of a situation" (p. 78). This seems to me to capture the essence of the reflective process in much expert practice. If we think of "materials" broadly, we can say that any professional needs to enter into a conversation with those persons, procedures, substances, and environments that define the problematic situation being addressed. And to participate in that conversation requires knowledge of the materials. The architect must be thoroughly familiar with the physical and visual properties of building materials and the site and surroundings of a proposed building. A doctor must know the configuration and conventional properties of the human body and the specific experiences and symptoms of her patient. And a teacher—though here for some reason I seem to be proposing an innovation rather than stating the obvious—must know the conventional patterns of human learning and the specific qualities of the student. But no one believes that knowledge of the materials constitutes competence. Until the practitioner has entered into a conversation with those materials—a give-and-take process of testing, evaluating, looking and listening, trying ideas, and observing consequences—expertise remains an abstraction. That conversation is what lets the practitioner frame the problem, then select the relevant information from the range of observed data, and act with integrity and a plausible claim of expertise. If expert behavior followed a mechanical algorithm, we would simply embed it into a computer program and save both money and time. It is through the ongoing, mindful, conversation with the materials of problematic situations that students learn to integrate knowledge and transfer it to new situations and hence develop practical expertise.

Performance Is the Natural and Necessary Mode for Realizing Intrinsic Goals

In the last chapter, we saw that a hot cognitive economy must emphasize intrinsic goals. The natural and obvious mode of seeking important goals is to act on them, to try to achieve them. Indeed, maintaining the flow experience requires that the individual attempt challenging tasks. If we want students to embrace significant learning goals, then we need to give students the ongoing opportunity to realize those goals. If we want students to become expert learners, we want them to pursue their curiosity and to follow their interests. In part for the reasons just summarized above, students can develop their interests only by acting on them.

Part of performance, as we are using the term here, is the attempt to bring tasks to completion. Is it possible to imagine not trying to finish a task if you are pursuing the task for its own sake? We may not finish the important tasks we start. But it is never part of our initial design to do only half of the envisioned job. We will drop tasks pursued for external rewards whenever the rewards disappear. How often do students go back and complete the partial paper or project after the grade is in? But if we are doing the task because we want to do it, we are doing it because we want to get it done, to finish it. Performance is the medium of action for doing what we choose rather than what we must. If we are to create a cognitive economy that promotes intrinsic goals, we must create an economy that requires performance. You can't have one without the other.

CREATING AN ACTIVE CURRICULUM

The effectiveness of extracurricular activities, as we noted before, flows from the fact that they are activities. But the quality of performance in those activities profits from the fact that they are extracurricular, outside the classroom. Even when the kinds of student performances called for in extracurricular activities are not strictly authentic, they often seem more authentic to the student simply because they aren't taking place in the classroom. An aura of inauthenticity hangs over the classroom like mist over a swamp. Extracurricular activities are structured around the activity, around a kind of student performance that is the object of the club, the competition, the public exhibition. And this by itself differentiates them from classes, which are usually not structured around student activity but around subject matter. Of course, good teachers at all levels go to great pains to make student performance the focal point of their classes. But even in the best classes, at most institutions, the classroom contains the performances. In extracurricular programs, the character and purpose of the performances contain the program.

Creating a curriculum that requires frequent student performances needs to be done at the level of pedagogy, of course. Colleges where teachers emphasize student performance more are better colleges than ones where teachers simply lecture and give tests. And classes that are organized around and emphasize student performances are better classes than those that are not so organized. This is one area where teachers within the classroom can make vast improvements right now—and I think many are doing so. Individual teachers can design their classes around the kinds of things they want students to do rather than simply the information they want students to know. Designing courses beginning with the student outcomes we aim for can result in dramatic improvements in pedagogy (Huba & Freed, 2000; Wiggins, 1993, 1998).

Russell Edgerton (1997) identifies "four strands of pedagogical reform" that have transformative potential. They are 1) problem-based learning (PBL), 2) collaborative learning, 3) service learning, and 4) undergraduate research. Three of the four explicitly and inherently involve student performance. The fourth, collaborative learning, nearly requires it. "All of these efforts," Edgerton points out, "represent streams of reform that are moving in the right direction, yet all remain marginalized pedagogies that operate on the sidelines of the dominant mode of lecture-based, didactic instruction."

Without at all diminishing the importance of what teachers can and should do in their classrooms, we need to face the fact that teachers acting independently cannot raise student performance to the level of authenticity, continuity, and connection it deserves in the Learning Paradigm college. Until the performance pedagogies that Edgerton has identified reach a critical mass of acceptance by faculty, they will remain marginalized—most significantly in the students' minds.

Individual teachers can require students to perform. But individual teachers cannot easily create a pattern of connection among the student performances. To the extent that whole faculties can do that, so that students repeatedly encounter the need to perform authentically in the classroom, the very nature of the classroom can change and the cognitive economy of the college will heat up in proportion to the consistency and vigor of the experiential curriculum.

ALVERNO COLLEGE: CREATING A PERFORMANCE-BASED CURRICULUM

Alverno College, a Catholic liberal arts women's college in Milwaukee, Wisconsin, has since 1973 been developing its ability-based curriculum. In addition to pioneering this distinctive approach, Alverno has conducted one of the best-documented experiments in the history of education. College faculty and staff members have published several books on the subject (e.g., Alverno College Faculty, 1994; Alverno College Faculty, 2000; Mentkowski & Associates, 2000; Riordan, 1994). The Alverno College Institute offers workshops on the Alverno approach to student learning and assessment, and Alverno staff travel the country explaining the approach and discussing it with others.

The Alverno system is rooted in the premise that student performances are what count:

> The principle of performance requires that we assess abilities in action, in the kind of integrated situation in which students will use them in their life beyond campus. This principle insists that if we are to assess our students' thinking, we must find ways to make their thinking observable. If we are

to assess their problem solving ability, we must observe them
solving problems. If we are to assess their interactive ability,
we must provide a situation and watch them interact.
(Alverno College Faculty, 1994, p. 19)

The Alverno approach is well known for its emphasis on assessment as
a responsibility of the whole college, not just individual faculty members.
The highly developed and comprehensive assessment system of the college
is justly famous. However, there is nothing inherently desirable about assessment per se, even frequent and systematic assessment, from the point
of view of the cognitive economy. If the college assessment system has the
effect of raising the profile and frequency of multiple-choice tests, it will
have the effect of cooling the cognitive economy. Assessment is a powerful
tool for shaping the cognitive economy, but the effects of that tool depend
entirely on how it is used. What is most important about Alverno's approach to assessment is that it requires frequent assessment of student performances; hence it requires frequent student performances. Furthermore,
it is designed to assure the authenticity of performance tasks.

The process begins by asking what students ought to be able to do,
and the answers to that question become the abilities that form the core of
the curriculum. Note that an ability-based curriculum does not begin with
the academic disciplines; it begins with the categories of student performance that are the intended outcomes of an education. The eight abilities
that shape the Alverno curriculum are 1) communication, 2) analysis, 3)
problem solving, 4) valuing in decision-making, 5) social interaction, 6)
global perspectives, 7) effective citizenship, and 8) aesthetic responsiveness. The abilities themselves are neither very surprising nor very innovative. A number of colleges, including Olivet, Valencia, and several others
that we will discuss later, have attempted to define corresponding sets of
abilities, and the lists differ more in arrangement and style than in substance (e.g., see Wilson, Miles, Baker, & Schoenberger, 2000). Where
Alverno has pioneered a distinctive approach is in integrating these abilities into all the courses in the curriculum so that the abilities run through
those courses as common threads that link connected learning experiences. While students at Alverno take classes, the abilities are prior to the
classes, and contain the classes, rather than being contained by them.

The design of student assessments at Alverno is governed by the master rubric that consists of the eight abilities, each one divided into develop-

mental levels. A set of design guidelines assists faculty in developing specific course outcomes and stimuli for assessed tasks. Here are the guidelines for designing an assessment mode:

1) Does it bring the student as close as possible to a situation within which the student will be using the ability outside the classroom?

2) Does it fit the level of the student? [This refers to the developmental levels under each ability.]

3) Will it engage the student?

4) Will it give the student an opportunity to demonstrate sufficient indicators of the ability? (Alverno College Faculty, 1994, p. 114)

The guidelines capture the elements of performance, authenticity, and developmental level, and they also address students' intrinsic goals. Performances might be to write a paper or present a report on a given issue for a specified purpose or to make a policy proposal and defend it before the class. Effective stimuli, ones that follow the guidelines, are framed so as to provide a context for the student performance that pushes students to conditionalize knowledge and connect it with frameworks of thought that make it accessible to transfer. Here is an example of a stimulus from a chemistry course:

> At a recent meeting of the Alverno Photography Club, one member, who was not feeling well, asked another for a specific brand of aspirin, whereupon, the vice president said "All aspirin is alike." A lively discussion followed, and you, as a chemistry student, were asked to give a short speech at the next meeting, outlining a chemist's perspective on the vice president's remark. (Alverno College Faculty, 1994, p. 127)

Among the outcomes that this stimulus seeks to assess are "Communicates effectively, using the language, concepts, and models of chemistry" and "Finds selects and uses appropriate scientific information to support her work."

Alverno has gone to some lengths to create a connection among student performances. Most faculty members serve not only in conventional disciplinary departments but in ability departments, in which faculty from across the disciplines review and refine the assessment approaches for a

The Learning Paradigm College

particular ability. So, unlike the arrangement at most colleges where faculty communication about pedagogy and assessment is locked into discipline-department loops, the Alverno faculty reflect upon, review, and revise student performance tasks and assessments from an interdisciplinary perspective. Alverno's faculty are pushed toward mindfulness by this system; they habitually approach the task of teaching as reflection-in-action. So the approach to communication or aesthetic responsiveness in business courses will cohere with the approach in education and philosophy courses.

While most assessment takes place within the classroom, students will—on a predetermined schedule—participate in outside-course assessment to mark progress on the development of their abilities in general education or the major. Outside-course performances (and sometimes in-course performances) are assessed by other faculty members and often by trained community assessors. Such assessments can be integrated in varying degrees with experiential learning activities such as internships and field experience. So a student might submit the business plan she developed in her accounting class not to the teacher of the class but to the loan officer of a local bank. And a science student might serve an internship at a local research company, integrating her work on the job with her science seminar. Surveys of student self-assessments and research on student reactions to the curriculum reveal that students find that such experiences have special value:

> Off-campus internships were key experiences for both older and younger students that validate these experiential learning principles and their learning in the ability-based curriculum. Important experiential features of off-campus learning situations are a complex performance-demand structure, in which students can test their ability to transfer what they have learned to actual work contexts; feedback from an independent environment; and the opportunity to observe oneself at work and to test the ability to appraise one's own performance. (Mentkowski & Associates, 2000, p. 231)

Leona Truchan and George Gurria (2000), professors of biology and chemistry respectively, relate the interesting case of a woman who was previously working at a pharmaceutical firm, before doing an internship there as a student. She wrote in her self assessment:

> I can honestly say that I learned more in this year's worth of internships than I have in all of my previous time [working at this site]. I learned a great deal about the modes of action and interactions of both pharmaceuticals and nutraceuticals, as well as a great deal of information and skill with regard to pharmacy management. As a result of the work that I have done on these internships, I have been given more responsibility in my job as a technician as well, which has brought me closer to the everyday clientele and professional colleagues. . . . (pp. 55–56)

Through creating genuinely authentic roles in which students affirm and advance their learning, colleges like Alverno are developing not just lifelong learners but reflective practitioners.

The connection that we want to achieve among student performances is the connection in the student's mind. Through reflecting on her own performance, the student can become mindful of the connections among learning experiences. Alverno has incorporated student self assessment, where the student is the assessor of performance, but the student as a person is not what is being assessed. The purpose of self assessment should be to get the student to reflect on her work as a learner.

Georgine Loacker (2000), professor of English at Alverno, describes the framework for self assessment:

> We have identified four components or skills inherent in self assessment: 1) observing, 2) interpreting/analyzing, 3) judging, and 4) planning. Although these components are not absolutely sequential—particularly in their development, which is an ongoing zigzag—we encourage students to form the habit of observing carefully and interpreting or analyzing their observations before they leap to judging. Planning seems to follow organically from the other components, yet a student might intuitively recognize the worth of some aspects of her work and continue to refine them without really understanding or even carefully observing them. (p. 3)

Self assessment so articulated focuses the student's reflection on the performance, its content and nature and quality, so that the component of judgment can function to guide future planning:

Self assessment focuses on a performance, whether product or process or both, including attitude as well as action. A student may be assessing a slide show she designed or her interactive performance caught on videotape. She may be assessing the problem-solving process she went through in her science lab or the paper she produced for English class and the thinking by which she produced it. In each case her instructor tries to assist her to focus on it as something she did on a given day in a given state of mind and feeling with a given set of other circumstances. That explicit emphasis on a specific performance as not necessarily being typical assists us in dealing with a beginning student's tendency to confuse performance with person. (pp. 4–5)

That "tendency to confuse performance with person" is what we discussed in Chapter 6 under the name of entity theory. The entity theorist sees a judgment on a performance as a fundamental critique of herself. Indeed, it is just this confusion of performance with person that leads entity theorists to develop performance goals, goals aimed at making a good appearance. The incremental theorist, in contrast, develops learning goals, goals aimed at improvement. Self assessment—by encouraging the student to focus on performances and to observe, analyze, and judge those performances in order to plan means of improving them—encourages students to set learning goals.

By creating an environment that highlights performance and promotes mindful reflection on performance, Alverno also encourages students to develop and pursue intrinsic goals. Donna Engelmann (personal communication, February 23, 2002), associate professor of philosophy and chair of the Arts and Humanities Division at Alverno, puts it this way:

Students see themselves as lifelong learners, but also as people who have their own goals for what they want to learn in life rather than having goal-setting imposed on them by other people, or even suggested by other people. We help them to develop from people who step into learning as something that's created by others to the point that learning is their own project. And I think that's the coolest thing in the world.

Alverno's ability-based curriculum is a framework for making student performances authentic, frequent, continual, and connected. It is designed on the principle that the curriculum is what students do at college. It provides a vivid example—one of the most notable examples available today—of how a college can put learning first, and keep it there. And that is certainly one of the coolest things in the world.

CHANDLER-GILBERT COMMUNITY COLLEGE: CREATING EXPERIENTIAL COURSES

Many colleges with more conventional curricula have created programs that seek to create increased opportunities for student performance. One way to do this, of course, is to encourage students to participate in extracurricular activities. Another is to create cocurricular programs that will involve students in going beyond or outside the classroom. We see this principle at work at both Alverno and Olivet. Alverno, as we have just seen, requires internships or other out-of-class activities for all students. At Olivet College, classes use Wednesdays to get out of the classroom. Olivet also has required one of Edgerton's performance-oriented pedagogies, service learning. Students are required to participate in service and reflect on that service. Olivet's Robert Petrulis (2002) points out that "service learning has emerged over time as a central component of the portfolio process" (p. 94).

Service learning, internships, and similar cocurricular activities can, of course, be done well or poorly. The mere fact of requiring students to go out into the community rather than come to the classroom does not guarantee that students are engaged in authentic performances. However, when experiential activities are linked to the curriculum, and when student reflection on their activities outside the classroom shapes their return to the classroom, and when students have the chance to engage in experiential learning and reflection repeatedly, then such programs have a real potential to change the cognitive economy.

There are many excellent examples of developing service-learning programs across the country. One of them is Chandler-Gilbert Community College in Chandler, Arizona, part of the ten-college Maricopa district that serves the city and suburbs of Phoenix. Chandler-Gilbert is interesting because its service learning program is an outgrowth of its prior commitment to collaborative and experiential learning. When I spoke with

Maria Hesse (personal communication, January 29, 2002), she was dean of instruction and had served for several years a faculty member. In the spring of 2002, she was chosen as the new president of Chandler-Gilbert. She reports that the college began in 1985 with a faculty interested in innovation and experiential learning. Faculty members began to explore collaborative learning early on, and many teachers and administrators were involved in community service. The college's service learning program began with a single English class and expanded through voluntary faculty participation. Now well over half of the college's 75 faculty members have taught a service-learning course, and a variety of options are available to students each semester. Over 100 community and nonprofit organizations are available for service-learning opportunities. These organizations have staff trained by college Student Services personnel to deal with the legal and practical challenge of employing college student volunteers. The college offers workshops for organizations on an ongoing basis.

Marybeth Mason (personal communication, February 4, 2002), who taught the first service-learning class at Chandler-Gilbert, is now interim dean of instruction. She says:

> I think Chandler-Gilbert is a wonderful model of student-centeredness in terms of philosophy and practice in classrooms with an emphasis on student performance. It probably started with our emphasis on trying to promote classrooms where students had a voice and where they were actively engaged in learning. That meant training our faculty in cooperative learning strategies.

This emphasis on faculty professional development that promoted experiential approaches to learning naturally led to trying out service learning:

> And before long, of course, you want them out there in the community. Service learning came along, and it was the logical next step for us in terms of providing students the opportunity to learn in meaningful contexts, no matter what their subject area. And I think that there is not a discipline at Chandler-Gilbert where someone hasn't used service learning. Everyone there has seemed to have been able to make a connection.

Chandler-Gilbert offers service-learning opportunities in a variety of fields, including writing, history, mathematics, child development, psychology, sociology, communication, music, foreign languages, American Indian studies, social work, and business. From its modest and experimental beginnings, the program has grown rapidly and consistently, but not according to a clearly articulated plan. Lois Bartholomew (personal communication, February 14, 2002), dean of students, suggests that service learning has been a way of realizing the pedagogical vision of the founding faculty:

> It was a way to teach and a way for the students to take what they were learning in the classrooms and go out into the community and actually experience it and then come back and write and reflect on the curriculum in the classes.

The impressive body of courses with service-learning links was built up incrementally over time. Hesse reports:

> There just wasn't an instance where we couldn't find some logical connection where students could see the value in what they were doing. And it just grew over the years until now, 12 years or so later, it's an integral part of the institution.

If the development of service learning at Chandler-Gilbert has not been according to a well articulated plan, it does seem to reflect a structural difference. Specifically, service learning has evolved as a joint activity of the academic and student services functions. The faculty and Student Services staff seem to have approached their work, from the beginning, as a team. I have suggested that one of the weaknesses of present approaches to curriculum development is an overemphasis on the classroom as a model. But viewed in a certain way, emphasis on the classroom can be liberating. Lois Bartholomew says, "I really believe that what's at the heart of this college is the classroom, and I think that everything needs to kind of surround that. And I really believe that we can rethink how we connect with each other and how we do things." The result, in this case, of seeing the classroom "at the heart" of everything has been to open up the classroom. Like Olivet and Alverno, but in a different way, Chandler-Gilbert has sought to expand the classroom by taking it into the world. The classroom, imagined in this way, can become a platform for active student performance and hence a forum for different and better learning rather than a cell with four walls that limits and constrains students in so many ways. Chandler-Gilbert students systematically work with real people facing real challenges, from the homeless and children in Boys and Girls Clubs to public agencies, museums, and schools. And they reflect on and discuss their experiences as a part of their class work.

UNIVERSITY OF MICHIGAN: RESEARCH AS A ROUTE TO LEARNING

Most college and university faculty members are or have been deeply involved in cognitive performance of a certain kind: academic research. Indeed, it has most often been the awakening of the spirit of discovery in the research process that has inspired us to enter academic life. Bruce Alberts (2000), president of the National Academy of Sciences, describes his own journey to science as a profession in a way that many will recognize:

> [E]ssentially every scientist whom I know remembers being utterly bored by the cookbook laboratories common to college biology, chemistry, and physics courses. My own experience is typical. After two years as a premedical student, I could stand these required labs no longer. I therefore petitioned out of the laboratory attached to the physical chemistry course at Harvard, seizing on an opportunity to spend afternoons in my tutor's research laboratory. This experience was so completely different that it soon caused me to forget about applying to medical school. Within a year I had decided to go to graduate school in biophysics and biochemistry, in preparation for a career in science.

The difference—at least one difference—between the cookbook laboratories that so many find tedious and the research laboratory is authenticity. Researchers are real people doing real work, and specifically, the work of discovery. "Why," Alberts asks,

> are we so fascinated to watch a live sporting event, sitting on the edge of our seats as the tensions builds in a close contest? And why, in comparison, do we have so little interest in watching the same event replayed on television, where the final outcome is already known? I conclude that human beings like to

confront the unknown.... Properly constructed, inquiry in education motivates students for the same reasons—it confronts them with an unknown puzzle, which can be solved only by a process that involves risk taking.

If we want students to learn to play the game of research, we have to let them onto the field. That, much simplified, is the conclusion of the Boyer Commission on Educating Undergraduates in the Research University (1998). The commission specifically addressed major research universities in the United States and found a dramatic difference between the work these institutions do in research and the work they do in undergraduate education. "[T]he research universities," the commission found, "have too often failed, and continue to fail, their undergraduate populations" (p. 5). While undergraduate tuition constitutes "one of the major sources of university income, helping to support research programs and graduate education . . . the students paying the tuition get, in all too many cases, less than their money's worth" (p. 5). I think it is fair to say that the commission found that most research universities continue to operate within the Instruction Paradigm:

> Many students graduate having accumulated whatever number of courses is required, but still lacking a coherent body of knowledge or any inkling as to how one sort of information might relate to others. And all too often they graduate without knowing how to think logically, write clearly, or speak coherently. The university has given them too little that will be of real value beyond a credential that will help them get their first jobs. And with larger and larger numbers of their peers holding the same paper in their hands, even that credential has lost much of its potency. (p. 6)

The Boyer Commission made specific recommendations to address the weaknesses of undergraduate education at the research universities. The central theme of those recommendations was that universities should let their undergraduate students in on the process of research and discovery. In other words, the commission endorsed the idea of involving students in more frequent, more authentic performance. The commission somewhat exaggerates, in my view, the distinctiveness of the research university and its difference from other colleges and universities. However, if its recommendations were followed in earnest it could indeed be possible to construct "a symbiotic relationship between all the participants in university learning that will provide a new kind of undergraduate experience available *only* at research institutions" (pp. 7–8). The commission recommends that research universities "make research-based learning the standard" (p. 15). It advocates inquiry-based learning beginning in the first year of college, continuing throughout the program, and culminating with a capstone experience. And many of its recommendations deserve to be considered carefully not just by research universities but by all colleges and universities.

In many ways, large research universities present the most difficult challenge for those seeking to transform undergraduate education simply because they have a substantial interest in perpetuating present arrangements, including the subsidy from undergraduate programs to research. This has led to an anomalous situation in which universities fundamentally dedicated to learning through research have been impervious, if not resistant, to the research about student learning, often research conducted by their own faculties and graduate students. So the institutions that are best at generating transformative discoveries about, among other things, human learning are often the worst at applying those discoveries to their own operations. However, in the wake of the Boyer Commission report, evidence mounts that at least some research universities are serious about addressing the problems of undergraduates. The arguments of the Boyer Commission have been reinforced by changes in policy by the National Science Foundation (NSF) and other federal agencies encouraging undergraduate research activity and by pressure from state legislators to show better results for undergraduate learning.

Many research universities have established programs to involve undergraduates in research, and the number has apparently increased as a result of the Boyer Commission's recommendations. But some such programs are little more than honors for already successful students, and many of them start at the wrong end. An administrator at one major research university, in describing what is certainly a very fine program for seniors, quotes one student as follows: "For the first time in my life, I felt passionate about an issue. . . . I wanted to dig deeper into the . . . questions; I wanted to search for my own answers" (The Reinvention Center, 2002). We can only rejoice for the student. However, it should give us pause when we hear a university senior declare that, in the last year of his undergraduate experience, he became passionately engaged with an issue for the first time in his life. What, we must wonder, was happening for the first three years of his university education? The Boyer Commission expressly recommended that inquiry-based learning begin in the freshman year. Several institutions have taken that recommendation seriously and implemented programs to engage freshman students in research.

One institution that began involving freshmen and sophomores in research nearly a decade before the Boyer Commission issued its recommendations is the University of Michigan at Ann Arbor. In its successful application for the NSF Recognition Award for Integration of Research and Education (RAIRE) (Universiy of Michigan, 1996), Michigan addressed the challenge just described:

> Ambitious science, mathematics, and engineering majors generally find means in their upper-class years to integrate research and education; the problem we seek to address is that, by that time, many students have been lost to these disciplines, and many even lost to higher education altogether. We want to engage underrepresented students in the intellectual community of the University as early as possible, to help them build the connections, understanding and confidence required to sustain them into their third year and beyond, and to provide bridging opportunities for students to graduation. (p. 1)

The long-term goal Michigan has set for itself is ambitious: "Ultimately, we envision at Michigan an undergraduate education wherein every student engages successfully in at least one direct, intensive experience in research, scholarship or creative activity before graduation" (p. 1). One is a good start and would be a cosmic leap from the present state of affairs at most research universities.

A major tool for approaching its goal of involving students in the actual performance of research is the Undergraduate Research Opportunity Program (UROP—pronounced as separate letters, not an acronym). The program began in 1989 as a small experiment with 14 students and has grown to involve about a 1000 students and 600 faculty members. The mission of the program is "to improve the retention and enrich the academic experience of undergraduate students during their first and second years at the University of Michigan through faculty/student research partnerships" (Universiy of Michigan, 1999–2000). From its inception,

UROP was targeted at first-year and second-year students. Indeed, it was initially targeted at students from underrepresented groups, as a strategy to improve retention and academic performance. In this respect, the program has been remarkably successful. In the early 1990s, "UROP students had an attrition rate 56% lower than underrepresented student in general" (Universiy of Michigan, 1996, pp. 11–12).

Students interested in UROP review the Research Project Book, which lists all of the available projects. They cover nearly the range of faculty research interests: a public health project in Detroit to track the effects of lead poisoning on teenage violence, a review of structural changes in Asian financial markets, a study of Afro Cuban religions since the revolution, the effect of treadmill exercises on children with Down syndrome (Universiy of Michigan, 2002). Undergraduate students are conducting literature reviews, Internet searches, surveys, data collection and analysis, and are often involved with the design as well as execution of the project. Students apply to the supervising faculty members, and once selected for a project they are assigned to a peer advisor and a Peer Research Interest Group of about 30 students grouped according to research interest. Student and faculty member sign a contract spelling out the nature of the student's responsibilities. Students keep a journal of their research activities and do a term project, which can be a research abstract, a paper, or an oral presentation or poster for the Spring Research Symposium held each year. They receive one hour of academic credit for each three hours worked per week (Universiy of Michigan, 1999–2000).

Evaluation of the outcomes for student participants indicates that "UROP appears to have the greatest benefit [for] students who are least prepared when they enter college" (Universiy of Michigan, 1996, p. 12). Comparison of UROP students with comparable control groups for 1990–1993 revealed that African-American UROP students had an attrition rate 51% lower than that of the control group and grades 7% higher. For White and Asian students with low grade point averages, attrition in UROP was zero, in contrast with 12% for the control group (p. 11).

Faculty participants in the program have responded very positively. "Seventy-two percent reported that their overall research productivity was enhanced by participation in the program" (p. 12). In excess of 90% of participating faculty said they would serve again as a research mentor and would encourage colleagues to do the same.

Undergraduate research at Michigan operates parallel to an extensive service-learning program. The Edward Ginsberg Center for Community Service and Learning offers a large array of service learning options to students. The center is developing an approach to service learning that seems especially compatible with undergraduate research. In their workshops for faculty, the center identifies "academic service-learning" as an activity that takes place at the intersection of relevant and meaningful service, enhanced academic learning, and purposeful civic learning. Jeffrey Howard (2001), assistant director of academic service learning at the center, who prepared the workbook that orients faculty to the program, encourages faculty members to embrace the pedagogy of service learning in the classroom:

> Classrooms and communities are very different learning contexts. Each requires students to assume a different learner role. Generally, classrooms provide a high level of teacher direction, with students expected to assume mostly a passive learner role. In contrast, service communities usually provide a low level of teaching direction, with students expected to assume mostly an active learner role. Alternating between the passive learner role in the classroom and the active learner role in the community may challenge and even impede student learning. The solution is to shape the learning environments so that students assume similar learner roles in both contexts.
>
> While one solution is to intervene so that the service community provides a high level of teaching directions, we recommend, for several reasons, re-norming the traditional classroom toward one that values students as active learners. (p. 18)

Both service learning and undergraduate research create models and motives for this re-norming of the traditional classroom. It is hard to tell how successful this re-norming has been at Michigan. But the 2000 NSSE report presented the University of Michigan as an example of a research university where freshman students reported a notably high level of academic challenge. Programs like undergraduate research and service learning are certainly part of the reason why.

UNIVERSITY OF DELAWARE: BRINGING DISCOVERY INTO THE CLASSROOM

While undergraduate participation in faculty research is an important way of involving students in authentic performance, it is hard to imagine such an approach addressing the needs of all students at most institutions. Undergraduate research can certainly change the cognitive economy, as can service learning and effective extracurricular activities. But to maximize the effect on the cognitive economy, performance pedagogies should also invade the curriculum, re-norm the traditional classroom, as Howard puts it. At the University of Delaware, this appears to be happening. Delaware, like Michigan, was a recipient of a RAIRE award from the NSF. Its application declares:

> The University of Delaware firmly believes that the development of its students into productive, proactive citizens is best accomplished in an environment of discovery, where research is an integral part of students' education and where students play an integral role in faculty research....The strategy to implement the institutional vision for the integration of research and education consists of two components: (a) involving as many undergraduates as is feasible in faculty research and (b) providing a discovery-oriented environment for those students who cannot be accommodated in research projects. (University of Delaware, 1997)

Delaware is implementing the first part of this strategy through the Undergraduate Research Program (URP), which was founded in 1980.

> Over 66% of the University's approximately 950-member faculty regularly participate in undergraduate research, including over 90% of the faculty in the sciences and engineering. From 600 to 700 students are estimated to be engaged in undergraduate research at any one time. (Bauer & Bennett, in press)

As part of its RAIRE grant activity, Delaware has done some interesting research on the impact of their undergraduate research program. In one study, a sample of alumni who participated in undergraduate research was surveyed along with a control group not involved in undergraduate research. Each group was asked a broad array of questions about their undergraduate learning experience, but no indication was given that the survey concerned undergraduate research. Karen W. Bauer, assistant director of institutional research and planning, and Joan Bennett, director of the URP (in press), found in this study that "there is a consistent trend throughout the survey that shows greater perceived enhancement of skills for those alumni who participated in undergraduate research." Furthermore, URP alumni went to graduate school at a higher rate. Bauer and Bennett conclude:

> The fact that alumni with research experience were significantly more likely to continue their educations beyond the bachelor's degree and were about twice as likely to complete doctoral study as were comparable alumni with no research experience suggests that skills and abilities enhanced by research contributed to their success as doctoral candidates.

In another study, Andrew L. Zydney, a professor of chemistry, along with Bennett, Abdus Shahid of URP, and Bauer (2002) examined faculty beliefs about undergraduate research in the mathematics, engineering, and science departments. They found that "The faculty . . . felt strongly that the undergraduate research experience yielded significant added value to the education of undergraduate researchers" (p. 296).

But not all students will have the initiative and courage to seek out research opportunities, and there simply aren't enough opportunities to offer to them if they did. Hence the second component of Delaware's strategy: creating a discovery-oriented environment in the classroom. One of the tools for this re-norming is problem-based learning (PBL).

In the larger, generic sense, research is problem-based learning, as are many other forms of apprenticeship that address real problems. But as the term is most widely used today, PBL refers to a particular approach to designing the classroom experience that emerged first in medical education. In 1966, the faculty of the medical school at McMaster University in Ontario, Canada, developed an alternative to the traditional lecture-and-notes approach to the foundational courses in medicine. They presented new students with the problems of actual patients and asked them to diagnose the symptoms and formulate treatment plans in small groups. PBL is now practiced in a number of medical schools including Harvard, Rush

Presbyterian in Chicago, and Southern Illinois University. It has also been taken up by a number of graduate schools in business and engineering.

Delaware began its involvement with PBL through a collaborative program begun in 1992 with the Thomas Jefferson Medical College in Philadelphia. The medical school offered early admission to Delaware undergraduates in the Medical Scholars Program if they were introduced to PBL in their undergraduate courses. After conducting some faculty workshops on the pedagogy, Delaware offered its first two PBL courses, physiology and physics, in the fall of 1992. The technique attracted the interest of a number of faculty members, especially in the sciences, and more faculty workshops led to more courses. With the support of an NSF grant, Delaware established the Institute for Transforming Undergraduate Education. The institute now conducts week-long sessions twice a year. According to Barbara Duch, director of the Math and Science Education Resource Center (personal communication, April 15, 2002), the more than 200 Institute Fellows who have completed the program constitute about one-third of the Delaware faculty. While the program began in the sciences, now every department offers some PBL courses. In Political Science, for example, 85% of the faculty are Institute Fellows. George Watson, professor of physics and astronomy, and Susan Groh, assistant professor of chemistry and biochemistry (2001), point out:

> In 1993, the term "problem-based learning" was virtually unknown on the campus of the University of Delaware. Seven years later, it has become a byword, and the university has established an international reputation as the leader in the development of problem-based learning in undergraduate education. (p. 21)

The essential value of PBL is that it makes students the explicit agents of their own learning. Problem-solving is performance, as we have defined it here. Kurt Burch (2001), associate professor of political science and international relations, says:

> PBL is a teaching strategy that shifts the classroom focus from teaching to learning. The central premise of PBL holds that most students will better learn information and skills if they need them; need arises as students try to solve specific, open-ended problems. Beyond an orientation to problems,

> a PBL course promotes learning via activity and discovery. Students interact with each other and engage course material in a shared enterprise of learning-by-discovery. As students explore problems, they discover much about their topics and themselves. A discovery-oriented course provides students with opportunities and responsibilities to make significant decisions about what to investigate, how to proceed, and how to solve problems. (p. 194)

The basic PBL process begins by presenting students with a problem. The problem might take the form of a description of a case, a research paper or essay, a videotape, or a novel. Students work in small groups to describe the nature of the problem.

> Throughout discussion, students pose questions called "learning issues" that delineate aspects of the problem that they do not understand. These learning issues are recorded by the group and help generate and focus discussion. Students are continually encouraged to define what they know and—more importantly—what they don't know. (Duch, Groh, & Allen, 2001, p. 7)

Using the learning issues as a guide, prioritizing them, and assigning research responsibilities, students proceed to limit, define, and explore the problem.

While PBL is one of Edgerton's four pedagogies, it also includes one of the others: collaborative learning. Like any other pedagogical technique, PBL is flexible and subject to many variations. However, it puts students in the center of classroom processes, involves students in conversation with one another not just about the facts of their subject but about the design of their classroom process. Certainly the role the teacher takes will have a significant effect on the experience. The nature and flexibility of the assessments used will be important. For example, the "triple jump" approach to assessment, developed in the medical context, uses the assessment process to focus and organize the problem-solving process. In this approach, students are assessed on dealing with or shaping the problem, independent study of the problem, and final formulation of the problem (Biggs, 1999, p. 210). To the extent that PBL is used consistently in a class but assessment focuses simply on declarative knowledge rather than on complex cognition, much of the value of the technique may be invisible to the assessment. There remains little doubt that PBL, like undergraduate research and service learning, is a significant means of transforming the classroom environment and raising the profile of student performance. The University of Delaware appears to be in the process of doing the re-norming of the classroom experience that can transform the cognitive economy of the college.

PROCESS FRONTIER: ACTIVITY

The Learning Paradigm college will require frequent, continual, and authentic student performances. As we have seen, there are many ways in which this can be done. The four performance pedagogies that Russell Edgerton identified can be infused throughout the curriculum in a variety of ways. None of the colleges we have considered in this chapter has completed the transformation—though Alverno has come far—but all have embarked upon changes that can make student performance the central and defining characteristic of the college curriculum. In the Learning Paradigm college the tables will be turned from Edgerton's description of present arrangements: lecture-based, didactic instruction will survive on the sidelines, while student performance defines and exemplifies standard practice. What is now the exception will become the default setting for pedagogy and course design.

13

A Learning Paradigm College Provides Consistent, Continual, Interactive Feedback to Students

ASSESSMENT, FEEDBACK, AND EVALUATION

All, or nearly all, significant interactions between students and their learning environments involve feedback, evaluation, or both. And those who exert the greatest control over the shape, direction, and effect of the information exchanges are the students. As Grant Wiggins (1993) puts it, "What matters in education is . . . the habits of mind that a student becomes disposed to use" (p. 9). We can say what we like to students, or about them, but it is ultimately the students' "habits of mind" that will determine what they hear.

As we saw in Chapter 6, students hear in large measure what they expect to hear, and what one student will perceive as evaluation another may recognize as feedback. I have defined feedback as information that illustrates the effect of a performance in light of some standard or goal and that the performer can use to improve future performances. Evaluation, on the other hand, is information that states or confirms a judgment on a performance or a person.

Two Differences Between Feedback and Evaluation

Feedback and evaluation differ in two important ways. First, feedback is about the learner's perceptions and beliefs about his or her performance while evaluation is about the perceptions of people other than the learner. Feedback is fundamentally information about what you are trying to do, information that you can use to do what you set out to accomplish. Evaluation is fundamentally information about what other people think about what you have done—and may or may not be even relevant to your purposes.

185

Second, feedback is dynamic. That is to say, it is information about an ongoing action or pattern of action. As I am using the term, feedback is defined by its relationship to contemplated future actions. Evaluation, on the other hand, is static. That is to say, it is information about a completed action. So feedback is about what you are going to do, while evaluation is about what you have already done. Feedback has the purpose of improving performances that have not yet occurred; evaluation has the purpose of reporting the quality of finished performances or the quality of other completed actions.

We should, on both counts, think of these terms not as describing absolute distinctions but as identifying the extreme points on continua. Indeed, I am inclined to say that there is an element of evaluation in all feedback and an element of feedback in all evaluation. The very design of the instruments of evaluation we use in conventional testing and measurement of student work contains feedback to the students about their own goals and beliefs. This must be true because these instruments were designed; they did not just evolve. As the National Research Council (2001) puts it, "every assessment is grounded in a conception or theory about how people learn, what they know, and how knowledge and understanding progress over time" (p. 20). The result, as Wiggins (1993) notes, is that:

> [E]very test teaches the student. It teaches the student what kinds of questions educators value, it teaches the student what kind of answers we value (correct merely? justified? chosen from our list? constructed by the student?), it teaches the student about intellectual relationship, and it teaches the student how much we respect student thinking. (p. 24)

Likewise, the degree and nature of feedback we give to students on their work implies an unstated evaluation of the student as an actual and potential performer. Even where it does not imply an evaluation of the performance it often implies an evaluation of the performer, which is a much more serious matter. Vague and nonspecific coaching sends the message that if the student does not already perform as we would like, then she must lack the potential to do so. Praise directed at the person rather than the performance implies that the performance already accomplished must express the highest level to which the student can aspire. Heavy reliance on extremely directive feedback places the student in the role of a novice who requires precise direction and has little capacity for discretion and discrimination. Specific feedback that the student is not in a position to act on in a reasonable time may imply unrealistic expectations, an evaluation that the student has reason to discount. Specific feedback that the student can address immediately implies a high estimate of the student's competence in a way that makes the student powerful in relation to the task. Overall, feedback that focuses on the performance rather than the person in a way that the person can reasonably address implies an evaluation that opens the door to improvement by seeing the student as someone capable of doing more.

THE FRAMEWORK FOR FEEDBACK

Feedback is information about the consequences of our actions that helps us to modify our actions to better achieve our goals. Feedback is not only important to learning; it is essential. Indeed, a rough but reasonable definition of learning might be "the process of responding to feedback in order to modify actions to better achieve intended consequences." The National Research Council (2001) puts it this way:

> Individuals acquire a skill much more rapidly if they receive feedback about the correctness of what they have done. If incorrect, they need to know the nature of their mistake. It was demonstrated long ago that practice without feedback produces little learning. One of the persistent dilemmas in education is that students often spend time practicing incorrect skills with little or no feedback. Furthermore, the feedback they ultimately receive is often neither timely nor informative. For the less capable student, unguided practice (e.g., homework in mathematics) can be practice in doing tasks incorrectly.... [O]ne of the most important roles for assessment is the provision of timely and informative feedback to students during instruction and learning so that their practice of a skill and its subsequent acquisition will be effective and efficient. (pp. 85–87)

In most activities that we pursue for their own sake, we systematically monitor feedback. We can see this in nearly all extracurricular, voluntary student activities, from playing video games or poker to performing in an orchestra or acting in a play. This does not mean that no evaluation takes place. Sometimes it does. In some activities, feedback and evaluation merge, and no judges are necessary. The baseball player who touches home base—or doesn't—and the singer who hits the right note—or doesn't—directly experience accomplishing the goal or falling short of it. Umpires and officials in most well-designed games serve the function of trained observers, watching and reporting what spectators cannot see from a distance. They do not judge performances; they report the exact nature of the performance, the meaning of which the rules have already defined. Carrying the ball out of bounds ends the play; that is a simple matter of definition. The business of the umpire or referee is to see where the ball is at any given point and report that information to the players and spectators. But even where a judge or evaluator intervenes, the evaluation of a single performance is subject to revision in the next performance. As with self-assessment, which we discussed in the last chapter, evaluation is best seen as focused on the performance rather than the performer. Evaluation is always for the moment, for this performance. Tomorrow is another day. Thus even evaluation takes on a quality of feedback and becomes a tool that can stimulate learning and improvement.

Feedback is a deceptively simple concept, deceptively because its simplicity allows it to be merged into similar but related concepts that change its valence significantly. In reflecting on the meaning and function of feedback, I will suggest two metaphors that illustrate how it functions in learning. The resulting picture of feedback will be consistent, I hope, but three-dimensional because viewed from different perspectives. We can think of feedback as road signs or conversation.

Feedback as Road Signs

The first metaphor is suggested by Grant Wiggins (1993). Imagine, he tells us, that you want to travel from New York to Sacramento for the first time. As a learner attempting a new task, you would probably seek some expert guidance (teaching). The first thing you would probably do would be to get a map, perhaps one from the Automobile Club with the best route already marked out. But once you get on the road, the map would be of little use if you did not have clear and accurate road signs. You have an objective: Sacramento. You have expert guidance as to how to reach the objective in the form of the map and directions. But to actually get where you are going, you need ongoing feedback to tell you whether you are approaching your goal. The road signs provide that feedback.

Think back to when you drove to a place for the first time. Recall the uncertainty and doubt that an unknown landscape inspires. You know you need to take Interstate 80 west, and you know it should be nearby. As you approach the next intersection, you are looking with fixed attention for that blue shield with the red cap and an "80" in the middle. If you don't see that sign, you probably won't turn. If you do turn, and as you enter the on-ramp you see that shield out of the corner of your eye, your decision to turn is confirmed and you advance with confidence. If you fail to see the hoped-for sign or see one that challenges your expectations—a round state highway sign with black letters and numbers—your decision is disconfirmed and you immediately begin to think of remedies. Feedback is not simply data from the environment, perceptions of the objects within view. Feedback is information; it informs your search for certain objectives.

I recently had the experience of driving through Salem, Oregon, seeking to make my way from the Interstate to a state highway. I had never been in Salem before. The map the rental car agent in Portland had given me showed only the main thoroughfares. Road signs identifying the route were intermittent, and at key points absent. As I entered the downtown area, I saw a sign pointing to the route I wanted, but following that road left me at a dead end facing the river. The street names were clearly marked, but my map didn't specify which streets to take. After getting incorrect directions from three different people and circling Willamette University four times, I finally got hold of a street map. That gave me specific enough guidance that street signs sufficed to let me know when I was on course, and I was able to move confidently—well, more or less confidently—in the direction of my goal.

The experience of using a map and road signs helps to illustrate the subtle but important relationship between guidance and feedback. "Guidance," Wiggins (1993) points out, "gives direction; feedback tells me whether I am on course. Guidance tells me the most likely ways to achieve my goal; feedback tells me whether I am on track or off track in a way that enables me to self-adjust" (p. 184). If we identify "teaching" with guidance, then we need to recognize that "teaching [is] never adequate to cause successful learning" (p. 184). Why? "Because no matter how well you 'guide' me in advance, I still need to determine whether I am successfully doing what you asked me to do . . ." (p. 184). In many learning situations, we need a roadmap or directions, guidance to point us in the right direction. But if we want to reach the destination, especially if we want to get there quickly and with a minimum of wasted motion, we also need landmarks or road signs that confirm or disconfirm our choice of route.

Guidance can be concentrated at the beginning of the trip or intermittent. But "feedback must be continuous, or almost so, if I am to achieve my goal with maximal efficiency and minimal reliance on ongoing guidance" (p. 185). When I was lost in Salem, I lacked both guidance and feedback. More precisely, the guidance I received and the data from the environment didn't match: One was more general, the other more specific. I could not connect them. So even though I was taking in a great deal of data from the environment—observing landmarks, reading street signs— none of it became usable feedback because I could not connect it with my goal. When I got a better map, I got more specific guidance: the specific street names and orientations on the route. This guidance transformed the data in the environment around me into information; street signs now informed my quest, became feedback that allowed me to confirm or disconfirm each choice I made as I proceeded along my route.

When you become an expert traveler in a given terrain, your reliance on guidance decreases and your ability to abstract usable feedback from the environment increases. One of the major functions of effective teaching, then, is to provide the kind of guidance that students can apply by reading the feedback from the environment. As we saw in the last chapter, one of the qualities of excellent student performances is that they are authentic. We spoke of authentic tasks as being embedded in a realistic context, so that knowledge is conditionalized, related to a context of action. The knowledge of experts empowers them to be better readers of the environment, makes them feedback literate, we might say. Most of us simply can't get as lost in our own neighborhoods as we can on the first visit to a new town because we have better mastery of environmental information that we can convert into effective feedback.

This suggests a couple of important points about the relationship between guidance and feedback. First, guidance is the most effective form— and perhaps the only effective form—of teaching. Second, guidance becomes meaningful and useful to the extent that it provides the performer information or tools that can then be used to follow feedback. Stop to reflect for a moment on how much teacher talk simply isn't guidance, as we have defined it here. To apply the metaphor at hand, teachers spend a good deal of time describing maps of places that their students will never visit and giving directions to places where their students will never go. But even when students are going to travel to the country being mapped, teacher guidance is much more useful when it is linked to specific road signs, when it is presented at a level of specificity and usability that will allow the student to apply it.

The master question that students bring into every class in the Instruction Paradigm college, of course, is "what do you want?" That question is an appeal for guidance, but for guidance of a certain kind. It reflects a deeply entrenched habit of mind that students bring to their classes. It says that, from the perspective of the students, their teachers are not working from the same map. Every class is a new country, offering a new set of roadways and landmarks to be learned. The confusion this causes students is reflected in the confusion and frustration it causes teachers. Even on a field laid out on as neat and abstract a grid as we can imagine, mathematics, many students seem to come into Algebra 2 looking for a new map—having apparently lost or discarded the one they picked up in Algebra 1. But if students are going to become more expert at making their way around the terrain of learning, they need to be working from the same map for an extended period of time. Hence, teachers, no matter how skillful or hard working, cannot lay out the basic guidance individually. The faculty, collectively and not distributively, needs to develop the guidelines, the rubrics, the standards that become the maps to learning.

Feedback as Conversation

This brings us to the second metaphor for effective feedback that I want to discuss: conversation. The weakness of the road sign metaphor is that it is static. Road signs just sit there, while the traveler moves past them. And they do not change when they are seen or missed. But feedback is often more interactive, more like a conversation between people. In the last chapter I quoted Donald Schön's characterization of the reflective process of design professionals as "a conversation with the materials of a situation." We can expand upon that idea by suggesting that the conversation that takes place involves probing and experimentation on the part of the performer and responsive feedback from the materials. We can see this even more clearly when the "materials" are human beings.

In an actual conversation, there is always an element of feedback. If there is not, it ceases to be a conversation. When I respond to what you say, one thing I reveal is whether or how I understood what you said. Sometimes this feedback is explicit and unmistakable, as in comments like, "I don't understand what you mean by that" or "What was that again?" or when I put on a bewildered facial expression or nod assent. In other cases, the clues may be less direct, as when my response suggests to you that I understood you to mean something other than you intended. But the element of feedback is always there. So central is feedback to conversation that its presence defines the difference between monologue and dialog.

Arthur Applebee (1996), professor of education at the University at Albany, State University of New York, explores the metaphor in his book *Curriculum as Conversation: Transforming Traditions of Teaching and Learning*. Applebee is explicitly addressing the challenge of creating environments for student performance, for what he (like Schön) calls "knowledge-in-action," which he contrasts to "knowledge-out-of-context." He suggests that many arguments about curriculum address the wrong issues:

> Discussions of curriculum in American schools and colleges have usually focused on what is most worth knowing: Should we stress the Great Books, the richness of multiculturalism, the basic literacy needed in the worlds of work and leisure? But these arguments have been based on false premises and reflect a fundamental misconception of the nature of knowing. They strip knowledge of the contexts that give it meaning and vitality, and lead to an education that stresses knowledge-out-of-context rather than knowledge-in-action. (p. 3)

Applebee offers an alternative vision of curriculum, one

> that redresses that balance, placing the emphasis on the knowledge-in-action that is at the heart of all living traditions. Such knowledge arises out of participating in ongoing conversations about things that matter, conversations that are themselves embedded within larger traditions of discourse that we have come to value (science, the arts, history, literature, and mathematics, among many others). When we take this metaphor seriously, the development of curriculum becomes

the development of culturally significant domains for conversation, and instruction becomes a matter of helping students learn to participate in conversations within those domains. (p. 3)

I think this is a useful way of framing the vision of the institutional response to student performance in a hot cognitive economy. We have too often conceived of the curriculum, as we have conceived of teaching, as a monologue that the institution or the teacher delivers to students. While I have presented the term "instruction" in a negative light in this book, there is really nothing innately bad about instruction, which can be a form of the guidance that is often necessary for learning. But the term has been corrupted by being yoked to the word "delivery." Instructional delivery imports the monologue model and presents the matter of learning as if it were a package that could be dropped on students' cognitive doorsteps. We should see the curriculum and the classroom not as a monologue but as a dialog, a conversation. And the difference between a monologue and a dialog is feedback.

Our purpose in assessment cannot be simply to measure performance. To do so is to treat the student as an object, as the audience for our monologue. As Wiggins (1993) puts it:

When our sole aim is to measure, the [student] is invariably treated as an object by any test. . . . The educative role of genuine assessment is always at risk if by test we mean a process in which we insist upon our questions, our timing, and our imposed constraints on resources and prior access to the questions and in which we see our scoring and reporting needs as paramount. (p. 7)

If the curriculum is a dialog, a conversation with students, then we will both give feedback and receive it. The student will become an interlocutor who both shapes and is shaped by the ongoing conversation. This interaction will allow the student to shape the curriculum to his or her ends, to engage the curriculum as a means of achieving intrinsic goals, which we discussed in Chapter 11. But it will also demand that students test their developing ideas and performances by exposing them to thoroughgoing feedback.

FEEDBACK AND THE COGNITIVE ECONOMY

We saw in the last chapter that colleges need to create a cognitive economy that requires frequent student performances. But the way students respond and grow in the process of performance will depend crucially on the kinds of feedback they receive.

A hot cognitive economy will be one in which the trajectory of student performance is upward, moving toward more complex cognition, deeper learning, fuller connections, and richer integration of learning with more fully realized intrinsic goals. Feedback is what will feed this process of growth. We saw in Chapter 11 that growth depends on a balance between challenge and ability in which the learner is constantly moving the zone of proximal development forward into new realms of possibility. It is feedback that fuels this forward movement. We saw in Chapter 6 that the ability to recognize data in the environment as relevant feedback on performance is rooted in the learner's self-theory, and that the learner's self-theory is likewise rooted in his or her experience of feedback. That is to say, an entity theorist, setting performance goals and pursuing them through surface approaches, can become an incremental theorist, can learn to set learning goals and pursue them through deep approaches, if the environment demands the conversion. That means that students need to be in an environment that respects their intrinsic goals and requires frequent and authentic performance. The key tool in integrating students into that environment is effective and consistent feedback. On the basis of what we have seen about feedback and its role, we can describe certain characteristics of an effective feedback system, one that will promote a hot cognitive economy.

Feedback Should Be Consistent Across the Curriculum

Feedback should be framed by a fundamental set of directions. Teachers and the institution should be giving guidance from the same map, speaking the same language. The objectives for learning that the institution values should be defined in a clear and consistent way, as should the common language about student performance and assessment. This suggests an institutional rubric or standard for key learning objectives across the curriculum and clearly articulated outcomes consistent with that rubric in specialized programs. We saw one example of such a rubric in Alverno College's core abilities, and we will see other examples in this chapter. Such a rubric, of course, is not feedback. But something like it is a prerequisite for effective feedback. By using a consistent framework for ongoing feedback, teachers and staff assure that students will be able to recognize the road signs on their route to learning objectives. Or to switch the metaphor, they assure that they are speaking the same language about learning, helping students to participate in the conversation about their own performances. Bowden and Marton (1998) frame the underlying issue this way:

> How can the university ensure that the relationships between the parts of a degree programme can be addressed by students so that the whole is greater than the mere sum of the parts? How can the university avoid having students merely collecting a series of unconnected educational experiences, however fine each might be in its own way, and graduating with a Bachelor of Bits and Pieces? Since the graduate's educational and personal attainments relate to the whole programme that has been experienced, there is a responsibility to ensure that the improvement process is not just at the subject level. Attention needs to be paid to how the parts relate to each other, how they fit the whole and how they contribute to the kinds of outcomes we expect for our graduates. (pp. 234–235)

Feedback Should Be Continual and Connected

To engage students in the conversation about their performance requires that teachers, staff, and other students engage in that conversation on an ongoing basis. One source of resistance to the very idea of creating a feedback-rich learning environment is the assumption by some faculty members that teachers must be the primary or even exclusive source of feedback to students about student performance. That assumption is based on the pattern of evaluation in the Instruction Paradigm college. Of course, if the main business of assessment is evaluation, then the burden of assessment tends to fall on the faculty. But if the purpose of assessment is to provide feedback, it is a positive virtue to involve a variety of agents. The more voices in the conversation, the better. Often, those not tainted with the burden of evaluation are more credible sources of feedback. Faculty who will not evaluate or grade the student, other students, or outside parties can give feedback free of the suspicion of bias or the desire for control. I am not aware of a single serious performance activity, in college or out, where coaches also serve as umpires and judges—except for nearly every classroom. The business of teachers should be to provide guidance toward effective performance and to design environments in which the activity itself generates feedback to the performer. Thus, providing consistent and continual feedback need not burden the faculty unduly. Indeed, it can liberate teachers for the crucial task of providing expert guidance and key feedback at crucial learning junctures.

Feedback Should Be Interactive

Feedback should be addressed to students as interlocutors in a conversation rather than spectators at someone else's performance. The problem with a systematic description of learning outcomes that provides clear guidance to students about learning objectives is that it will hardly ever be set at the right level for most students. Unless the rubric is dumbed down to the level of students low on the developmental scale, it can easily be pitched too high for them to reach. This problem can be addressed to some extent by laying out the rubric of expected learning outcomes at different developmental levels. Alverno does this, as do other colleges we will discuss in this chapter. The objective and end product of all assessment, of course, should be self assessment. So the rule of thumb guiding the development and application of rubrics and standards should always be that the student can apply them continuously to his or her own performances. Thus the work of learning becomes interactive in the sense that the college speaks to students in the language of learning outcomes and students speak back in the same language. The curriculum genuinely becomes a forum for reciprocal feedback, a real conversation.

The question of developmental levels is especially important because it is hard to get hold of today. I am convinced that our own understanding of our students and their potential is warped by the information that most existing assessment regimes provide. In the Instruction Paradigm college, where evaluation is valued consistently over feedback, we tend to exaggerate the disparity between students in a variety of ways. Wiggins (1993) puts it this way:

> The consequences of years of norm-referenced testing and grading on a curve go deeper than we imagine. Two generations of relentless norm-referenced testing have caused many

teachers to believe in the inevitability of vast differences in student achievement and in the inevitability of current levels of
total performance. We have an educational system built upon
an increasing "prejudice," in the literal sense of a sweeping
"prejudging": teachers and administrators assume that they
can predict all future results on past performance. (p. 169)

He is referring to teachers and administrators in elementary and secondary education. The skewing of expectations is even more pronounced
in higher education. We have so long been conditioned to see students as
SAT scores with legs that we have forgotten that the entire purpose of
norm-referenced testing is to exaggerate differences, to discriminate more
boldly than simple observation can. If we fall back into the habit of reifying test scores, of seeing them as the real ability and potential of our students, then we have committed ourselves in advance to an ontology of failure. If we accept the verdict of testing that is both the cause and the product of surface approaches to learning, we have trapped ourselves in a vi-
cious cycle of testing and judging that will inevitably confirm the decline
we have taught ourselves to expect.

The large plurality of students entering college—perhaps now a majority—who come deficient in the knowledge or abilities that should define
the college student are not newly cast minds, fresh from the genetic
foundry. They are the products of a dozen or more years of schooling.
Many of them have been tested from infancy, tracked on the basis of multiple-choice tests into programs designed to prepare them for more multiple-
choice tests that in turn locked them into paths that systematically precluded the development of higher-order thinking skills and complex cognition. In short, many entering college students have been nearly evaluated to
death, have suffered an education that has trivialized their engagement with
learning to the point that they are almost disabled for seeking or recognizing significant feedback on their own performances in an academic setting.
The Instruction Paradigm response to these students is, by and large, more
tracking: To shunt them into developmental or remedial classes, usually
severed from and uncoordinated with the curriculum proper, to teach them
to do long division and write paragraphs with topic sentences. That is, they
are most often excluded from participating in the curricular conversation.
The cognitive economy of many developmental programs is hypothermic.
And this is often true in spite of the best efforts of talented and dedicated

teachers. It is like driving around Salem with a map that doesn't tell you how to get where you want to go. They drop like flies.

The challenge that colleges face is to engage every student in the curricular conversation, beginning at the level at which the student is prepared to engage, but operating from the same rubric of ultimate learning outcomes. If developmental education is to offer students a rising spiral of accomplishment rather than a funnel down the drain of failure, it must engage them from the very beginning in the unending cycle of model-practice-feedback-refinement that Wiggins describes. Indeed, ongoing feedback is more important for less well prepared students. As Bandura (1997) points out, "The less individuals believe in themselves, the more they need explicit, proximal, and frequent feedback of progress that provides repeated affirmations of their growing capabilities" (p. 217). To provide this, the feedback system of the college must be interactive from the very start; it must listen to what students say and respond seriously to it. I am not so unrealistic as to believe that every student will reach the same level of performance in every field. But the predominant problem that developmental students face today is not that they run the race and don't reach the finish line; that is a statistical illusion. The predominant problem is that they never reach the starting line. They never enter the race. They run in circles on a separate track until they give up and go away. They drive around Salem until they run out of gas.

Those students who enter college with explicit, testable developmental deficiencies are just the tip of the iceberg of those students, discussed in Chapter 5, who enter college with an ingrained surface orientation to learning. For all of these—and they amount I think to a very substantial majority of incoming college students—the first priority is to engage them in an interactive cycle of performance and feedback, an ongoing conversation about learning.

The Feedback System Offers Many Opportunities for Reevaluation

Evaluation, of course, is necessary. At many points in the student's progress through college, someone must make judgments on that progress, must rate performances. And in the end, someone must say whether the progress is sufficient to justify the granting of the degree. It would be foolish to suggest that we can do without evaluation. The problem with evaluation as it is practiced in the Instruction Paradigm college is not so much that there is too much of it as that it is poor, intermittent, uncoordinated, and final. Indeed, more frequent student evaluation—rather than less frequent—could be a good thing because then evaluation could take on the quality of feedback, giving students information that they could use in a practical way to improve their next evaluation. The key defect of the evaluation in the Instruction Paradigm is that it is usually final; it can seldom be repeated. This corrupts it into a mere judgment on the performance and prevents the student from seeing it as feedback.

Evaluation gains value by being repeated. If a student can be reevaluated, then she gains the power to correct the errors of the first effort, and evaluation takes on some of the quality of feedback, or it can. It is the finality of evaluation, the final examination followed by the final grade, that trivializes education.

KING'S COLLEGE: MAINTAINING GOOD MAPS VIA A DELIBERATE PLAN OF LEARNING

The foundation for an exemplary feedback system consists of clear, consistent guidance, across the curriculum, as to what the institution's learning expectations are for students. All the teachers should be giving directions from the same map. We have already seen one example of a college that has developed such a system: Alverno, with abilities articulated at different developmental levels. Another such system is the Comprehensive Assessment Program at King's College. King's is a Roman Catholic liberal arts college founded in 1946 by the Congregation of Holy Cross priests and brothers from the University of Notre Dame. In the 1970s King's adopted a new core curriculum that had many of the features of the conventional college general education program. It soon became clear, however, in faculty surveys and discussions, that the curriculum wasn't working:

> The core allowed students too much choice among a smorgasbord of courses; students often avoided the exact courses they needed to repair serious weaknesses in their thinking and writing skills as well as courses many faculty regarded as essential to the liberally educated person; the core was politicized as departments vied for "representation"; the core had no sequence, no integrity, no character that would give students both a common experience and a distinctive King's College education. (King's College, 1998, p. 2)

This description of the curriculum could be adopted with minor amendments by a majority of colleges and universities, then and now: no sequence, no integrity, no character. What is distinctive about King's is that they moved aggressively to do something about it. It is also noteworthy that, unlike many colleges that have adopted major reforms, King's was not impelled by some impending catastrophe. As Jean O'Brien (personal communication, April 2, 2002), professor of psychology, puts it, "King's has been lucky in that we have been in good shape. These changes came from a focus on 'How do we become better teachers?' and 'How do we help our students to become better learners?'"

The Curriculum Committee asked the faculty to redesign their courses, beginning by spelling out the objectives ("measurable within the course") and goals ("not measurable in a conventional sense but desirable nonetheless") of each course. What should students know and be able to do after completing a course? It soon became apparent

> that certain objectives appeared repeatedly; those repeated objectives came to be translated into eight "transferable skills of liberal learning," that is, skills the faculty obviously wanted students to transfer from assignment to assignment, course to course, Core course to major courses, college experience to life and work after college. (King's College, 1998, pp. 2–3)

The eight transferable skills of liberal learning are 1) critical thinking, 2) effective writing, 3) effective oral communication, 4) library and information literacy, 5) computer competence, 6) creative thinking and problem solving, 7) quantitative reasoning, and 8) moral reasoning. These skills came to define the new core curriculum, adopted in 1985 and continuously modified and refined since then. The skills of liberal learning are all addressed in specific course sequences.

The tool King's has used to implement the core program is assessment. The late Donald W. Farmer (1999), former academic vice president at King's, captured as well as might be hoped for the role of assessment in the Learning Paradigm college: "Assessment best serves as a strategy for improving student learning when it becomes an integral part of the teaching-learning equation by providing continual feedback on academic performance to students" (p. 199). Assessment at King's

means defining goals for their learning that students can understand; designing performances that provide students with
multiple opportunities to achieve those goals; and defining
criteria to judge student performance that can be shared with
them so that they can meet faculty expectations. King's faculty believe it is not enough for a teacher to know excellence
when he or she sees it; students need to be empowered both
to recognize excellence and consciously to aim for it. (King's
College, 1998, p. 5)

Assessment at King's is "aimed first at enhancing student learning
rather than at only measuring and documenting for others" (King's College, 1998, p. 19). One of the guidelines for developing assessment criteria
is that "they provide a starting point for feedback to students, a jumping-off
place for continuing conversation" (King's College, 1998, Appendix C).

The conversation, of course, needs to be extended across the curriculum and throughout the program. To achieve consistency, to make sure
that all students are getting directions from the same map, project teams
that consist of faculty members teaching the courses do the development
work. O'Brien points out that

the faculty who teach a particular component of the core
work together, first to design the courses. Then, once assessment data comes in, they meet to make whatever changes
they deem necessary. It really is a team developing what they
think needs to be included in their own courses.

One product of the project teams is a set of specific criteria for assessments. These criteria are the street-level maps of intended learning. According to O'Brien, the use of criteria for learning assessment has by now
pervaded not only the faculty but the student culture:

It's been very helpful, when faculty can develop specific criteria and we give it to students with the assignment. At least
with my students, if I don't do that, the students ask "What
are the criteria?" They call us on it if we get lazy.

To provide an ongoing conversation based on consistent feedback,
King's has developed the Comprehensive Assessment Program. It

focuses on a plan for the student's systematic development of transferable liberal learning skills, on practical connections between courses in the Core and courses in the major, and on the student's command of both the subject matter and methodology of the major discipline at critical junctures in the degree program. (King's College, 1998, p. 19)

The first component of the Comprehensive Assessment Program is pre- and post-assessments in many Core courses. "Generally, these assessments ask the student to demonstrate competence in a particular area by responding to a question or problem that is real world or practical rather than a question in the narrow test or academic sense" (King's College, 1998, p. 20). "The post-assessment is administered to students two weeks prior to the end of the course in order to provide ample time for faculty to give feedback to students. The post-assessment usually counts as twenty percent of the final examination grade" (Farmer, 1999, p. 200).

The larger framework for feedback is developed in Competency Growth Plans for the eight transferable skills of liberal learning. As Farmer (1999) points out,

Since most students cannot master a skill at the expected level for a graduating senior by taking a single freshman-level course, faculty in each major program must assume responsibility for helping students further develop their skills within the framework of the discipline in their respective major programs. (p. 201)

Thus, to develop the Competency Growth Plan for each of the eight skills, "each department or program defines the skill into specific competencies students develop from freshman through senior years in both core and major courses" (King's College, 1998, pp. 20–21). The plans are specific maps of the course of learning that list not only the courses students will take but the assignments they will do and the criteria for assessing those assignments. "When read sequentially, the criteria from freshman to senior year reveal the developmental nature inherent in acquiring and promoting a skill" (King's College, 1998, p. 21). These plans are tools for faculty members to use in coherently planning and executing feedback in their courses; they appear to students in the syllabi of courses as they move through the curriculum. But what appears in the syllabus for each class is explicitly linked to what appeared in other syllabi. In the King's course-embedded assessment program, students only receive a portion of the detailed map of learning at a time, but the portion fits with the general map they received in the first year.

At two points in the curriculum, more comprehensive tasks present more integrated assessment possibilities. The sophomore/junior diagnostic project is "conducted within a required sophomore or junior course for the major, to determine the student's ability to transfer critical thinking and effective communication . . . to a project related to the major . . ." (King's College, 1998, p. 65). Each department develops and refines its own project. For example, in political science,

> the department embeds its . . . project in a required course in public administration at the sophomore level. The instructional purpose of the project is to provide students an opportunity to explore a specific career in public administration. Students select a profession in government service to study by designing surveys, conducting interviews, and doing a literature search. Students then submit a written report and collaborate with peers to present and compare their findings in a panel discussion. (Farmer, 1999, p. 202)

Some departments ask for a portfolio of work, some for a specific kind of performance. All aim to assess student thinking and communicating skills in the context of the chosen major. Students receive feedback on the project—usually several times in the course of its development—from their fellow students as well as teachers. And they do a self-assessment based on the explicit criteria for the project.

The sophomore/junior diagnostic project points toward the senior integrated assessment. This is the capstone experience. It "allows department faculty and students to examine the latter's success at integrating learning in the major with advanced levels of the transferable skills of liberal learning" (King's College, 1998, p. 86). As with the sophomore/junior diagnostic project, students in most departments do detailed self-assessment as well as assessing the work of other students at several stages in the development of the projects.

To translate clear criteria into effective feedback, of course, requires that faculty use the language of the criteria in a clear and consistent way and guide students to do so as well. So connected feedback across the curriculum depends in large measure on effective communication among the faculty. Within project teams,

> Each faculty member records the number of students scoring on the assessment at the highest, middle, and problematic levels and reports this data to the project team leader. In addition, each faculty member also submits three samples of student performance on the assessment activity at each of the three levels for review by other faculty members on the project team for the purpose of inter-reader reliability based upon the use of common criteria. The members of the project team attempt to identify common student problems and to use these assessment findings as a basis to design strategies to improve student learning. (Farmer, 1999, p. 203)

To achieve clarity in the development of criteria in the major, project teams in the core offer six-week workshops for faculty in the disciplines on a rotating basis, one each semester.

King's Comprehensive Assessment Program is designed explicitly to create a single, coherent map to guide feedback in order to increase student learning. As Farmer (1988) notes, "Education in most colleges and universities is fragmented. Students experience the curriculum as a collection of courses rather than as an integrated plan of learning" (p. 53). Like Alverno, King's has sought to create an integrated plan of learning. However, the King's approach is to integrate the plan into separate courses. The result is to create a developmental map that students can follow through the curriculum. Jean O'Brien puts it this way:

> Assessment has enabled us to articulate more effectively what we expect of students, to ourselves and to them, so that there is a clear progression as someone goes through a King's education. It really is cumulative. I've been at colleges where there are classes, many of them, where there are freshmen through seniors in the same class. And we have some of that, but that's not the plan. So we are able to have classes that are junior or senior level where the expectations are clearly higher, and the students and faculty are aware of it. That's a really big difference. It's cumulative; it's sequential. It really is a plan of learning, not a collection of courses.

The integrated plan of learning at King's College illustrates how clear maps of the terrain of learning and attention to providing clear and consistent feedback can create an environment that moves the conversation of liberal learning forward.

INVER HILLS: IDENTIFYING THE ESSENTIAL SKILLS AT AN OPEN-ACCESS COLLEGE

The task of mapping the curriculum is one thing at a small liberal arts college like Olivet, Alverno, or King's, but it takes on a different complexion at an open-access college. It is more difficult to provide consistent feedback where many students are part-time and/or working off campus and all or most are commuters. But it is correspondingly more important to create a coherent framework for student feedback when students' experiences are more likely to be fragmented.

Inver Hills Community College is a comprehensive community college in Inver Grove Heights, Minnesota, a suburb of Minneapolis-St. Paul. After several years of planning, Inver Hills initiated its Liberal Studies/Professional Skills (LS/PS) program in 1998. The basic format, the Minnesota Skills Profile, was created by David Shupe with Jennifer Lundblad when both were at the University of Minnesota. The format was then given content by faculty teams at Inver Hills. The framework for LS/PS is the list of ten essential skills: 1) appreciation, 2) collaboration, 3) conceptual, 4) implementation, 5) inquiry, 6) presentation, 7) materials, 8) technology, 9) qualification, and 10) quantification. Each of the ten skills is defined and broken down into five subordinate skills. For example, inquiry is defined as "finding, evaluating, and assimilating new information" and consists of the following five modes: 1) learning through observation, 2) learning from people, 3) learning through information inquiry, 4) learning from texts, and 5) learning from recorded data (Inver Hills Community College, 2001, p. 8).

Faculty in the program assess students in appropriate skills at one of five levels of mastery. 1) Incidental occasion: "These are short, often informal activities without attention to explicit standards, often accomplished while attending to something else" (Inver Hills Community College, 2001, p. 11). A student might demonstrate an ability quite by chance in the course of classroom activities. 2) Assessed effort. Here, the student performance is a response to a designed activity intended to be assessed,

usually a classroom assignment. 3) Substantial accomplishment: "Here
you will find extended projects of larger scope, requiring more effort and
attention to complete and stringent standards. . . ." 4) Broad ability. Here
the student has demonstrated the skill consistently, in multiple contexts.
5) Personal mastery: "At this level, a given skill becomes a part of who you
are and what you bring to any setting. . . ."

In practice, level 1 serves as a kind of benchmark. Teachers do not
record level 1 performance in the database, but it does help them to define
the minimum standards for a level 2 performance. In its overall design, the
template is intended for use not just at one college, but for transfer and ar-
ticulation among colleges. (We will discuss this application of the system
in Chapter 16 on alignment.) Because Inver Hills is a community college
it records in the LS/PS database level 2 and 3 performances. And at each
level, for each subskill, the faculty is developing rubrics that rank student
performances on a scale from one to four. Because they contain four levels
of performance, the rubrics might be taken to correspond to conventional
letter grades "D" through "A." However, the rubrics were all developed
collaboratively by faculty members from different disciplines and can
apply to performances in extracurricular activities as well as in the classroom. Julia McGregor (personal communication, February 6, 2002), English instructor and coordinator of the LS/PS program, points out:

> The key in developing the rubrics was to make them content-
> and discipline-free, so that a rubric for "seeing something
> from several points of view"—that's one of the Appreciation
> skills—could be used in sociology, could be used in art, could
> be used in biology, or psychology.

By developing and applying the rubrics, the program encourages
teachers to begin to articulate certain standards and to agree to certain
standards across the curriculum.

Faculty members teaching classes in LS/PS rate students on specific
skills, also recording the context, date, and method of assessment. In a
case where a student has not demonstrated a skill, or where the teacher
has observed it only on level 1 (Incidental occasion), no rating is
recorded. The product is a skills profile, accessible to the student online,
that records up to three skill ratings (by different faculty members) for
each subskill. The skills profile also contains the narrative describing the
nature of the assignment, the date, and the method of assessment. The

skills template, including the rubrics, constitutes an interdisciplinary map of the curriculum. It can be a powerful tool to provide consistent guidance and feedback to students. Ratings on a given skill at levels 1 or 2 in the rubric for that skill are recorded in the database but do not appear on the student's skills profile. The skills profile shows only skills that have been demonstrated at levels 3 or 4 of the rubric.

The skills profiles of all students constitute an interactive database tracking student achievement over time and across the curriculum. McGregor points out:

> The database is constructed so that data can be aggregated in a variety of ways; at the individual level, the aggregation is the student's skills profile. But a teacher could aggregate data for a class—around a particular skill, for instance. And, this could be done for a course, a program, a particular cohort of students (the class of '02, for example), or for the whole college.

The LS/PS essential skills template will guide the faculty-student conversation effectively only if it guides the faculty-faculty conversation. As the program has evolved, this feature of shaping the faculty conversation has taken on an important role. McGregor points out that "this is really at heart a faculty development program, and it has to be so. If we lose sight of that we start going off track." And the aspect of professional development that it addresses most importantly is the design and execution of assignments, the shaping of the student tasks that become the context for feedback. According to McGregor:

> It's a faculty development program that is most of all focused on assignment design. We thought this was focused on assessment; it's not. It is focused on assignment design, because you can't assess anything unless you have an assignment designed in a particular way.

The program began in 1998 as a pilot with about 200 students. By 2002, roughly half of Inver Hills' full-time teachers had begun to use the LS/PS template and about 1,200 students had skills profiles.

For the program to be the foundation for consistent, clear feedback on learning, students as well as faculty members must understand it. McGregor explains:

We developed brochures we could hand out to students and a video we could use in each of our classrooms just to give students a quick look at this because we found it was very difficult to explain to students in a meaningful way what this was during the first few days of class, when their heads were spinning with a lot of information.

The college commends the program to students by urging them: "Distinguish yourself!" The skills profile adds value for students: "in addition to your transcript with its record of courses, credits, and grades, you will also have a skills profile that will document the skills that you have mastered—those skills that distinguish you from other students" (Inver Hills Community College, 2001, p. 3). The institution is selling the program to students, and to faculty, on the basis of one of its most important features. Because the skills profile is a much more specific and detailed language about learning outcomes than the language of grades, it allows for a much more individualized picture of each student. The *LS/PS Student Guide* (Inver Hills Community College, 2001) explains it this way:

> For instance, two students may have accumulated the same number of credits in, say, sociology or psychology, but because they took courses from different teachers, they learned different skills: one student may have learned how to design a valid experiment and to research the latest academic journals; the other may have learned how to interview sources and display information graphically. A transcript does not communicate those differences, but a skills profile does. (p. 3)

One of the appeals made to students is explicitly to the evaluative element of the program: It will confirm students' abilities in a way that will be credible to potential employers, transfer institutions, and the students themselves. And, by implication, it will be both more specific and more credible than grades. What Inver Hills is promising its students here is an evaluation system that can correct the growing deficiencies of the transcript as an evaluation system. However, because of the design of the new evaluation system, it also has a strong element of feedback because it allows for frequent reevaluation. Grades, of course, are once-and-for-all, final marks. But the skills profile can be improved by working on the same skill in future classes. Thus it can serve to connect the learning objectives in different classes and redress some of the finality of the grading system.

The framework of LS/PS at Inver Hills—a template of skills with detailed, interdisciplinary rubrics developed and supported through ongoing professional development focused on assignment design—offers a model that could lead to a consistent, connected feedback system. Such a system will change the cognitive economy of the college.

CALIFORNIA STATE UNIVERSITY, MONTEREY BAY: LAYING DOWN ROAD SIGNS AT A STATE UNIVERSITY

California State University, Monterey Bay (CSUMB) is one of the youngest universities in the largest state university system in the country. Founded in 1994, it set out to be different in a number of ways from its sister universities. The fundamental difference was to be a commitment to assess and document achievement of learning outcomes rather than just course credits. "[T]he 'outcomes-based education' model being implemented at CSUMB begins with a statement of 'what students should learn' as the framework for conceptualizing, defining, and organizing its academic programs" (California State University, Monterey Bay, 2000). Defining and designing its operations in terms of learning outcomes "both reflects and reinforces the basic premise that *student learning is the primary business of this institution*" (California State University, Monterey Bay, 2000).

The outcomes-based model at CSUMB entails three institutional commitments that, taken together, constitute a commitment to create and maintain a coherent and comprehensive feedback system. First, CSUMB requires that all programs explicitly state what the learning outcomes for the program will be. Second, "These learning outcomes are to serve to focus and guide program curricular design, course design, instructional pedagogy, student learning, and learning assessment" (California State University, Monterey Bay, 2000). And third, "All programs are to assess student learning in relation to their prescribed learning outcomes."

In the general education program, the intended learning outcomes are spelled out in 13 University Learning Requirements (ULRs). CSUMB sets these requirements out for incoming students in this way:

> We have established learning requirements differently at CSUMB than you may be used to. Rather than graduating based on which courses you have taken, you will graduate based on what you have learned.
>
> Our system works a little bit like getting your driver's license. To get a driver's license, you need to demonstrate that you know how to drive and that you know the rules of the road. You can learn these things in a variety of ways, for example, taking private lessons, doing trial and error, or some combination. When you do get your license, you are not held accountable for how you learned to drive, but rather for demonstrating that you are able to drive. (California State University, Monterey Bay, 2002a)

For each of the ULRs, students are given specific learning outcomes, criteria for demonstrating the outcomes, and evidence acceptable for the outcomes. For example, one of the ULRs is ethics. Among the outcomes for the ethics ULR are "Identify and analyze real world ethical problems or dilemmas, and identify those affected by the dilemma" and "Describe and analyze one's own and others' perceptions and ethical frameworks for decision-making." The criteria for assessing these outcomes are spelled out in language that is used consistently across all of the outcomes.

Students may fulfill ULRs through course work or through independent assessment of the requirement without taking courses. "If the student does not already possess the required knowledge and skills," she may develop "a plan to gain the required knowledge in some way other than taking one of the designated courses" in coordination with an advisor (California State University, Monterey Bay, 2002a). To this point, most students fulfill the ULRs by taking courses.

While ULRs define general education learning outcomes, major requirements are spelled out in Major Learning Outcomes (MLOs). Both are implemented in courses in Course Learning Outcomes (CLOs). MLOs are set by centers (similar to colleges or divisions at most universities) and institutes (which would be called departments at most universities).

If learning outcomes are to be a guide for consistent and coherent feedback to students, of course, they need to be understood in the same way by faculty members and students across different programs. The University Strategic Plan (California State University, Monterey Bay, 2002b) sets as an intended outcome under the strategic theme of student learning that "Learning opportunities and expectations are clear to all concerned" (p. 11). Among the success indicators for this outcome are the following:

> Because it is impossible to gauge what students "know," "are able to do," or "believe" except by observing the actions and products of those students, all CLOs, MLOs, and ULRs state what students DO or PRODUCE (i.e., deliverables) to demonstrate that they have acquired associated knowledge, skills and perspectives. . . .
>
> The syllabus for each course clearly states CLOs for that course, as well as the methods, criteria, and standards by which each student's mastery of each CLO will be assessed. . . .
>
> The language and organization of documents describing outcomes (ULRs, MLOs, and CLOs) are sufficiently clear, unambiguous, and free of jargon to assure that all who read them—students, faculty members, parents, employers, and other community members—articulate substantially similar understandings of what students must do to achieve each outcome. (p. 11)

To implement these admirable goals, to assure that everyone is working from the same map, requires ongoing monitoring of the relationship between the outcomes expressed by the institution and student performances. In 2000, about half of the faculty participated in the Alignment Project. As Amy Driscoll (personal communication, March 14, 2002), director of the Center for Teaching, Learning, and Assessment, describes it, teachers took their course syllabi and entered the content on a spreadsheet:

> Across the top of the spreadsheet were the outcomes for the course. Down the side in a vertical column they listed their class sessions, all their readings, all their assignments, any service-learning component, a lab—everything they did in that class. Then they worked on this grid to see which sessions were working on which outcomes, which readings were working on which outcomes, or where there was a reading that wasn't working on any outcome, or where there was an outcome that wasn't getting any attention. . . . Now many of the

outcomes have been clarified and rewritten, and we're going
to do it again, as a check to see whether what they're doing in
the course really is working on the outcomes.

CSUMB has established faculty learning communities to monitor and
develop outcomes, assessment, and pedagogy for each of the ULRs. Periodically, these learning communities, sometimes more than one, will review samples of the evidence produced in courses for the ULRs. In day-
long work sessions, they will analyze student work for quality and for relevance to the desired outcomes. In such sessions, faculty are explicitly engaged in the ongoing conversation with students shaped by ULRs. They
are listening to what students have said in response to their prompts, listening to the feedback from students generated by the feedback from faculty, making assessment a channel of communication rather than simply a
protocol for evaluation. Participating faculty members will often review
student evidence several times to calibrate the outcomes and criteria. In a
recent such review, according to Driscoll,

> Most of our outcomes came out with such clarity that we
> didn't change those. We did find changes that need to be
> made in the courses and in the way assignments are given and
> the kind of assessment, so that they're more carefully aligned
> with what students are trying to produce as evidence. But
> those came from faculty doing that work of review and analy-
> sis, so it's been a really powerful learning experience for fac-
> ulty, and they're making the changes because they got to see
> it in the student evidence.

Swarup Wood (personal communication, May 10, 2002), a faculty
member who teacher chemistry in the Institute of Earth Systems Science
and Policy, participated in one of these review sessions and took an interest
in the process. He subsequently began to interview the other participants
to attempt to gauge their response to the experience. At the time of our
conversation he had interviewed 13 other faculty participants. Overall, he
found:

> People have just been very turned on by the process of sitting
> with a group of colleagues and looking at student evidence,
> and asking themselves: "How is it that we know that this
> work actually meets the outcome? What is it that we can

point to in this work that we know meets the outcome? And what is evident in this work that says it meets the outcome at this level? What can we point to in the work that really says, 'Oh, here's complexity?'"

The process has revealed differences as well as similarities in the way different faculty members view the outcomes and view their student work. Wood points out:

> Different departments and different groups of people deliver courses that meet the same ULR. And if you're teaching towards the same outcomes, that requires a dialog, a common understanding of what those things actually mean. People were amazed. We thought we were on the same page, and we were not on the same page. You've got people from different disciplines that use words completely differently. But people don't know that. I mean, they know it, but they don't know it.

Wood relates an example of the kind of confusion that lies beneath the curriculum of every college, often invisible to all but the students:

> I was very intrigued and excited by a conversation that happened with my colleagues in which five other Ph.D. scientists sat around and argued intensely about what the word "fact" meant. We had a geologist, a couple of biologists, I'm a chemist, and we're all scientists, but we were all using this word differently. So what does that mean? Well, it means that we took it out of our outcome because if we couldn't agree on it, to pretend that our students could meet it, that just doesn't work.

Thus the conversations among faculty members shape the conversation with students. And all move toward a vocabulary of shared understanding that can clarify rather than simply multiply meanings.

It is through the ongoing, interactive conversation with students through a clearly defined assessment system that a faculty can get better at framing student tasks, generating feedback on student performances, and understanding and responding to feedback from students. To the extent that this dialogue comes to shape pedagogy, assessment in the classroom will become more sophisticated, performance-oriented, and interactive. According to Driscoll, that is happening at CSUMB:

> This is a faculty that's getting pretty clear that the assessment has to be aligned with the outcome, and for most of our outcomes an exam wouldn't be the appropriate thing to use. It wouldn't really assess the outcome. And this is also a campus where a majority of our faculty are very committed to innovative and student-centered pedagogy, and traditional assessment doesn't fit very well in that model.

CSUMB is still a small state university—fewer than 3,000 undergraduates. But it plans to grow following the design for learning laid out in its formative years. It is a public institution that gives grades and produces student transcripts that very much resemble those of other state universities. But it has created a pattern of information flow and feedback loops that have the potential to give meaning to the transcript by making it a product of a real conversation with students about the purposes and methods of learning.

PROCESS FRONTIER: INFORMATION

The Instruction Paradigm college, as we saw in Chapter 9, emphasizes evaluation and diminishes feedback in its information system. The cognitive economy that results promotes a surface orientation to learning. Colleges that want to create a hot cognitive economy will reverse the ratio, will emphasize feedback to students about learning over evaluation of student knowledge, and will do so systematically, across all programs and disciplines.

The structural feature of Instruction Paradigm colleges that appears to lock them into processes that value evaluation over feedback is the system of letter grades and transcripts. Substantial evidence suggests that this system creates or reinforces a bias toward evaluation and conveys to students that grading is a major priority of the college. Some colleges, Alverno and a few others, have taken the obvious and bold step of simply eliminating the whole apparatus of letter grades and conventional transcripts in favor of a more nuanced and meaningful system of evaluation. The case for such a step is strong. However, the grading system is one of the most entrenched features of modern higher education. Simply removing it would be difficult for all institutions and currently impossible for many because of public policies and systemic rules. Furthermore, some institutions that have eliminated letter grades have failed to take other significant steps away from the Instruction Paradigm. At the same time, many institutions that have maintained letter grades have been able to make significant changes in the way they value, channel, and express information about student performances. While I can find very little positive to say of the conventional grading system, I think we must admit that its outright elimination is neither a necessary nor a sufficient condition for creating a hot cognitive economy. The three colleges discussed in this chapter were chosen in part because each is an institution that has maintained letter grades and the GPA but attempted to transform them by creating sophisticated systems for conveying feedback about student learning across the curriculum.

These colleges have attempted to transform the grading system in two somewhat different ways. Two of them—King's and CSUMB—have embedded feedback on student learning in the grading system itself. They have created frameworks, supported by ongoing professional development and faculty conversations, for rationalizing and giving meaning to letter grades within classes. The rubrics for learning outcomes developed at King's and CSUMB are used in classes as tools for assigning letter grades, so that grades become indices of clearly defined learning outcomes, often based on designated kinds of evidence of those outcomes. "The standards," says Amy Driscoll at CSUMB, "are very closely related to grades." This approach attempts to salvage the grading system by giving it real meaning, and hence raising the grade in a course to the level of significant evaluation of specific abilities. Thus grades become feedback on the development of knowledge and abilities the pursuit of which extends beyond the class.

The Inver Hills approach is somewhat different. Here, rather than embedding the rubric for outcome evaluation in the course grades, they have created a parallel structure for assessing the development of core abilities alongside the existing structure of grading in courses. This structure is also supported by ongoing professional development and a continuing conversation about learning outcomes, assessment, and feedback. The PS/LS program at Inver Hills will almost certainly change the way teachers assign grades in courses, and if it is to be effective it must change the way students think about their transcripts. But it will affect the meaning of the transcript more indirectly, through creating a rich and ongoing source of feedback about learning that will enliven the curricular conversation.

These two approaches and several possible variations of them are much superior to the standard practice of letting course grades stand alone as the only authorized evaluation of student work. They move toward consistent feedback across the curriculum on student performances. They provide for continual feedback on ongoing development of abilities and knowledge. They provide for interactive feedback in a system that allows faculty and staff to respond to what they hear from students. And they provide for frequent reevaluation of developing abilities. There is room for development in all of these areas. But these colleges are pushing the process frontier, are changing their feedback systems in ways that will change the cognitive economy for the better.

14 A Learning Paradigm College Provides a Long Time Horizon for Learning

MOTIVATION AND THE LONGEVITY OF CONSEQUENCES

Small children have very little sense of the future. That is to say, they tend to think in terms of the immediate consequences of their behavior only and not to consider the implications for subsequent events. Likewise, promises of reward in the long term—even as long a term as an hour—become meaningless. This explains in part the "Are we there yet?" phenomenon, which every parent who has traveled with children has experienced. The answer "We'll be there in an hour" usually succeeds in postponing a repetition of the inquiry no longer than a minute.

As we grow older we develop a sense of the future and of the relative distance in time of future events. We come to realize that a week is longer than a day, a month longer than a week, and we develop a sense of the approaching proximity of these milestones in time. Even as adults, of course, we do not maintain a scientifically accurate sense of distance in time, which no doubt accounts in large measure for the frequent occurrence of procrastination, not only among our students but among ourselves. We do, however, come to consider time as a flexible factor in our decision-making. One way we consider it is to weigh, consciously or unconsciously, the length of time that the consequences of a decision will stay with us. We generally hold choices that will have long-term consequences to a higher standard than choices the effects of which will dissipate in a relatively short time. A young man or woman will make a date with a potential partner on much slighter evidence of compatibility than he or she would commit to marriage with the same person, in large measure because the date will last only an evening while the marriage portends an involvement surviving for years. Most of us would examine the consequences of signing a mortgage more carefully than those of a lease. We

217

differentiate decisions all the time on the basis of their significance and one of the major elements of significance is the longevity of the consequences. Our major investments of both time and money are usually made with the expectation of long-term consequences. People who thrive in the money economy are generally those who plan and invest with a long time horizon.

Students do this too. In fact, we might summarize many of the distinctions between surface and deep orientations to learning by saying that a surface orientation is learning for the short term, while a deep orientation is learning for the long term. Students who adopt a surface orientation seem to be operating on the assumption that they won't have to live with the consequences of their academic decisions for very long. Academic work, for the student with a surface orientation, has a short time horizon. Students who adopt a deep orientation, on the other hand, seem to have a long time horizon; they seem to assume that the consequences of their academic decisions will stay with them for quite some time.

Conversations between teachers or counselors and students are often muddled by this factor. Teachers, advisors, and mentors almost always assume a long time horizon in talking with students about academic work. One reason for this is that we who are doing the teaching and the advising are well advanced on the time path of academic work. We have passed through undergraduate and graduate education and on to work in an academic institution. With perfect hindsight, we know quite well that the skills and the attitudes our students are shaping now are laying the foundation for either problems or solutions for them in years to come. We know that really mastering algebra or calculus or French verbs or the thesis statement now will save them the hours of suffering in graduate school caused by not mastering those fundamentals as undergraduates. So we urge our students quite sincerely to take their studies seriously, to lay the foundation for building what they want. Much of the time, our students do not seem to hear what we are saying, or if they hear it don't seem to believe it. We often use expressions such as "It's like talking to a brick wall" or "They just don't seem to care."

In fact, the problem is that most of our students have a short time horizon. The distant future that we describe to motivate them is lost in the fog; they can't see it. And this short time horizon, while sometimes a product of emotional immaturity, is also reinforced by the cognitive economy of the Instruction Paradigm college. Consider some of the factors of the cognitive economy we have already discussed.

Intrinsic Goals

Intrinsic goals tend to have a long time horizon simply because they relate to things that we want today and expect to keep wanting. Furthermore, genuinely motivating intrinsic goals tend to involve cumulative challenges, ones that call for growth in abilities to meet higher standards. Just consider most extracurricular activities, the arts and games and skills that motivate many students to continual effort throughout their college careers. Do soccer players ever finish becoming better soccer players, contrabassoonists or journalists or painters ever finish practicing their skills? They may, of course, stop doing the activity because they aren't improving or because other activities demand too much time. But the mental model of such activities does not include a terminal point built into the design of the activity. Likewise consider highly experiential activities like those we discussed in the last two chapters such as research and service. A research project may be completed, or a particular service activity, but that project simply points to the next project, lays the foundation for the work yet to be done. Almost any activity that can become a stable medium for the flow experience has a long time horizon. The time limits for intrinsic goals, especially the most powerfully motivating ones, are the limits that time itself imposes, the limits reached by failing physical and mental capacities or conflicting demands. We never stop wanting to get better at what we really value and enjoy. Intrinsic goals have a long time horizon.

Extrinsic Goals

Extrinsic goals, on the other hand, come with built-in time limits. They declare, in the manner of the tapes on *Mission Impossible,* "This goal will self-destruct in 16 weeks." The time is variable, of course, but the extrinsic goal always carries a predefined performance as the index of goal accomplishment. You perform the task at a certain level, and you receive the reward. Once you have received the reward, or not, the goal evaporates. If my goal is an "A" in American history or a high score on the SAT, after final exams or test day, my goal dies as a functional motivator for my behavior. In the Instruction Paradigm college, of course, the cognitive economy is shaped by extrinsic goals, specifically grades in courses, each of which is partitioned off from the others: my grade in Algebra II is in no way dependent on my grade in Algebra I. (My performance in Algebra II is strongly dependent on my learning in Algebra I, but that will be visible only to one whose time-horizon extends beyond the semester. It is obvious to teachers, apparently not so obvious to students.) So the class grade system creates a time horizon of about one academic term for the external reward of the grade. We discussed in Chapter 9 the role of the final examination in reinforcing this short time horizon.

An atomized learning environment reinforces a short time horizon; a holistic learning environment reinforces a long time horizon. To the extent that courses are hermetically sealed, independent, self-sufficient modules of content, they encourage students to adopt a time horizon for the learning that ends with the course. To the extent that courses or other learning experiences are connected and cumulative, they encourage students to adopt a long time horizon. Most well-designed extracurricular activities are holistic in this sense, and that is one of the reasons why most students experience extracurriculars as more motivating and involving. My class in German or biology will end after finals week, but the choir will keep singing, and the swim team will keep swimming. Extracurriculars have a longer time horizon than courses in the Instruction Paradigm college.

WHY A LONG TIME HORIZON IS IMPORTANT

Important learning tasks take longer than a semester. This is generally true, and it is certainly true of those foundational tasks that lay the groundwork for more advanced work. As we saw in Chapter 12, learning requires practice, and practice—all other things being equal—leads to improvement. But the route to improvement, especially in complex skills, is not simple or linear.

Substantive learning takes time because it involves changing fundamental patterns of thinking or information processing. We have already seen that deep learning involves moving knowledge from episodic to semantic memory—or to use different but parallel terms, from working memory to long-term memory. It also involves the creation of flexible and resilient frameworks for organizing information in long-term memory: schemas. As the National Research Council (2001) points out, schemas organize information into coherent patterns that facilitate easy recall. As a result, "Schemas help move the burden of thinking from working memory to long-term memory" (p. 70). Developing schemas is an iterative process.

It often involves going back and forth, reverting to a previous framework of thinking and then testing the new one. It takes time for new cognitive schemas to become established as the default structures of thinking.

Not only do students need to develop and refine their cognitive schemas; they need to become aware of this process of refinement and testing so that they can consciously reproduce it in response to new problems. That is, students who take a deep approach will develop their metacognitive abilities. Metacogniton is the thinking about thinking that allows us to regulate our own learning process. The National Research Council (2001) lays out some of the consequences for learning of developing more sophisticated metacognition:

> Strong learners can explain which strategies they used to solve a problem and why, while less competent students monitor their own thinking sporadically and ineffectively and offer incomplete explanations. Good problem solvers will try another strategy if one is not working, while poor problem solvers will hold to a strategy long after it has failed. (p. 78)

The student who is learning to self-regulate his cognitive processes begins to attend to the results of his learning experiments, abandoning failed strategies or adapting them to get different results. Students do not develop metacognitive skills all at once. The process is cumulative. So students do not necessarily develop metacognitive abilities at a steady rate but may experience spurts of improvement after long periods of trial. Metacognitive learning comes, for most of us, only through consistent and persistent effort, and after consistent and persistent failure—and felt failure at that.

In most Instruction Paradigm colleges, the short time horizon reveals itself in the students' tendency to compartmentalize classroom learning in a special academic space in their minds, severed from their fundamental, long-term beliefs and concerns. Eric Mazur (1992) is a Harvard physicist who has conducted interesting research into classroom learning. After teaching successful lecture classes in introductory physics for many years, Mazur came across research suggesting that perhaps the knowledge that freshman physics students were gaining did not go very deep. He set out to explore the question in his own classes by giving students a brief, qualitative test of physics concepts, based on simple questions using everyday examples developed by David Hestenes at Arizona State University. He also administered his highly quantitative exam in which students solved challenging physics problems using the algorithms they had learned in class. In response to the conceptual test, one student asked a revealing question: "Professor Mazur, how should I answer these questions? According to what you taught us, or by the way I *think* about these things?" If that query were not unnerving enough, the results were even more unsettling: About 40% of the students actually did better on the "difficult" quantitative problems than on the "simple" conceptual ones. "Slowly," Mazur reports, "the underlying problem revealed itself: Many students concentrate on learning 'recipes,' or 'problem solving strategies' as they are called in textbooks, without bothering to be attentive to the underlying concepts." In other words, these Harvard students had become skillful in using a surface approach to learning. They had learned to compartmentalize, as Mazur's student so aptly put it, "what you taught us" from "the way I *think* about these things." "The way I think" is the way my mind works for the long term, the way I frame, shape, and use knowledge for activities that have a long time horizon. "What you taught us" is compartmentalized into the short-term knowledge I need to get through this class, and then will need no more.

Another Harvard professor, psychologist and cognitive scientist Howard Gardner (1991), has commented on essentially the same phenomenon that Mazur discovered. The experiences of schooling, Gardner points out, often leave "the unschooled mind" untouched. The unschooled mind consists of the set of primitive schemas that form the foundational apparatus of long-term understanding. Students learn from their earliest years of schooling to compartmentalize school learning for use in specialized "debriefing contexts." To challenge the assumptions of the unschooled mind with school knowledge would be risky, and "neither teachers nor students are willing to undertake 'risks for understanding'; instead, they content themselves with safer 'correct-answer compromises'" (p. 150). Those correct-answer compromises take the form, in mathematics and science, of rigidly applied algorithms and in the arts and humanities of stereotypes and simplifications. In physics classes, many students learn in their earliest engagements with the subject that the safer course is to adopt such compromises:

> On the one hand, the lessons in physics class are learned in
> such a way that they can be produced in certain debriefing

> contexts, specifically on homework assignments and in class-room tests. Memorization of certain key demonstrations, def-initions, and equations suffices, particularly when the stu-dents know in advance the form that such debriefing will take. . . . So long as the questions are put in a certain expected framework, the students will appear to understand, and the essential bargain of science teaching will have been honored. The correct-answer compromise prevails. (p. 156)

It prevails, as Mazur discovered, well into college—even Harvard College. The correct answer compromise and dividing into separate mental compartments "what you taught us" and "what I think" are the strategies of a surface approach to learning. Indeed, learning for the narrow debrief-ing contexts of schooling is inherently surface learning. The reason stu-dents make this compromise is that, in the cognitive economy of the school and the college, risks for understanding are simply too costly. Those risks are the necessary cost of developing metacognitive skills; to discour-age students from taking risks for understanding deflects them from the path toward cognitive maturity and mastery of essential skills. One of the chief reasons such risks are too costly is that the time horizon of learning is so short. The debriefing rituals of academic life come like clockwork every term, and the results of those rituals are what the institution values and preserves. The risk that must be taken for understanding, the risk of test-ing the unschooled mind by ongoing experimentation, offers no clear pro-tocol of reward. The learning that matters in the long run, the learning that can change your life and change your mind, will almost always come too late for the course and the term. Only a fool, students might reason-ably think, would risk aspiring to wisdom in a place like college.

CREATING A LONG TIME HORIZON

To the extent that we make the framework of the one-semester course with its final exam the dominant learning environment for students, we model for them a short time horizon for learning. To the extent that we design learning environments as if the learning will live beyond the course—and beyond the degree—we model a long time horizon. We have already examined a number of ways in which institutions are doing this. In discussing student performances in Chapter 12 and feedback in

Chapter 13, I emphasized the importance of connection. Student performances and feedback to students on those performances need to be connected across time. If we make those connections we are extending the time horizon because we are making clear to students that this semester's learning will matter in the future. Institutions like Alverno, Olivet, King's, Inver Hills, and CSU, Monterey Bay that identify the core learning outcomes of the curriculum and provide ongoing feedback in consistent and clear language about progress toward those learning outcomes are extending the time horizon. They are doing so by explicitly identifying the learning that matters throughout the curriculum and repeatedly reminding students that this core learning does matter. They may have final examinations at these institutions, but the whole design of their curriculum makes clear that no course assessment is really final; rather, every assessment is a step toward greater mastery.

If students are to approach learning with a long time horizon, then they need to think of their own learning holistically rather than atomistically. They need to see their learning process as a coherent whole that determines the choice of parts, rather than as a collection of parts that, by being glued together in a makeshift pattern, will determine some hodgepodge whole. But of course these polarities are artificial. We all see the whole in the parts and the parts in the whole. We make some sort of sense out of things by imposing a system (or whole) on them in our minds even when there is little rational justification for doing so. So it is useful to consider the problem of time horizon both from the perspective of the parts and from the perspective of the whole—from the micro and the macro perspectives, we might say. The micro perspective strongly determines the time horizon students will adopt: what sense of connection they get from their experience of the parts, from their work and feedback in individual classes and other activities. The framework that these micro experiences fit into, the image of the institution as a whole that the institution projects to its students, constitutes the macro perspective.

A college career is something like a baseball (or soccer or golf or tennis) season. At the micro level, each game is important. Indeed, the games are what make up the season. But the games are given meaning and importance by the whole season, the complex system of interaction that frames them and connects them. To change the metaphor, a college curriculum should be like a ladder. It should rest on the surface that we want to reach, but the rungs should be spaced for easy access by the user. If the rungs are too far apart or too close together, we will be discouraged from climbing. If the rungs are spaced properly, then we can reach very high places. In designing a curriculum with a long time horizon we need to attend to the micro perspective, make sure that the ladder is designed so that the individual rungs or steps are appropriate for the user. But we also need to consider the macro perspective, to make sure that the ladder is not resting flat on the floor, but rises to the height that we eventually want to reach.

The Macro View: Projecting a Long Time Horizon from the Start

Beginning with the macro view—the vision of the whole that the institution projects to students—the root problem of many institutions is that they don't project such a vision very well at all; the ladder is leaning against a blank wall or lying on the floor. The planning documents of most institutions avoid referring to learning goals in a way that would be meaningful to students.

Perhaps it is unfair to judge colleges on the basis of documents that most students probably don't pay much attention to anyway. We should look at programs aimed at students specifically, such as freshman seminars and orientation-to-college classes. How does the college convey to students the long-term purposes and possibilities of a college education? And I emphatically do not mean the usual propaganda about the amount by which they will increase their lifetime earnings by acquiring a B.A.

At many institutions, first-year or orientation programs begun with the best of intentions have degenerated into lessons in how to play the Instruction Paradigm game of surface learning, but play it skillfully. It proves to be difficult to introduce students persuasively to a vision of the whole college experience if the college doesn't have one. That is to say, if the curriculum is a distributional grab bag of isolated courses in the lower division and an array of hermetically sealed departmental boxes in the upper division, there is no whole there. If students are to adopt a deep orientation to learning and sustain it throughout a degree program, they must continuously reshape their cognitive schemas and refine their metacognitive skills. We call upon them to take the risks for understanding involved in revising the unschooled mind. To do so, they need to believe that they are engaged in a continuous project of learning rather than an intermittent engagement with random subjects.

If what institutions should offer students is a ladder to higher learning, distributional general education requirements are more like a collection of boxes spread around the floor. We can do step exercises to the point of exhaustion, but we cannot climb very high. We need a ladder to do that. That means something like a deliberate plan of learning, such as we have seen at King's, CSUMB, and Alverno, for example. Programs that try to introduce students to an institutional integrity and coherence that doesn't really exist are likely to make things worse by persuading students of the conclusive split between the institution's espoused theory (liberal education, preparation for life in the 21st century, lifelong learning) and its theory-in-use (pick the requisite number of three-unit classes, and good luck).

If colleges are to persuade students to adopt a long time horizon, they should lay out for entering students a vision of the whole college experience that they can illustrate and support with evidence from their own programs. They should show students what is at the top of the ladder. This vision should be sewn from the fabric of students' experience at the college, not tacked together from fragments of the whole cloth of wishful thinking.

When I speak of a long time horizon, I mean a *long* time horizon. I do not mean four years. I mean to suggest that we should take quite literally that much-abused term "lifelong learning." That long. So the model of ongoing learning that the college projects should be embodied in the curriculum and the experience of college, but should go beyond it. The horizon of college learning should extend beyond the degree, into the world of work, family life, citizenship, and moral choice. Only if the time horizon of the student extends beyond the degree can college become real life, and hence raise real life to the level of an ongoing, deliberate engagement with significant meaning through learning.

The Micro View: Experiencing Connection

A long time horizon does not emerge just from setting distant goals, even intrinsic goals. The student must believe that she can achieve those goals, and that means she must have the experience of incrementally approaching them. She must be able to climb the rungs on the ladder, one at a time. Thus the view of the whole is always mediated through the experience of the parts. Bandura (1997) points out:

> The motivating power of personal goals is partly determined by how far into the future they are projected. Short-term, or proximal, goals provide immediate incentives and guides for current pursuits. Distant goals are too far removed in time to be effective self-motivators. Usually, there are too many competing influences in everyday life for distant aims to exert much control over current behavior. By focusing on the distant future, it is all too easy to keep putting off difficult activities to some future time. Self-motivation is best sustained by combining a long-range goal that sets the course of one's endeavors with a series of attainable subgoals to guide and sustain one's efforts along the route. (p. 217)

Recall that the flow experience depends on a balance between challenge and ability. Long-term goals provide the challenge, but we meet the challenge by moving incrementally toward subsidiary goals. When you write (or read) a book, you need to work from a coherent design of the whole, but you have to write it (or read it) one chapter at a time. So the principle of breaking the curriculum up into manageable chunks is an entirely valid one. The key to making it work is to design the chunks so that they are aligned with a coherent long-term purpose. A long time horizon is sustained by an ongoing experience of connection with significant goals as one incrementally approaches them. That means that a coherent curriculum should be like a well-designed ladder. The rungs should be spaced so that the user can reach each one in order.

In reflecting on the steps toward holistic learning goals, we should consider three questions: 1) What standards or goals should the step achieve? 2) How should those standards be connected to the larger (macro) goals of the learning experience? and 3) How much time will it take for the student to reach the goals? We have already examined the first two questions and seen several examples of their application. Standards for individual learning experiences should be expressed as learning outcomes of the experience, stated in terms of what students should do. And those experiences should be connected in a developmental sequence to the larger goals of the program. And defining the learning experience in terms of learning outcomes opens up new possibilities for answering the third question, which is especially crucial when we consider the time horizon of learning.

In the Instruction Paradigm college, as the National Education Commission on Time and Learning (1994) put it, "The rule, only rarely voiced, is simple: Learn what you can in the time we make available." This generally means, learn a predetermined chunk of content in the standardized period of weeks we designate, a quarter or a semester. As we have already seen, this inflexible framework doesn't fit all students any of the time, and doesn't fit any student all of the time. It is a Procrustean bed upon which we break the will to learn.

The root problem is that different students will learn in different domains at different rates. To think again of the learning progress of students as a ladder, one size will not fit all. Some students need rungs that are closer together, some rungs that are farther apart, if they are to climb effectively. And the same student may need a different sized ladder in a different discipline. I always found, for example, that my math legs were considerably shorter than my verbal legs. This problem is most acute for students who need more time to develop foundational skills and metacognitive strategies. They will take longer to do that. Yet developmental programs at many colleges propose that students who have failed, for example, to develop proficiency in arithmetic in 12 *years* of formal schooling will do so in the first 16 *weeks* of college and then move on. Worse, distributional general education requirements often allow students who enter college without a solid grasp of quantitative thinking to take courses that assume an understanding of, say, statistical concepts such as regression and averaging. Or they allow students who have only a very limited ability to synthesize matter from disparate sources to take courses that demand research from many sources to produce an organized overview. And unless the learning outcomes of such courses are clearly spelled out in advance in terms that students understand, they have no way of knowing what they are getting into. These students find themselves grasping a ladder that has no rungs, hoping their arms will hold them until the semester ends and they can drop to the ground again, to take their chances next semester.

Vary the demands on students. One way to adapt the rungs to students' reach is to keep the length of the term the same but vary the demands on the students. If we can define the developmental level of the student in some reasonable way, we can adapt what the student does in a given course to that developmental level. One way to do this is to offer students who need more time classes that cover less material, allowing more time in the conventional term for practice and performance. Some developmental programs have moved in this direction by increasing the number of courses that cover a given body of material.

This can be a good strategy if pursued in the right way. But it is easily abused in the Instruction Paradigm context. We have seen a steady evolution over the past two decades from no developmental courses in writing at most colleges, to one, then two, and in some cases three semesters of developmental work. The value of such courses, of course, depends on the first two factors indicated above: whether the course objectives are clear and achievable and whether they are well coordinated with the larger goals of the curriculum. Too often, the multiplication of the developmental courses has had the effect of obscuring the intended learning outcomes of the individual courses as well as their connection to the curriculum at large. For example, many institutions have expanded their developmental writing programs by offering prewriting courses that consist largely of studying the rules of grammar and taking multiple-choice tests. The research on how students learn to write provides no rationale for such courses (Hillocks, 1986). Indeed, such developmental courses sometimes seem expressly designed to reinforce a surface approach to learning and to undermine the development of precisely the metacognitive skills that developing writers require. Correcting the punctuation in other people's prose involves mental operations that fairly well exclude attending to developing schemas of expression through experiment and self-monitoring. Revision cannot precede invention. Having taught for several years now students who have completed developmental writing courses, my own impression is that many of them have been set up for failure in significant college work by such courses. We might make the same objection to mathematics courses that emphasize memorizing and applying problem solving algorithms prior to developing the conceptual framework for quantitative reasoning. Life, as the saying goes, is a word problem. Developmental courses that do not clearly lead to the larger objectives of the whole curriculum risk shortening the time horizon for students by obscuring the long-term meaning and application of their learning in a fog of ultimately trivial testing. If courses are well coordinated with one another and with larger curricular goals, however, breaking down content into smaller chunks can be an effective way to give students the time they need to develop foundational skills and habits.

Extend the course time. A second approach to addressing the problem of too much material in a course is to extend the time for the course. An example of such an approach that is currently being tried is to give students the option of taking Algebra I, say, in a year rather than a semester. Another is to break courses up into modules and let students register for more time to complete a certain number of modules. Another, and for many subjects the most obvious approach, is to make the completion of the course dependent on the completion of the learning outcomes rather than the date of the end of the semester.

One of the major determinants of the time horizon that students adopt in their studies is the approach of the institution to failure. When the student falls short of expectations or requirements, what happens? The least satisfactory response to this question is the one that Instruction Paradigm colleges most often make: Leave it to the single faculty member teaching the class to resolve at the end of the semester, and then if the student fails, make the student repeat the course. This approach seems almost willfully nonfunctional. There are a number of points at which the institution can intervene. First, in the course of the normal semester, the institution can take steps to reverse the failing trend. Second, the institution, as suggested above, can offer supplementary time where appropriate to allow the student to do the necessary work. And third, if the student fails a conventional course, the institution can create alternative paths that specifically address the causes of the failure rather than ignoring them and mechanically repeating the learning design that has already failed. All three of these approaches seek to integrate the particular course or experience into a larger whole, to set the student on a trajectory that will bear her above the course.

INDIANA UNIVERSITY PURDUE UNIVERSITY INDIANAPOLIS (IUPUI): PARTS INTO WHOLE

Most large universities are fragmented and radically decentralized; that is one of the things that makes it hard to resist the atomizing tendencies of the Instruction Paradigm. Judging by superficial signs and administrative structures, it would appear that one of the most fragmented universities in the country must be Indiana University Purdue University Indianapolis (IUPUI). Even the name speaks division: two universities yoked together. And historically, this has been the case. Scott Evenbeck (personal communication, April 11, 2002), dean of the new University College at IUPUI says, "We grew out of a stapling together of professional schools that had very long, varied, and separate, histories. So there's a lot of autonomy within the schools." Today, the composite university houses 20 schools, 16 of which offer undergraduate degrees. All told, the university maintains 180 degree programs. Its graduates—depending on their major—get degrees from either Indiana University or Purdue University. Furthermore, IUPUI is an urban university; more than 60% of its 20,000 undergraduates are first-generation college students. It has "the state's largest population of first-generation, low-income, and minority students" (Evenbeck, 1999). What sets IUPUI apart from many other highly decentralized universities is a determination to convert its weaknesses into strengths and a clarity of purpose unusual even in much smaller institutions. The impetus of much of IUPUI's innovation over the past several years has been to create a whole from the parts in a way that will extend the time horizon of learning for its students.

The central unifying move, one that we have already seen repeatedly among colleges engaged in serious transformation, was to identify the learning outcomes that should define a successful college experience for students. These Principles of Undergraduate Learning were adopted after several years of intensive discussion and development, in 1998. "These principles describe the fundamental intellectual competence and cultural and ethical awareness that we believe every graduate of an IUPUI baccalaureate degree program should attain" (Campus Statement: IUPUI, 2001). The principles are core communication and quantitative skills; critical thinking; integration and application of knowledge; intellectual depth, breadth, and adaptiveness; understanding society and culture; and values and ethics. All of the schools in the university have made assessment of the principles a central project.

In 1998, the same year the Principles of Undergraduate Learning were adopted, University College opened its doors. According to its mission statement, "University College is the unit at IUPUI that provides a common gateway to the academic programs available to entering students. University College coordinates existing university resources and develops new initiatives to promote academic excellence and enhance student persistence" (Indiana University Purdue University Indianapolis, 2001).

How can a highly decentralized university provide a gateway experience to students that both introduces them to the core purposes of liberal education and helps them to see beyond the next semester? Evenbeck, the dean of University College, puts it this way:

It's the opposite from what people think. They think, well, general education is what you do in the first year or two, and then you get it over with, then go on with your real education in the major. Our approach has been to say that these Principles of Undergraduate Learning cut across the entire curriculum, and since we do have such varied schools, we need to start by spinning them out in the majors and then working backwards.

Learning Communities

The tool for introducing new students to the long-term purposes and processes of collegiate learning is the first-year learning community. At IUPUI a learning community is a first-year seminar linked to a subject-matter course. Learning communities are taught by an instructional team consisting of a faculty member, a librarian, an academic advisor, and a student mentor. Because the first-year seminars are linked to a variety of different subjects, there is no common syllabus for the course, but University College has developed a template that spells out the intended learning outcomes, recommends pedagogical strategies, and explains the required content. The first learning outcome of first-year seminars is that "students will begin to develop a comprehensive perspective on higher education" (Indiana University Purdue University Indianapolis, University College, 1999). Among the components of this outcome are that students will "demonstrate an ability to see relationships among academic disciplines" and "be familiar with the IUPUI Principles of Undergraduate Learning in the context of their course work and/or major." In other words, the first-year seminar aims to give students a vision of the whole college experience, to connect the parts in a coherent pattern.

The Principled Scavenger Hunt. Many of the learning communities use the Principled Scavenger Hunt as an assignment. Students, after their introduction to the Principles of Undergraduate Learning, look around the institution to find those principles reflected in practice, "in your coursework, lectures, interactions with fellow students or faculty, or in some other academic, artistic, or sporting event that occurs at or in connection with IUPUI" (Indiana University Purdue University Indianapolis, n.d.). Students then describe the example and explain how it demonstrates the principle. They then report their findings in small groups and prepare a presentation to the class on a given principle.

The purpose of the freshman learning communities is in large measure to project to students the long-term purposes and potential of their engagement with the university. It is an effort to instill the macro vision of learning that has a long time horizon of connected activities. The Principled Scavenger Hunt, in several variations, is an example of a micro-level student engagement that reinforces the macro vision. The actual application of such assignments is an ongoing work of learning, feedback, and revision for the instructional teams. But the design models an excellent approach to using the work in a specific class to initiate a process of discovery through which students find and pursue connections between what they are doing now and what they can do in the future.

Introduction to the institution. One task that good first-year seminars should perform is to introduce students to the nuts-and-bolts organization of the college, including the campus itself, the homes of the educational and support programs, and the curriculum and requirements. Thus one of the objectives of the first-year seminars is that "Students should make full utilization if IUPUI resources and services which support their learning" (Indiana University Purdue University Indianapolis, University College, 1999). This entails knowing where to go on campus to get services and how to negotiate the various documents that contain information students will need.

This is especially important for students who come from backgrounds that have prepared them poorly for the collegiate experience. Bandura (1997) notes, for example, that in high school

> Students from low-income families are much less likely than more advantaged ones to receive informative guidance on what they need to gain admission to college and to realize occupational aspirations. Deficient information leads to poor academic preparation, which can foreclose entire classes of pursuits requiring advanced competencies. (p. 65)

In other words, students who developed a short time horizon in high school often did so because they were shrouded in a fog of silence or misinformation on the questions that mattered in planning their futures. Colleges have an obligation to these students to show them what is around them and ahead of them, to let them see what the future can hold. That means making sure they know where the tutoring center and the advisors' offices are on campus, how to access the online library resources, and who they can safely ask for guidance when they are confused. But it also means connecting those places and people and the functions they serve with the range of educational choices they represent.

We discussed the importance of good maps in the last chapter. We can extend this concept to mapping the geography of future options and the tools to realize them, which extends the time horizon for students. Assignments like the Principled Scavenger Hunt and other such experiential engagements bring the map of learning that will be the framework for learning feedback together with the maps that describe the geography—literal and figurative—of the campus and its ongoing work. This permits the student to look ahead. The fog lifts.

If learning communities are the basic approach to the macro challenge of giving students a long-term view, then those learning communities need to be linked as closely as possible to the long-term goals of the students. That means that where the student has a major in mind on entry, the best introduction to the university is one that emphasizes the goals and purposes of the major. Thus schools and departments, working with University College and following the template for first-year seminars, have developed their own introductory learning communities. According to Evenbeck,

> Every one of our undergraduate degree-granting programs participates in orientation; every one of the 15 undergraduate degree-granting schools offers a learning community for first-semester students, even though they won't see them again until they're juniors. So we get them off to a good start and connect them with that faculty from the very beginning.

Support systems. If orientation and introductory learning communities instill the macro vision of future possibilities, the ongoing experience of students at the university needs to support them in approaching that long-term vision. At the micro level, IUPUI is pursuing a number of approaches to maintaining a long time horizon for students, some well developed and some in the formative stages as of this writing.

IUPUI has used the recommendations of *Involvement in Learning* (Study Group, 1984) and Russell Edgerton's (1997) white paper as blueprints for the directions in which to move in faculty development and pedagogy. They have expressly supported Edgerton's four powerful pedagogies: 1) collaborative learning, 2) service learning, 3) problem-based learning, and 4) undergraduate research. The institution has established an extensive service learning program and an undergraduate research program.

One of the major challenges at the course level, as we have seen, is to make sure that students can succeed in their individual courses, to support them in reaching the rungs of the academic ladder as they climb to their long-term goals. To support students in their course work, University College offers supplemental instruction (SI) in many courses. Developed in the 1970s by Deanna C. Martin at the University of Missouri-Kansas City, supplemental instruction is a technique for supporting and assisting students in challenging courses (University of Missouri-Kansas City, 2000). An SI leader acts as a model student, attending class meetings and then meeting with students in small groups outside of class, serving as a facilitator to help students understand and integrate their learning. A considerable body of research confirms the potential effectiveness of SI as a support mechanism for students who otherwise might be overwhelmed or defeated by course work. SI is generally voluntary for students, but IUPUI has made it a requirement in certain math courses where students are at high risk of failure.

IUPUI has initiated an early warning system in an effort to identify challenged students early in the term and bring support mechanisms to bear:

> [F]aculty in all courses are asked to identify students whose performance suggests difficulty within the first three to four weeks of the semester. Midterm grades, though also helpful, are too late for students to be able to modify their behavior or for interventions from advisors and others to make much of an impact. (Evenbeck, 1999)

Many IUPUI students come to the institution with a certain kind of long-term goal: productive and rewarding employment. Recall that a substantial majority of IUPUI's students are first-generation college students. "They and their parents," Evenbeck says, "are very pragmatic in their thinking about careers." A career focus, of course, is not an unqualified good in a university setting. But immersing these students in a general education program that has no clear connection with their career goals can encourage the students to view each course as something to get out of the way. This attitude imposes a short time horizon on the student and greatly reduces the chance of developing and revising the schemas that will survive in long-term memory. IUPUI is attempting to address that problem. Evenbeck points out:

> What we're trying to do is to say, yes, they're very vocationally focused, but how can we harness that motivation and intrinsic interest in having a career to help them get on with the business of learning? And so we've moved the career center into University College. We've hired four new advisors whose primary responsibility is to work with beginning students in learning communities and other contexts to help them think through majors and career choices at the beginning, with the idea that that will help sustain them and get them more interested in learning through their undergraduate careers. And so far, so good.

IUPUI, through a variety of programs, is making an explicit and systematic effort to lay out the long-term prospects of education for entering students and to support those students in incrementally moving toward their goals. It is, in other words, systemically seeking to create a long time horizon for learning.

MADISON AREA TECHNICAL COLLEGE: LINKING WITH A LARGER WHOLE

The motivation to begin or advance a career is very strong for most students in two-year technical colleges. While many of the students who enter such institutions will eventually complete a baccalaureate degree, most do not have that intention clearly formed when they arrive. The majority of technical college students, and most who enter vocational programs at community colleges, intend to prepare for moving directly to some kind of work. In other words, most students enter the process with their long-term thinking pointed toward vocational concerns. We just discussed how a four-year college tries to turn these vocational concerns into educational energy. The challenge is somewhat different, however, for a two-year college. Indeed, community and technical colleges face serious challenges when it comes to designing programs that promote a long time horizon simply because many students do not expect to be at the college for more than two years, and hence tend to compartmentalize the whole engagement with the college. This is a challenge with students who plan to transfer to a four-year college as well as with those who are seeking a vocational degree or certificate. We will discuss the generic problem of transfer under the issue of alignment in Chapter 16. But it has specific and obvious implications for the effort to create a long time horizon. And the challenge is in some ways most acute for students who do not have clearly articulated plans to transfer to a baccalaureate institution but are preparing for immediate employment.

Madison Area Technical College (MATC) in Madison, Wisconsin, is one of the largest of Wisconsin's 16 technical colleges. (Another, by a perverse coincidence of naming, is Milwaukee Area Technical College, also a large and excellent institution and also, unavoidably, MATC.) It has about 50,000 students in credit and noncredit courses and the equivalent of about 17,000 full-time students in credit programs. Most of its students who are in a program are seeking a certificate with a vocational focus or a one-year or two-year degree. How can a technical college project a long time horizon for the most fundamental metacognitive skills and transferable schemas of learning when students tend to focus on the immediate technical skills they need to get a job?

Vocational students often formulate the relatively short time horizon of their studies because they see employment as the terminal point of learning. That is to say, they often think more in terms of getting a job than of keeping it or thriving in it. Employment is an autonomous goal for many. And any of us who have suffered the trials of unemployment or underemployment can surely empathize with this attitude. Yet we know that such an approach does not serve students very well, and the first ones we hear that from are employers. I had the opportunity a few years ago to sit in on a focus group of community stakeholders discussing the programs of a California community college. A captain in the local fire department expressed a view that echoes much of the employer community. Prior to this experience I would probably have said that firefighting was close to being a pure vocational program, hard to connect with the liberal learning that we often see as central to college education. But when asked what he would like to see in graduates from the college who came to work for him, he responded: "I wish that more of the people who come to us would get the degree and not just the certificate. They come with good skills as firefighters, but often they don't add as much as they could to the organization." When asked for examples of the kinds of skills he would like to see, he said, "I'd like the people I hire to be able to write an executive summary of a report that I can trust to contain the essential information. I'd like people who can work together to solve a problem or come up with a plan without constant supervision and guidance." In other words, this employer wanted people who had developed cognitive and metacognitive skills that resemble many of those that repeatedly show up in the lists of the core abilities of liberal education.

MATC has addressed the needs of employers and employees in the workplace in the same way that many other institutions we have discussed have addressed the needs of baccalaureate education, by identifying the core abilities that students need to thrive in the contemporary world. The result is the Core Abilities Assessment Program. The Core Abilities at MATC are communications, critical thinking, ethics, global awareness, mathematics, science and technology, self-awareness, and social interaction.

The Core Abilities enter the educational process in course development. When developing a new course or revising an old one, faculty members in all programs prepare a Course Analysis Form, a matrix that lists the learning outcomes of the course, the assessment methods, and the Core Abilities that are being assessed. Then, in addition to giving conventional letter grades, they rate students on a three-point scale in terms of the Core Abilities. Each year, students receive, in addition to course or program feedback, a Core Ability Rating Sheet that indicates their ratings in the Core Abilities for each completed course.

The system is similar to that at Inver Hills, another two-year college, and has the same advantages in terms of providing a consistent template for feedback. Its use at a technical college also has special applications to extending the time horizon for learning. Paul Anjeski (personal communication, May 20, 2002) is coordinator of the Assessment and Evaluation Department, which is charged with administering the Core Abilities program. He notes that, "being a technical college, we have groups of students who come in and are very narrowly focused. They just want to learn what they need to know to do a job." Students at MATC hear early on that the Core Abilities are crucial to their career goals. Catherine Wilson (personal communication, March 19, 2002), who teaches in the Occupational Therapy Assistant (OTA) program and served on the original team that developed the system, describes the effect on students in her program:

> The core abilities are embedded in any of the professional development tools that we use and in course assessment. So when students get feedback on a project, they get feedback using those terms, and they also routinely self-assess using those terms. So what has happened is that they have greater skill in talking about their own general education and these lifelong learning skills. They have always had quite a bit of ability to talk about their technical background and their skills specific to OT, but I think they have more strength in actually talking about and critically looking at their Core Abilities.

And that the Core Abilities transfer to the world of work is an easy lesson to teach, because students are applying them in work-related contexts and assessments, leading to their direct application in the workplace. The Occupational Therapy Assistant program, like many others, culminates in an internship. Wilson says:

> The fourth semester is in the field, and once you get out there, this whole process maps very well over any work evaluation and any of the assessments used for interns. They may not call it the same thing as "Core Abilities," but the major elements are there. So the supervisors in the work situation have not had any difficulty providing another layer at that level.

Indeed, employers in general have welcomed the Core Abilities and the authentic assessment of them. Students are encouraged to incorporate the Core Ability Rating Sheet into their resumes and use the assessment of Core Abilities in their job search. Anjeski's office conducts periodic surveys of the employment community to gauge their degree of satisfaction with the program. He reports that "Every employer we ever talked to in our evaluation process said, 'absolutely, this is what we want you to be giving students feedback on.'"

The explicit endorsement of employers, of course, tells students that the Core Abilities will not be going away when they graduate, that the cognitive schemas they are revising and reinforcing through Core Ability assessment will remain active and required when they go to work. Thus, vocational students in two-year programs find that the time horizon of their classroom learning extends beyond the degree or the certificate.

It is interesting to note that the Core Ability Rating Sheet has had a very different reception among the transfer institutions that receive MATC graduates than it has had among employers. Anjeski (personal communication, March 19, 2002) has found:

> We get wonderful lip service from our educational colleagues, particularly at the four-year institutions, who say "We want a more self-aware student; we want a student who has these qualities. Gee, we're glad you're doing this." But not a one, to date, has ever said to us, "Yes, we'll use these ratings in determining admissions or advanced standing." They completely discount the artifacts that come out of this, where the employers embrace them. The least practical response we've gotten is from our own educational colleagues.

> Philosophically and conceptually, they agree with us. But when our students have gone to any university with their Core Ability Rating Sheet or tried to use it in the system, we hear that they have either discounted it or just kind of looked at it and said, "We don't know what to do with this; what's your GPA?" "So you're a critical thinker? What's your GPA?"

Many in universities tend to view both their colleagues at community and technical colleges and the business community at large with ill-concealed condescension. So we can hardly fail to note the ironic implications of the fact that the business community seems sometimes to take the core outcomes of liberal learning more seriously than the research universities. It is not, of course, that university faculty or staff members who praise the Core Abilities are insincere. It is that their espoused—and no doubt deeply held—theory of the function of a college education is quite different from the theory-in-use imposed upon the admissions office. Instruction Paradigm universities are locked in the structural constraints of the credit hour and the GPA. It is not a framework that anyone in the institution necessarily respects or understands, but it is the one that controls their practice.

From the point of view of students at MATC, however, the Core Abilities have the potential to dramatically extend the time horizon of learning. When they began tracking the program in 1998, 132 courses were actively rated for Core Abilities. By the fall of 2001 that had increased to 161. Sixty-two faculty members rated 922 students in 1998; by 2001, 101 faculty members rated 3,271 students. The goal is to have all students in two-year associate degree programs rated by 2004.

Through professional development activities, MATC has made a consistent effort to raise the quality of pedagogy and to incorporate authentic assessment into the curriculum. That is in many ways easier in vocational and technical programs because authentic assessment has a long tradition there. Apprentices in the skilled trades have from time immemorial been assessed on the basis of their ability to do the work, rather than pass a test on the work. Authentic assessment presents the greatest challenge at a place like MATC in the general education program, in the arts and sciences. But it is a challenge that the institution is pursuing with much energy and creativity.

NORTHCENTRAL TECHNICAL COLLEGE: LOOSENING THE BOUNDARIES OF THE CLASSROOM

Perhaps the structural feature of colleges that most constrains the time horizon is the rigid academic calendar. I believe that a plausible argument could be made that the skewed bell curve of student outcomes in many academic programs, with a substantial number of students failing to achieve real learning success, is more a product of the academic calendar than of students' native abilities. Students who take longer than the designated term to achieve given learning objectives look incompetent at term's end because their learning is not completed. Students who take less time than the term assigns often lapse through boredom or distraction. The standardized academic term exalts the hypothetical average student while punishing the living, breathing students who diverge, almost inevitably, from the norm.

Another technical college, also in Wisconsin, has initiated an experiment to test the possibilities of flexibility in the academic term. At Northcentral Technical College (NTC) in Wausau, two programs—Graphic Communication Technologies and Computer Information Technology—have begun what they call "barrier-free learning." At the invitation of NTC's president, Robert Ernst, the faculty of these programs brainstormed and explored the possibilities of alternative scheduling beginning in 1999. They initiated the barrier-free curriculum in these programs in the fall of 2000. The choice of a name for the project is instructive because it explicitly acknowledges that the traditional academic calendar is precisely a barrier to learning for many students. At NTC, they found that there was much room for more flexible scheduling, but that much depended on the particular course and the students.

Faculty in the Graphic Communication program concluded that there were three different kinds of courses in their own program—excluding, that is, general education courses and others over which they had no immediate control.

Some courses, they found, require teachers to instruct students in specific cumulative tasks, so that they have to be done in a certain order, and with practice following directly on instruction. These they called step-by-step progressive training courses. This is the category of courses that is most difficult to offer in a self-paced format. They require demonstration or explanation of a specific skill or task followed by student practice, and the tasks that students learn in these classes are often cumulative, so that the student needs to move step-by-step through the progressive tasks (Northcentral Technical College, 2000).

The second category of classes is demonstrations and self-paced project courses. These classes combine tasks that students need to practice following faculty demonstration with larger-scale projects that students can pursue on their own.

Finally, there are self-paced courses. Such courses consist almost entirely of projects that students can carry out on the basis of instruction they have previously received or with written instructions or intermittent conferences with faculty members. Sometimes, of course, at least in a program like Graphic Communication, students will need to use equipment or supplies in campus labs to do the projects, so those labs must be available when the students need them. Likewise, students will need to meet with faculty or staff members to ask questions and get feedback on developing projects. But the student can basically schedule the work at his or her convenience. And in a sequence of self-paced courses, the student is free to move faster or slower than the semester framework would have allowed. "After completing all the requirements for the first self-paced course, the student will immediately begin work on the projects for the second self-paced course, regardless of when this occurs in the semester" (Northcentral Technical College, 2002).

Computer Information Technology has taken a different approach to barrier-free courses. Jayne Rowe (personal communication, May 2, 2002), who teaches in Computer Information Technology, explains that the program keeps the length of the term stable, but allows the student to choose the start date. After beginning the course, the student has the prescribed number of weeks to complete it, but he or she may begin at nearly any time during the year. So a student who starts in the middle of the semester has roughly until the middle of next semester—or the summer session—to complete the work. This allows the students to adapt their academic schedules to the circumstances of their lives. The student who has to cope with illness or surgery or work demands can schedule academic work when it is compatible with other needs. And in a program like computer technology, students often need to get new equipment or new software in order to do the work of the course. They can begin the course after they have been able to buy and set up the equipment. All of the barrier-free courses in Computer Information Technology are online courses, while none are in Graphic Communication.

Courses in vocational programs like these are, of course, very different from many college courses. However, viewed from the perspective of student learning, most of the differences point to the superiority of such vocational programs. Students in Graphic Communication learn how to design and prepare print jobs and then print the work using current technology. The work students do in such classes is almost inherently problem-based, in the broad sense of the term. It frequently requires collaboration with others. It is inherently experiential. So, as with most well-designed vocational programs, the cognitive economy of the course is considerably warmer than that of the average lecture class. I know of no research on the question, but I strongly suspect that the average student of offset lithography is much more likely to be a deep learner, after demographic and background factors are controlled for, than the average student of introductory sociology or history. The specific issue we are considering here, of course, is the time horizon. It is interesting to reflect on the possible parallel between barrier-free learning in vocational courses and in subject-matter courses.

The constraint that applies to some vocational courses—the need for the instructor to demonstrate an operation or a piece of equipment and then observe while the student practices the skill—hardly ever applies in subject-matter courses. Indeed, the requirement that all the students in a given course be present at the same time and in the same place for lectures is exclusively an artifact of the Instruction Paradigm calendar and course design, without any apparent justification in terms of learning. To the extent that the instructor talks and students listen, the instructor's talk could be heard over audiotape or videotape or online as well as in person. The ability to replay confusing sections would more than make up for the loss of the ability to ask questions contemporaneously. The inability to view the backs of between dozens and hundreds of other students' heads would be no loss at all. The requirement for all students to be in the same place at the same time for tests is an artifact of test security needs, not learning or assessment needs. So most conventional lecture classes could easily be self-paced. The pedagogical limitations on self-scheduling of course work are the ones that the barrier-free design acknowledges. Sometimes students need to be present with the instructor for demonstration or instructions, and sometimes students need to be present with each other for hands-on collaboration. Those requirements need to be respected in the design of learning environments and will limit the freedom of students to schedule their own activities. However, those requirements are not barriers to learning but necessary rungs on the ladder of learning.

The programs involved in barrier-free learning at NTC have made a number of modifications in their courses to facilitate self-paced work. Lectures and demonstrations have been condensed wherever possible so as to reduce the time students have to spend in mandatory class meetings. In Graphic Communication, according to Daniel Seanor (2001), an instructor in the program, students have been given a voice, whenever possible, in scheduling lectures and demonstrations. Faculty have been developing comprehensive course packets to be given to students at the beginning of the program that, according to Seanor, "allow students the flexibility to work at their own pace if they desire. This also allows students to easily make up projects that they miss due to unforeseen events."

The barrier-free scheduling has been implemented for only two academic years, as of this writing. As Seanor puts it, "it has been a process of trial and error for us and we continue to work towards perfecting this concept." But the experiment has yielded several insights. The chief among these, perhaps, is that different students and different groups of students respond to the barrier-free environment differently. "Some groups of students need barrier-free opportunities more than others." Some students put their new opportunities to better use than others. And the amount of time required for faculty to facilitate the work in this new environment varies a lot from one group of students to another.

I suspect that these lessons reveal a couple of things that colleges contemplating increased flexibility should take into account. On the one hand, variation in the student response to a barrier-free environment is precisely what we should expect and is in a way encouraging. After all, the motivation for creating the flexibility in the first place was the realization that current lockstep arrangements do not respect student differences. If we give students the freedom to respond differently, we should anticipate that they will.

But some of the differences that the NTC faculty have seen have not been the product of innate student differences, I suspect, but of the fact that many students will take time to learn to use their freedom. Students are not accustomed to having the freedom or the responsibility to devise their own schedules and plan their own work. Beth Ryan (personal communication, May 22, 2002) a Graphic Communication instructor, reports exactly what we would expect, that younger students, just out of high school, tend to have more problems with self-paced projects than older students who have worked for a few years. Many students have adopted a radically short time horizon. They think in terms of the next test or the next assignment. To complete a major project that may take weeks or months, and to schedule and monitor the work themselves, requires them to think much further ahead than they are accustomed to, especially in a school setting. Indeed, the complaints of employers about the quality of college graduates frequently flow from precisely this weakness: Even after they have completed a degree, many students seem unable to take personal responsibility and motivate themselves to get a job done. You do not develop a long time horizon by never having to think more than a week ahead. The problems that the barrier-free environment brings to the surface are not problems that it created. The self-paced lab class merely reveals problems that have been concealed in the lecture hall. They are real and important problems, and we need to see them in order to solve them.

At this point, barrier-free learning is an experiment limited to only two programs at NTC. If the flexibility and extended time horizon that it embodies were extended across the curriculum, where appropriate, it would be interesting to see how students would respond.

UNIVERSITY OF MARYLAND'S GEMSTONE PROGRAM: BEGINNING WITH THE END IN MIND

We move now from programs at two-year technical colleges to an elite honors program at a research university. The idea that became the Gemstone Program at the University of Maryland began to germinate in the mind of Dr. William Destler, then dean of the A. James Clark School of Engineering and now university provost, in reaction to feedback from the employment community. Employers were reporting that engineering graduates, while well educated in the technical aspects of engineering, seemed less well prepared to work in collaborative teams in the problem solving contexts that working engineers had to face on the job. The root idea behind Gemstone was to model some of the aspects of professional work in the undergraduate years by integrating students from different disciplines and engaging them in meaningful research with a long time horizon:

> The basic concept was to team the most talented freshmen students from engineering and the sciences with students in business and management, the behavioral and social sciences, and the humanities and challenge them to pursue the solution to a major societal problem over their four-year undergraduate career. (University of Maryland, 2000, p. 2)

Gemstone, initiated in 1996, is a variation on undergraduate research in which the students themselves collaboratively formulate the research question and conduct the research, under the mentorship of a senior faculty member, with support from a librarian, and with facilitation in the early stages by upper-division students in the program. The team thesis, which is presented at a thesis conference in April of the senior year and—following final revisions—placed in the university library (and in some cases published in a professional journal), is a quintessential capstone project, a project that concludes ongoing and connected work begun in the first year of college.

Students enter the Gemstone Program as freshmen, by invitation. James Wallace (personal communication, May 17, 2002), professor of mechanical engineering and director of the program, describes Gemstone as a living-learning environment: "Nearly all the Gemstone freshmen live in a dorm where we also have the Gemstone offices and team spaces. We try to integrate instructional activities, their living activities, some extracurricular and social activities, all in a kind of a seamless educational package." In the fall of 2001, 189 students began the program.

Freshmen take the first of the 20 credit hours dedicated to Gemstone in the form of an orientation course, an introduction to the university and the honors program that, beginning in the fall of 2002, will be specifically designed for Gemstone students. This course will include exercises in team formation and topic selection.

In the spring semester, students participate in a Gemstone seminar focused on developing topics for the team research projects. Faculty members make brief presentations on research ideas and students meet in groups chaired by upper-division Gemstone students to discuss various topic ideas. Students engage in an extensive interactive process for topic selection and team formation in which, according to Wallace, "they brainstorm topic ideas, refine the ideas, vote on them, narrow them down, and eventually end up with 14 topics and 14 teams of from eight to 14 students." Also during the second semester of the freshman year, students take a three-credit course in the history of science and technology that involves original research. One formulation of the course is "Technology and the City," in which students explore the infrastructure of Washington, DC.

In the sophomore year, teams meet to pursue research on their topics under the supervision of senior faculty mentors. They formulate mission statements, study team dynamics and research methodology, and develop Web pages. A series of team deliverables shapes the schedule of activities. In May of each year, teams present a research update in poster sessions and update their Web pages. Some students integrate study abroad, other course work, and service activities with their Gemstone projects. In the senior year, students present several iterations of the team thesis. In February there is a thesis rehearsal, and in early April at the thesis conference, teams present and defend their theses. Teams invite three outside discussants to the conference, often experts in fields relevant to the thesis, who serve as a panel to start the questioning following the presentation and then confer with the team on plans for their final revision. The thesis is submitted for publication at the end of April.

The Gemstone Program is interdisciplinary from the outset. Invited students are a mixture of applicants from different schools, and teams combine students with different majors. The program aims to move students beyond specialization to problem solving in multidisciplinary teams. The result is research topics such as emergency telemedicine, the disposal of nuclear waste, antibiotic resistance, and urban revitalization.

Not all Gemstone teams are equally successful. The program faces the same challenges as any new program in that it needs to develop and refine its ability to recruit, select, and train faculty mentors who can maximize the potential of the program. When it works, it works spectacularly well. Some success stories are remarkable, such as that of the young graduate who was contacted by a federal agency and offered a position—they had found her team thesis on the web while doing research on an ongoing project. Wallace reports:

> What I have heard from the seniors who were in the most effective teams, who really achieved a lot with their research and produced really very substantial theses, is that their team experience, their experience with each other, overcoming all the problems that any group of disparate people can have trying to work together and making themselves an effective team, was by far the most important educational experience that they had in their four years at the university, that nothing else was even close. It was a source of satisfaction, of bonding, of support. They really speak in glowing terms of what this meant to them.

Stephen Covey (1989), the management consultant and author, gives some excellent advice for both personal and organizational practice: "Begin with the end in mind." His point is that if you know what you're trying to do you have a much better chance of actually accomplishing it—with a minimum of frustration, wasted motion, and false starts. Another way of putting it might be to suggest that we should look ahead, think of the consequences, and adopt a long time horizon. But it is advice that students will often be hard pressed to take in the process of getting a college education. The Gemstone project attempts to implement that advice by radically intervening to change the cognitive economy for some students. It puts them in a context in which they must describe the end at the beginning and shape much of their behavior toward achieving that end. In other words, it provides a long time horizon as a foundational characteristic of the cognitive economy for those students who participate. In the case of Gemstone, the program is for a limited number of students. But the principle is a sound one for every student at every college.

PROCESS FRONTIER: TIME

Students who believe that they are engaged in a long-term process will invest more of themselves and their resources in education than students who believe that what they are doing now will soon be over and finished. A long time horizon for learning heats up the cognitive economy of the college; a short one cools it down. The structural atomization of the Instruction Paradigm college creates a learning environment that breaks educational processes into small pieces and obscures the connection between those pieces. To create the Learning Paradigm college we need to open the long-term meaning and purpose of the whole of a college education to students at the very beginning and engage them in connected and clearly relevant activities that approach that purpose. That means that at the macro level we need to make collegiate learning as a conduit to lifelong learning a concrete option for new students. At the micro level we need to design specific learning experiences that will be steps toward holistic goals. The educational ladder needs to be resting on a high place, a place where students want to go. And the rungs need to be spaced at reasonable length, so that students can climb it.

A Learning Paradigm College Creates Purposeful Communities of Practice

THE PARADOX OF COLLABORATION

We should not need reminding of the fact that students are people, but the design of our institutions and the shape of our work suggests that we do. The Instruction Paradigm college seems designed as if students were the products of some strange and perverse experiment in artificial intelligence; it seeks to create autonomous, and indeed interchangeable, thinkers programmed to operate as isolated automata. Real people live and thrive with other people; human thought, language use, and creativity are inherently social. We have created a cognitive economy for strange academic beings unlike any born on this planet.

Or perhaps it is simpler than that. Perhaps we have just imitated a design we found. This story captures the problem nicely: The professor spends most of the class period explaining how they will set up collaborative groups for the work of the following class session. He explains the rationale and process of collaborative learning and does his best to inspire the students in the large class to approach the task with hope and enthusiasm. A young woman from the class comes up to the front right after the session concludes. "I really enjoyed your lecture," she tells the professor, "and you made a number of excellent points. But I just wanted to let you know that I won't need to participate in the collaborative work. It doesn't really apply to me. I'm going to be a college teacher."

No work is more inherently and unavoidably collaborative than academic research. Some are still burdened with the myth of the lone scholar isolated in his turret of the Ivory Tower. (It is always *his* turret, in case you haven't noticed; Rapunzel, who was no scholar, has a near monopoly on the female turret.) The myth is almost entirely illusory. This is not to deny the importance of periodic, and sometimes extended, solitude and withdrawal for creative work. But such withdrawal forms the other pole of intense involvement with others. It is no accident that the modern university is still organized around academic disciplines, which are more than anything else groups of scholars doing similar work, using similar language, and generally accepting collaboratively developed standards to govern both the process and product of their work. Not only is the research enterprise built from the ground up on an infrastructure of collaboration; the work of most creative artists is collaborative as well. Michael Schrage (1989), in his book *No More Teams: Mastering the Dynamics of Creative Collaboration,* goes so far as to define collaboration as "the process of shared creation" (p. 33) and to illustrate the principle by the examples, not just of Watson and Crick, Rogers and Hart, and Braque and Picasso, but with the less evident cases of T. S. Eliot, Vincent Van Gogh, Neils Bohr, Werner Heisenberg, F. Scott Fitzgerald, and many others. He quotes the conclusion of sociologist Harriet Zuckerman, who interviewed 41 Nobel laureates and compared their research with that of a control group of scientists in the same fields: "Nobel laureates in science publish more and are more apt to collaborate. . . . Comparison of their research output with the output of the matched sample indicates that these patterns hold at every stage of the lifework cycle" (p. 40). The point is not that collaboration always works well or that it is easy. It is, however, usually a necessary process in the development of creative work. The air is not always sweet, but those who live, breathe. If you want to live in the world of academic research, you learn to breathe the air of collaboration.

But, as the story of the undergraduate who didn't need to learn to collaborate illustrates, perhaps no field of work in the modern world is less collaborative than college teaching. Here, community colleges provide valuable evidence simply because they are institutions in which the design of the teaching role specifically excludes research. They often offer themselves as teaching institutions to indicate that the whole focus of faculty activity is on teaching. W. Norton Grubb (1999) and his associates at the School of Education at the University of California, Berkeley conducted an extensive analysis of community college teachers for their book *Honored but Invisible: An Inside Look at Teaching in Community Colleges.* The team observed 257 classes and interviewed over 300 administrators and teachers at 32 community colleges across the country. One of their most striking conclusions is this:

> A defining aspect of instructors' lives in community colleges is their isolation. Except in a small number of exemplary institutions, most instructors speak of their lives and work as individual, isolated, lonely. A teacher's job is a series of classes, with the door metaphorically if not literally closed. Some faculty view isolation as an inherent part of teaching: "Teaching is a very individualistic endeavor, and people are often secretive and unwilling to seek out or utilize a different approach." (p. 49)

My own experience teaching at a community college for over 20 years entirely confirms this assessment. It is not that collaboration is impossible, but to attempt collaborative work is like trying to swim upstream.

Community colleges may be an extreme case, yet they are an extreme case of a tendency that is inherent in the Instruction Paradigm. At most colleges and universities, collaboration among faculty is much more extensive in research than it is in teaching. Research, as we saw in Chapter 3, has become increasingly interdisciplinary, largely through the need for colleagues from separate disciplines to work together in order to get to the bottom of anything. For the most part, teaching has been slow to follow the trend. I will choose the example of the University of Michigan, in part because we have already seen it as a positive example of transformative change in some areas. The President's Commission on the Undergraduate Experience (2001) at Michigan concluded that "interdisciplinarity is much more strongly rooted in faculty scholarship and graduate pedagogy than in the undergraduate experience. According to the reaccreditation self-study, the barriers to team-teaching and course selection across college lines remain high..." (p. 29).

We will return in Part V to the issue of faculty collaboration for teaching. However, we should keep in mind this radical disjunction in the nature of faculty roles as we consider the way the cognitive economy rewards and conditions students.

COMMUNITIES OF PRACTICE

All learning is a social activity. If this does not seem obvious to you, spend a moment on this question. If human beings were raised in isolation from other human beings, is it possible to imagine the development of language, either for the race or for the individual? How? The tools and artifacts of thought are all fundamentally vehicles of communication. Speech, language, writing, the visual arts, modes of transcription and recording—none of them is imaginable in the absence of the need to convey to others what we value and what we perceive. Without a universe of discourse, a common framework and vocabulary of thought, how could we think at all?

The culture in which we live, the groups and organizations through and in which we act—our friends and families, clubs and teams, workplaces and schools—these are the media of learning for us, in large measure because they are the media of meaning for us. Nearly all of our learning is negotiated with the other agents in the communities in which we live. In this sense, every community is a learning community, and all learning is a social act.

Overwhelming evidence shows that students who live on campus among their peers persist in college and graduate at much higher rates than students who live away from college and commute to their classes. Residential students develop social connections with other students: They create a peer group consisting of students at the same college, facing similar challenges and difficulties. They help each other. Commuting students often rely for social support on groups of peers formed in high school or at work, many of whom are not attending college at all. But even at residential colleges, a distributional lower-division curriculum separates students from their potential peers by allocating them to separate classes, often each with a completely different group of students. The larger the institution, the more severe is this barrier to peer-group formation: the larger the total number of students the smaller the chance that any will fall by chance into the same classes; and the larger the classes, the smaller the chance that students will be able to recognize and connect with other students at all. As one student at the University of Washington put it, "The way the university is set up, it is practically impossible to meet people unless you subdivide it into smaller groups" (Tinto, Goodsell-Love, & Russo, 1994, p. 5). As we have already seen, Astin (1993) concludes from an analysis of extensive longitudinal studies that the single most powerful influence on college students, in their cognitive as well as social development, is other students. A college that does not support the formation of peer communities chills the cognitive economy.

While community formation among students is vitally important, not all communities affect learning in the same way. Communities engaged in purposeful action shape the participants' expectations and goals differently than simply social communities, such as many fraternities and sororities. Going to a party with several other people and writing an article with several other people are both communal activities, but one is likely to prove a much more powerful engine of learning than the other. Knowing, trusting, and communicating with people are important, but sharing tasks with them creates a special opportunity for learning.

"We learn what we do," as John Dewey said, but we also learn in order to do. We learn what we need to know in order to accomplish what we want to accomplish. And what we want or need to do is invariably shaped by the social units that set the boundaries of our productive action. We may speak of the "kind of community created over time by the sustained pursuit of a shared enterprise" as a "community of practice" (Wenger, 1998, p. 45). The term has its roots in the analysis of learning from an anthropological perspective. Jean Lave and Etienne Wenger (1991), in their book *Situated Learning: Legitimate Peripheral Participation,* examine modes of apprenticeship in a variety of societies and settings, including those practiced to train midwives among the Yucatec Mayan Indians of Mexico, tailors among the Vai and Gola of West Africa, and quartermasters in the United States Navy. They find that apprenticeship is a process by which newcomers are gradually introduced, through what they call "legitimate peripheral participation," into the practices common to experts. Novices are introduced to a community of practice through observing the actions of more experienced practitioners and gradually assuming more responsibility for practice themselves. Their participation is legitimate: They have a right to be there, where the work is done or the decisions made. But it is peripheral: They stand initially on the outer rim of the circle. They observe a lot at first, and gradually assume increasing responsibilities. But they are, from the very beginning, participants and not merely spectators. Initially, they may only watch, but they watch in order to learn, and they learn in order to do. This concept of the process of gradual socialization to skills and knowledge through peripheral participation is an important and useful one.

Wenger (1998) has developed a detailed and valuable framework of analysis in his book *Communities of Practice: Learning, Meaning and Identity.* Here I will draw on it for some key ideas without attempting to summarize the entire theory. A community of practice is a group of people who identify with one another because they share common purposes. A group becomes a community of practice when it becomes a forum that its members use to negotiate meaning. "Practice," Wenger points out, "is, first and foremost, a process by which we can experience the world and our engagement with it as meaningful" (p. 51). This process of negotiating meaning is a central function of communities of practice.

Participation in a Community of Practice

The dynamics of negotiated meaning involve two opposed but complementary processes: participation and reification. I participate in a group or activity when I share in it. Participation is playing the game, whatever the game may be. Teachers and students use the term all the time in essentially this sense. When we say a student is not participating we mean he or she is standing outside the group as an observer, not sharing in the work or engaging in the common effort. We see on a daily basis a whole range of degrees of participation, from apparent noninvolvement to genuine and enthusiastic investment. Part of what we see when we see participation is an inclination to take seriously the participation of others, a recognition of the status of other participants. Wenger points out:

> [W]hat I take to characterize participation is the possibility of mutual recognition. When we shave a piece of wood or mold a piece of clay, we do not construe our shaping these objects as contributing to their experience of meaning. But when we engage in a conversation, we somehow recognize in each other something of ourselves, which we address. What we recognize has to do with our mutual ability to negotiate meaning. (p. 56)

We used the metaphor of conversation in Chapter 13 to discuss feedback. In conversation, we expect and accept feedback. But the point here is a bit larger. The mutuality we experience in conversation involves not just the refinement of our personal purposes and aims; it involves us in a process of developing shared meanings through identifying with the others in our community and acting with them. If I am participating in a community of practice, I recognize you as a peer. That doesn't mean that I agree with what you say, for example, but it does mean that I recognize what you say as calling for acknowledgement and response. I may refute your views, but I cannot ignore them. To do so would be to withdraw rather than participate. Participation in a community of practice makes meaning flexible and malleable, subject to revision and reshaping.

Reification in a Community of Practice

But meanings cannot be infinitely malleable or we would never be able to act on them. We must agree on some settled meanings as a basis for moving forward or our conversation becomes aimless wandering. Reification is the act of making an abstraction concrete. If participation is playing the game, reification is the rules and tools and records of the game. It is, Wenger says, "the process of giving form to our experience by producing objects that congeal this experience into 'thingness'" (p. 58). We reify when we translate a concept or idea into concrete form by writing it down or embodying it in a symbol or when we create a tool to facilitate repeating a process. Written history is our reification of past events. A constitution is our reification of our political process. In developing a curriculum the official course outline or syllabus reifies the process of the class. In the classroom, a textbook is the reification of the intended content. The student participates in the class discussion by explaining her point of view; she reifies her views by recording them in her journal or writing an essay about them.

Participation and reification are complementary, reciprocal processes. Both are required to negotiate meaning. Without reification, activity is not participation; it is random movement. At a party or in casual conversation there is often activity that never leads to reification; hence there is no real participation, though there may be bonding and enjoyment and mutual respect. If there are no rules, running around the field may be exercise, but it isn't a game. Without participation, tools and symbols are merely static objects; they cease to bear meaning if no one uses them.

Balancing Participation and Reification in a Community of Practice

For a community of practice to productively negotiate meaning on an ongoing basis, participation and reification must be in balance. The community must occasionally marshal the meanings it has negotiated by reifying those meanings in public objects. But those reified meanings must then be subject to ongoing negotiation through the active participation of community members.

It is through accepting and adopting the reifications of a community of practice that we come to identify ourselves as believers in certain ideas and followers of certain principles. It is through participating mutually with the other members of a community of practice in the refinement and application of these reified principles that we come to identify with the other members. We shape our individual identities and negotiate our sense of ourselves through the complementary processes of participation and reification.

Is a classroom a community of practice? The answer, I think, has to be "It depends." It depends on whether there is a possibility of genuinely negotiating meaning, of real participation. The conventional classroom in the Instruction Paradigm college tends to value reification over participation to such an extent that it calls into question the very existence of a community of practice. Wenger points out that the traditional classroom "offers unusually little texture to negotiate identities: A teacher sticking out and a flat group of students all learning the same things at the same time." In such a context, "Competence, thus stripped of its social complexity, means pleasing the teacher, raising your hand first, getting good grades" (p. 269).

Let us assume for the sake of argument that a classroom is a community of practice. What are the meanings it is negotiating? Surely students talk to one another, at least to some extent, in even the most traditional of lecture halls. But what do they talk about? What is the range of meanings that they can negotiate? Wenger describes the danger: "If school practices become self-contained, then they cease to point anywhere beyond themselves. School learning is just learning school" (p. 267). Yes, students communicate with other students. But the meanings that they can negotiate are about the tactics of successful surface learning in the settled bounds of reified content. What does this teacher want? How can you ace her tests? How does she respond to questions? How can you distract her? What page are the answers to the study questions on? So perhaps it is not that students are not participants in communities of practice, but that the communities of practice to which they have access do not aim at the kind of learning we had in mind. Perhaps the traditional classroom has created a community of practice that will prepare students to become tacticians of bureaucracy, to manipulate the inflexible rules they do not respect in order to get through the system. In the cognitive economy of the Instruction Paradigm college, students will tend to form opportunistic communities of practice that aim to reduce the cost of a credential. Students will collaborate all right. They will form teams to play the game of surface learning.

We should consider one final point about the classroom as community of practice. It rarely allows any form of legitimate peripheral participation, the gradual increase in responsibility and activity that marks the learning process of almost all communities of practice in almost all societies. There is only one master or expert practitioner in the conventional classroom: the teacher. But with rare exceptions the teacher is not modeling the activity she wants from the students. So the students do not observe and imitate; they listen to instructions or explanations. There are no masters for the apprentices to watch. And there are usually no advanced learners to model for them the incremental steps toward mastery. In one sense, the apprentice midwife among the Yucatec Mayans finds herself in a richer learning environment than the average college freshman.

A FRAMEWORK FOR PURPOSEFUL COMMUNITIES OF PRACTICE: LEARNING COMMUNITIES

If we want to see the kinds of purposeful communities of practice that set worthwhile learning goals, we can find them at almost any college. Such communities abound. The theater group and the debate team, the newspaper and the literary journal, the jazz ensemble and the math club are communities of practice in which meaning is negotiated on an ongoing basis and students consciously grow as learners. Such groups involve new members in legitimate peripheral participation in a community of practice that includes a range of expertise—from the coach, director, or editor through experienced upper-division students, to those with little but some experience who are just a step above the novice. The new participant enters the outer circle and can gradually approach more closely.

Communities of practice are not, of course, limited to extracurricular activities. To the extent that colleges have moved to create a hot cognitive economy, they tend to become friendly environments for purposeful communities of practice. All of the principles we have discussed so far reinforce and support the creation of such communities of practice. Students who are pursuing intrinsic goals will tend to form communities of practice, in and out of the classroom, with others who share similar goals. If students are involved in performance—especially if they are aiming for public performance—they will need to practice, and those who practice together will become, not surprisingly, communities of practice. If students get clear, consistent, connected feedback they will be engaged in the process of negotiating meanings. And to the extent that the reifications that form the framework for feedback make meaning clear to students, they encourage those students to form or join communities that can enact and negotiate those meanings. Students who adopt a long time horizon for learning will be more likely to join together with other students for common interests and purposes. And they will have more incentive to do so because they will believe that their communities will have the time to do the work they seek to do.

We have already seen many examples of institutions that have created purposeful communities of practice. The Bailey Scholars Program at Michigan State and the Gemstone Program at the University of Maryland are very different, but both are explicitly designed to create ongoing communities of practice for students and to involve the students in the ongoing negotiation of meaning. The first-year learning communities at IUPUI and the portfolio seminars at Olivet seek to create such communities of practice. All the efforts we have discussed to define the desired learning outcomes of a college education seek to provide the infrastructure for negotiating meaning focused on valued learning goals.

Likewise, the powerful pedagogies we have discussed all tend to promote purposeful communities of practice. Problem-based learning and collaborative learning aim to create communities of practice in the classroom, to put students in groups, reify the challenge and at least some rudimentary rules for addressing it, and tell the students to negotiate the meanings they generate through participating in the problem solving process. Undergraduate research embeds students into new or existing communities of practice. Service learning also places students in roles as participants in ongoing work, the meaning of which they must negotiate. When students write reflective journals or essays about their experience in the field—in internships, research, or service—they reify their formative meanings. And when they discuss those reflections, they participate in the ongoing negotiation of meaning.

In addition to the obvious step of strengthening extracurricular activities, colleges should seek to modify the classroom to make it a vehicle for productive communities of practice, in much the same way that

many extracurricular activities already are. The basic format for purposeful communities of practice is not hard to see: It will be communities that
bring students together for more than a single class, in learning communities. We have already encountered that term several times in slightly
different uses. Most of the time, however, it means what I will use it to
refer to in this chapter: groupings of students and teachers in interdisciplinary or nondisciplinary courses involving much collaborative work. So
the IUPUI first-year learning communities fill the bill, as do many of the
other examples we have considered. The primary goal in creating a learning community is to bring students together for a longer time, to do
more work, with more chance to talk and listen to each other than the
conventional class affords. So at its simplest, a learning community can
be two classes linked together with the same students in both and some
coordination between the teachers. In creating learning communities,
colleges are tapping into the same principle that causes students to do
better in small colleges than in large ones and better in residential than in
nonresidential colleges. At colleges where the odds are low that students
will accidentally find a common group of students in several classes, you
manipulate the odds by linking the classes together.

Patrick Hill (1985) began what came to be called federated learning
communities when he was a philosophy professor at the State University
of New York (SUNY), Stony Brook. The federated learning community is
so called because it "federates" three courses with a discussion seminar
headed by a Master Learner, a faculty member from outside any of the disciplines taught in the three courses. Hill later became provost at The Evergreen State College in Washington State, where he still teaches, and which
offered learning communities on a somewhat different design (which we
will discuss in more detail below.) Many of the flaws and dysfunctions of
the modern college, he believes, flow from "the atomism—the social
atomism, the structural atomism—which isolates people and enterprises
from each other." Acknowledging the great variety of designs possible for
learning communities, Hill points out that "the fundamental structural
move is to link related enterprises and to make structural changes which
release, for faculties and students, the powers of human association." The
university or college as presently designed, he says, "is set up to discourage
communication across boundaries, and is even set up to discourage people
from having time to talk to each other."

> It is common to coordinated studies, to clusters and linked courses, and to the federated learning communities, to put people with related interests together and give them time and space—real time and space—to learn from each other. You are releasing the capacity of people to learn from each other, and it is as simple as that.... (Hill, 1985)

For their primary function of creating communities of students, learning communities work remarkably well. Vincent Tinto, Anne Goodsell-Love, and Pat Russo (1994) conducted a study of learning communities at three different institutions for the National Center on Postsecondary Teaching, Learning, and Assessment at The Pennsylvania State University. They found: "In all cases, ... the structure and continuity of program activities provided a space for the emergence of a supportive community of peers that continued outside the program" (p. 6). One program they studied was at LaGuardia Community College in New York where "students enroll as a group in a thematically linked cluster of courses where professors integrate the content across courses according to a unifying theme" (p. 2). One student they interviewed at LaGuardia summarized the principle nicely:

> In the same class you see the same faces, and you make friends. And you discuss anything whenever you want.... If I have a class, like writing, and the next class is different, then I have to make friends in that class, and I can't discuss the things that I want. [In this learning community] it's easier to talk about different ideas or whatever you want. (p. 7)

How do you negotiate meanings in a community of practice? Simple. "You discuss anything whenever you want." Another LaGuardia student contrasted the learning community experience with the return to the conventional separate classes in the following semester:

> In the cluster we knew each other, we were friends, we discussed everything from all the classes. We knew things very, very well because we discussed it all so much. We had a discussion about everything. Now it's more difficult because there are different people in each class. There's not so much—oh, I don't know how to say it. It's not so much togetherness. In the cluster, if we needed help or if we had questions, we could help each other. Now we're just, more on our own. (p. 8)

What I hear in these accounts—and what I have seen first hand in the learning communities in which I have taught—is something that most teachers will recognize. If a class goes well, there is a certain point in the term where it awakens, grows up, takes charge of itself, becomes a class instead of a group strangers yoked unwillingly together. The manifestations of this transformation are so varied that I despair of proof or even much clarity and leave it to the reader to decide. I am inclined to turn Tolstoi's aphorism about families on its head and say that unhappy classes are all alike, but each happy class is happy in its own way. A class that is working is never quite like any other because it really is negotiating its own meanings, negotiating itself. Sometimes, the resulting new thing is aggressive or critical or positively disagreeable. But it is of a piece, has a certain integrity. Like poor Justice Potter Stewart with pornography, I can't define it, but I know it when I see it. And you can see it. When students come into the room, you can see that they know where they are, that it is no longer a strange place.

This coming together as a new thing seems to me to happen sooner in learning communities. And I think that it happens more strongly too. A learning community will sometimes more readily make its tendencies into excesses, get drunk on itself, carry things too far. But we can almost say of learning what Mark Twain said of whiskey, that too much is just enough. The power of the ongoing negotiation of meaning through participation is so great that it can breathe life into the reified corpses of academic practices that would otherwise be entirely inert. Even studying for a multiple-choice test becomes less shallow if you discuss it enough and with enough passion. The test may be formatted for surface learning, but the discussion has the potential to give it substantive meaning. In a learning community, many more students can say, with that anonymous LaGuardia student, "We knew things very, very well because we discussed it all so much." Tinto, Goodsell-Love, and Russo found that participation in learning communities significantly increased the persistence of first-year students into the second year of college, even after controlling for other factors known to influence persistence. The value of learning communities has been confirmed by a substantial body of research (Gabelnick, MacGregor, Matthews, & Smith, 1990; Tinto, 1997). And this is, of course, just what we should expect.

At the beginning of this chapter I suggested that one reason we deny meaningful communities to our students is that we, as college teachers, do not participate in them ourselves. At many institutions there is no living community of practice among the faculty that is actively negotiating the meaning of teaching and participating in revising the tools they use and rules that govern them. Patrick Hill (1985) points out:

> The individual, isolated course, standing on its own and too often created out of the research interests of the professor, deprives the students and the teacher of the widest system of coherent curricular support which would relate the fragmented disciplines to each other and reinforce the significance of what is being taught. That lack of coherence—I think we understand what it does to the student—but few people have focused on what it does to the teacher. It deprives the teacher of a support system.

The reified artifacts that define our roles as teachers—the course outlines, the calendar, the departments and divisions—are fossilized beyond all negotiation. Whether they have meaning or not is often beside the point; they are like the seats of the lecture hall, bolted to the floor. They are not merely concrete; they are set in cement. We have, as I suggested in Chapters 2 and 3, made the means the end. We have made the tools of our work the object of our work, and in doing so, have vitiated our own freedom to negotiate meaning. We cannot create genuine communities of practice for students until we allow faculty to participate too. Learning communities that bring together faculty members from across disciplines are a powerful way to address this challenge. Only if the teachers are learners too, and if they are seen to be learners, can they genuinely model deep learning for the apprentice learners in the community. That is why the design of federated learning communities, for one example, makes teachers into learners in the seminar, allows them to support students by modeling a learning process, not as subject matter experts, but as master learners.

The best design for learning in classrooms, it seems to me, is the combination of several teachers with a group of students who are addressing a theme that none of them quite has charge of, the meaning of which must be negotiated by the teachers as well as the students. This means that the best learning communities will be thematic, shaped to address a question or issue, not cut out by some disciplinary cookie-cutter. This is not a new insight. *Involvement in Learning* recommended: "Every institution of higher education should strive to create learning communities, organized around specific intellectual themes or tasks" (Study Group, 1984, p. 33).

Implicit in this advice, however, is the more fundamental recommendation to keep searching, to continue our own participation. We need to think seriously about the things and processes that make up the learning environment. Our goal should be to design so as to promote participation: discussion, involvement, and the negotiation of meaning. I am inclined to think that this works better when the objects themselves are somewhat ambiguous or problematic, objects that need clarification or refinement, so that they invite from the onset the negotiation of meaning.

THE EVERGREEN STATE COLLEGE: BREAKING OUT OF THE CLASSROOM INTO COORDINATED STUDIES

The attempt to create purposeful communities of practice among undergraduates has a long and noble history. One of the most noteworthy of these efforts, and one from which we still have much to learn, was Alexander Meiklejohn's Experimental College at the University of Wisconsin. The Experimental College, founded in 1927, dispensed with courses, credit units, and grades. It offered an integrated program designed for the first two years of college, what Meiklejohn called a "moral curriculum." Its purpose, in Meiklejohn's (1932/1981) words, was "by using scholarship— its fruits or processes or both of these—to so cultivate and strengthen the intelligence of a pupil that he may be ready to take responsibility for the guidance of his own behavior" (p. 9). He set out to avoid making "the mistake of thinking that the fundamental lesson to be learned in a college is identical with the 'studies' which we teach" (p. 10). Rather, "It is a general process of human learning of which our education by books and teachers is only a special limited phase" (p. 11). Faculty and students lived together in the same dormitory. The first year was devoted to the study of ancient Athenian civilization of the fourth and fifth centuries B.C., the time of Pericles and Plato. The second year focused on 19th-century America. Students read books concerning the period in question and discussed them in seminars. The program was thematic, nondisciplinary, and relied on original sources rather than secondary textbooks. The Experimental College closed its doors in 1932, when the faculty senate of the university withdrew its support. Meiklejohn's experiment was a precursor of what we now think of as learning communities.

Joseph Tussman (1997) was a student of Meiklejohn's at Wisconsin, though only after the demise of the Experimental College. He came to the University of California, Berkeley in 1964 and set out to create a similar experiment. Tussman's Experimental College Program was also short-lived, but inspired many in the higher education world of the time, and subsequently. The Experimental College Program was also intended for just the first two years of college. In Tussman's view, the undergraduate college had been overwhelmed by the research university. "The college is everywhere in retreat," he wrote, "fighting a dispirited rear-guard action against the triumphant university. The upper division, dominated by departmental cognitive interests, has become, in spirit, a preparatory run at the graduate school, increasingly professional" (p. 53). The only enclave for a college that cultivates human understanding was the first two years: "Only the lower division remains outside the departmental fold—invaded, neglected, exploited, misused. It is there that the college must make its stand." To do so, Tussman created a curriculum that focused on "times of cultural crises throughout history, periods that produced a rich and varied literature in which powerful minds grappled with fundamental human problems" (Trow, 1998, p. 9). The extensive reading list of some 35 original sources covered Greece in the time of the Peloponnesian Wars, 17th-century England, 18th- and 19th-century America, and contemporary America (Trow, 1998). The centerpiece of the program was the seminar, in which small groups of students worked through the books and discussed them, sometimes with faculty members who were reading them for the first time as well. "We begin cold with the *Iliad*," Tussman wrote, "but everything after that is read in a steadily thickening context of insights, questions, ideas[,] . . . a growing sense of relation and interconnection as we progress" (Trow, 1998, p. 10). Tussman's college at Berkeley was closed in 1969 when the administration refused to create tenured faculty positions dedicated to it, and Tussman was unwilling to continue the program without this assurance of continuity.

The following year, the founding faculty and administrators began to plan the curriculum of a new public college for the state of Washington. The founding dean for social sciences, Mervyn Cadwallader, was formerly a faculty member at San José State University in California. By chance, Cadwallader was a cousin of Joseph Tussman's wife. He attended a dinner party at Tussman's home in 1963 where he met the 90-year-old Alexander Meikeljohn, then also living in Berkeley. "Cadwallader recalled being 'bowled over' at how vital Meiklejohn was at 90 years.... Cadwallader was immediately taken with Meiklejohn's energy and ideas and particularly his account of the Experimental College at the University of Wisconsin" (Smith, in press). Ongoing contacts between the three men led to discussion of Tussman's formative Experimental Program at Berkeley. Cadwallader took up the idea and established a similar one, called the Tutorial Program, as San José State. Cadwallader left San José State and arrived, in 1970, at the new college in Washington State. He urged the founding faculty to read Tussman's book *Experiment at Berkeley.* In one of the first planning meetings for the new college—held in a trailer—after a fair amount of vague and directionless discussion about floor plans and lecture halls, Cadwallader requested that he be allowed to develop a "coordinated studies" program offering thematic courses not bound to traditional disciplines for about 100 students. Another of the founding deans, Don Humphrey (sciences), responded: "if it's good for 100, it's good for a thousand" (Smith, 2001, p. 68). The idea caught on. The Evergreen State College adopted the interdisciplinary coordinated studies learning community as its entire curriculum. And 25 years later, that curriculum survives, with some ongoing experimentation and development, in essentially the same form.

In its statement of expectations for graduates, headed "Evergreen is about learning" (The Evergreen State College, 2002), the college says that "It is about creating a community that works together to build knowledge, experience and insight. Everything we do is designed to foster collaborative learning among students, among faculty and between students and faculty." Rather than offering individual classes, Evergreen offers a curriculum consisting chiefly of coordinated studies programs. These programs preserve the essential form—though not the content—of Meiklejohn's and Tussman's experiments. And that form applies not just to the lower division but to all of the college's offerings. Instead of taking four or five separate classes, students will take a single coordinated studies program, team-taught by three to five faculty members and designed to explore a single theme or issue. Students may attend lectures or labs, for example, on Tuesday and Thursday and hold reading seminars on Wednesday and Friday. The total program may have 100 students, but for reading seminars 20 to 25 students meet with a single faculty member to discuss the books. Most programs continue for the entire academic year, others for one or two quarters.

The theme of a coordinated studies program may be a place or a time, as in "Japanese Language and Culture," "Russia: Empires and Enduring Legacies," or "Silver Sky: Poetry and Place in the Pacific Northwest." It might be a subject matter that resembles a conventional disciplinary unit, as in "Freshwater Ecology," "Foundations of Visual Art," or "Great British and Irish Moderns: Poetry and Fiction." Or it might be a problem or question that clearly crosses disciplinary lines such as in "Bilingual Education and Teaching" or "Pillars of Fire: Jewish Contributions to European and American Culture."

The reading lists for coordinated studies courses are often eclectic and extensive. The art of designing a coordinated studies program, as of teaching a more conventional course, consists in large measure of selecting appropriate books. But here, where courses do not follow the predetermined disciplinary outlines to which most textbooks are written, the preponderance of reading consists of real books, rather than books written to fit the standardized design of conventional college classes. In "Power and Limitations of Dialogue," for example, the reading list includes Peter Senge's *The Fifth Discipline,* Deborah Tannen's *You Just Don't Understand,* Desmond Tutu's *No Future Without Forgiveness,* and a biography of Martin Luther King, Jr. "Morality and Political Life: Classical and Modern" uses Aristotle's *Nicomachean Ethics* and Kant's *Fundamental Principles of the Metaphysics of Morals.* (All of the examples, by the way, are taken from Evergreen's offerings for the academic year 2002–2003, posted on its web page.)

The Evergreen model of coordinated studies is widely known, and information about it is readily available. The essential principle is simple. It brings a group of students together and, as Patrick Hill (1985) put it, gives them "time and space to learn from each other." Yet, it is more than just bringing a group of students together so that they take all of their classes together—though that can be done too, and is done in some places. The Evergreen curriculum is not exactly what most of us would think of as interdisciplinary. This is a point that Katherine Trow (1998) makes about Tussman's college at Berkeley. It was not, she says, "meant to be interdisciplinary, but since it drew from a variety of perspectives . . . it was often mistaken for an interdisciplinary program. Instead, it was independent of all these common curricular characteristics . . ." (pp. 9–10). While no Evergreen coordinated studies program aspires to the depth and breadth of Tussman's two-year program, they are in design not so much interdisciplinary as what a colleague of mine calls "transdisciplinary": They seek to transcend academic disciplines, to aim above them. Perhaps this is not an unambiguous good. It may mean that some faculty members bring less depth and less dexterity to some topics than they would have had they been pursuing the subject and testing it against student questions for a while. But it also means that the negotiation of meaning among the teachers that begins in the planning of the learning community and continues through its execution is much more likely to really model a process of discovery for students.

While there is a certain amount of repetition in the Evergreen curriculum, it seems likely that the curriculum itself is much less reified, much more a product of ongoing participation, than that of most institutions. This, again, is both good news and bad news. The bad news we will discuss below, but the good news is that a curriculum consisting of coordinated studies programs is much more likely to generate and support a living community of practice. The ongoing negotiation of meanings that are never fully settled assures—to the degree that it can be assured—that the larger community of practice that students enter as novices will be, really, a learning community.

There is a danger, of course, in having too little reified as well as in having too much. Our goal in designing purposeful communities of practice should be to achieve a balance between reification and participation, to create communities that negotiate meanings, but negotiate the meanings that are most productive and important for educational purposes. Thus, while extracurricular activities are often valuable communities of practice, they are not enough to constitute a curriculum because they allow students to become so focused on one purpose or meaning that they may neglect other important meanings. The jazz ensemble or the math club may be a powerful community of practice, but we want college graduates to be more than specialists. The danger in a program that is so thoroughly negotiated on an ongoing basis as Evergreen's is that it can fail to reify some of the central processes or knowledge that should characterize a college education. One way of addressing this problem is to monitor the student experience for the appropriate balance. This is something Evergreen has done and continues to do, using, for example, the College Student Experience Questionnaire developed by Robert Pace at UCLA and the NSSE. The results support Evergreen's commitment to the coordinated studies model (Meld & Hunter, 1998).

Another approach to maintaining the balance of the curriculum is faculty development. Barbara Leigh Smith (personal communication, June 27, 2002), former provost and currently a faculty member at Evergreen, points out, "We do very extensive summer institutes. We run a little college for our faculty in the summer: ten to 25 institutes every summer to inform and consolidate team planning. And that's partly also because as we now are larger, with lots of turnover; you won't have a community of faculty if you don't keep rebuilding it all the time." Maintaining the correct balance requires ongoing attention, but that attention is the price of freeing professional educators from onerous regulation and standardization. According to Smith,

> It's partly about balance in your faculty, and it's also about trying to insure through the way they develop programs and the way they're assigned that the balance is there. Basically we don't have requirements, but we also highly constrain choice, so people can't eat only desert. We think that constrained choice that has a smart vision behind it is often a better way to go because then you don't have that motivational issue around requirements.

Evergreen seeks to maintain and renew the faculty community as a means of supporting and balancing the development of student communities. It is committed to involving students in the ongoing negotiation of the significant meanings that shape and direct their education. That commitment, it seems to me, lies at the core of the Evergreen design for learning.

WAGNER COLLEGE: DESIGNING COMMUNITIES FOR REFLECTIVE EXPERIENCE

Wagner College is a private liberal arts college in Staten Island, New York. It has pioneered an interesting and promising approach to building communities of practice in a way that puts special emphasis on the importance of practice. Wagner was a small campus in a state of malaise in 1996, when Richard Guarasci became provost. (In 2002, Wagner selected Guarasci as its next president.) A political scientist, Guarasci had previously served at St. Lawrence University and Hobart College, where he had been involved in the development of first-year programs with a special emphasis on service learning. Upon his arrival at Wagner, Guarasci led an effort to develop a curriculum that would combine community building with experiential programs. The result was the Wagner Plan for the Practical Liberal Arts. The first class to follow the Wagner Plan curriculum graduated in 2002.

The curriculum at Wagner is designed around three required learning communities: one in the first semester of the first year, a second—usually—in the second year, and a third in the senior year. The foundation of the Wagner Plan is the first-year learning community required of every entering freshman. The college offers a variety of learning communities in different disciplines, but all follow a common form. Each consists of two subject-matter courses linked together and team taught; a "reflective tutorial," in which small seminar groups (10 to 14) meet separately, facilitated by one of the instructors; and an experiential learning component. The reflective tutorial involves a lot of discussion and writing, and involves shared reflection on the experiential component: students are required to spend about 30 hours during the semester, roughly three hours each week, in fieldwork related to the theme of the course. The instructor for the reflective tutorial also becomes the student's academic advisor.

Julia Barchitta (personal communication, May 31, 2002) is dean of experiential learning at Wagner. Her office coordinates the scheduling of fieldwork at more than 60 off-campus sites: museums, hospitals, public-service agencies, schools, and businesses. Working with the faculty teams teaching a learning community, the experiential learning staff assists in designing field experiences that complement the goals of the program. Most students do their fieldwork in teams formed from their reflective tutorial groups.

One of the learning communities is "Living on Spaceship Earth." It combines Environmental Biology and Introduction to Literature. In one formulation of this learning community, fieldwork was focused on the Toms River, New Jersey, Superfund site, location of a chemical plant for many years. Students met with and interviewed residents—including cancer victims, officers and employees of the chemical company, and officials for the Environmental Protection Agency and local utility companies. They discussed and wrote about the case in their reflective tutorials and made a presentation of their findings to the Toms River community. In a learning community called "The Spanish Connection," combining intermediate Spanish and Introduction to Literature with a reflective tutorial, students interviewed Spanish-speaking immigrants to prepare for reflection and essays on the immigrant experience. A learning community formed from an education and a theater class worked with students at an elementary school to present a play. Various learning community groups did fieldwork supporting groups feeding and housing the homeless, tutoring adults in literacy programs and school children in after-school programs, doing research on developmental disabilities and mental retardation, and providing assistance and support to AIDS patients. Students have worked on political campaigns, in businesses, and on individually designed fieldwork.

As with service-learning programs, this kind of experiential fieldwork is neither as predictable nor as controllable as life in the isolated classroom; it is subject to the uncertainties that plague real life and that make it real. A course combining history and art history that deals with the immigrant experience and the Holocaust used Ellis Island as a fieldwork site for three years. But in the fall of 2001, Ellis Island was closed. As it happens, the World Trade Center was visible from the Wagner campus. "Our students," Barchitta says, "could watch the towers going down." In the aftermath of the disaster, Wagner's learning communities were among the many aspects of people's lives in the greater New York area that were immediately affected. "We did" Barchitta acknowledges, "have to change some of our plans." While students were unable to do fieldwork at Ellis Island, most of the material recovered from the disaster site was brought to Staten Island. Between 30 and 40 Wagner students did fieldwork serving food to rescue workers, moving supplies and equipment, and doing miscellaneous support tasks. A distinctive kind of fieldwork, not possible to plan for.

The second learning community comes in the sophomore or junior year, though most students do it in the sophomore year, and the college encourages that option. It consists of two linked classes, without the reflective tutorial. As with the first-year program, the degree and mode of integration between the two classes is largely left to the faculty members who are teaching the learning community.

The senior-year learning community consists of the capstone course in the student's major linked to a reflective tutorial and a minimum of 100 hours served in a field-based internship or significant research project. Students in the senior program have done internships or volunteer work at a variety of businesses, churches, television studios, social service agencies, newspapers, and hospitals. As with most successful internship programs, students periodically move into employment with the agencies where they worked on a volunteer basis. As of this writing, only one class has reached senior standing under the Wagner Plan, so the senior program remains somewhat more experimental than the first-year learning communities.

The Wagner Plan is distinctive in a number of ways. The most obvious, perhaps, is its linking of experiential work not just outside the classroom but outside the college as a component of the learning community. It recalls Etienne Wenger's (1998) critique of the conventional classroom, quoted earlier in this chapter: "If school practices become self-contained then they cease to point anywhere beyond themselves. School learning is just learning school" (p. 267). Certainly programs like service learning and undergraduate research do point beyond themselves. And such programs almost inevitably involve students in communities of practice. But the idea of linking the communities of practice, in the classroom, to active involvement in the world outside seems to me an especially powerful one. It has not only the power to change the way students engage with learning, but also the power to change the way students engage with schooling. It may also have the power to change the way society thinks about colleges and students. The experience of college begins by looking actively and explicitly beyond college, by negotiating the meaning of new knowledge from perspectives not bound by the walls of the classroom. All students, of course, have experience—in fact, most of their experience—outside the classroom. And in any good class discussion, one of the primary goals is to bring that outside experience into the classroom, to get students to renegotiate the reified meanings that the class presents to them. Their own experience is the yeast that causes the bubbling ferment of meaning that rises to the top in vivid and transformative dialogue. Yet to connect the experience of life with the reading of books and the study of school matter is not an easy task for most students. They come trained to compartmentalize. By making experiential fieldwork a part of the study, both an object and a method of study, we begin to break down the compartmental walls. By making it a shared study, by having a group of students bring their experience back to one another and reflect upon it as a group, we help to create the kind of community of practice that can broach the secrecy of deeply held meanings, that can hazard negotiating the unexamined proclivities of the unschooled mind.

A key forum for participation in this negotiation of meaning is, of course, the reflective tutorial. It is something like a combination of the book seminar in a coordinated studies program and the reflective seminar in a service-learning program. It is writing-intensive by design. (Writing-intensive tutors are integrated into the freshman learning communities to support students in the writing.) These tutorials provide what Hill identified as the central structural need: time and space for students to learn from each other. If the fieldwork can break up the reified assumptions of the classroom, the reflective tutorial can provide a space for negotiating revised meanings.

The Wagner Plan is still new. But like Evergreen's coordinated studies curriculum, it is a coherent design to address the need to create community throughout the college experience. Richard Guarasci ("Transforming Undergraduate Education," 2001), the architect of the plan, says that "this is a moment in which Wagner takes seriously the challenge for coherence and efficiency in redirecting teaching and learning toward measurable educational outcomes. For Wagner, that means placing reflective practice at the center of a practical liberal education."

PORTLAND STATE UNIVERSITY: SERVING STUDENTS BY SERVING THE URBAN COMMUNITY

It is one thing to create a comprehensive, connected program for supporting communities of practice in a small liberal arts college. To do so at a large urban university is something else again. But that is the project that Portland State University (PSU) in Oregon embarked upon in 1994. Portland State has an enrollment of around 17,000 students. Its main campus adjoins the central business district of Portland. It offers doctoral degrees in 32 fields and bachelors' in 55. It is, in other words, a big downtown research university.

In 1994 then-president Judith Ramaley appointed a faculty committee to examine the general education program, which was at the time much like most university general education programs. The committee "spent several months reviewing the literature on student learning, retention and graduation, on learning communities, and general education" (Association of American Colleges and Universities, 2001). The new model for general education was to be called University Studies.

University Studies is not a conventional lower-division general education program. Instead, it extends general education through the entire college experience. The goals or intended learning outcomes of the program fall under four headings: 1) inquiry and critical thinking, 2) communication, 3) the diversity of human experience, and 4) ethical issues and social responsibility. These are the goals of the entire University Studies program, freshman through senior levels.

The foundation of University Studies is Freshman Inquiry, "team-taught, interdisciplinary thematic courses supported by undergraduate student mentors" (Portland State University, 2000). Freshman Inquiry is described to students on the University Studies (2001) web page as follows:

> Freshman Inquiry consists of a year-long course developed by a team of faculty from different disciplines. Freshman Inquiry has a maximum class size of 40 students and each class is divided into three small-group, peer mentor sessions led by specially selected upper-division students. Class material is introduced and explored during the full class sessions and then assignments are developed and discussed in the peer mentor sessions.

These year-long learning communities include "The Power of Place," which "explores interaction between humans and the physical landscapes they inhabit, ranging from scientific understanding to changing representations of landscape in culture and society over time" (Portland State University, University Studies, 2001). In "The Columbia Basin: Watershed of the Great Northwest," "students will acquire an overview of the natural and human history of the Columbia River Basin, examine the ethical, political, and social issues surrounding human/environmental interaction in the region and make informed judgments about our stewardship of the region." "Entering the Cyborg Millenium [*sic*]: Transformations in Technology and Society" "explores the impact of Twentieth Century revolutions in information technology and genetics on our lives and on diverse cultures by looking at change in relationships, work, privacy, reproduction, and personal responsibility."

Freshman Inquiry leads to Sophomore Inquiry. Students select a Sophomore Inquiry course from a number that are offered. Each Sophomore Inquiry course is linked to a cluster of upper-division courses. Students will select three interdisciplinary courses from the cluster. Some of these Sophomore Inquiry courses "were developed as gateways to upper division clusters of courses to help guide students in their choice of majors" (Portland State University, 2000). Like the Freshman Inquiry courses, Sophomore Inquiry includes seminars conducted by mentors, but these mentors are graduate students. In Sophomore Inquiry, students develop a theme that they can pursue in the Upper Division Cluster. Students are encouraged to select their Sophomore Inquiry course with an eye to the Cluster of junior- and senior-level courses to which it is linked. Cluster areas range from Medieval history through American or African studies to family studies and technology.

The Sophomore Inquiry program, in addition to carrying through the pursuit of the University Studies goals initiated in Freshman Inquiry, addresses a major weakness in many university general education programs: how to deal with transfer students from other institutions. Carol Geary Schneider (personal communication, February 20, 2002), president of the AAC&U, characterizes the problem—and solution. Many institutions, she points out,

> invent these lovely, fancy first-year programs, and then nine out of ten students that they graduate . . . are transfer students who did not have that first-year program. Portland picked up that point when they were working on their program and designed it so that significant pieces of it would occur in the junior and senior year and that there would be an alternative to Freshman Inquiry for students transferring in the sophomore year. So in a sense there are various doorways in. But the general design of it is that there's an elaborate first-year program, then in the sophomore year you would take Sophomore Inquiry if you missed Freshman Inquiry.

Transfer students may be required to take a one-term Transfer Transition course depending on their number of transfer credits. Transfer students are also are required to take one, two, or three Sophomore Inquiry courses, depending on how many units they have accumulated when they transfer. All transfer students are required to take at least one Sophomore Inquiry course and its associated cluster.

University Studies culminates in the Senior Capstone. This is an interdisciplinary course in which students work in teams on community-based projects, under the direction of a faculty mentor. Capstone projects are generally carried out with one of the university's many "community partners." For example, one capstone team conducted an oral history project on the Gifford Pinchot National Forest, interviewing men who had worked in the Civilian Conservation Corps and the Forest Service before the Second World War. They posted a number of the interview transcripts on the Internet. Another studied the ecosystem and human communities surrounding Johnson Creek, which flows from the foothills of the Cascade Mountains through Southeast Portland. The community partners for the project were the Portland Parks and Recreation Agency and the Portland Police Bureau. Capstone courses have dealt with cancer diagnosis and treatment, cultural issues in the workplace, grant writing, family court, and learning disabilities. Community partners include schools, public agencies, social service groups, and businesses (Portland State University, 2001).

The Senior Capstone creates communities of practice for students, communities that extend beyond the classroom and engage the larger community. This particular mode of learning community came about in part because Portland State sees its mission as an urban university as intimately linked to the local community:

> The idea of Senior Capstones arose out of the university's mission to make connections with the community in which it lives, and the general education program's mission to engage a student's sense of civic responsibility. It allows for the university and the community to interact on projects that are beneficial to each. Often times, capstone classes are providing service to organizations that they normally would not have the resources to accomplish on their own. At the same time, the students get to see the direct application of what they are learning in the classroom. (Portland State University, 2002)

As of 2000, 86% of Portland State's undergraduates were completing their general education through the University Studies program. (Honors students follow a different track.) It serves not only students who come to this large state university as freshmen; transfer students from other universities and community colleges are integrated into the program when they arrive.

In addition to its comprehensive reach, University Studies has some distinctive characteristics worth noting. Incoming first-year students are immersed in a substantial and extended community of practice—a year-long program by design. In the first year and second year, students are involved in seminar groups that are mentored, not by faculty members, but by advanced students. In addition to its obvious financial advantages, peer mentoring is a powerful tool for integrating students into communities of practice. Environments where advanced students model the negotiation of meaning for novice students introduce an element of legitimate peripheral participation into the classroom setting that is difficult to achieve otherwise. That is to say, the fact that new students can see their more advanced peers at work in the academic setting encourages the apprentice learner to emulate that work, but without the pressure of judgment implied by the presence of the master faculty member. This is what happens on athletic teams, in the band, on the newspaper, and in much collaborative research: Newcomers observe and interact with their more experienced peers as well as with the experts. Thus they see the work at hand done by those not too many years removed from their own level of practice. And they have access to a gradation of peers, peers who are fundamentally like themselves, but with different levels of experience. This range of peer experience encourages legitimate peripheral participation because it highlights the legitimacy of the novices as genuine participants. Peer mentoring is a powerful mechanism for building purposeful communities of practice. Portland State has made it a permanent feature of its general education pedagogy.

Another interesting feature of University Studies is that it varies the mode and intensity of collaborative work. At the beginning, students are fully involved in an extended community of practice. At the next stage, they are involved in a seminar group similar to the one they have already participated in, but without so large a supporting community. The Sophomore Inquiry course, recall, is freestanding, not linked directly to subject-matter courses taken at the same time. But this freestanding sophomore course points forward to the cluster in the junior year. These courses are linked differently than those in the Freshman Inquiry course. They are not linked together by the teacher; they are linked by the student, by the student's interests and chosen theme of exploration. Then in the Senior Capstone, the student is again explicitly a member of a team, but a different kind of team. The community is less tightly drawn than in the Freshman Inquiry course, but it is more participatory; it reaches out to the surrounding community and joins up with others, explicitly leaves the classroom and goes into the world.

I do not know if the system was intentionally designed for the purpose, but this variation in the level and nature of involvement can be of value. In the first year, students need comprehensive and explicit community support: total immersion in a community of practice focused on meaningful academic goals. Only such a community, I suspect, can give students the support and resources they need to adopt a deep approach to learning. Freshman Inquiry potentially provides that needed support. Sophomore Inquiry also provides a stable community of practice, but the focus shifts to preparing students for individual choices; they should use Sophomore Inquiry to bring their personal intrinsic goals to the surface and to let those goals manifest themselves in the selection of the cluster. Then, as seniors, again as members of a community of practice, they participate in a larger community, but as more mature and independent carriers of meaning—negotiating the reified meanings not just of the course community or even the university community but of the larger and sometimes looser communities, some of which will not be communities of practice at all but opportunistic groupings created by chance and need. The design of University Studies seems to me an interesting and worthwhile experiment in sequencing collaboration in varied communities of practice in a developmental pattern through the student's life at the university.

PROCESS FRONTIER: COMMUNITY

A hot cognitive economy requires that students participate in purposeful communities of practice linked to their academic work. Many students find such communities already through extracurricular activities. And collaborative pedagogies such as service learning, undergraduate research, and problem-based learning tend to create communities of practice. But the barriers that keep academic communities of practice small and weak in the Instruction Paradigm college are the walls of the classroom. I mean, of course, the physical walls that separate students and teachers from one another in their separate rooms, but also those other walls: the walls in time that calendars and schedules build; the organizational walls that separate disciplines and departments from one another; and the walls of perception that rise between two students sitting next to each other, eyes fixed on the lecturer, cut off from the minds of their peripheral peers. To build purposeful communities of practice in academic programs, we need to take down these walls.

We have seen several examples of how this can be done. Learning communities are a growth business in higher education today. The Washington Center for the Improvement of Undergraduate was founded in 1985 at The Evergreen State College to promote the wider use of learning communities and support other institutions in adopting them. The Washington Center is the home of the National Learning Communities Project, funded by the Pew Charitable Trusts. The project has compiled a directory of over 100 colleges and universities that have ongoing learning communities.

As we have seen, colleges have a broad range of options in constructing communities of practice for students. It seems to me that almost all of those options are inherently superior to the one-teacher/one-class form that overwhelmingly dominates higher education. This is not to say that learning communities cannot be done badly. Rather, all other things being equal, courses that bring students together in purposeful communities are likely to add more educational value than those that do not. And, as we have also seen, learning communities facilitate and are facilitated by programs that emphasize the other characteristics of a hot cognitive economy: intrinsic goals, student performance, feedback, and a long time horizon.

Learning communities will work best when they best facilitate legitimate peripheral participation, when they give students more freedom to negotiate the ongoing rules and processes, when they maintain a balance between participation and reification in the process of negotiating meanings, and when they allow students to move developmentally toward more mature participation. But at base, learning communities are a wonderful design for learning when they serve the fundamental function that Patrick Hill characterized so well: They give students time and space to learn from each other.

16

A Learning Paradigm College Aligns All of Its Activities Around the Mission of Producing Student Learning

INTEGRITY: HONESTY, WHOLENESS, SOUNDNESS

On September 2, 1994, most of the faculty of Olivet College met at the home of their president, Michael Bassis, for the Labor Day barbecue. Since his arrival a year and a half earlier, Bassis had guided the faculty through the process of developing a new vision of Education for Personal and Social Responsibility. A faculty group had formed teams that had traveled to several other colleges to study innovative practices that seemed relevant to that vision. The first day of the faculty forum that ended with the barbecue had been designed to sort out and select some approaches to put flesh on the bones of the Olivet vision. The day had gone badly. After hours of sometimes impassioned debate, the faculty had split in several different directions and seemed no closer to a meaningful consensus than ever. An air of failure hung over the group. As one participant commented, "People were milling around the yard . . . and everyone was very sullen-faced. It was just a depressing atmosphere . . . very depressing" (McLendon, n.d.). The next session of the faculty forum was scheduled to begin the following morning.

After dinner, Bassis called together the leaders of the faculty work groups and a few other faculty leaders, along with the vice president, and asked them to remain behind after the others left. He ushered the group into his study. According to one participant, he "basically . . . locked the doors, and said 'No one's getting out. Nobody's going home until this thing is done. We have come too far for this to fall apart. We're going to stay here until we reach some agreement.'" Taped to the walls of the study were the poster-sized pages describing the alternative models of college education that they had discussed all day. While some present expressed surprise at being, in effect, detained, they overcame their astonishment and settled into the task. They argued the virtues of the alternative approaches for three more hours, with the leaders of the different faculty working groups tending to support the plans they had proposed and to criticize the others, selecting and advocating the ideas on one or the other of the posted sheets of paper. Bassis said little. But after the deadlock had persisted for some time, he stood up. He took a pen and approached the sheets posted on the wall and began to circle the ideas on each sheet that had received the most favorable faculty response, as indicated by gold stars pasted next to them. According to one of the participants:

> [He] then said, "Why can't we do all of these things simultaneously? Why can't we have a first-year experience *and* a senior experience *and* learning communities *and* service learning? It seems to me that this would give us a very powerful and truly unique curriculum that could drive the whole thing forward." . . . And [we] looked at it, all the items that were circled, and [our] mouths dropped open.

Thus began what became the Olivet Plan, a comprehensive reorganization of the college and its curriculum that did and does include learning communities, and a first-year seminar, a portfolio developed through the entire college program that culminates in a capstone senior experience, and more. Indeed, the Olivet Plan, and today's Olivet College curriculum, contains much more than the items that were circled on those sheets taped to the walls in Michael Bassis's study the night of the Labor Day barbecue. The plan grew in the planning. The whole became more than the sum of the parts, and hence the parts became different through their membership in the whole. But the key step, the transformative moment, was to see in a particular list of parts the potential for a new whole. And once it was seen, once the outline of something integral and meaningful began to come together, well, everything began to come together. Here a community of practice that had been vigorously negotiating the meaning of their own institution saw the meaning of all that they had done become new before their eyes, reified in an integral framework that as yet existed only in their shared understanding. One participant described that moment as magical.

I have no doubt that it was. To find the integrity hidden in the fragments is to be inspired, and empowered.

For many who work in colleges and universities, a vision of the whole is so distant from our daily experience that the very idea seems magical, in the sense of impossible, beyond and outside the world we live in. But to see it, to watch the haze clear and the parts form themselves into an image of integrity and purpose, would leave us transfixed, spellbound. The power of the epiphany comes from the sudden and utterly persuasive vision of many become one.

What has happened at Olivet, and several of the other colleges we have discussed in the preceding chapters, is indeed magical—wonderful—but hardly impossible. Indeed, contrasted with the task of carrying the burdens of incoherence and waste that drag us down daily, it is not even difficult. What it requires is a certain kind of vision, held in common: a vision of an undergraduate college as a whole, as a coherent community acting from a consistent and unifying purpose. A vision of integrity.

The *Random House Dictionary* offers three definitions, very closely related, for the word "integrity": "1) adherence to moral and ethical principles; soundness of moral character; honesty; 2) the state of being whole, entire, or undiminished; and 3) a sound, unimpaired, or perfect condition. . . ." Honesty, wholeness, soundness.

Perhaps the most fundamental critique we can make of the Instruction Paradigm college is that it lacks integrity, in all three senses. It is not a whole; in many cases it is hardly even a sum. It is a basket of parts, often disconnected parts. The life sciences instructor does not know what the sociology instructor is doing, and neither knows what the counselors are telling their students. Faculty members, isolated in the solitary cells of their classrooms, learn only through hearsay and complaint what their students experience in the rest of their academic lives.

Because it is not a whole, the college lacks soundness. If the Instruction Paradigm college is a knowledge factory, it is not a very efficient or effective one. It is not a well-oiled machine, but a creaking assemblage of unsynchronized units, as likely to be working against as with each other, a Rube Goldberg contraption that produces a good deal more heat than light.

And, as an institution, the Instruction Paradigm college is not honest. I certainly do not mean to suggest that the people who work in the institution do not do their best to tell the truth. In my experience, most of them try to be honest, some making heroic efforts to do so. It is the institution itself, in its very design, that imports falsehood into its practices. College presidents and college teachers usually say what they believe. But the espoused theories of educational leaders, as we discovered in Chapter 2, are misaligned with the theory-in-use that controls institutional behavior. The result is that the college gives the lie to its leaders. Practice contradicts precept at every turn. Students learn that the unwritten rules are the ones that determine your future and learn to cast a jaundiced eye on the noble espousals of their well-intentioned professors and deans.

Many institutions—we have seen several examples in the preceding chapters—have initiated new programs and innovative strategies that hold real potential to change the cognitive economy for students. In each of the cases that we have examined, the changes illustrate and advance a principle that will make the learning environment more friendly to deep learning, more supporting of incremental self-theories and mindful reflection on the learning experience. In other words, they tend to create a hot cognitive economy. But some institutions have gone farther than others in aligning institutional policies. The Bailey Scholars Program at Michigan State and the Gemstone Program at the University of Maryland are both well-integrated programs; each has considerable integrity on its own terms. And each is at odds with the larger system on the large campus where it resides. At Inver Hills Community College, the Liberal Studies/Professional Skills Program expands along with professional development initiatives that are almost certainly changing the cognitive economy, but only intermittently for many students. Many fundamental structures still remain locked in inflexible Instruction Paradigm frameworks. Valencia Community College has articulated a vivid and inspiring vision, which it has made substantial first steps toward achieving in terms of advisement and support, while the future of the curriculum remains obscure.

Some institutions have advanced far toward achieving systemic integrity. CSU, Monterey Bay's University Learning Requirements have shaped the curriculum there and freed the faculty from many of the constraints that inhibit change in the cognitive economy. The university now will test the effects of growing enrollment on a coherent framework for learning. At Wagner College, and longer at King's College, a comprehensive overhaul of the curriculum seeks to align the entire system in one direction.

The University of Michigan in many ways offers an especially interesting example of the challenge of alignment. The UROP program and service learning can claim extraordinary success in changing the cognitive economy for many students. Yet Michigan is a large research university, and so the barriers to creating communities of practice and requiring connected performances across the curriculum are substantial. We heard the testimony of a Michigan graduate in the first chapter who found little coherence in the curriculum: "They don't add up to anything. It's just a bunch of courses. It doesn't mean a thing" (Willimon & Naylor, 1995, p. 58). But many at the university seem to be aware of the problem and are consciously grappling with it. The President's Commission on the Undergraduate Experience (2001) at Michigan characterizes the challenge with both candor and clarity:

> Our concern is not simply with the anonymous classroom or the routinized instructor. Rather it is with the larger tendency of the undergraduate experience at the University of Michigan to become fragmented into disconnected pursuits, discrete subcultures, and generational enclaves. The proposals in this report are designed to undo that regime of separations, to braid together the academic, social, and residential strands of the undergraduate experience. Doing so means making the campus and the faculty role more permeable, creating new linkages between disciplines, teaching and research, academics and student life, between the university and the "outside world." (p. 24)

Characterizing the challenge of alignment isn't the same thing as meeting the challenge, but it is probably a useful first step. Indeed the beginning of systemic integrity is probably to explicitly address and acknowledge the misalignment of existing structures. Honesty comes before wholeness and soundness, because until we honestly acknowledge the atomization of our structures and the misalignment of our functions, we can hardly address them. And again, when I speak of honesty, I mean primarily being honest with ourselves, learning to see what is really there, so we can describe accurately the reality before us. If we can see our institutions through the lens of the Learning Paradigm, we can describe them as they are.

The problem with seeing the nature of our policies clearly and whole is that the essential reality of our educational programs is hidden, obscured under layers of debris, the detritus of Instruction Paradigm processes that are largely circular and uninformative. Almost any college administrator can give you enrollment figures with considerable confidence: how many students, headcount or FTES, how many in various programs and in each class. Almost no college administrator can give you any information about how those programs affect students. We know a lot about the enrollment economy of the college, almost nothing about the cognitive economy.

Most of the information gathered at Instruction Paradigm colleges is collected in order to feed the never-ending, self-referential processes that support the enrollment machine. The operations of most curriculum committees are a vivid example. Josina Makau (personal communication, July 20, 2002)—a founding faculty member at CSU, Monterey Bay—describes her experience at a major research university where she taught earlier in her career in this way:

> Faculty seeking to develop new courses were expected to wait up to two years before their proposals would be considered. The review process itself—mired in detail—often focussed primarily on issues of disciplinary turf, rather than issues of education. Notably, no mechanism was offered to insure alignment of the syllabus to what actually happened in class.

A colleague of mine who served on a community college curriculum committee actually had the temerity to raise the question: "But how do we know whether students are actually learning what's prescribed in the syllabus?" The curriculum chair set him straight: "That's not our job." And, of course, it isn't anybody's job. Which is why it doesn't get done.

To be honest with ourselves, we need not create a massive apparatus for measuring what we now ignore; we must simply recognize that we are ignoring it. If we can disenthrall ourselves from the trivia of the knowledge factory, then we can begin to move toward a vision of the whole. We begin by asking the right questions, then keep asking and answering them, and things will come together.

Most new colleges have years to plan their initial offerings and to hire staff and organize their operations. But it was different for CSU, Monterey Bay. When the Fort Ord military base was closed, the site came available to the state of California for a new state university. But the decision needed to be made and acted on very quickly. Makau was one of the 12 founding faculty members who came together in January 1995. She recalls:

We were placed in what could have been construed—and by many was construed—as a highly untenable position: that in eight months, by that August, we would start a university at all four levels, with as yet undefined majors, and an as yet undeveloped general education program.

While the originating staff did not have the luxury of time, it did have something more important: they were asked the right questions.

The very first day that the founding faculty got together, the very first thing we were told was, "Just answer the question: What if the purpose of the university were learning?" And everything we did was in response to that question. . . .

Our first month we were told: "Don't think about constraints. Think only about what it would mean to create a leaning-centered university. What would you do? What kind of majors would you have? What kind of general education would you have?"

These are the questions that generate a vision of the whole, that make the integral possible.

Of course—as is clear from the examples of Olivet; CSU, Monterey Bay; Alverno; Evergreen; and several others—just having a vision of the whole is not the same as achieving it. Much hard work intervenes. But it is the vision of the whole, the framework that gives meaning to all of its constituent elements, that makes it possible to do the work well. This is not to imply that the vision is rigid and unchangeable. Quite to the contrary, it will probably be in a constant state of development. When we begin with the parts and screw or glue them together to make a machine that we hope will run, the best that we can hope for is that the mechanism will move in the prescribed ways and no parts will fall off. Perhaps, when we seek a vision of the whole, when we envision our hoped-for integrity, we should think of our work not as a machine but as an organism, a living thing. And living things grow; they actualize the design implicit in their origin, sometimes in surprising ways.

If we think of the institution as an organic unity rather than an extravagantly complex widget, we come to see that integrity does not imply rigidity or inflexibility. It is precisely the integral wholeness of the organism that gives it the wherewithal to grow, to develop into more and better.

In fact, soundness—that third leg of integrity—in the organic world implies growth and development. This should not surprise us. Growth and development are supposed to be our stock in trade at colleges. But if we see our colleges, the institutions themselves, through the Instruction Paradigm lens, what we expect is growth without development. We expect our colleges to get bigger, to grow in size. We do not expect them to get better. We expect them to grow out without growing up. We are inured to the rhetoric of development when it is applied to our students; we hear it all the time. But that our colleges themselves might get smarter as well as bigger, that seems a stretch.

In the end, if we want to understand what integrity means for colleges, we had best set all of the analogies aside and see a college for what it literally is: a community of people. Integrity, in all three of its meanings, is a quality that we find only in persons and communities of people. A college is a community of practice seeking to negotiate the meaning of itself. To purposefully negotiate that meaning, the members of the community must participate—this is where the honesty comes in. We must be willing to speak the truth to one another, and to mutually recognize one another as bearers of meaning. We must test our ideas and beliefs together rather than withdrawing into the secret solace of isolated expertise and atomized opinion. Through this negotiation we come to reify shared meanings and especially the central meanings that become the touchstone and standard for future negotiations—this is where we shape a vision of the whole. And as we continue to negotiate those meanings, we revise and correct our vision, test it in practice, and negotiate the solutions to the problems our vision has created. (A vision that doesn't create problems is not worth having.) Achieving and maintaining the soundness of our work, revising the vision to keep it healthy, changing and adapting to circumstances, is part of integrity, too. Some readers may be thinking here, "Well, this sounds all well and good. But it doesn't sound anything like the place where I work." Precisely.

It is a rough outline of what happens at colleges, or even within programs in colleges, that are transforming themselves in a way that moves them toward institutional integrity. It is an iterative process, involving much back-and-forth. Once you have a vision of the whole, you must continuously be willing to revise it, to renegotiate it. Indeed, the real work of alignment is this ongoing renegotiation that aims at achieving a sound, a healthy embodiment of the vision. We can see this vividly in the ongoing work of colleges that have been negotiating a coherent vision for many years. At Alverno and Evergreen, both of which have been moving toward a transformative vision for over 30 years, we see that the central vision of the whole survives, but maintaining the soundness of the institution as a healthy embodiment of that vision requires constant conversation and on-going adjustment. At Portland State, the Curriculum Committee (that's right, the Curriculum Committee!) requested a progress report on the effectiveness of the University Studies program. That report, *Progress Report: University Studies* ((Portland State University, 2000), entails a thorough analysis of the program and an assessment of its effectiveness based on many kinds of evidence and specific recommendations for how the institution should continue to study the effects of the program on students and how it might experiment with modifications. In the spring of 2002 Olivet College modified its portfolio program to put more emphasis on fieldwork, especially in the major. Integrity, in other words, entails that we continuously maintain the vision by changing practices, by adjusting the work on the periphery so that it makes a good fit with the core.

Of course, this general outline of organizational integrity could apply to almost any organization, from a bowling league to a clothing store to a fire department. But a college, certainly a Learning Paradigm college, has a distinctive object. If a college exists to produce student learning, then the conversation of the college as it seeks to become integral and aligned must be about students. The vision of the whole must be a vision of and for students. And it must begin with a recognition of their integrity, as persons. Indeed, the vision of the whole purpose of a college needs to be a vision about the whole learning experience of students.

Honesty, wholeness, soundness. That is what makes up institutional integrity. It is not a static state; it is an ongoing process. You are not honest because you told the truth once; you are honest because you keep speaking the truth. Because maintaining the soundness of any system in a changing world requires constant maintenance and adjustment, integrity means an ongoing willingness to change. But integrity is more than efficiency; the soundness it calls for is soundness for a coherent and consistent purpose, movement toward a vision of the whole. That vision is what we move toward, and what we come from. A vision of the whole assures a long time horizon for a community because no such vision will ever be fully realized. But the vision, if we can see its outlines in our daily work and lives, is also a place we can always return to. We go to it to come back to it. It is the place where we live; it is the place where we are going. We are always where we belong, and we are always going there. Always journeying. Always coming home.

THE AFFORDANCES OF THE LEARNING ENVIRONMENT: A TEST OF ALIGNMENT

Technologists and designers speak of the "affordances" of an object. Donald Norman (1993), founding chair of the Department of Cognitive Science at the University of California, San Diego, who has subsequently worked on technology design for Apple Computer and Hewlett-Packard, puts it this way: "The 'affordances' of an object refers to its possible functions: A chair affords support, whether for standing, sitting, or the placement of objects. A pencil affords lifting, grasping, turning, poking, supporting, tapping, and of course, writing" (p. 106). Norman points out that the affordances that matter are those that users perceive easily, not those that are perhaps powerful, but hidden: "We tend to use objects in ways suggested by the most salient perceived affordances, not in ways that are difficult to discover..." (p. 107).

Organizational structures also have affordances. When an institution adopts certain tools and processes, settles on a set of objects that it will use, it affords certain kinds of participation. The architecture and the furniture, the textbooks and the syllabus, the calendar and the curriculum all afford certain kinds of learning experiences and impede others. In large measure, what I have attempted to describe in the last five chapters are the organizational practices that afford a deep orientation to learning rather than a surface orientation. To achieve alignment, we need to look at everything about the learning environment in terms of how it affects these five principles, and how they combine to affect the overall learning experience of the student.

To change the cognitive economy of the college we must change the affordances of the organization. Norman (1992) presents a photograph taken in the cafeteria of the University of California, San Diego (p. 24) that illustrates the power of affordances. It shows an ice cream freezer, a rectangular box sitting on the floor. The whole top of the freezer consists of two flat glass doors that open from the top. It stands by itself near a wall. The right-hand glass door has been cracked all the way across and has a piece of glass missing; the cracks are covered with wide tape. Just below the taped cracks is a printed sign that reads "PLEASE DO NOT PUT YOUR TRAY HERE!" Alas, too late. The design of the freezer affords only one place where the diner seeking dessert can put down a tray in order to open the freezer with one hand and pluck forth ice cream with the other: the glass top. But the glass top was not designed to hold weight. Hence the sign, explicitly contradicting the clear affordance of the device, saying in effect, "Don't do the obvious! Refrain from taking the logical step! Before you do the only thing that makes sense, stop!" Instruction Paradigm colleges are like that freezer. They have signs all over telling students to study hard and long, not to cram, to think in the long term, to seek feedback, to form communities, to connect. Students don't pay attention to the signs. They pay attention to the design. They follow the affordances of the organization, not the advice.

What, for example, are the perceived affordances of the conventional classroom? I mean the room itself. The chief affordance of a lecture hall is—no surprise here—lecturing. A raised platform before a black or white board defines itself as the front of the room. All the chairs face this focal point, probably tiered in rows to allow everyone to see the focal point. The chairs are usually bolted to the floor and immobile. A lecture hall affords sitting among a mass and listening. The overwhelming message sent by the room to the entering student is "sit down and watch what happens at the front of the room." It affords observation, spectatorship, but not participation. It can be used for other things, of course. But to so use it is to resist the perceived affordances.

At a deeper level, one of the fundamental affordances that physical objects suggest is their availability to manipulation. When you enter the room, do you have the sense that you can move the furniture? How would the student react upon entering a classroom with no chairs? That would afford confusion leading to some kind of decision and active participation: sit on the floor, stand, or go looking for a chair. As multiple students entered the room, the absence of furniture would almost certainly lead to communication, and more than that, problem solving communication. It is inconceivable that the presence of chairs, conventionally arranged, could lead to communication. Students would come in and sit down quietly, unlikely to speak to anyone they didn't already know. But the absence of chairs would lead to: "What's this?" "Hey, where are the chairs?" "Are we supposed to sit on the floor?" I do not necessarily recommend the experiment, the logistics of which would be cumbersome at most institutions. And the location of furniture, taken apart from the whole context, is a trivial matter. (Of course, anything taken apart from the whole context is a trivial matter.) The question I am suggesting with this example is an important one, however. Do the objects students encounter in the environment they enter afford participation, or do they afford passive observation?

Contrast the conventional lecture hall with the Bailey Common of the Bailey Scholars Program at Michigan State University, which we discussed in Chapter 11. The common is a large room with modular furniture, easily maneuvered. Often the tables are arranged in a rectangle, but they can be broken apart and configured differently. Strung around the top of the room, like an enormous ticker tape above the windows and just below the ceiling, is the Declaration of Bailey: "The Bailey Scholars Program seeks to be a community of scholars dedicated to lifelong learning. All members of the community work toward providing a respectful, trusting environment where we acknowledge our interdependence and encourage personal growth" (*Bailey Scholars,* 2001). The objects reified in the Bailey community of practice afford very different modes of participation than those of the conventional lecture hall.

The same principle applies to the tools students use—like textbooks, computers, and software—and to the rules that govern their behavior. These rules produce all the artifacts of the Instruction Paradigm college, all of which should be reexamined: the three-unit class, the dominant format of one teacher-one class, final exams, study sheets, and review sessions. It seems to me beyond debate that the most powerful learning environments for promoting a deep orientation to learning will not be three-unit classes—perhaps especially three-unit classes taught by brilliant and entertaining lecturers, who largely preempt the negotiation of meaning.

We have seen many examples of institutions that have changed the affordances of their institutional structures. When Valencia puts the assessments it uses to guide students through LifeMap on the Internet, it affords access to the system for students who can't make it in to campus easily or who are embarrassed to take such an assessment in a public place. When the Gemstone Program allows a full semester for students to select teams and topics, it affords reflection on goal setting and collaboration. When Evergreen offers year-long coordinated studies programs, it affords thinking in the long term and valuing collaborative communities. In each case we have discussed, changes in organizational structures afford changes in the modes of student engagement.

The problem of alignment consists of shaping the affordances of all organizational structures and policies in light of an integral vision of the whole, so that they consistently encourage a deep orientation to learning. Consider the case of problem-based learning (PBL), certainly one of the most promising of pedagogies we have discussed. It was first developed in medical schools, where there is a kind of inherent connection among the parts of the curriculum. The human body is interdisciplinary. When PBL was translated to the undergraduate context, a number of problems arose. One of those is that the design of the conventional three-credit class— meeting three hours per week—does not afford thorough and extensive exploration of a problem. It is limiting. It fragments student attention rather than focusing it. It denies students the time and space to engage in shared reflection. In other words, the affordances of the class conflict with the affordances of the pedagogy. Posing students a problem to resolve collaboratively affords a certain kind of student behavior; asking them to do the work from 9:00 a.m. to 9:50 a.m. on MWF affords quite another kind of behavior.

Two of the institutions we discussed in previous chapters have joined with a third to seek funding to explore the potential of combining two powerful pedagogical techniques. The Evergreen State College pioneered learning communities, and the University of Delaware and Stamford University have developed an extensive program of problem-based learning. The three institutions would like to investigate how learning communities work with PBL. The environment of collaboration, rich feedback, and time to explore that learning communities offer should help student to meet the demands of PBL. In other words, the affordances of these two designs complement one another. Barbara Leigh Smith of Evergreen puts it this way:

> We think that it's a marriage waiting to happen because the undergraduate schools that have implemented PBL have found that the three-credit course is a big issue. It not only limits the problems, the depth and scope and interdisiplinarity of the problems, you have a real culture problem, because the students are getting just a little snippet of it embedded in a whole set of courses that are completely different. It's like incompatible cultures.

Every college should examine the affordances of its system for consistency and alignment around its learning objectives. By doing so, they can change the cognitive economy for all students.

THE CHALLENGE TO ALIGNMENT IN THE LARGER SYSTEM

One of the challenges institutions face in trying to achieve organizational integrity around a mission of producing student learning is that no college or university exists in isolation. Most college students today complete their college education somewhere other than where they started it. One of the purposes and rationales of the standardized formal processes of the Instruction Paradigm is that they facilitate transfer between institutions. Transfer, in many ways, is a good thing. The possibility of transferring from one college to another increases access to higher education in a highly mobile society. But there is a price to pay for the formal, standardized structures that facilitate transfer: They reify form and ignore substance; they facilitate credentialing at the price of educational value.

The one structure of the Instruction Paradigm that is perhaps more influential than any other, especially in terms of efforts to create institutional alignment, is the student credit hour. The student credit hour first came into use at the end of the 19th century in an effort to provide some standard measure of the high school experience. It was only after the Second World War, however, that the credit hour came to be used for budgeting, accreditation, and regulation. In the 1970s, the federal government began to use the credit hour as a device to measure and account for financial aid and has increasingly relied upon it since. The rapid growth of transfer in the post-war period also increased reliance on the credit hour as a common metric that different colleges could use to translate courses into a standardized code (Wellman & Ehrlich, 2001). Indeed, we can fairly say that the increased use of the credit hour as a metric of educational accomplishment has been one of the main indices of the growth and pervasiveness of the Instruction Paradigm. Peter Ewell (n.d.), senior associate at the National Center for Higher Education Management Systems (NCHEMS)—and one of the most acute observers of the state of higher education—characterizes the role of the credit hour today:

> For better or worse, the student credit hour... has become
> ubiquitous as a unit of measure in American higher education.

At this point, the credit hour is used for purposes as divergent as allocating costs, accounting learning gain, assigning workload and assuring quality.

But, of course, the student credit hour is not a measure of learning; it is a measure of instruction. Actually, it is not even that. It is a measure of classroom time. The use of the credit hour as a measure of faculty workload, for example, has no foundation in research or logic. The credit hour has become the standard not because it means anything about educational value, but because it allows for the easy translation of instructional information within and between institutions. As Robert Shoenberg (2001), senior fellow at the AAC&U, notes, the credit hour has become "the standard unit of academic currency" (p. 2). The result has been to devalue measures of real value: "the convenience of the credit hour as common currency has driven out the better but far less fungible currency of intellectual purpose and curricular coherence." Most institutions have made compacts with other institutions to recognize credit hours as evidence of educational attainment. However, as Shoenberg points out,

> None of these transfer agreements addresses in any meaningful way the purposes of the general education curriculum, much less the purposes of a baccalaureate degree. Uniformly they assume a general education program consisting of a loose distribution requirement plus competence in writing, mathematics, and increasingly, computer use. They give some definition of the content of courses that meet the requirements, but they offer few details as to the goals to be reached through study of that content. As far as these transfer agreements are concerned, all social science or science or humanities courses are created equal. Never mind that the introductory political science course at one institution addresses a different set of purposes than the introductory course at another—they are identical in the eyes of the transfer agreement. Never mind that some schools offer a rigorous and integrated general education program while others do not. Any collection of courses from whatever source, no matter how lacking in coherence, must be accepted for transfer if they are in the same subject matter domain. (p. 3)

Because the credit hour is a measure only of time spent in a classroom, and because the information that the Instruction Paradigm values and preserves is largely self-referential, there is no agreed-upon standard of the meaning or significance of a credit hour. Indeed, it is used quite differently in different institutions and even within the same institution.

Jane Wellman, senior associate at the Institute for Higher Education Policy (IHEP), and Thomas Ehrlich, senior scholar at the Carnegie Foundation for the Advancement of Teaching (2001), are directing a study of the student credit hour for the IHEP. As I write, their work is in progress. But they have reached some interesting, if tentative, conclusions. One of their first discoveries was that the credit hour is not easy to pin down:

> The research into the uses and definitions for the [credit hour] has been akin to the inquiry of the myth of the blind men and the elephant: Each audience understands the measure to mean something slightly different, and the different audiences do not talk to one another. Like the laws in the Red Queen's croquet court, the [credit hour] is often mandated but not defined. (p. 12)

This is what we should expect. Because the credit hour is an Instruction Paradigm form without educational substance, it can easily be used in the self-referential exercises that sustain the operations of the knowledge factory. But because the form has become independent of any educationally significant referent, it is nearly impossible to define it functionally. We would expect, then, that the credit hour would be a major barrier to institutional innovation and would impair the ability of institutions to make changes rooted in the needs of students and the nature of the cognitive economy rather than the credit economy. That, in fact, was the core hypothesis that Wellman and Ehrlich attempted to support. But in a review of many innovative colleges (which included several of those we have discussed in the previous chapters), they were unable to confirm that hypothesis. They found:

> [I]nstitutions that are committed to campus-wide innovations in teaching and learning are able to work around the measure. In reflecting on why this seems to be true, we concluded that those involved in leading innovative institutions had a clear idea of what they wanted to do and how they wanted to do it.

They developed visions of the learning modes they sought to encourage, visions that had relative institutional cohesion and coherence. They faced numerous and troublesome hurdles in developing their programs because of the accounting metrics associated with the [credit hour], and some still face major problems. But they did not allow a particular metric of student and faculty workload to interfere with their broader visions for their institutions. (p. 13)

In other words, institutions that have a functional vision of the whole, that know what they want to achieve in terms of learning, can manipulate the façade of Instruction Paradigm requirements while doing real and important work. Institutional integrity gives institutions power over the formal barriers to alignment for learning.

Institutions still face the challenge of gaining recognition by conventional standards for programs that rise above the conventional. As we have seen in the case of Madison Area Technical College, when a two-year college actually begins to assess outcomes in a way that provides more substantive and important evidence of student learning than grades associated with credit hours, universities tend to ignore the substance and demand the hollow form. But that can change.

THE POTENTIAL FOR SYSTEMIC ALIGNMENT

There are signs on the horizon that not only individual colleges but higher education systems are recognizing the hollowness of Instruction Paradigm forms and seeking alignment on more substantive grounds.

We have already seen an example of how one university is addressing the transfer problem in Portland State's Sophomore Inquiry program and the accompanying Transfer Transition course. It is an attempt to retain the integrity of the University Studies program even for students who come to Portland State from other institutions. But Portland State has taken this principle even further. It has supported community colleges and high schools in its region in preparing students for a learning-focused university education. Portland State has worked with Clackamas Community College just outside Portland to develop its own version of the Freshman Inquiry learning community. As Terrel L. Rhodes (personal communication,

June 5, 2002), vice provost for Curriculum and Undergraduate Studies at Portland State, describes the program:

> The faculty at the community college who teach Freshman Inquiry meet with the faculty here who teach it on that theme. They meet as a team; they design the course together. There is now a peer mentor there at the community college who works with their students just as they do here. They're doing portfolios, and we have a FIPSE project underway where their student portfolios and our student portfolios are being evaluated on the same criteria and the same rubrics to see what kind of experience there is and continuity.

This is hands-on alignment, extending the integrity of a purposeful plan of learning to other institutions.

The high school program is conducted somewhat differently. There the Freshman Inquiry learning community becomes Senior Inquiry. At four local high schools, Portland State faculty members actually join the teaching team: one Portland State instructor with two faculty members from the high school. Upper-division Portland State students serve as peer mentors. The program reaches about 250 high school students each year and is growing. This program is creating alignment between institutions in the most effective possible way: by actual collaboration with faculty, staff, and students at the other institutions. Portland State is expanding the purposeful community of practice outside the institution, to other schools and colleges.

Such experiments in local institutional alignment and cooperation perhaps offer the best hope for substantive curricular development across campus boundaries. Of course, alignment between institutions one at a time could take a while. Alignment between colleges and between systems can be achieved on a broad scale only by cooperation across systems and between colleges. Higher education systems in a number of states are exploring approaches to such improved alignment.

The California State University is the largest campus-based system of four-year colleges in the United States. It has 23 campuses and 40,000 faculty members. It also resides in the state with the most heavy-handed regulation of higher education in the country. (I know; I live here.) One faculty member from a CSU campus told me, "Faculty in this system, basically they're working as if they were on an assembly line. It is just a stunningly bad system." I am not endorsing this view nor disputing it. There are certainly many brilliant and talented teachers and scholars in the CSU system. And campuses have much independence. But it is a highly bureaucratized system in many respects. Historically, the bulk of its campuses have been locked quite firmly in the Instruction Paradigm. Today, there are signs of change, and they are worth noting because if CSU can change, anybody can change.

One sign of change is a system-wide project called Cornerstones. The process began in 1996 and produced a set of "general principles and supporting recommendations designed to guide CSU into the next century" (California State University System, n.d.). The first principle states that "The California State University will award the baccalaureate on the basis of demonstrated learning as determined by our faculty." In order to implement this principle, the plan proposes, "Each university will have a faculty-determined, comprehensive set of general education outcomes that are sufficiently specific to support a public declaration of educational results...." The plan recommends a comprehensive system of learning assessment, and calls upon the faculty to involve students as "active partners with faculty in the learning process" and to "provide opportunities for active learning throughout the curriculum." The proposed completion date for developing comprehensive general-education outcomes is the fall of 2002.

The Cornerstones process would not achieve instant alignment among different institutions. It would, however, focus attention on the learning outcomes of programs and thus give institutions something to align. It would move institutions toward giving functional meaning to the formal processes of curriculum and instruction. It would therefore reveal, for the first time, where institutional activities are aligned in terms of learning outcomes and where they are not. It would provide a vocabulary that not only the CSU system but community colleges and high schools could use to meaningfully discuss and plan for their own alignment with the universities.

It is difficult to see just what the outcome of this process will be. According to Gary Hammerstrom (personal communication, February 18, 2002), associate vice chancellor for academic affairs of the CSU system, campuses have been submitting accountability reports every two years, and the system's board of trustees has been actively monitoring progress. Josina Makau of CSU, Monterey Bay receives the email on the department chairs listservs in several disciplines. She reports:

> Department chairs are aware [of Cornerstones]. Under-
> standably, there's a combination of responsiveness and resist-
> ance. Some cadres are making efforts to develop learning
> outcomes and assessment mechanisms. Most, however, are re-
> sisting. We experienced similar responses at CSUMB. In the
> absence of a thoughtful pedagogical framework within which
> to develop learning outcomes, most faculty who care deeply
> about student learning and academic freedom resisted the
> mandate. It was only after we were able to demonstrate a
> commitment to development of a learning-centered model
> with academic integrity that faculty came to embrace the
> process.

How much will happen how fast is hard to tell, but what we see in
Cornerstones is a substantial, sustained effort at the system level of a very
large system to realign fundamental processes in the interest of learning. If
the theory-in-use displayed by institutional practice were to lag far behind
the espoused theory expressed in the Cornerstones plan—well, it wouldn't
be the first time. But if this initiative can create and sustain substantial
pockets of innovation and initiate broad-based conversations on many
campuses about how well the system serves learning—that would be news
worth reporting.

An even more interesting approach to alignment among colleges and
universities within a system is being discussed in Minnesota. We have already seen an example of the basic framework for alignment proposed for
Minnesota in the Liberal Studies/Professional Skills program at Inver
Hills Community College. Inver Hills is a part of the Minnesota State
Colleges and Universities (MnSCU—pronounced "MIN-skew"), which
includes state universities, community colleges, and technical colleges—
but not the University of Minnesota. David Shupe is director for Academic Accountability for the system. He notes that while faculty members
often assess student learning in a sophisticated and meaningful way, no
record of those assessments survives in the transcript: "even when faculty
can assess students well, there is no good way to gather and display evidence of that" (Shupe, 2001a, p. 9). This is more than a problem of external accountability:

> It is learning—the personal, professional, and intellectual de-
> velopment of individuals—that is the primary process for

the creation of value in colleges and universities, yet this is the
one process about which colleges and universities, *as organizations,* have little or no data. Most learning is invisible, because our institutions do not have the means to capture or retain the crucial information: what a student has learned—
that is, has demonstrated that he or she knows and can do—
while being one of our students. (Shupe, 2002, p. 1)

Data about actual student learning provide the benefits of an improved feedback system to students that we have already discussed. But
they would also provide much better evidence for institutions, departments, and faculties to use in planning: "Instead of indirect indicators of
an otherwise invisible process, each college and university would have real
data that can be usefully aggregated" (Shupe, 2001a, p. 10). In the past,
Shupe points out, "Many assessment efforts have been caught in an ei-
ther/or decision, either creating data for institutional purposes that has little or no meaning for students or facilitating student evidence that provides little or no data for the institution" (2001b, p. 7). As I indicated in
Chapter 13, the priority of these two objectives should be clear: Feedback
to students is more important than feedback to institutions. However,
these alternatives are not mutually exclusive, which is good news if we
want to achieve institutional alignment: "Both are needed and can be simultaneously achieved if a college or university chooses to organize its
outcomes data carefully enough." In the Inver Hills system we see the
principle applied: Evidence of student accomplishment once entered in
the skills template can be aggregated for a variety of purposes and is also
used to produce an ongoing Skills Profile for each student.

Shupe has developed a template for learning outcomes that individual
institutions can adapt to their own purposes and that could also be used to
translate information about learning outcomes from one institution to another in a coherent way. If many institutions in a system implemented
such a template of outcomes, it would help to achieve alignment both
within and between institutions.

Shupe's template is based on a framework for categorizing learning
outcomes that facilitates identifying and clarifying the kind of outcomes a
course or program aims for and also assists in differentiating outcomes
that should be expected from the general education program and those
that are more appropriate to the major. This is not the place for a detailed

discussion of the template, but the basic framework is worth considering. Shupe makes two basic distinctions among student proficiencies:

> One is between what a student has demonstrated that he or she knows and what a student has demonstrated he or she can do. The other is between an outcome that is specific to a particular context (e.g., discipline or profession) and one that transcends that context and can be brought to bear on (or transferred to) others. Taken together, these yield four types of learning outcomes:

> *Understanding:* a student's demonstration of what he or she knows and understands within a specific context (discipline or profession)

> *Performance:* a student's demonstration of what he or she can do that is specific to a context (discipline or profession)

> *Perspective:* a student's demonstration of what he or she knows and understands that can be carried from one context to another

> *Capability:* a student's demonstration of what he or she can do that can be carried from one context to another. (2001a, pp. 4–5)

Some seven colleges and universities in the MnSCU system are working on trial implementation of the template, or parts of it. If faculty from different colleges and universities can use a common framework for defining the sometimes distinctive learning outcomes that they want their curricula to produce, they achieve, of course, all of the advantages of creating a system that provides more meaningful feedback to students and extends the time horizon for learning. But they also create the possibility of informing other institutions what their degrees and programs mean. Credit hours and grades are now counters in a system that is fairly well sealed against meaning: They are formal mechanisms and processes that refer to other formal mechanisms and processes. A shared template for defining the outcomes of courses and programs has the potential to give substance to the forms, to point to the value added in an education rather than just the hours accumulated. This means that colleges could be accountable, but not by the vague and ill-defined standards of those who do not understand their work. They could be accountable for what they aim to do, and for what they do well, and could at the same time do it better. As Shupe puts it, they could achieve "a thoroughly academic accountability and a thoroughly accountable academy" (2002):

> [T]he future to be imagined is one in which a college or university can more completely develop and demonstrate its distinctiveness, more fully reward individual strengths in both faculty and students, more rigorously maintain academic standards across the curriculum and offer a creative and more dynamic curriculum—and do all of these not in spite of but precisely *because* of systematically and continuously produced data on student achievement. (2002, p. 2)

Both institutions and systems are working with the formal Instruction Paradigm processes to try to find or create more meaningful standards and processes that truly reflect information about learning. One of the most pervasive processes for peer review in the academy is institutional accreditation. Increasingly, the regional accrediting organizations are moving to a model of institutional excellence that owes more to the integral vision of institutions that have taken learning seriously than to the formal processes of the Instruction Paradigm college. Perhaps the clearest example to date of this movement is to be found in the newly revised standards of the Accrediting Commission for Senior Colleges and Universities of the Western Association of Schools and Colleges. Under the leadership of Ralph Wolff, executive director, the commission has engaged in several years of intense collaborative effort among faculty and administrators from the whole range of colleges and universities in the region. The product of this effort, the *WASC 2001 Handbook of Accreditation,* envisions nothing less than a complete redesign of the accreditation process, giving individual institutions much more freedom and autonomy to define their own purposes and goals. The new standards, however, call upon institutions to focus on learning outcomes rather than simply describe institutional processes, to define the terms of institutional integrity for themselves. The accreditation process, they propose, has the aim of "[p]romoting deep institutional engagement with issues of educational effectiveness and student learning..." (p. 8). In the past, institutional accreditation has been a process largely driven by the need to comply with bureaucratic requirements. Accreditation self-studies have often consisted of masses of data that present a static snapshot of institutional processes, proof that the atomized organization has all the appropriate parts. The new WASC standards propose to radically change the process by shifting the focus from formal compliance to "educational effectiveness." The process of self-development the standards propose for institutions entails three stages or "lenses" for viewing institutional processes: "Articulating a Collective Vision of Educational Attainment," "Organizing for Learning," and "Becoming a Learning Organization" (pp. 6-7). At the core of this process is the development of an institutional vision that is about students and their learning, that focuses on "the degree to which the institution sets goals and obtains results for student learning both at the institutional and program levels..." (p. 6).

The new standards propose to promote the creation of "a culture of evidence where indicators of performance are regularly developed..." (p. 8). To support institutions in this process, the commission has developed and distributed an evidence guide that outlines the process and standards for seeking, evaluating, at using evidence about student learning (Western Association of Schools and Colleges, 2002). (Peter Ewell, who has worked with WASC throughout the development process, is the primary author.) The guide proposes that "The process of accreditation... should result in more than an external validation of 'quality'; it should 'add value' to an institution by providing an important opportunity to inquire deeply into student learning..." (p. 6). Indeed, the standards and the evidence guide taken together constitute a forceful invitation to institutions to define and describe that vision of the whole purpose of the institution, rooted in a coherent vision of student learning, that is the foundation for institutional integrity.

Individual colleges can move toward their own visions of integral alignment more rapidly and more effectively if the systemic framework of interaction between colleges can advance beyond hollow formal categories and become a medium for the exchange of educational meaning. There are many ways this can happen. As more institutions come to define what they want an education to mean, the pressure for educationally meaningful standards among and between institutions will mount.

PROCESS FRONTIER: ALIGNMENT

The colleges and universities we have seen that have made real progress toward alignment for learning have approached the task from different directions. In some cases, like Evergreen and CSU, Monterey Bay, they have started a new college and designed it from scratch with a coherent vision. In other cases a college was in crisis, or at least discomfort, and had reached consensus on the need for a dramatic break with the old ways. This was the case with Olivet and Wagner—and even Alverno back in the 1970s. In some cases, an individual leader emerged who shaped the conversation: Donald Farmer at King's and Michael Bassis at Olivet come to mind. Places like the University of Delaware and Chandler-Gilbert exhibit substantial movement over a period of years. And in both cases, the movement began with the faculty. At Delaware, a small faculty development program in problem-based learning grew consistently for years and created a substantial constituency among the faculty. At Chandler-Gilbert, likewise, a small group of faculty interested in experiential learning began an approach that grew over a period of years with the support of an effective and well-executed professional development program.

Some institutions, of course, have created innovative programs that change the cognitive economy for some students and then simply stop. These programs may persist for years and become integrated into the fabric of institutional life, become reified both in terms of their advantages and their limitations. And it is certainly better to warm up the cognitive economy for some students than for none. Yet, in the final analysis, an institution must move toward integrity as a whole—or away from it. Transformative change will always be movement toward a coherent vision of the whole. And systems like colleges must begin movement toward becoming integral wholes by meeting the first condition of integrity: honesty. The road to alignment with integrity begins by seeing what we are doing, and then saying it.

PART V

TRANSFORMING THE COLLEGE

....

At the beginning of Part I, I described my experience of getting eyeglasses. Prior to getting them, I was unaware of the fact that I did not see clearly, having nothing with which to compare what I saw. The world was a vague place of indistinct things, and I had no way of knowing that it might seem otherwise. My understanding and my expectations were shaped by how I saw. When I first put on eyeglasses the first effect was simple amazement, but the second was an eagerness, a hunger to look at things and for things. After being overwhelmed by the sheer multiplicity of shapes and sizes and delineations, I began to realize that there was so much out there that I couldn't possibly take it all in. It required attention and sometimes persistence to get what was in plain view. Never mind getting to the bottom of things. Just getting to the surface was a long-term task. It was a labor of love, but labor nonetheless. I think I was probably lucky that I didn't fall down and break something or get hit by a car in those first weeks of corrected vision. Seeing became a quest. If it's there, I should look at it. My expectations of the world were radically altered. I now expected the world to bear variety and multitude, and I was not disappointed.

I did not, at the age of 12 or so, draw any coherent conclusions from all of this. What I remember from that time is the world I saw. I remember, of course, the blender. And so many different kinds of trees. The experience of seeing clearly, and the expectation of seeing new and remarkable things, stayed with me and shaped my thinking.

When I first read Parker Palmer on the grace of great things, the personal embodiment of that concept that sprung up, unbidden, in my mind was the day I put on my first pair of eyeglasses. It was certainly an experience of grace: I hadn't asked for the experience, and I had no idea what it would be like. It came to me totally unexpected, a gift. And the gift was the fundamental subject, the world itself. To see all that was there—that had been there all along—humbled and changed me. I mean, beyond the obvious differences of being able to read what was on the blackboard and recognize friends at a distance. When I applied the right tools to looking, I discovered that there was much more to what I had been looking at than I had realized. All of a sudden, my expectations were blown away, completely disqualified as a valid limit on the visible world. I saw with my own eyes—aided by the proper tools, of course—that the world itself burst the narrow confines of my constrained expectations. The lesson, I suppose, was that there's more there than meets the eye.

Seeing is not believing. Seeing is more like asking. Seeing is what gives us the wherewithal to look for more. This is, in one formulation at least, the grace of great things: the gift of expecting more. If we expect more, we hone our tools, look more closely, examine the subject from different angles, explore. "We expect" as G. K. Chesterton put it, "the unexpected."

The Learning Paradigm has affected me in much the same way. It has been a tool that I have been able to use to discover the unexpected, the potential in the commonplace, the patterns in what had seemed random. It has changed my expectations. Looking at higher education as it exists today in much of the world, I see a system that seems in many ways perversely at odds with itself. The only future I can imagine for it, if I assume that the present design and structure are inevitable, is one of decline and increasing insularity. But to look at the world of higher education through the lens of the Learning Paradigm opens up a whole new realm of possibilities.

17 Barriers to Transformation

THE TENACITY OF PARADIGMS

I once attended a meeting of a college planning committee at a college that had a general education program in a very conventional distributional mode. Someone suggested that the college needed to define what students should be learning; it needed to clarify to itself and declare to its students what the outcomes of a college education should be. Another individual spoke up. This fellow, as it happened, was both an intelligent and level-headed scholar and a thoughtful person. "But," he said, in genuine confusion, "don't we already do that?" This talented teacher had worked in Instruction Paradigm institutions all of his professional life. He genuinely could not see the difference between a list of courses and a description of learning outcomes. He was not dishonest or foolish or stupid. But the institution where he worked obscured student learning behind the façade of Instruction Paradigm structures so thoroughly that he took the formal surrogates it had put in the place of learning for learning itself.

Organizational paradigms are not easy to change. They are tenacious. And, one reason they are tenacious is that they are invisible. Like the professor mentioned above, most of us cannot see the paradigm that governs the institutions where we work. For one thing, we did not choose the structure and rules of our institutions; they were that way when we arrived. So the structures and processes of the Instruction Paradigm do not appear to the casual observer to be chosen at all. They are just part of the environment, the ongoing background of our lives. Like the white noise of traffic outside our offices or the rain that comes down as we are running to our cars, we may or may not *like* the institutional structures of the places where we work, but we seldom think in terms of *changing* them, any more than we contemplate changing the weather. As the saying goes, everybody talks about it, but nobody does anything about it. The Instruction Paradigm has been our institutional weather for so long that we simply live with it. Rain or shine, night and day. The three-unit class, the credit hour,

307

the GPA. Change these things? We might as well try to stop the sun in its course. The task of moving the foundational furniture of our institutional world seems positively Biblical in its scope.

But that is an illusion. The Instruction Paradigm is not an act of God. It is not even a natural disaster. It is an artifact of human ingenuity. We made it and sustain it. We can unmake it. It survives and persists only because we consent to it; if we withdraw our consent, it loses its force. But to say that we can control the paradigms that govern us is not to say that we can control them easily. Paradigms are tenacious. Consider three different perspectives that illustrate why they are so tenacious. A paradigm is a lens, and a habit, and a language.

It is a lens because we don't see it under normal circumstances; we see through it. A paradigm raises certain objects into bold relief and causes others to fade into the vague background. It makes some things vivid and some things obscure. It shapes our options by allowing us to see the objects that are available for our use. It shows us what we can act upon and what we can use for tools, and therefore it shapes our choice of actions. Probably like you, I was born and bred in the Instruction Paradigm. I attended only Instruction Paradigm colleges and have worked only at Instruction Paradigm colleges. Of course, as a student I had some extraordinary teachers who resisted the paradigm, and I have myself tried to resist the paradigm, sometimes alone and sometimes working with colleagues. But the exceptions prove the rule. It still conditions, in large part, the way I tend to see things. I have to remind myself that I am looking through a lens. When I see a college, I see a place where people congregate in classrooms for the purpose of meeting classes. Through the lens of the Instruction Paradigm, a classroom looks like a space designed for a teacher to fill. A classroom looks like a place in which I, as a teacher, should exercise control and provide information, should instruct.

And my habit, as a teacher, is to do precisely that: to tell the other people who are in the classroom at the same time as myself what to do, frequently what to think, and sometimes even how to feel. A paradigm is a habit, or a set of habits. That is to say, it implies a pattern of behavior that is so familiar as to seem normal: normal not just in the sense of average but in the sense of proper and expected. When I walk into one of my classes, the normal thing for me to do is to talk. Indeed, it is so easy for me that it requires little or no effort to do so and considerable effort to refrain from doing so. If you are a college teacher, try the experiment: Walk into your class at the beginning of the prescribed session and don't say anything for a full minute. How does it make you feel? It still makes me feel a little like I'm breaking the rules, going against some unwritten law, doing something wrong. As if I have just stepped out of bounds in the educational game. If there were a referee present in the classroom, I would fear a penalty. Parker Palmer (1998) puts it this way:

> Like most professionals, I was taught to occupy space, not open it: after all, we are the ones who know, so we have an obligation to tell others all about it! Even though I have rejected that nonsensical norm, I still feel guilty when I defy it. A notso-small voice within me insists that if I am not filling the available space with my own knowledge, I am not earning my keep. (p. 132)

Lining up the chairs in rows is an Instruction Paradigm habit. I have for many years now followed the procedure of rearranging the furniture when I come into the classroom. I ask the students at the beginning of each class to join me in putting the chairs in a circle, so that everyone can see everyone else, and indeed can look everyone else in the eye. When I was a relatively new part-time instructor, I came into the office one day early in the semester to find a note in my mailbox from my department chair, requesting that I come to see him. He told me that he in turn had received a note from another department chair, call him Dr. Smith, requesting that I contact him. Completely at a loss, I made my way across campus and located Dr. Smith. I introduced myself. Noting that his office was in the same building as my Tuesday-Thursday class, I had figured out that the classroom where I had been teaching for about three class sessions was a room normally assigned to Dr. Smith's department. "Ah, Mr. Tagg," he said, "do you teach a class in room Z-12?" I allowed that I did. With a bit of shuffling and milling, Dr. Smith came to the point: "Mr. Tagg, are you the individual who arranges the chairs in that room in, uh, a . . . less than traditional manner?"

Dr. Smith, I found out later, was a thoughtful man and a good teacher. But I can never think of him without recalling his revealing choice of words when he wanted to know if I had put the chairs in a circle. Our paradigm determines the norms we seek to maintain. Behavior that differs from the prescribed norm falls short. By the norms of the Instruction Paradigm, a room in which the chairs are not lined up in rows looks, not just different, but less: less traditional certainly, less normal, less of a classroom. Changing old habits is hard.

A paradigm serves as a kind of a language. When we talk about our work, we tend to use the terms that have referents within the organizational paradigm. A number of states have initiated programs to reward or encourage better outcomes for higher education or some sort of accountability. But if we look at what those programs are referring to as outcomes, we see things such as retention, persistence to the degree, number or percentage of degrees granted. In other words, the outcomes of college, in the Instruction Paradigm language, are things that happen in college, usually numbers of students who have gone through the formal processes of college. It is as if a hospital were to report as the outcomes of care what operations and medicines were prescribed and the numbers of patients who were discharged, ignoring whether they lived or died, thrived or failed after discharge, or for that matter whether they were healthy or sick on discharge. A body out the door is an outcome.

Of course, I realize that the reason higher education systems have to use procedural surrogates instead of real evidence about what students have learned at the college is that most colleges have no idea what students have learned. But that is because the Instruction Paradigm is a closed, self-referential system in which the only language available is the language of educational processes. So even terms like "outcomes" and "learning" take on special and limited meanings. The Instruction Paradigm has provided us with a language that will let us talk about higher education forever without ever making any falsifiable, and therefore meaningful, claims about what students in fact learn.

This creates a language barrier when people begin to move outside the paradigm. I have a lot of experience with this. One of the reasons I mention so frequently my dislike of multiple-choice tests is that for several years I encountered many educators who took me to be advocating their wider use. For many, the word "assessment" means testing and "test" means bubble-sheet, machine-gradable test. I would mention the importance of assessment in passing, and people would rise up, sometimes on high horses, to condemn the culture of testing and the commercialization of higher education. No, I would say, I don't mean testing; I mean assessment. Sure, sure. It was too late. They already had me pegged. The consistent misunderstanding of the term "assessment" is one factor that has led me to frame the argument in terms of the importance of feedback rather than evaluation. But confusion still persists.

The fundamental barrier to changing organizational paradigms is that the governing paradigm is the lens through which we see, the habit pattern that governs our behavior, and the language we use to speak about our work. That is changing. For example, many people in higher education today know just what you mean when you refer to learning outcomes. (State legislators, unfortunately, still seem to be fuzzy on the point.) When the Boyer Commission report came out in 1998, many research universities (not all) reacted defensively—sometimes with seemingly willful misunderstanding. But today most of those institutions have or are developing serious undergraduate research programs, and they are beginning to focus some of their research skills on assessing and evaluating the results of those programs. As the examples of institutions explicitly breaking out of the Instruction Paradigm grow, it becomes easier to talk about outcomes and assessment and learning without being misunderstood. One challenge that still remains is to get faculty and administrators to talk to one another about these things, to increase the number of educators who can put on their Learning Paradigm glasses, so to speak, and see the word around them through a different lens. The resistance to doing this takes several forms. I believe that it is becoming easier in many places. But we need to address the barriers to doing so. I mention just a few of the more prominent ones here.

ORGANIZATIONAL DEFENSIVE ROUTINES AS A BARRIER TO TRANSFORMATION

I attended a workshop some years ago conducted by faculty members from Alverno College, explaining Alverno's ability-based curriculum. The attendees were faculty members and administrators from two California community colleges. After the initial presentation, which included an explanation of learning outcomes and an outline of the Alverno abilities, we broke into small groups. The task we were given was to come up with a list of what we thought were the most important outcomes of lower-division education. What should community college graduates know and be able to do? We went to our separate rooms. Those of us in my group introduced ourselves. After a few moments of silence, someone said, "Well, what do you think?" Again, a moment of silence, then one faculty member spoke up:

"You know, the reason we could never do anything like that here is that we can't create prerequisites. Without prerequisites, this sort of outcomes-based curriculum would just be impossible for our students."

The speaker had a point. The system for creating prerequisites for a course in the California community colleges is Byzantine in its complexity, lengthy, and ultimately daunting. He was suggesting that without prerequisites to compel students to take courses in the right order, it would be impossible to develop student abilities in a developmental sequence, as Alverno does. Perhaps, perhaps not. But my first reaction to the comment was that this teacher was like the student who writes an essay on why he can't write an essay: He wasn't doing the assignment, wasn't answering the question we had been asked. We had been asked what we thought the outcomes of college should be. He responded by changing the subject and giving a reason why it was pointless to talk about the outcomes of college. I thought it was odd at the time. Subsequently, I have discovered that it was not odd—in the sense of unusual—at all. Indeed, changing the subject in this way is a very conventional response that we often hear to questions that aim to move toward a vision of the whole purpose of a college education. This kind of comment is a particular case of an organizational defensive routine.

You may recall that we discussed defensive routines in Chapter 3. As noted there, Chris Argyris (1992) defines a defensive routine as "any action or policy that prevents human beings from experiencing negative surprises, embarrassment, or threat, and simultaneously prevents the organization from reducing or eliminating the causes of the surprises, embarrassment, and threat" (pp. 102–103). This is not the place to discuss the whole panoply of defensive routines that the Instruction Paradigm college generates. But such defensive routines function to derail movement toward transformative change at many institutions. So we might consider why they appear so often.

Why would a college teacher want to avoid talking about the meaning and purpose of his work? Why would such a discussion be a potential source of embarrassment or threat? We touched on this in Chapters 3 and 4 in discussing John Biggs's idea of the three levels of thinking about teaching. Level 1, you may recall, focuses on what the student is. It is the job of the student to learn. This leads to the blame-the-student response to failure or problems. If students don't learn, it is because they didn't study hard enough, they watch too much TV, they never mastered the basics, etc. Level 2 focuses on what the teacher does. It is the job of the teacher to teach. It leads to the blame-the-teacher response to problems. If the students don't learn, the teacher isn't motivating them, isn't interesting, etc. As I suggested in Chapter 3, the Instruction Paradigm tends to lock us in a box with only these two options. They become the poles of possible explanation for failure (or success) if our thoughts are framed by what goes on in a conventional classroom, where the teacher is in control and the job is to master a discrete body of knowledge.

We might see these alternatives in a little broader sense now. The Instruction Paradigm pushes us to assume several things: the extrinsic goals that the course seeks to impose on the student, a very constrained scope for student performance, the priority of evaluation over feedback, a short time horizon, and the absence of an active community of practice in the classroom. This constrained and artificial reading of the academic environment forces us into a two-valued system where failure must be either the student's fault or the teacher's fault. So, why is a discussion of the goals of college threatening to many college teachers and administrators? Because they have a fairly good intuition that if those goals are not achieved it will be their fault! If we define substantial goals for student learning, and we don't reach them, we will have to blame either the teachers or the students. (Blaming the administration is a variation on this defensive routine, appealing to the faculty because administrators are easier targets to aim at than the student body, which is all over the place.) In the long term, we will end up blaming both, sometimes alternately, sometimes simultaneously. Thus the subject of the whole aim of a college education is an inherently threatening one; it calls forth defensive routines that will protect us from the blame we can see coming if we start down that road. And I might add that those who have this defensive response are not wrong. If we are thinking in the framework of level 1 and level 2 thinking about teaching, they are absolutely right that teachers are in for it if we allow the question of the serious objectives of student learning to be raised. Our only hope is to change the subject. But changing the subject, as with all defensive routines, assures that we will never resolve the underlying problem. It protects us, as individuals, from facing the immediate source of embarrassment or threat, but condemns us, as institutions, to encounter the underlying source of embarrassment or threat over and over again.

INSTITUTIONAL STRUCTURES AS BARRIERS TO TRANSFORMATION: THE CASE OF THE CREDIT HOUR

It should go without saying that the rules and regulations, the bureaucratic dicta of the Instruction Paradigm college, are a major barrier to realignment for learning. At many colleges, interdisciplinary courses and team teaching are difficult—if not impossible—to schedule because the computer programs that produce the schedule of classes won't accept them, or the rules governing submissions for the schedule prohibit them. Institutions like Inver Hills and Madison Area Technical College that have decided to provide meaningful evidence about student performance in specific abilities have had to create a whole separate apparatus for recording and reporting such data because the existing information system is designed for grades and nothing but grades. New management information systems, if we are not especially careful, can magnify these barriers. The examples are legion in which people who wanted to do things differently at colleges have been told that it is impossible simply because the system isn't designed for it. Not to put too fine a point on it, we can't do things differently because we're too busy doing them the same old way.

The apparatus of the Instruction Paradigm, recall, creates an information and administrative process that is almost entirely self-referential. What does a semester or a course or a grade mean? We can define these and the multitude of other structural features of the Instruction Paradigm college only in terms of one another. A semester is so many weeks, and the reason it is so many weeks is that that's how long it takes to complete a course. A course is the body of work you do in a semester. A grade is the evaluation you get at the end of a course. A course is a semester-long exercise resulting in a grade. But what does any of it mean? In the Instruction Paradigm college, the meanings of fundamental structures are purely self-referential and hence non-negotiable. And that is one reason it is hard to create a genuine community of practice about teaching and learning at many colleges: All the apparatus is terminally reified, fossilized, so what is there to negotiate?

We discussed the effect of the credit hour in the last chapter on alignment. We found that institutions that have a vision of the whole and a strategy for pursuing it can work around the structure. This is not as easy for some institutions as for others, however. Wellman (personal communication, March 11, 2002) points out that it is easier for research universities and private institutions to work around the credit hour than it is for more strictly regulated institutions: "In highly regulated systems, in particular the community colleges, the measure tends to be much more consistently enforced and used as a basis for external control and audit." This does not mean that these colleges do not innovate. "I think," she says, "there's a lot more innovation going on in teaching in the community colleges than the enforcement of the credit hour would have us believe." But at the same time,

> the regulatory systems and control mechanisms that surround the community college are absolutely inflexible. So what that means is that everybody's lying about it. Everybody has words they use to characterize what they want to do that fit within the regulatory structure and then they do what they want to do, or they work around it as best they can.

While there may be much innovation going on at community colleges—and we can add, many state universities—the pressure of regulation does impede transformation. It keeps innovation in the closet, so to speak, makes it private rather than public, and hence impedes the development of an open conversation about transformative ideas. And, of course, it makes it harder to achieve institutional honesty and hence to move toward integrity if you have to consistently misrepresent what you are really doing. If you are really paying attention to learning rather than counting credit hours, it just doesn't fit on the form from the state budget office. You must pretend to be doing less than you really are, in some cases, to be funded. Some existing state funding mechanisms demand the trivial and would penalize the substantive. It's hard to maintain integrity under those circumstances.

The greatest damage that the student credit hour does, however, is not to institutions that have formulated a vision of the whole aligned for learning. The greatest damage is that the credit hour and other Instruction Paradigm regulations do is to deter institutions from forming the vision, from taking the prospect of transformation seriously. The credit hour and other structures of the Instruction Paradigm cause many in higher education to reify the barriers to transformation that they represent. Wellman says:

> It is the behaviors that have grown up around the measure with respect to teaching and learning in many, many institutions that really are the problem. Because the measure is such

an easy way to document that you've done what you're supposed to do that alternative ways of defining teaching and learning are not required. So that an institution where you don't have energy around alternatives or more robust measures of teaching and learning, you've got the credit hour.

The behaviors that have grown up around Instruction Paradigm structures and rules are significant barriers to alignment for learning. Many colleges have offered learning communities. Many colleges have promoted experiential pedagogy. Many colleges have at least attempted to create better and more consistent feedback. Why have more colleges not tried to put the pieces together? Why have more educational leaders not, like Michael Bassis after the Labor Day barbecue, looked at the handwriting on the wall and said "Why can't we do all these things simultaneously?" Why is it so hard to see the whole, to envision a transformed college that really does put learning first? If we allow our vision to be bounded by Instruction Paradigm structures, we will not see a vision of the whole; we will spend ourselves counting beans, making educational widgets, punching our time cards in the knowledge factory.

THE SACRAMENTO SYNDROME AS A BARRIER TO TRANSFORMATION

It is only when we look at the substantive outcomes of a college education or the substantive experience of the students—I mean the living, breathing persons, not the FTES, the beans that get counted in the knowledge factory—that we see how horribly misaligned the practices of the Instruction Paradigm college are. To align them requires that we participate in the conversation about what our practices really mean. At many Instruction Paradigm colleges, that conversation doesn't take place. We have just considered two factors that inhibit such conversations: organizational defensive routines that deflect questions about substance and organizational structures that impede change. I want to suggest that these two factors combine at many institutions to produce a particular psychology that deters conversations leading to purposeful change.

I gave the example above of a faculty member in a workshop about learning outcomes who used a defensive routine to deflect the question. What happened as that conversation proceeded was very interesting.

While he was willing, and apparently eager, to avoid a conversation about student outcomes, several of us in the room were equally eager to have that conversation. So we pressed him. As the conversation progressed, it became clear that the faculty member who had deflected the question of outcomes with the point about prerequisites did not approve of the difficult and cumbersome process for creating prerequisites. He believed that the absence of appropriate prerequisites for many courses condemned many students to failure and misinformed them about what would be expected of them. Furthermore, he thought that it had the effect of dumbing down his own courses and that he could not resist the pressure to do so. Indeed, there turned out to be nothing that he liked about the regime that (he believed) precluded our consideration of student outcomes. Yet he kept bringing the conversation back to what we could not do and why we could not do it and the pointlessness of whatever positive steps we might consider. He kept rationalizing and returning to policies that it became increasingly clear he did not like and could not defend. Yet he was nonetheless, implicitly, defending them—if not defending their wisdom, then defending their inevitability. He seemed to regard the regulatory structures that he abhorred as inviolate and unchangeable, the educational practices he admired as impossible and undiscussable.

This is an example of a pattern of behavior that is fairly widespread among college administrators and faculty members. I will call it "the Sacramento syndrome" even though it is not limited to California but can—and does—arise anywhere educators have long been captive by excessive regulation and Instruction Paradigm processes. Those who suffer from it protect their captors and fight against their own liberation. They rail against their captivity, but when offered freedom, won't take "yes" for an answer.

I have come to believe that the Sacramento syndrome is widespread in Instruction Paradigm colleges. And I am inclined to believe that the more disheartened and dispirited a college is about the perpetual drill of meaningless processes, the more they will cling to those processes and hide from open discussion of them. Organizational defensive routines become epidemic. At one institution, a president who raises the issue of learning is attacked savagely by faculty members who claim that academic freedom is at risk; party lines are drawn, accusations made. Learning is not discussed; the subject has been effectively changed. At another institution, a faculty group proposes conversations about learning. Others rise up in high dudgeon, about as high as dudgeon can get, and attack the administration, which must be behind the whole thing. The conversation becomes about who really started the effort and whether the administration is committed to the business model of management. Learning is not discussed; the subject has been effectively changed.

Many cases are less dramatic. But the structures of governance in Instruction Paradigm colleges support a variety of strategies for changing the subject. Those structures, both the organizational chart of administration and the faculty committees, were designed to execute the formal practices of the Instruction Paradigm. Learning is not on the agenda. And efforts to put it on the agenda can often be deflected by pointing out that learning is not the charge of the committee. Indeed it is not. Learning is not the charge of the college. I once raised a question about the effect of certain policies on student learning in a committee that dealt with staffing. Another member of the committee waved the comment off (literally, she raised her hand and flapped it up and down as if to blow away the offending comment) with the remark, "Oh, of course, we're always doing what we can for learning, but that doesn't have anything to do with this issue." It certainly didn't have anything to do with the way the issue was resolved, but that was a self-fulfilling prophecy. Some will deflect conversations about learning on the grounds it is so important: We're always doing everything we can to promote learning; therefore we don't need to talk about it. Some will deflect these conversations on the grounds it is irrelevant: that isn't the issue here. Sometimes, they will use both rationales. All of these practices—defensive routines, hiding behind organizational structures, pounding on the table—are manifestations of the Sacramento syndrome. We embrace our captors and close our ears to the calls of those who would rescue us. We use the irrational rules and limiting structures that imprison us as protective devices, so we don't have to talk about learning.

Part of the explanation is that, like hostages who have been imprisoned under strict restraint, we have been isolated for so long. There are probably some college teachers who like the privacy and secrecy of the conventional classroom. But nearly all of us are accustomed to it. We have been conditioned to believe that it is a normal state of affairs. As Parker Palmer (1998) explains it:

> When we walk into our workplace, the classroom, we close
> the door on our colleagues. When we emerge, we rarely talk
> about what happened or what needs to happen next, for we

have no shared experience to talk about. Then, instead of calling this the isolationism it is and trying to overcome it, we
claim it as a virtue called academic freedom: My classroom is
my castle, and the sovereigns of other fiefdoms are not wel-
come here. (p. 142)

Is it any wonder we get cranky? The artificial isolation of the teacher
in higher education may be average, may be statistically predominant, but
it is not normal. It exacerbates the Sacramento syndrome by denying us
the reality check that most people get in their work by contact with peers.
Palmer notes:

The growth of any craft depends on shared practice and
honest dialogue among the people who do it. We grow by
private trial and error, to be sure—but our willingness to try,
and fail, as individuals is severely limited when we are not
supported by a community that encourages such risks.
When any function is privatized, the most likely outcome is
that people will perform it conservatively, refusing to stray far
from the silent consensus on what works—even when it
clearly does not. (p. 144)

It is exactly the character of the consensus about learning and teaching
in many colleges that it is a silent consensus. Nobody talks about what
everybody knows. Procedures that would seem to be inherently valuable in
a democratic society—defining your terms, questioning for clarity, restat-
ing the views of others to test your understanding—are seldom practiced
in terms of faculty work, and in fact are sometimes regarded as suspicious.
The only way to protect a silent consensus is to be quiet about it. So the
consensus, the reified rules of the game, is not negotiated, it is merely
known. It doesn't change.

I certainly do not mean to blame the victims. And I hope it is clear
that I am suggesting that the faculty and staff of the college—nearly as
much as the students—are victims of the Instruction Paradigm. Furthermore, I believe that many college administrators are as much victims of
the system as their faculty colleagues. Because one of the most entrenched
defensive routines in many colleges is to change the subject by blaming
the administration, and because administrators are the designated en-
forcers of the Instruction Paradigm, it may sound strange to speak of

them as victims of the system. But they often are. Many administrators, like many faculty members, have learned that open conversations about the meaning of our work are a dangerous idea. So administrators, like faculty members, reify the rules, hide behind the regulations, do only what they have to do, embrace the limitations that they hate. The Sacramento syndrome can affect any of us.

There is one group of administrators who I believe have been particular victims of the Sacramento syndrome: college and university presidents. The same point applies in many cases to provosts and vice president and deans, but at most institutions, presidents effectively set the tone for organizational behavior—whether they want to or not. And presidents are in a particularly precarious position: They are in most cases charged, by law and oath, to maintain the Instruction Paradigm. It is their job to maintain the institution as a healthy, functioning, enrollment-generating machine. So the president with a coherent vision for the institution is drawn into the practical defense and enforcement of processes that obstruct and impede the achievement of that vision. Distinctive learning programs can be a barrier to transfer. Really valuing deep over surface learning can damage enrollment. Extending the time horizon for learning can bring down the state regulators.

The easiest way out is to say one thing and do another. My guess is that there are few job classifications in which the breach between espoused theory and theory-in-use is more pronounced than it is for college presidents. My point, however, is not that presidents are bad people. Like the rest of us, they are a mixed bag. My point is that they, like the rest of us, are captives, hostages to Instruction Paradigm structures and rules not of their making. They, as much as their faculties, are subject to the Sacramento syndrome.

We should not blame the victims. But neither should we leave the victims to their bondage. In the next chapter we will discuss some approaches to overcoming the barriers to transformational change in the service of learning.

18 Scaffolding for Change

Seeing Through a New Lens

In the country of the blind, the one-eyed man is really annoying. He continuously spouts nonsense. He is always seeing things. In the country of the severely nearsighted, perhaps a better analogy, the first one with corrective lenses is likewise a pain to most folks. She sees things that obviously aren't there. She is constantly telling you about her imaginary visions. And she frequently burdens you with unwanted advice. If everyone is wearing the lenses of the conventional paradigm, those who adopt the corrective lenses of a new paradigm discover that they can see vividly things that previously were obscure. And conceptually, they perceive in a better and clearer way how the world around them is organized. They feel empowered, informed, refreshed. But normal folks, still looking through the lenses they grew up with, just going about their business and doing their jobs, often have a low tolerance for the busybodies with the fancy new lenses. Ultimately, the only way to get people to embrace a shared project with you is to get them to see things the way you see them. That means that they must try on your lenses. We know how that happens: through conversation, dialog, the ongoing negotiation of meaning. But, as we have just seen, there are many defensive barriers set up in most colleges to looking through the Learning Paradigm lens, to learning the new language, to examining our old habits and experimenting with new ones. How, then, can colleges begin to build a hot cognitive economy?

We often speak of providing students the scaffolding they need to support their growth as learners. The real task of transformation, of course, is to learn about ourselves and our institutions. We need to provide the support apparatus—the scaffolding—for our institutions as they learn to change. Scaffolding is a temporary structure that we stand on to change the permanent structure. Some of what is described below as scaffolding will become a part of the permanent structure of the organization, such as ongoing learning assessment, while some can be disassembled as its func-

321

tions are supplanted by a more permanent edifice. The main purpose of this scaffolding, then, is to facilitate institutional learning, to help those of us who work at the college to learn more about our work, to help us to see the college through the lens of the Learning Paradigm, and then to bring about fundamental structural change that will create a hot cognitive economy for undergraduate learners.

CREATING A COLLEGIUM: SHAPING A COMMUNITY OF PRACTICE

We saw in the last chapter that Instruction Paradigm structures and ways of thinking put us in a box that limits our options and inspires defensive routines that deflect creative conversation. How do we get out of the box? Level 1 and level 2 ways of thinking about teaching see the classroom as an isolated cell and the prisoners of the classroom as isolated individuals. There is no such thing as a community GPA. So it is the war of all against all, positively Hobbesean. The escape route is to move to level 3.

Level 3 sees the teacher and the student as partners in the quest for learning. The teacher seeks to support the student in learning—not to make the student learn, not even necessarily to teach the student what she needs to know, but to create an environment in which the student learns. And here I would go beyond Biggs. I think we can say now that level 3 requires that we see the learning transaction as being played out on a larger field than the classroom. Indeed, the arena for level 3 is the college as a community of practice. The teacher—in the classroom or out—is a member of the community of practice, the learning community, that is the college. The teacher, if you will, is a member of a team—or of overlapping teams. To really move to level 3, to really get beyond the two-valued structure of blame that the Instruction Paradigm classroom puts us in, we need to look at the student—and the teacher—as a whole, and as part of a larger, integral community. And we have to see that learning—deep learning, learning that matters, learning that lasts—is not something that teachers do to students or even that students do for themselves. Rather it is the product of action in a context shaped by goals, performance, feedback, time horizon, and community—of all of the principles that define the cognitive economy, acting to create an environment that empowers and engages students.

Faculty members, administrators, and staff locked in the box of level 1 and 2 will continuously generate defensive routines to deflect and avoid the task of seeking alignment for learning. To get beyond these defensive routines, we need to move to level 3, where we can see learning not as the job of teachers or of students but of everybody who makes a claim to membership in the larger community of practice that is the college. This, it seems to me, is a liberating view, for faculty, administrators, and staff. We are no longer sitting on the bull's-eye, waiting for the next critic to take aim. If we think of ourselves as part of a community that shares responsibility for creating a hot cognitive economy, then asking what learning we want to achieve is no longer a threat to our being able to do our job: asking and answering that question is our job.

Organizational defensive routines are a threat to the institutional honesty that integrity requires of us. But we will never overcome the barrier they present to moving toward a vision of wholeness until we can begin to see our own work as part of a larger whole, as involved in something greater than the classroom. Parker Palmer (1998) speaks of "the grace of great things." He uses the phrase, which he borrows from Rilke, to describe the subjects that we study: "not the disciplines that study these subjects, not the texts that talk about them, not the theories that explain them, but the things themselves" (p. 107). For me, as I said earlier, the phrase calls to mind the day I got my first pair of glasses. To see that the world I had walked through, unseeing, for so long was such a place as this—so full, so intricate, so richly figured—was to be in the presence of something larger than I could easily compass. In later years, I found that same feeling, that sense of being the recipient of a surprising gift, in other people, and especially in communities. In a sense, the grace of great things is the key to transformation. "I wonder," Palmer says, "Could teachers gather around the great thing called 'teaching and learning' and explore its mysteries with the same respect we accord any subject worth knowing?" (p. 107).

There is, I think, another approach to calling upon the grace of great things to break the patterns that hold us back. We can gather, as educators—not just faculty, but all of us who do the work of the college—around our students. Put them in the center. As Palmer points out, we want to bring our students into the circle, to become a community with them. But to do that, before we do that, we need to see them clearly. As I will suggest again in the next chapter, to see our students, and to see them whole and clear, is to invite the grace of great things to fill us. If we can focus for a while on them, instead of ourselves, it will help us to clear our heads, so that we can address one another with a sense of a common purpose that is larger than any of our divisions and that can overcome our fears.

When I say we should try to focus on our students rather than ourselves, I do not mean to suggest that we are selfish or self-centered as a rule. What I mean to suggest is that we are afraid. The Sacramento syndrome is a response to fear. And it is fear, over and above all else, that inspires the defensive routines that lock us in and keep us from changing. We are afraid of embarrassment, afraid of failure, afraid of being held up to ridicule, afraid of feeling inferior. I could go on. I am not so unrealistic as to believe that these fears are unique to college staff. They are widespread, and they take a certain shape in almost anyone who works for a large organization. But there seems to me no doubt that the Instruction Paradigm college reifies these fears in a particular way. Yet, if we stop to reflect on the fact, there are few people in the world who have more security and stability and ongoing stimulation in their daily work than a tenured college teacher. It is, in many ways, an extraordinarily privileged position. Then why are so many of us so afraid, so defensive?

We have discussed the reasons why already. We are isolated in our work, cut off from the shared community, locked in the box with level 1 and level 2 thinking. The word "college" comes from the word "collegium": "a group, the members of which pursue shared goals while working in a framework of mutual trust and respect" (*American Heritage College Dictionary,* 3rd ed.). To become that again, we must move to level 3 thinking, to seeing the work we do as a work we all share in common: the building of a cognitive economy that will liberate the best efforts of our students—and of ourselves.

All of the examples of colleges I have seen that appear to be moving toward genuine transformation have one thing in common. I cannot think of a single exception. They have created structures that bring at least the faculty, and often the whole college community, together outside of their departments or disciplines to negotiate as a group the terms and means of student learning. At Alverno College the faculty ability committees meet every week. At CSU, Monterey Bay faculty learning communities negotiate the meaning of the University Learning Requirements and their assessment. At Inver Hills, faculty in the LS/PS program receive two extra professional development days to meet together and discuss the assignments they have developed to assess the skills. At King's, interdisciplinary project teams come together to develop and refine courses in the core curriculum. At Evergreen, IUPUI, Portland State, and Wagner, faculty and sometimes others work together to teach learning community courses as teams.

Olivet College has adopted the idea that all of the college staff are educators. If the arena for learning extends beyond the classroom, then all of the educators on campus are members of the extended community of practice that create the cognitive economy of the college. Kathy Fear (personal communication, January 24, 2002) explains:

> Many people on campus beyond faculty will work as coteachers for the portfolio sections. So, for instance, many of the secretaries who have students working for them will help teach the portfolio sections and help students develop their student work as part of their portfolio exhibit. . . . Many of our campus staff have volunteer projects that they work on in the community with students. So they'll generate projects and get students involved.

Of course, the staff at every college is deeply involved in the education of students. At some institutions, I suspect, department secretaries do more actual student advisement than counselors or faculty mentors. The staff in the library and the admissions office, the groundskeepers and the nurses in the student health center, see and hear and speak to students, often at times when students are seeking crucial information or facing important decisions. The entire staff of the college shapes the cognitive economy. If we extend the community of practice beyond the classroom in order to nurture a hot cognitive economy, we should recognize the role of those college staff who are outside the classroom. Being outside the classroom does not put you outside the community. Or it should not.

What all of these institutions have in common is that they have created structures that bring together educators in working communities of practice. They break down the isolation, in one way or another, and throw people together to assume shared responsibility for the real work of the college. There are many ways in which this can be done. And I do not claim that to do so will magically transform institutions in a minute. But it does appear to me that creating such working communities, across conventional organizational lines, is essential scaffolding for building toward purposeful change. It seems, to a considerable degree, to inoculate people against the Sacramento syndrome. It helps them to find the courage to move to level 3. It puts people in a circle, often with students in the middle, so that they can be open to the grace of great things.

GOING SOMEPLACE WITH CURRICULUM

At most institutions, the term "curriculum" refers to what teachers are expected to cover in various classes. This way of thinking about curriculum flows from the Instruction Paradigm assumption that the basic business of the college is offering instruction. It is a prescription for a cool cognitive economy. In a Learning Paradigm college, we would think of curriculum as being about what students learn, not what teachers teach. The curriculum should be the institution's systematic plan for what and how students will learn. The guiding principle in restructuring curriculum should be that the whole is more important than the parts. Individual courses are of trivial importance. What matters in terms of the students' whole experience is how the courses—or other learning experiences—fit together. Colleges should seek to create a curriculum that leads somewhere rather than spinning in an infinite variety of nonintersecting circles. A curriculum should not be a list of classes; it should be a description of learning outcomes. In the Instruction Paradigm, curriculum is what teachers do; in the Learning Paradigm curriculum is what students do.

Unless the students' experience of classes is connected, it is trivialized. Any course that isn't part of a larger journey is a dead end. The conventional design of bifurcated curriculum, the first two years devoted to general education, the last two to the major, may have some structure and coherence in the upper division—though that is largely a matter of luck—but lacks any recognizable shape at all in the lower division, which is where students need structure the most. Carol Geary Schneider (personal communication, February 20, 2002), president of the AAC&U, characterizes the movement away from this failed format:

> This conventional division between general courses in the first two years and specialized work in the last two years is a bankrupt design. And many of the interesting designs that we're seeing in four-year institutions have a different configuration to them, with something very strong in the first year,

and then milestones in the second and third year, culminating in integrative work in the senior year, which strikes me as the way it should be.

We can see this kind of pattern, in different configurations, at Olivet, Alverno, Wagner, IUPUI, Portland State, and several other institutions. They all treat the curriculum as a whole and seek to design the student's participation in a way appropriate to the student's developmental stage. This kind of a curriculum extends the time horizon for learning by creating a sense of progress toward a meaningful goal and allows for feedback at one stage to be clearly relevant to the next stage.

It is much more difficult, of course, for community colleges to design a curriculum as a whole, since they only have the lower division to work with. Nevertheless, we have seen a number of cases where community colleges have put shape and substance into the curriculum by defining the learning outcomes intended for a degree or program. Inver Hills and Madison Area Technical College have, in slightly different ways, defined the overall outcomes intended. As more four-year colleges define intended learning outcomes of their curricula, they should work with the community colleges to assure that transfer students do not lose coherence. The excessive regulation of community colleges in many states that prevents them from creatively designing curricula serves no useful purpose. It would be much easier for institutions to build the scaffolding they need to create a hot cognitive economy if they had the freedom to do so. It would also, to return to an earlier point, be easier to combat the Sacramento syndrome with a little help from Sacramento.

USING ASSESSMENT TO CHANGE THE COGNITIVE ECONOMY

In order for the scaffolding for a new curriculum to be effective, institutions must assess student performances continually. By "assessment" I mean significant feedback on and evaluation of student performance. Institutional assessment in a hot cognitive economy will always be primarily for feedback to students. However, such assessment can also supplant, support, or supplement the role of grades in providing evaluations of student performance. I take it as obvious that testing, in the conventional sense, will play a very small role in any institutional assessment program that aims to promote a hot cognitive economy. I see no danger that most colleges will rely too little on testing. Today, they rely on it far too much.

Institutional assessment has been mixed up with issues of accountability, program assessment, and accreditation. These are all-important issues, but secondary. Institutional assessment may or may not be useful for public relations or compliance with external requirements. But it is essential to build a hot cognitive economy.

My advice as to accountability would be to forget, for a moment, about what the state legislature wants to know, about what the chancellor's office or the board of trustees wants to know, and for that matter what employers want to know. Let us ask ourselves, with the utmost seriousness, these questions: What do we want our students to know about their own learning, about the state of their knowledge? What are the goals of knowledge and ability that we hold for them? And what do they need to know in order to achieve those goals? If we can design a system of assessment feedback that will tell our students in a meaningful and coherent way what they need to know about the progress and the process of their own learning, then we will have created a system that simultaneously tells everyone else what they need to know. We have been haunted and harassed and nagged by the shibboleth of accountability for so long that we have lost our bearings. We should not forget what is of value in this work.

In saying this I do not mean to diminish at all the importance of or the necessity for accountability. I believe that taxpayers, legislators, employers—and even administrators—have a right to know what the real consequences of our investment in higher education are. However, the interests of all of these stakeholders, important though they may be, are derivative, secondary. If we want to achieve a meaningful and productive and constructive accountability, then we will recast the concept in terms of those stakeholders whose interests are supreme over all others: our students. If we are clearly and fairly accountable to our students, then we can answer everyone else's questions without evasion or apology. If we do our duty to our students, then our duty to all others will be done. And if we do not do our duty to our students, then no manipulation of our management information systems or juggling of standardized test results will conceal our fundamental failure at the mission that justifies our institutional existence.

Alverno College and King's College and Olivet and CSU, Monterey Bay and Inver Hills have designed feedback systems to tell students what is most important about their progress toward significant learning goals. For these institutions, accountability will not be a problem. For institutions that can report only grades and graduation rates, accountability will always be a problem. Institutions that have defined for their students high expectations for collegiate learning and have created assessment systems that can tell students how they are progressing toward meeting those expectations have solved the problem of accountability and simultaneously constructed some of the essential scaffolding for building a Learning Paradigm college.

The scaffolding for institutional assessment may become a permanent structure of the institution, or it may serve as a transition to a more stable and expansive structure. For example, an institution might create an experimental framework for assessment to try on a significant cohort of students and then phase in a more permanent structure incorporating lessons learned from the experiment. A structure of institutional assessment will be important scaffolding for other changes, as well: a place to stand in order to see how a variety of structures affect learning.

INSTITUTIONAL LEARNING THROUGH COURSE DESIGN

While a well-designed curriculum supported by an institutional assessment system can begin to raise the level of feedback and extend the time horizon for learning, such a system will be more effective if the design of courses themselves promotes a hot cognitive economy. The discrete course poses a major structural barrier to an extended time-horizon for learning and to the creation of communities of practice among students. But at most institutions, the entire academic program is structured around discrete courses, from counseling and advisement through the transcript; the academic calendar and the administrative processes of the college are designed for producing and delivering three-unit classes. The simplest way of addressing this problem in the short term is by merging and connecting existing classes. The scaffolding to allow for this is not complicated to construct, but it may require setting up a parallel process in the computer and the registrar's office to establish classes in a different format. Many colleges have done this already, offering linked and team-taught courses, coordinated studies programs, freshman interest groups, first-year experiences, service-learning courses, and other alternative course designs either replacing some conventional courses or superimposed over them.

A major focus of course redesign should be to create communities of practice among students. This means grouping students in a way that makes sense in terms of the curriculum and making those groups relatively stable over time. This is most important for new students at risk of dropping out or failing. Institutions should also test flexible scheduling options, allowing students whenever possible to learn at a pace that leads to successful growth. As institutional assessment develops and student performances take a larger role in the curriculum, course design will become more flexible and responsive to evidence of learning.

Many of the innovative designs for courses we have examined here have been simple extensions of practices that work well. Chandler-Gilbert found that service learning works well and has simply linked it to an increasing number of classes. Chandler-Gilbert has now begun to experiment with learning communities as well. Wagner took the two ideas and put them together: learning communities linked to service or other experiential fieldwork. Northcentral Technical College extended the time horizon by the simple expedient of extending the semester, or starting it at the student's option. Innovation within these alternative frameworks can lead to better results. So IUPUI introduced a librarian and an academic advisor to the team. IUPUI and Portland State have incorporated a peer mentor in the learning communities, though in slightly different roles. There is ample room for experimentation in designing courses that involve students in continual performance, provide ongoing feedback, and extend the time horizon for learning.

COLLABORATING TO SHAPE A LEARNING PEDAGOGY

My impression, based largely on anecdotal evidence, is that college teachers over the past couple of decades have changed their beliefs about classroom teaching significantly. Research on learning is widely translated into practical advice on how to teach. Ideas like collaborative learning and problem-based learning are no longer very controversial, in theory. Hardly anyone is willing to publicly defend the standard lecture course as an effective learning environment for most students. It is much harder to tell how much practice has changed. As mentioned earlier, the classroom is still largely a private domain. According to the National Center for Education Statistics (2001) of the U.S. Department of Education, as of the fall of

1998 the primary instructional method in 82.7% of college and university classes in the United States was lecture.

As George Kuh (1999) suggested in Chapter 9, many students and teachers have reached a disengagement compact: "You leave me alone, and I'll leave you alone." Given the characteristics of incoming college students and the institutional protections for a cool cognitive economy, it is easy to see why such a disengagement compact is appealing to faculty and to students. However, such an agreement to low learning expectations chills the cognitive economy even further. The issue of faculty engagement in teaching is vital because any mode of pedagogy can be used as a cover for disengagement. Collaborative learning can serve as a front for the passive instructor as easily as old lecture notes. To create a hot cognitive economy, teachers must be involved in active, feedback-heavy, real-time coaching—in and out of the classroom. The scaffolding for change must support pedagogies that treat students as active learners, but it must as well support active, engaged teaching as a superior, more highly rewarded option for faculty.

The range of changes in faculty support and reward systems that would produce a hot cognitive economy are worth discussing but would take us too far afield here. However, we can safely say that many existing professional development programs fail to provide the necessary scaffolding for change. But those systems could be expanded and extended. The appropriate scaffolding here requires as a minimum rich feedback to teachers on the results of their classroom activities. Today, teachers at many colleges are as feedback-deprived as are students. We seldom receive any information about the consequences of our teaching after the term is over—in other words, we seldom receive any information about the real and significant consequences of our teaching. Given a developing system of institutional assessment, it would become possible for colleges to provide teachers feedback on the ongoing performance of their students. Colleges that have moved to more experiential pedagogies have often improved the flow of information to faculty members. At Madison Area Technical College, not only does the student receive a report, the faculty member teaching a course receives a report indicating the range of ability ranking in a course or a section of a course. The institutions that are involved in collaborative portfolio review or review of the evidence of student abilities are engaged in providing feedback to teachers so that they can provide better feedback to students. Portfolios can be as powerful a tool for teachers as they can for students in structuring and organizing learning feedback.

The basic scaffolding for professional development to promote active and effective pedagogy should emphasize feedback to teachers, not evaluation of them. As with students, rich feedback leads to learning, while frequent evaluation often deters it. Such scaffolding would initially focus on pedagogical strategies already shown to be effective: collaborative learning, PBL, apprenticeship, and other strategies for increasing the frequency and interconnectedness of student performances and improving the quality of feedback. Feedback systems to teachers and administrators about the quality of teaching should seek to hold conventional pedagogies to the same standards as innovative ones. PBL should not be scrutinized for effectiveness while conventional lecture classes are merely assumed to be effective. The characteristics of a hot cognitive economy translate easily into pedagogical practices and can provide a framework for the scaffolding that professional development should provide.

USING TECHNOLOGY TO CREATE A HOT COGNITIVE ECONOMY

I have not said much explicitly about technology, and that is by design. This is not because I am suspicious of technology or doubt its efficacy. I have taught online classes for several years now and use computer technology extensively in my face-to-face teaching. I believe that technology has enormous potential to facilitate a hot cognitive economy. But it has an equal potential to reinforce and further reify processes in a cool cognitive economy. Everything depends upon how the institution uses technology, whether it reinforces the cool cognitive economy that thrives in most institutions today or raises the temperature. For example, computer technology has the potential to hasten the delivery of feedback to students on an array of performances and to build communities of practice by increasing communication. On the other hand, if we look at many online courses offered today, we see a very cool cognitive economy, where students are isolated and denied significant feedback for most of their activities. Many institutions have developed the initial scaffolding for applying technology to the curriculum on the template of the cool cognitive economy that pervades the classroom.

To establish the technological scaffolding for a hot cognitive economy, institutions need to keep certain fundamental requirements in mind. First, if the goal is to facilitate and highlight student performances, the tools that count most are the tools that students use. For teachers to deliver their lectures with state-of-the-art audio-visual effects, or to deliver them over the Internet instead of in the classroom, is an exercise in mildly interesting gadgetry. What counts most is what students, the learners, do with the technology. Word processing is more important than PowerPoint in terms of the way technology affects the cognitive economy—unless, of course, the students are using PowerPoint. Second, technology will most powerfully and positively shape the cognitive economy when it reinforces student habits already established. The student who can't write down his ideas in longhand will not profit from word processing, but word processing will allow the student who can produce a reasonable draft to revise more quickly and effectively. Students will collaborate by email more effectively with people they already know than with people they have not met. Getting to know people through email requires more support and direction than it would if students were face-to-face. Students will use computer-mediated feedback well if they are accustomed to receiving and responding to feedback already. Technology should not be viewed as an alternative to a hot cognitive economy on campus, but as a toolbox to maintain and extend the patterns of interaction that the campus already embraces.

Technology can provide scaffolding to support a hot cognitive economy in several ways. For example, one barrier to requiring frequent and connected student performance and using the products of those performances in multiple courses is the difficulty and expense of storing vast numbers of essays, videotapes, drawings, or other records. Such records can be stored digitally for a long time at little expense. Thus server capacity for the electronic or digital portfolios that link courses and extend the time horizon of learning is an obvious form of technological scaffolding for building a hot cognitive economy. Alverno has recently created an electronic student portfolio and IUPUI is in a consortium of colleges that includes Chandler-Gilbert developing a template for such a portfolio. Portland State is experimenting with an electronic portfolio.

Software can be designed to facilitate rapid and effective feedback to students, can increase feedback, and can make student work public. And communication technology can reinforce and support communities of practice. In all of these applications of technology, of course, the effectiveness of the technology will be multiplied if it is not contained by the classroom but broadens and extends the students' reach beyond a single learning environment. Hence much of the impact of technology on the cognitive economy depends on the consistency and distribution of technological applications. If students have to learn new programs for each class, for example, it will reinforce the expectation of a short time horizon for learning experiences. If students can apply their technology learning consistently to many courses and build increasing expertise with experience, the use of technology will model the long time horizon that the institution seeks to create for all student learning. If students do not have access to the tools required at home, the institution should make sure that they can have easy, convenient, and inexpensive access to those tools on campus or elsewhere.

DARE TO BE DIFFERENT

Learning Paradigm colleges, unlike their Instruction Paradigm counterparts, will not all be shaped from the same mold. To adopt the Learning Paradigm is to put mission above method, to shape form to function. If the Learning Paradigm were to take hold, colleges would be more different from one another than they are today. Colleges and universities that define themselves in terms of standardized formal processes end up looking a lot alike. "Diversity" is one of the god-words of the academy, but there is precious little of it in the organization and functioning of our colleges.

Colleges that put the ends before the means, though, end up being different—not just different from the standard college, but different from one another. Contrast King's College with CSU, Monterey Bay or IUPUI with the University of Delaware or Evergreen with Portland State. Each has taken a distinctive approach to reform and has come at it from a different direction. What they have in common is clear enough. They have all addressed the same question, the question that was posed explicitly to the founding faculty of CSU, Monterey Bay: What if the purpose of the university were learning? In answering that question, different colleges have come up with different answers. In seeking alignment for learning, they will pursue different priorities and emphases.

The great research universities of ancient lineage and sterling reputation often serve as the models for others in formal characteristics. But the characteristics that make a research university great—Nobel laureates on the faculty, vast endowments, institutes and linkages—are almost completely irrelevant to the mission and purposes of undergraduate education. There is no reason that our leading universities could not become model learning environments. They could and should. But the barriers to change at institutions that are doing notably well staying the same are considerable. Given the enormous resources available to the elite research institutions, their potential to serve the mission of deep learning is great, but unrealized. A university like Harvard or Princeton could, with application and commitment, become the Alverno of the East. But they have set their sights lower.

Yet already, today, we can see the standards of academic reputation changing. New and better evidence is becoming available through tools like the NSSE that provide much more solid indications of the real quality of the learning environment at colleges than have ever been available before. We may hope that the powerful examples of learning-focused programs and institutions that are emerging today and the weight of the accumulated evidence about what works for learning will embolden more colleges to reexamine what they do in light of the central question: What if the purpose of the college or university were learning?

Part of the scaffolding for change that today's institutions require is attitudinal: the willingness to break the mold, to be substantively different, to experiment in fundamental ways. This does not mean that institutions should be reckless or foolhardy. To use Howard Gardner's language, it means that we, like our students, should stop settling for the correct-answer compromise and be willing to take risks for learning.

LEADERSHIP FOR LEARNING

Few words are more frequently misused in discussions of organizational change than "leadership." It is with some trepidation, then, that I raise the issue. But certainly we need it. Part of the essential scaffolding for changing institutional structures and processes is leadership. Sometimes what is needed is for formal leaders, persons vested with authority, to use their authority to remove barriers and open new possibilities. Sometimes what is needed is for persons to step up on a particular issue or problem and assume local, temporary leadership. Sometimes what is needed is just for a member of the group to speak up and say what everybody is already thinking or to raise a question that nobody was thinking about. By raising the issue of leadership, I do not mean to introduce the issue of the kinds of people who are conventionally thought of as leaders. I mean to highlight a process that is often useful in getting communities of practice to do their work.

I won't try for a comprehensive definition of leadership—that task has defeated better minds than mine—but I would characterize a couple of the things I mean by it. There are certainly different types of leadership. In a hierarchical organization, there are folks who make decisions and give orders, which other people then follow. That's a kind of leadership. In political organizations there are folks who make proposals, persuade others, compromise with opponents, and get policies adopted. That's a kind of leadership. But what I want to talk briefly about here is leadership in a collegial organization, in a purposeful community of practice. In such an organization, it seems to me, a leader has two important roles—other than whatever else is listed in his or her job description and hence becomes a part of his or her leadership role. To the extent that the organization is genuinely collegial, the members negotiate the ongoing meanings of its work. The leader has two important roles, and they are derived from the two coordinate functions of a community of practice: reification and participation. In an effective and purposeful community of practice, reification and participation are in balance. The function of leadership is in large measure maintaining this balance.

Clarifying Agreed-Upon Meanings
The first role of leadership is to clarify the reified meanings that the community has adopted. That can involve explaining the rules and the mission to new members. It can involve periodically reminding old members what has been agreed to. And it can involve clarifying the challenges and confusions and failures of practice that require ongoing negotiation. So the president at the opening convocation may remind everyone of the mission statement and review some of the recent history that has helped to define it and clarify it. Or a member of the task force may recap what was decided at the last meeting so that those not present are brought up to date. Or a department chair may chat with a few members of the curriculum committee to make sure that they understand the new policy in the same way. It doesn't have to be someone with an office or a title who exercises this kind of leadership. It requires no authority. The reified meanings that the community has adopted are not the property of the president or the

dean or the chair; they are the property of everyone. So anyone can remind us what we did. Anyone can ask for clarification of what we meant. But this process of putting before the community the meanings that it has settled on is an essential leadership role, no matter who performs it. When it doesn't get done, institutional memory blurs; some members come to formulate what we believe differently than others. Gaps in interpretation open between groups: For some the mission or the goals mean one thing; for others they mean quite another. If the reified meanings that the community has settled on are not clear and current, participation is nearly impossible. Everybody has to be on the same page even to have a coherent argument. This is probably why so many arguments at our institutions are not very coherent. Note that the leadership role here is not to provide for the community or impose on the community reified meanings. The president cannot unilaterally adopt a mission or manipulate the system to produce goals she likes. Wrong word: of course she can. But if she does, she dramatically undermines the credibility and potential of her own leadership by undermining the fundamental functioning of the community of practice. The role of the leader is to clarify to the community what it has chosen to say and chosen to be by articulating and making present to the members the reified meanings they have embraced.

Promoting Ongoing Participation in Articulating Meaning

The second and corresponding role of leadership is to promote ongoing participation in the continuing negotiation of meanings. This is the other side of the coin of clarifying the meanings that have been settled. In a purposeful community of practice, meanings are settled only for the interim; meaning is a work in progress. The reified meanings that describe the history and accomplishment and process of the community are open to renegotiation when they come in conflict or when they fail to satisfy the community. For the community to thrive, the members must participate in negotiating the living meaning of their practice, testing the artifacts of their history against the daily application of purposes to problems. The leader's role is to facilitate that participation and to elicit it where it is not forthcoming.

These two roles, clarifying reified meanings and eliciting participation to revise and advance meaning, are coordinate. One requires the other. If the meanings negotiated through participation never get reified, if it's all talk, talk, talk, and the group never reaches consensus on anything, well, nothing gets done. If the reified meanings are put in a book or a report to sit on everybody's shelf but nobody talks about them, then they die, and the actual process of negotiating live meaning becomes covert. That invariably means that the community breaks up into subgroups, frequently working at cross-purposes. Nobody has a handle on things. For a community of practice to thrive as an agency of purposeful action requires that meanings get periodically reified, and that they get continually negotiated. Leaders are the people who support those processes.

The dynamic interaction of these coordinate leadership roles illustrates an important characteristic of effective leaders. As Parker Palmer says of teachers, the most effective leader is not one who fills space, but one who opens it. Certainly, the leader must sometimes take center stage. The president's convocation speech can clarify the reified meanings the group has settled upon, define the challenges for ongoing practice, and inspire participation. But if the speech fails to facilitate and inspire participation, it has simply failed. The provocative email or the extended comment in the committee meeting can set forth the problem that has to be resolved or the confusion of meaning that needs to be negotiated. Leaders will sometimes take the stage. But the purpose of doing so should be to open up the conversation on the floor, to create the conditions for participation. Without participation, leadership has failed.

Kinds of Leaders: Structural and Functional

There are two kinds of leaders we should think about: structural leaders and functional leaders. A structural leader is someone who has a leadership role because of her position in the organizational structure. Examples are the university president, the provost, the deans, the department chairs. A functional leader is someone who assumes a leadership role because he wants to accomplish something, to achieve a purpose, and must elicit the participation of others in order to do so. An example is the faculty member who suggests starting a roundtable on teaching topics and talks it up with colleagues. A structural leader leads because it is her job to do so. A functional leader leads because it is his mission to do so. An individual can be both a structural and a functional leader. Indeed, the best and most effective structural leaders are almost certainly those who sought leadership position because they wanted to accomplish something, not just to have a bigger office.

Structural leaders affect the workings of the institution because they have substantial authority. But they do not necessarily affect it in the ways that we have just defined as leadership. The person in a position of structural leadership who does not promote participation in the ongoing negotiation of meaning is simply involved in maintaining institutional structures as they are and making them bigger. This kind of maintenance-and-growth role—the most common format for institutional leadership in the Instruction Paradigm—seldom involves the campus community in any genuine negotiation of the meaning and purposes of the institution. Yet the burden of day-to-day duties in Instruction Paradigm colleges makes the maintenance-and-growth mode of leadership tempting. It is also safer, in the sense that negotiating substance is likely to be long, complicated, and perhaps sometimes rancorous. To pose the challenges of learning to a faculty gripped by the Sacramento syndrome risks nasty confrontations and serious efforts to derail the conversation at all costs. But the future of the maintenance-and-growth approach to leadership is probably not very bright. The Instruction Paradigm college offers no promising approaches to the mounting challenges that beset higher education. It has been called to my attention that, while ostriches do not in fact hide their heads in the sand when threatened with danger, some college presidents still do. As a leadership technique, this approach does not hold much promise.

Effective structural leaders are also functional leaders. That is to say, they will use the authority of their offices to achieve the mission of institutional transformation. The central role of leadership for transformation is to help the college community to form and shape a holistic vision of the institution they want to become. And this can only be done well by leaders who both reify the challenges and commitments that present themselves and elicit ongoing participation from the community on how to address the challenges. Parker Palmer (1998) describes the challenge as it applies to the conversation about teaching and learning among the faculty:

> Community does not emerge spontaneously from some relational reflex, especially not in the complex and often conflicted institutions where most teachers work. If we are to have communities of discourse about teaching and learning—communities that are intentional about the topics to be pursued and the ground rules to be practiced—we need leaders who can call people toward that vision.

Good talk about good teaching is unlikely to happen if presidents and principals, deans and department chairs, and others who have influence without position do not *expect* it and *invite* it into being. Those verbs are important because leaders who try to coerce conversation will fail. Conversation must be a free choice—but in the privatized academy, conversation begins only as leaders invite us out of isolation into generative ways of using our freedom.

This kind of leadership can be defined with some precision: it involves offering people excuses and permissions to do things that they want to do but cannot initiate themselves. (p. 156)

Indeed, it would be a bit of an oversimplification—but only a bit—to say that one of the central roles of structural leadership for learning is to provide for the college community what learning communities provide for students: time and space to learn from each other. If structural leaders do that, functional leaders will emerge from the community to help shape the negotiation of new meanings that will lead the institution forward.

If we think of the role of a functional leader not as making decisions but as sparking conversation, the role seems less daunting. And the problem at many institutions is not a lack of ideas or talent but an inability to bring either the ideas or the talent into the shared space of community practice. Whether from the Sacramento syndrome or the simple force of habit, many faculty members and administrators repeatedly deflect and avoid the conversation about learning. At many institutions, the prime role that calls for leadership is simply to get a purposeful conversation going. It is only by talking and listening that groups of individuals come to recognize themselves as communities. These conversations can start in a hundred different ways, but it requires leadership to start and sustain them.

We can all be functional leaders in the effort to create a working community of practice around the issues of teaching and learning. The task of genuine leadership requires no special titles nor extended seniority. Every Learning Paradigm college will be a distinctive product of a living community of practice moving purposefully to realize its own vision of the Learning Paradigm. It is the central role of leadership to bring those communities to conscious action.

THINGS ARE CHANGING

Colleges and universities are changing. The change has not reached critical mass yet, but the growing number of clear examples of institutional movement toward learning, and the growing body of evidence to support further movement, is beyond dispute. We have seen a dozen examples of institutions where transformative change is taking hold—or already has. There are dozens more examples, some every bit as persuasive as those we have discussed here. The 22 colleges and universities in AAC&U's Consortium on Quality Education and the 12 Vanguard Learning Colleges of the League for Innovation in the Community College are all worthy of study, as are the recipients of the Hesburgh Awards and other thoughtful recognitions of educational excellence. Higher education is changing. As Peter Ewell (1998) points out, "we appear to be right in the middle of a major renaissance of interest in the nature of collegiate learning itself and with it, in the things that institutions can do to occasion and create collegiate learning."

The task of transforming our institutions is not and will not be easy. But we never embark upon important tasks because they are easy. We do important work because it is important, because it changes the world for the better. When we act in and on the world in ways that make a difference, we inevitably encounter resistance. When we seek to move things, things push back. Inertia is a natural phenomenon. How we conceptualize it is a personal choice. We can view the inertia of current practice as an irresistible barrier that banishes further effort or as the weight of the resistance that becomes the measure of our effort—as the barrier that ends our work or the clarifying challenge that guides us as we begin and advance that work.

The Golden Rule

BUILDING EXPECTATIONS

If there is one bit of advice that we hear from nearly everyone who is dedicated to substantial improvement in education, it is this: We must maintain high expectations of our students. Pedagogues, scholars, commencement speakers, presidents, deans, faculty leaders, and outside critics all agree that high expectations are a necessary condition for progress. Indeed, it ought to go without saying (but does not) that if we don't expect much, we won't get much. But if this is the nearly universal espousal of higher education leaders, it is advice that is rarely followed in practice. Most of us don't have very high expectations, not really. There is just too much evidence against it. We see these students every day, and we know that, with the few exceptions that keep hope alive, they do not have very high expectations for themselves. They are, to oversimplify only slightly, in college to get out of college. They are cutting their losses and bargaining for the best deal they can get. We hope for the best, we do what we can, but we don't expect a lot. And those who do expect a lot find the ongoing disappointment hard to bear and don't bear it well for long.

Perhaps the first recourse when we cannot maintain high expectations is to blame the students. And this makes a good deal of sense. It is, in a significant way, their fault, their choice. What I am suggesting here, however, is that students are the way they are for a reason. We cannot easily reject the premise that, on average, they are average. They are not significantly smarter or dumber than previous generations of students. They are, if not well educated, basically rational beings. Students are the way they are in school largely because schools have made them so. Being in school, that is how it made sense for them to become.

If we want to raise our expectations of college students, we must raise our expectations of college. We need to make colleges and universities the kinds of places where undergraduate students learn the power of learning, and relearn the power of education. That means making them places

342

where we, along with our students, unlearn the false lessons that the calcified and nonfunctional patterns of schooling have taught us, lessons that serve us all so poorly.

I have suggested here an outline of what a hot cognitive economy would entail, what a robust learning environment would be like. The details are not important. What is important is this: As we change the way we do the work of education, we must at every step move towards expecting more, never less, of our students and of ourselves. A college or a university should be, and can be, a place where people come with high expectations and learn to surpass them. Learning, after all, is discovering that you are more than you thought you were.

SEEING WHAT YOU EXPECT TO SEE

In a writing class it is useful to have an initial assignment that doesn't require a lot of reading or research, so students can begin to perform and get feedback as quickly as possible. Some years ago I began to experiment with topics that would be good to start out with. One subject, I reasoned, about which students have quite a bit of information already is education, since they have all gone to school for many years, in most cases recently. So I assigned the first essay on education, and we started the unit by having everybody in class tell us something about his or her high school experience. I didn't ask for any particular information, just what did they think about school, what was it like? We'd go around the circle and everybody would talk for a few minutes. In many ways, it proved to be an excellent assignment, so I continued to use it for several years and still use a variation of it. For one thing, everybody would talk. They all had experience, and once it got started and people heard what others said they would loosen up and begin to react to things they heard from others and ask each other questions. Over a period of several years I heard from several hundred students. From the very first, the experience affected me powerfully.

I had always prided myself on having high expectations for my students, and hence setting high standards for them. And in a sense this was true. But I was also, and perhaps increasingly, appalled at the low level of preparation they brought to class and their lack of skills and lack of motivation. "What's wrong with them?" I asked myself. So when I had them discuss their experience of schooling, I was interested and amazed and disturbed. Disturbed in part because of the content of their discussion, the narratives of their school experience, the belief that they almost uniformly conveyed of the essential pointlessness of their schooling, the waste of their time, the meaninglessness of it all. There were exceptions, of course—the remarkable teacher, the special class, the group of friends who worked together and found value. But the overwhelming image that emerged from these discussions was of time spent under compulsion for no good purpose.

I was disturbed too because of the way they talked. As they got more relaxed, came to feel that they could speak freely, they began to talk with each other in a more natural and spontaneous way. They talked about the tactics of getting through school: learning what a teacher wanted, distracting teachers to lessen the workload, studying for tests in the most efficient way possible. What I heard unfolding before me was a thought-out and deliberate strategy for what I came later to call a surface approach to learning. Occasionally a student would mention a book, but rarely. The strategy of getting through high school, for most of them, had been a negotiation of teachers' requirements. I was surprised by their honesty—and I said as little as possible so as not to give them reason to hold back. There was nothing really devious or mean-spirited in their approach. It was like listening to a team recap the game. Sure, they tried to win. But they played within the rules, as they understood them. (I'm sure some didn't, but they never brought that up in class.)

At the time I had never heard the distinction between deep and surface learning, was unaware of the term "cognitive economy." So I had no theory to explain my observations. But some formative ideas emerged from the experience. In one class, I even asked the question that had been growing in my mind for some time. A student had just explained how he managed to find out what a teacher wanted and to identify what would be on the test without ever looking at the text. I couldn't hold back. "Are you doing this to me?" I asked. The class laughed, and the young man who had been boasting of his effort-avoidance skills smiled a broad smile and said, "Sure! Of course! It's a proven method." Full marks for honesty.

I brought away two conclusions. One was—and this was a hard learning—that I hadn't really been seeing my students. I had been looking right at them, but I had never seen them. What had been invisible to me was the way they thought about school, and the way they thought about themselves in relation to school. The experience of being an eavesdropper on their conversations with one another gave me a new lens through which to view them. Suddenly they came clear. It was a genuine epiphany. And what I saw, then and since, had much more detail and nuance than what I had seen before. Chiefly, it answered the question that I had implicitly formed: What's wrong with them? And the answer was, there's nothing wrong with them. They're playing the game they learned and playing it well. It was just not the same game I had thought we were playing.

My second conclusion was that I was wrong not just about them but about me. I was wrong about the kind of work I was doing. As a teacher of writing, I had conceived of my work as educating students in writing, especially revision, and what it would now be fashionable to call "critical thinking." I thought of what my class was for in terms of developing abilities like close reading of texts, analysis, synthesis, and invention. Basically, learning to take apart and examine texts and produce your own in response to them. I might say now, though I didn't use that language then, that my goal was to get students to do deep learning with written text. Not a very original view, and not a very controversial one either. But, I realized, completely wrong.

My whole repertoire of means to elicit involvement and engagement were entirely circumventable. Not to put too fine a point on it, these folks could play me like a flute. They knew every trick in the book. They knew how to skim an assignment rather than read it, and soon would find out where to go to get the preskimmed material with even less effort. They had experience divvying up the reading assignments to designated readers who could summarize it for everyone else. They were past masters at going right to the essentials of an assignment that were grade-related and pushing the necessary buttons. Many of them showed enormous intelligence and ingenuity in their approach to avoiding any real engagement with ideas while navigating the teacher-infested waters of that dangerous time-and-effort trap, school.

No, I realized, I was not teaching writing or critical thinking. There would not be much point to that, under the circumstances. Looking at the students in front of me through my new lenses, I saw what I needed to be teaching. I needed to teach them a completely new way of thinking about what they were doing. I needed to change the way they conceived of school, and of themselves in relation to school. I needed give them new lenses through which to see the academic world.

I wasn't going to give up without a fight. I studied their tactics and planned my strategy. Gradually, over a period of years, I made changes. I stopped giving letter grades and gave number scores, and then I stopped giving grades on individual assignments completely. I stopped lecturing—I'll give you no clues! I had them keep journals on all of their reading, and I read the journals. I had them do increasing amounts of collaborative work. I required revisions and required that they respond to my feedback on their papers. I required they give more feedback to each other and that they self-assess all their work. I held individual conferences with each student so that I could look each one in the eye when she told me what she had been doing.

At some point, I don't recall just when though I do recall the moment of awareness, I realized that what I was trying to do was not merely difficult and time consuming; it was impossible. I couldn't do it. Nobody could do it. Not alone. No teacher acting independently, no number of teachers acting independently, could work the transformation that was called for here. That didn't mean that I was wasting my time, of course. My class could still help students. It might, in a few cases, even be the class that opened their eyes to a new approach and showed them they could do things they hadn't known they could do. It was a good thing, not a bad thing. But even if some students left thinking this was a great class and it planted the seeds for future development, most students would leave my class with the same basic attitude toward school learning they had when they entered it. And that meant that the chances were that they would fall back into the pattern of strategic thinking to achieve maximum rewards for minimum costs.

My thinking on these matters has developed, but I still believe that my job is impossible. The only way to do it at all is to redesign it. I've done what I can within the constraints of the classroom. It isn't enough.

The problem is one of expectations. But the root problem isn't our expectations of our students: It is our students' expectations of us. Our students expect the Instruction Paradigm. They count on it. They're prepared for it. If we expect them to behave on any other assumptions we should ask ourselves with the utmost seriousness: Why?

We cannot raise our expectations for our students' performance until we change their expectations of us, of college. And we cannot change their expectations until we change our behavior. They expect to see what they have seen before. They will expect something different when they see something different.

THE GOLDEN RULE

The subject of this book is how and why to change the nature of our institutions so that students can and will expect more. It can seem a long and complicated task, but perhaps I have made it seem too complicated. At root, I think, it is simple. Not easy, mind you, but simple. What we need to do to achieve transformative change for learning can be expressed in a single dictum. I call it, with some temerity, "the golden rule." It is a variation on the Golden Rule of ancient lineage: Do unto others what you would have them do unto you. That is exactly the principle. But we can perhaps articulate it more clearly for the application to colleges. I would put it this way: Do what you want your students to do. Be what you want your students to be. It is a rule that can be applied to and by everyone who works at the college. It can also be applied to and by the college or university as an institution. It is simple. It is testable—we can easily find out whether we are following it. It will not lead everyone to the same answers, but it will lead everyone to discussable answers, ideas that can be shared and tested.

There are many reasons why this is a useful rule, not the least of which being that it is a way of bringing our practice in line with our avowals, and thus achieving the honesty that is ultimately required to achieve integrity. We, as individuals, must have integrity before we can achieve it for our institutions. But another reason for applying the golden rule is that to do so, we must first see our students as they are and then see them as they might be. We must see them, that is to say, as learners. We must see them through the lens of learning. The rule, note, is not "do what you *expect* your students to do." It is "do what you *want* your students to do." Our expectations will not raise us to a higher level unless they are linked to our aspirations.

IMAGINING WHAT TO EXPECT

One of the reasons that we expect so little of our students is that we cannot expect what we cannot first imagine. To expect something, after all, is to project onto an envisioned future the shape of what we have seen yet only in our minds. We must first be able to see it in our minds. We must have the internal vision to project into the imagined future world. This is why so many people expect only what they have already seen. The power of expectation is so great that many stop looking beyond their expectations, fail to see even what is already there, so that life seems an invariant cycle of repetitions. It is not so. Or perhaps it would be better to say that whether it is so or not is entirely in our hands. To purposely create a future that differs from the past in the ways we hope requires two things. We must see what is before us clearly. And we must be able to imagine how it could be better.

To inspire imagination in this sense is one the central purposes of college. I quoted Whitehead (1929) on the point in Chapter 7 and it is worth recalling what he said:

> This atmosphere of excitement, arising from imaginative consideration, transforms knowledge. A fact is no longer a bare fact: It is invested with all its possibilities. It is no longer a burden on the memory: It is energising as the poet of our dreams, and as the architect of our purposes. (p. 93)

If we can see the bare facts of our studies enlivened by imagination, how much more important is it that we see our students in this way? And that is what I am suggesting that we do.

First, we must see our students as they are. "Imagination," says Whitehead, "is not to be divorced from the facts: It is a way of illuminating the facts" (p. 93). To see the thing itself clearly and in focus is the foundation for all useful reflection. And in the case of our students, that means knowing them one by one, attending to them. This is not an easy thing to do, even for one teacher with a class of 30 students. But it is an important foundation for seeing what they could become, for the exercise of imagination founded in what is real.

I am asking the perennial question that students ask of their teachers, but am asking it quite seriously of all educators: What do you want? Not just what do want your students to do, though that is important, but what do you want them to be? What do you want them to become? This is not, I realize, an easy question to answer. To answer it seriously requires serious reflection. When we pose the question in earnest, it implies something that is unstated, but has always been true, about the nature or our work in educational institutions. It suggests that we need to take some responsibility for what our students become. I think that is true—indeed, it is one of the central premises of this book. But I am not at the moment urging you to take responsibility. I am urging you to do the foundational work of deciding what you would like to be responsible for. What kind of students should come out of the experience? How would you imagine the successful student?

This question is similar to the one that began Chapter 1: What are colleges for? But it is asked at a level of detail that allows a more complete and nuanced answer. This is also very similar to the question that many of the institutions we have discussed have posed to themselves: What should our graduates know and be able to do? What should the outcomes of collegiate learning be? And the answers they have produced are often very coherent, if partial, answers. But I do not intend here to impose anyone else's answers on you. Make your own.

You apply the golden rule this way: You reflect in earnest on what you would like your students to be able to do, then you do that. You don't tell them to do it; you don't lecture about it; you don't explain it. You can do any of those things at the appropriate time, of course, but that's not the point. The point is, you do it yourself. You live it. And as a member of the college, you try to get your institution to do it.

Deep Learning

Do we believe that our students should take a deep approach as learners, that they should seek the meaning of the signs, look below the surface? Then we should be deep learners. Not just in the classroom, though certainly there, but in the lab and the library and the curriculum committee and the cabinet. We should not accept formal and conventional signs, including the self-referential code that may describe the functions of our colleges, as sufficient. We should ask for meaning. We should do it as individuals, and the colleges where we work should do it. If we want our students to approach the objects of their learning as isolated bits of factual knowledge—signs without substance—learned for short-term retention, then that is the way we should treat knowledge in the academy—the way that, in large measure, we do. But if what we want to emerge from our colleges is students who seek the meaning of the signs, dig for substance, seek to connect, then we need to seek the meaning, dig for substance, connect. We need to do it in our classrooms, and we need to do it in our curriculum, and we need to do it in our assessment, and we need to do it in our governance and planning.

Active Learning

Do we want our students to be active learners, becoming the self-conscious agents of their own understanding? Then we need to be active learners, and take responsibility for our own agency as seekers and formulators of knowledge. If we want our students to be passive learners, taking in inert knowledge and acting only in response to external demands, then we should certainly follow that policy. But if we do not want that, if we want our students to take the initiative in learning, then we need to take the initiative. We need to do this as researchers and scholars and teachers, certainly, but also as curriculum planners and course and program designers. We need to be active learners about our students and about the learning process itself, for these are the objects of our work. We need to exercise initiative in finding out how well the formal processes that govern our institutions work. We cannot with credibility and integrity call upon our students to be agents of discovery while claiming helplessness about the very process of discovery we are asking them to enact. We must be discoverers, explorers, and experimenters too as the shapers of the learning environment for our undergraduate colleges.

Integrated Learning

Do we want our students to integrate their learning into a holistic framework, to see the elements of their studies as interconnected and relevant? Then we must seek to integrate what we know and what we learn about our own institutions into a coherent whole, to test the connections between the parts of our knowledge and the parts of our institutions. If we want our students to approach the world as a set of atomistic fragments, disconnected and irrelevant, then we should proceed to offer and support a curriculum that does precisely that, and to do our work in the isolated cells of our classrooms and the cellblocks of our departments. But if that is not what we want for our students, how can we possibly justify imposing such a regime on ourselves? If we want them to see the world whole, must we not at least see our colleges whole? Are we not called upon by our own values to connect the disconnected parts and seek to find the linkages in what is now broken?

Incremental Learning

Do we want our students to be incremental theorists, people who believe that effort pays off and that they can build understanding through incremental movement toward clarity? Then we should be incremental theorists. We should believe—and act on the belief—that we can improve with effort, that we can move beyond what we have already done. If we want our students to be entity theorists, to believe that their capacity is set by genetics or upbringing and their potential is predetermined, then that is what we should be. We should regard our own abilities as fixed and regard our institutions as set in an unchangeable pattern that is beyond anyone's control. But if that is not how we want our students to live their lives, then neither should we live our working lives like that. The core belief of incremental theory is the simple faith in the possibility of change. We are not locked by destiny in either our abilities or our limitations. We can do more if we try to do more. If we want our students to believe they can live into new possibilities, then we must believe that we can too. If we want our students to believe they can become what they can imagine for themselves, then we must have the courage to imagine new possibilities for ourselves and our colleges—and try to make them real.

Mindful Learning

Do we want our students to be mindful—to seek the continuous creation of new categories, be open to new information, and to look at the world from more than one perspective? Then we must be mindful as well. We need to learn to take our own work and hold it up, turn it around, look at it from all angles. If we want our students to adopt a mindless approach, reacting to a world of preformatted, one-dimensional stereotypes, then by all means we should adopt a mindless approach to our planning and decision-making. But if we do not want that, then we need to be mindful ourselves. We should look at issues of college governance and curriculum from more than one perspective. Rather than using defensive routines to deflect the search for new information, we should embrace open inquiry. Rather than being locked into a single perspective, determined by the formal structures of our institutions, we should try to understand these structures themselves from multiple perspectives.

Self-Direction and Collaboration

Do we want our students to be self-directed persons who are self-conscious members of working communities? Do we want them to realize both their individual power and responsibility as persons and their irreducible dependence on and need of one another? Do we want them to know their own minds while being capable of empathy and understanding for others? Do we want them to be collaborators, joining together to negotiate the meanings of their learning and their work? If that is what we want for them, that is what we must do, must become ourselves.

DESIGNING FOR OUTCOMES

In Chapter 5, I examined some of what we know about today's students and found them wanting. They are not, by and large, as we would wish them to be. But the way they are is the product of our institutions and of other institutions very much like ours. We have conducted the experiment with institutions designed on the Instruction Paradigm, and we don't seem to be entirely happy with the results. Maybe we should approach it from the other direction. Maybe we should ask what we want to do, and then work backwards to design a system to do it. That is the approach that is taken in outcomes-based education—as we have seen illustrated many times in these pages. These institutions begin by asking how we want the students to end up, and then try to design a system to make them that way. They ask what outcomes we want, and then design a system that is likely to generate them.

The golden rule works on the same principle, but is more expansive in its application. It says that we should be as we want our students to be. It is not just addressed to teachers. It should apply to all the educators who are doing the work of the college. And it should apply to the college or university itself, which is the collaborative structure created and maintained by the educators who do its work.

Today, most colleges and most who work in colleges do not follow the golden rule. Indeed, they employ another imperative with a long tradition: "Do as I say, not as I do." Colleges maintain fixed and fossilized structures, and tell their students to be flexible and open to new things. Colleges reify a set of self-referential, indefinable signs, and tell their students to look for meaning. Colleges break all of reality into tiny parts, locked in hermetically sealed boxes, and tell their students to make connections and see how everything fits together. Colleges impose rigid and permanent, though un-defined, labels through their pervasive evaluation structures, and tell their students to avoid stereotypes and always seek to improve. Colleges isolate their employees and their students into separate, noncommunicating units, and tell their students to collaborate and work as teams. The weakness in this approach is that students are not infinitely credulous.

The verdict, I think, is in on "Do as I say, not as I do." It doesn't work. It never works. A thousand generations of parents have tried the experi-ment, and it fails with a consistency that makes the operations of the law of gravity look random. Yet still we follow it. We say one thing and do an-other. We present an espoused theory that our theory-in-use consistently contradicts.

When I refer to what "we" do in the previous paragraph I mean we as the agents of colleges as institutions. The very hopeful news is that we, as individuals and as educators, often try to follow the golden rule in our per-sonal lives and in our academic practice. Indeed, it is the effort of individ-uals to embody the principles that they believe in that creates the immense misalignment of the Instruction Paradigm college. This misalignment is a most encouraging sign. Because it points to a system that is not content with itself, that has not reached equilibrium but is in a state of potential realignment.

PARADIGMS AND DESTINY

Perhaps the most intractable barrier to institutional change to create a new equilibrium and an alignment around learning is the simple belief in the inevitability of present practices. One defensive routine that is often used to deflect a discussion of change that creates an innovative process rather than just random innovations is what we might call the appeal to destiny: "It'll never happen!"

At root, the defensive routines, the Sacramento syndrome, the various rhetorical tactics that deflect us from talking about learning are manifesta-tions of the Instruction Paradigm defending itself. This is especially clear with the appeal to destiny. It says, in effect, "You can't change, because you can't!" We must be what we are now. We cannot try to become more. We cannot even talk about it.

Yet few claims could be further from the truth. It seems overwhelm-ingly likely that colleges and universities will change. I need not recount the arguments for this view because you have heard them already. You know that the technological revolution and competition and the changing economy and a dozen other factors are changing the climate and character of colleges. Higher education will change. The only question is how. And how soon.

One could make a powerful argument that the economic, technological, demographic, and political pressures that are impelling colleges to change pose a threat to whatever self-determination our institutions have. One could recount the pressures for accountability that threaten to create external mandates that will limit the autonomy and impair the effectiveness of our institutions. Many of these arguments are persuasive and hard to set aside. However, these are not the grounds that I have offered for change here, because I don't think that they are the right grounds for change. If our goal is the right kind of change, we should make that change for the right reasons. And to find the right reasons, we should use the golden rule.

We should ask what we want our students to believe and how we want them to behave on issues of organizational change. Do we want our students to form a vision of the whole that can inspire and engage those around them? Or do we want them to find hiding places in highly structured organizations and do their jobs as defined by others? Do we want them to engage the fundamental issues of their time and their organizations? Or do we want them to deflect conversation about mission and avoid engagement on purposes? Do we want them to take the initiative to create their own communities of practice for purposeful change in the organizations where they work? Or do we want them to seek out protective isolation? Do we want them to take responsibility or shift it down the line? We should try to be the way we would want our students to be and to do what we would have them do.

Finally, we should ask ourselves what we really believe about leadership. As I defined it in the last chapter, any one of us can be a leader. Any one of us can help to clarify and reinforce the meanings that guide our community. Any one of us can participate in negotiating and refining those meanings to better shape our practice to our purpose. What do we want for our students? Do we want them to become functional leaders? Do we want them to actively negotiate the meanings that will shape their choices and their lives? We say that that is what we want. Isn't that what we tell them?

Do we really believe what we say to our students? Many of us do. Many of us feel the frustration of the student who holds back, who steps aside and lets others set the agenda, who reacts defensively and so obscures the issue. We think, of many of them: "You can do it. You can make your point. You can question where you doubt. You can offer a better way. It's in you—I've seen it—so let it out!" We see, in the living, breathing students in our classrooms, the potential, the seed. And at our best we nurture it. At our best we open the space and open the way for them to step in and grow, to become leaders: leaders for the moment, leaders for a cause or for a person or for a belief.

We may or may not believe that the students we have in our classes today are likely leaders. But we want them to be, don't we? We want our students to have the presence and the courage and the trust—of themselves and of one another—to try to move the world to a better place, to take on the burdens, to attack the barriers, to quell the doubts, to inspire others to engagement. We want them to try great things. We want them to believe in themselves, so they can serve, and lead, others.

For too long, we have expected too little of our students. And the reason is that we have expected too little of ourselves. One way or another, we are linked to them. We cannot escape them. If we look at them as they are and find them wanting, inventory their faults and their weaknesses and are appalled, they become our excuse for inaction and our rationale for disillusionment. But if we look at them as they might be, as we would want them to become, as they can be, then they can be our models for right action. The people our students could become, if only we sustain them on the journey, can be our mentors and guides.

Colleges and universities can transform themselves into genuine learning communities. The argument that it can't be done, that transformative change is impossible—the illusory dream of those removed from the realities of life—is clearly refuted. Because many colleges are changing, have embarked upon transformation, are in fact shifting the very paradigm that governs them. We have seen some of those colleges here. Research universities, state colleges and universities, private colleges, community colleges—there are examples in every category that show us what change looks like and what transformation does. It can be done, because they are doing it.

It hasn't been easy. And it won't be. It will take courage and dedication and time. But it can be done. We can do it. This way: Ask what we want our students to do, to become. Do that. Be that.

References

Alberts, B. (2000). *Some thoughts of a scientist on inquiry.* Retrieved February 16, 2002, from http://www.sunysb.edu/Reinventioncenter/Alberts%20article%20for%20web.htm

Alverno College Faculty. (1994). *Student assessment-as-learning at Alverno College.* Milwaukee, WI: Alverno College Institute.

Alverno College Faculty. (2000). *Self assessment at Alverno College.* Milwaukee, WI: Alverno College Institute.

Applebee, A. N. (1996). *Curriculum as conversation: Transforming traditions of teaching and learning.* Chicago, IL: University of Chicago.

Argyris, C. (1982). *Reasoning, learning, and action: Individual and organizational.* San Francisco, CA: Jossey-Bass.

Argyris, C. (1992). *On organizational learning.* Cambridge, MA: Blackwell.

Argyris, C. (1993). *Knowledge for action: A guide to overcoming barriers to organizational change.* San Francisco, CA: Jossey-Bass.

Argyris, C., Putnam, R., & Smith, D. M. (1985). *Action science: Concepts, methods, and skills for research and intervention.* San Francisco, CA: Jossey-Bass.

Argyris, C., & Schön, D. A. (1974). *Theory in practice.* San Francisco, CA: Jossey-Bass.

Argyris, C., & Schön, D. A. (1978). *Organizational learning: A theory of action perspective.* Reading, MA: Addison-Wesley.

Argyris, C., & Schön, D. A. (1996). *Organizational learning II: Theory, method and practice.* Reading, MA: Addison-Wesley.

Association of American Colleges (AAC). (1985). *Integrity in the college curriculum: a report to the academic community.* Washington, DC: Author.

Association of American Colleges and Universities. (2002). *Campus statement: Portland State University.* Retrieved June 3, 2002, from http://www.aacu.org/gex/campusstatements/portlandstatement.cfm

Astin, A. W. (1975). *Four critical years.* San Francisco, CA: Jossey-Bass.

Astin, A. W. (1985). *Achieving educational excellence.* San Francisco, CA: Jossey-Bass.

Astin, A. W. (1993). *What matters in college? Four critical years revisited.* San Francisco, CA: Jossey-Bass.

Bailey Scholars Program. (2001). Retrieved December 6, 2001, from http://www.bsp.msu.edu/

Bandura, A. (1997). *Self-efficacy: The exercise of control.* New York, NY: W. H. Freeman.

Barr, R. B. (1995). From teaching to learning: A new reality for community colleges. *Leadership Abstracts, 8* (3).

Barr, R. B. (1998, September/October). Obstacles to implementing the learning paradigm. *About Campus,* 18–25.

Barr, R. B., & Tagg, J. (1995, November/December). From teaching to learning: A new paradigm for undergraduate education. *Change, 27,* 12–25.

Bauer, K. W., & Bennett, J. S. (in press). Alumni perceptions used to assess undergraduate research experience. *Journal of Higher Education.*

Biggs, J. (1999). *Teaching for quality learning at university: What the student does.* Buckingham, England: Society for Research into Higher Education and Open University Press.

Bowden, J., & Marton, F. (1998). *The university of learning.* London, England: Kogan Page.

Boyer Commission on Educating Undergraduates in the Research University. (1998). *Reinventing undergraduate education: A blueprint for America's research universities.* Retrieved May 12, 2002, from http://naples.cc.sunysb.edu/Pres/boyer.nsf/

Burch, K. (2001). PBL, politics, and democracy. In B. J. Duch, S. E. Groh, & D. E. Allen (Eds.), *The power of problem-based learning: A practical "how to" for teaching undergraduate courses in any discipline* (pp. 193–205). Sterling, VA: Stylus.

California State University, Monterey Bay. (2000). *CSU accountability report.* Retrieved April 17, 2002, from http:// iar.csumb.edu/campus_reports/CSU_accountability_report.pdf

California State University, Monterey Bay. (2002a). *University learning requirements.* Retrieved April 17, 2002, from http://csumb.edu/academic/ulr/

California State University, Monterey Bay. (2002b). *Strategic plan.* Retrieved July 20, 2002, from http://csumb.edu/strategicplan/strategicplan.pdf

California State University System. (n.d.). *Cornerstones implementation plan.* Retrieved January 15, 2002, from http://www.calstate.edu/cornerstones/reports/implment.html

Conway, M. A., Perfect, T. J., Anderson, S. J., Gardiner, J. M., & Cohen, G. M. (1997). Changes in memory awareness during learning: The acquisition of knowledge by psychology undergraduates. *Journal of Experimental Psychology: General, 126* (4), 393–413.

Covey, S. R. (1989). *The seven habits of highly effective people: Restoring the character ethic.* New York, NY: Simon & Schuster.

Covington, M. V. (1992). *Making the grade: A self-worth perspective on motivation and school reform.* New York, NY: Cambridge University Press.

Covington, M. V. (2000). Goal theory, motivation, and school achievement: An integrative review. In S. T. Fiske, D. L. Schacter, & C. Zahn-Waxler (Eds.), *Annual review of psychology* (pp. 171–200). Palo Alto, CA: Annual Reviews.

Cross, K. P. (2001). *Motivation: Er... will that be on the test?* Mission Viejo, CA: League for Innovation in the Community College.

Csikszentmihalyi, M. (1990). *Flow: The psychology of optimal experience.* New York, NY: Harper & Row.

Csikszentmihalyi, M. (1997). *Finding flow: The psychology of engagement with everyday life.* New York, NY: Basic Books.

Csikszentmihalyi, M., Rathunde, K., & Whalen, S. (1993). *Talented teenagers: The roots of success and failure.* New York, NY: Cambridge University Press.

Drucker, P. (1968). *The age of discontinuity: Guidelines to our changing society.* New York, NY: Harper & Row.

Drucker, P. (1993). *Post-capitalist society.* New York, NY: HarperCollins.

Duch, B. J., Groh, S. E., & Allen, D. E. (2001). Why problem-based learning? A case study of institutional change in undergraduate education. In B. J. Duch, S. E. Groh, & D. E. Allen (Eds.), *The power of problem-based learning: A practical "how to" for teaching undergraduate courses in any discipline* (pp. 3–11). Sterling, VA: Stylus.

Dweck, C. S. (2000). *Self-theories: Their role in motivation, personality, and development.* Philadelphia, PA: Psychology Press.

Dykman, B. M. (1998). Integrating cognitive and motivational factors in depression: Initial tests of a goal-orientation approach. *Journal of Personality and Social Psychology, 74* (1), 139–158.

Edgerton, R. (1997). *Education white paper.* Retrieved April 11, 2002, from http://www.pew undergradforum.org/wp1.html

Education Trust. (2000). *Youth at the crossroads: Facing high school and beyond.* Retrieved April 11, 2002, from http://www.commissiononthe senioryear.org/HSReportfinal.pdf

Eliot, T. S. (1943). *On poetry and poets.* New York, NY: Farrar, Straus & Giroux.

Entwistle, N. J., & Entwistle, A. (1991). Contrasting forms of understanding for degree examinations: The student experience and its implications. *Higher Education, 22,* 205–227.

Evenbeck, S. (1999). *University College 1998–1999: The first year.* Retrieved February 28, 2002, from http://uc.iupui.edu/Pubs/State UC/Report1998-99.htm

The Evergreen State College. (2002). *Evergreen is about learning . . .* Retrieved June 4, 2002, from http://www.evergreen.edu/expectations. htm

Ewell, P. (n.d.). *Some notes on the credit hour.* Retrieved June 4, 2002, from http://www.pewundergradforum.org/Credit%20Hour%20Notes. html

Farmer, D. (1999). Course-embedded assessment: A catalyst for realizing the paradigm shift from teaching to learning. *Journal of Staff, Program, & Organization Development, 16* (4), 199–211.

Farmer, D. W. (1988). *Enhancing student learning: Emphasizing essential competencies in academic programs.* Wilkes-Barre, PA: King's College.

Fear, F. A., Doberneck, D. M., McElhaney, K., & Burkhardt, P. (1998). *Students and faculty growing together: How might it be?* East Lansing, MI: Michigan State University, Liberty Hyde Bailey Scholars Program.

Fear, F., Latinen, L., Woodward, D., & Gerulski, K. (2000). Fusing competence and character: Celebrating postmodern expressions in higher education. *Journal of College and Character, 1.* Retrieved February 6, 2001, from http://www.collegevalues.org/articles.cfm?a=1&id=373

Gabelnick, F., MacGregor, J., Matthews, R. S., & Smith, B. L. (1990). *Learning communities: Creating connections among students, faculty, and disciplines.* San Francisco, CA: Jossey-Bass.

Gardiner, L. F. (1994). *Redesigning higher education: Producing dramatic gains in student learning.* Washington, DC: George Washington University, Graduate School of Education and Human Development.

Gardner, H. (1983). *Frames of mind: The theory of multiple intelligenses.* New York, NY: Basic Books.

Gardner, H. (1991). *The unschooled mind: How children think and how schools should teach.* New York, NY: Basic Books.

Gardner, H. (1999). *Intelligence reframed: Multiple intelligences for the 21st century.* New York, NY: Basic Books.

Gow, L., & Kember, D. (1990). Does higher education promote independent learning? *Higher Education, 19,* 307–322.

Grubb, W. N. (with Worthen, H., Byrd, B., Webb, E., Badway, N., Case, C., Goto, S., & Villeneuve, J. C.). (1999). *Honored but invisible: An inside look at teaching in community colleges.* New York, NY: Routledge.

Hagen, A. S., & Weinstein, C. E. (1995). Achievement goals, self-regulated learning, and the role of classroom context. In P. R. Pintrich (Ed.), *Understanding self-regulated learning* (pp. 43–55). San Francisco, CA: Jossey-Bass.

Hill, P. (1985). *The rationale for learning communities.* Retrieved May 18, 2002, from http://learningcommons.evergreen.edu/pdf/rationale.pdf

Hillocks, G., Jr. (1986). *Research on written composition.* Urbana, IL: ERIC Clearinghouse on Reading and Communication Skills.

Howard, J. (2001). *Service-learning course design workbook*. Ann Arbor, MI: OCSL Press, University of Michigan.

Huba, M. E., & Freed, J. E. (2000). *Learner-centered assessment on college campuses: Shifting the focus from teaching to learning*. Boston, MA: Allyn and Bacon.

Indiana University Purdue University Indianapolis. (n.d.). *Principled scavenger hunt*. Retrieved May 14, 2002, from http://www.iport.iupui.edu/OLD%20SITE/scavAssmt.htm

Indiana University Purdue University Indianapolis. (2001). *University college program review and assessment committee report*. Retrieved April 11, 2002, from http://www.planning.iupui.edu/prac/00-01school reports/uc/01ucannualreport.html

Indiana University Purdue University Indianapolis, University College. (1999). *Template for first-year seminars*. Retrieved April 17, 2002, from http://www.universitycollege.iupui.edu/UC/Assessment/Template.pdf

Indiana University Purdue University Indianapolis, University College. (2001). *Campus statement: Indiana University Purdue University Indianapolis*. Retrieved February 28, 2002, from http://uc.iupui.edu/Pubs/StateUC/Report1998-99.htm

Inver Hills Community College, Liberal Studies/Professional Skills Program. (2001). *Liberal studies/professional skills student guide*. Retrieved September 22, 2001, from http://www.inverhills.mnscu.edu/lsps/LSPSStuGuide.pdf

King's College. (1998). *Handbook on assessment for King's College facutly*. Wilkes-Barre, PA: King's College, Office of Academic Affairs.

Kuh, G. D. (1999). How are we doing? Tracking the quality of the undergraduate experience, 1960s to the present. *The Review of Higher Education, 22* (2), 99–120.

Kuhn, T. S. (1970). *The structure of scientific revolutions*. Chicago, IL: University of Chicago.

Langer, E. J. (1989). *Mindfulness*. Reading, MA: Addison-Wesley.

Langer, E. J. (1997). *The power of mindful learning*. Reading, MA: Addison-Wesley.

Lave, J., & Wenger, E. (1991). *Situated learning: Legitimate peripheral participation*. New York, NY: Cambridge University Press.

Lazerson, M., Wagener, U., & Shumanis, N. (2000, May/June). Teaching and learning in higher education, 1980–2000. *Change, 12–19.*

Leamnson, R. (1999). *Thinking about teaching and learning: Developing habits of learning with first-year college and university students.* Sterling, VA: Stylus.

Levine, A., & Cureton, J. S. (1998). *When hope and fear collide: A portrait of today's college student.* San Francisco, CA: Jossey-Bass.

Light, R. J. (2001). *Making the most of college: Students speak their minds.* Cambridge, MA: Harvard University Press.

Loacker, G. (2000). Introduction. In G. Loacker (Ed.), *Self assessment at Alverno College* (pp. 1–22). Milwaukee, WI: Alverno College Institute.

Logan, R., & Geltner, P. (2000). *The influence of session length on student success.* Retrieved July 15, 2002, from http://www.smc.edu/research/T20000410.htm

Lopez, C. L. (1999*). A decade of assessing student learning: What have we learned; What's next?* Retrieved July 14, 2002, from http://www.ncacihe.org/AMpastmaterial/ASSESS10.PDF

Marchese, T. (2000, May/June). Undergraduate Reform. *Change, 4.*

Marton, F., & Booth, S. (1997). *Learning and awareness.* Mahwah, NJ: Lawrence Erlbaum.

Marton, F., & Säljö, R. (1976). On qualitative differences in learning I: Outcome and process. *British Journal of Educational Psychology, 46,* 4–11.

Mazur, E. (1992). Qualitative versus quantitative thinking: Are we teaching the right thing? *Optics and Photonics News, 3,* 38.

McClenney, K. M. (1998, August). Community colleges perched at the millennium: Perspectives on innovation, transformation, and tomorrow. *Leadership Abstracts, 11.*

McKeachie, W. J. (1999). *Teaching tips: Strategies, research, and theory for college and university teachers.* Boston, MA: Houghton Mifflin.

McLendon, M. (n.d.). *Olivet College: Reinventing a liberal arts institution.* Retrieved February 14, 2002, from http://www-personal.umich.edu/~marvp/facultynetwork/cases/olivet/olivet1.html

Meiklejohn, A. (1981). *The experimental college.* J. W. Powell (Ed.). Washington, DC: Seven Locks Press. (Original work published in 1932).

Meld, A., & Hunter, S. (1998). *Environment, experience, and outcomes: Using the College Student Experience Questionnaire for assessment and accreditation.* Retrieved May 20, 2002, from http://www.evergreen. edu/institutionalresearch/ pdf/CSEQpresentation98.pdf

Mentkowski, M., & Associates. (2000). *Learning that lasts: Integrating learning, development, and performance in college and beyond.* San Francisco, CA: Jossey-Bass.

Milton, O., Pollio, H. R., & Eison, J. (1986). *Making sense of college grades.* San Francisco, CA: Jossey-Bass.

National Center for Education Statistics. (2001). *Condition of education 2001 in brief.* (NCES Publication No. 2001-125). Washington, DC: National Center for Education Statistics, U.S. Government Printing Office.

National Center for Postsecondary Improvement. (1999, September/October). Revolution or evolution? Gauging the impact of institutional student-assessment strategies. *Change, 53–57.*

National Commission on the High School Senior Year. (2001). *The lost opportunity of senior year: Finding a better way (preliminary report).* Washington, DC: Author.

National Education Commission on Time and Learning. (1994). *Prisoners of time.* Retrieved June 2, 2002, from: http://www.ed.gov/ pubs/PrisonersOfTime/Prisoners.html

National Research Council. (1999). *How people learn: Brain, mind, experience, and school.* Washington, DC: National Academy Press.

National Research Council. (2001). *Knowing what students know: The science and design of educational assessment.* Washington, DC: National Academy Press.

National Survey of Student Engagement (NSSE). (2001). *Improving the college student experience: National benchmarks of effective educational pracice.* Bloomington, IN: Indiana University Center for Postsecondary Research and Planning.

National Survey of Student Engagement (NSSE). (2002). *The college student report.* Retrieved July 15, 2002, from:http://www.indiana.edu/~nsse/

Nellis, P. (n.d.). *TRS: Teaching in college, an online facutly development program.* Orlando, FL: Valencia Community College.

Nellis, P., Clarke, H., DiMartino, J., & Hosman, D. (2001). Preparing today's faculty for tomorrow's students: One college's faculty development solution. In D. Lieberman (Ed.), *To improve the academy: Vol. 19. Resources for faculty, instructional, and organizational development* (pp. 149–168). Bolton, MA: Anker.

Newmann, F. M., & Archbald, D. A. (1992). The nature of authentic academic achievement. In *Toward a new science of educational testing and assessment* (pp. 71–83). Albany, NY: State University of New York Press.

Norman, D. A. (1992). *Turn signals are the facial expressions of automobiles.* Reading, MA: Addison-Wesley.

Norman, D. A. (1993). *Things that make us smart: Defending human attributes in the age of the machine.* Reading, MA: Addison Wesley.

Northcentral Technical College. (2000). *Barrier free learning: An analysis for the restructuring of the printing/publishing department.* Wausau, WI: Author.

O'Banion, T. (1997). *A learning college for the 21st centry.* Phoenix, AZ: Oryx Press.

Olivet College. (2002). Retrieved February 14, 2002, from http://www.olivetcollege.edu/

Palmer, P. J. (1998). *The courage to teach: Exploring the inner landscape of a teacher's life.* San Francisco, CA: Jossey-Bass.

Pascarella, E. T., & Terenzini, P. T. (1991). *How college affects students: Findings and insights from twenty years of research.* San Francisco, CA: Jossey-Bass.

Percy, W. (1954). The loss of the creature. In *The message in the bottle: How queer man is, how queer language is, and what one has to do with the other* (pp. 46–63). New York, NY: Farrar, Straus & Giroux.

Perkins, D. (1992). *Smart schools: Better thinking and learning for every child.* New York, NY: The Free Press.

Perkins, D. (1995). *Outsmarting IQ: The emerging science of learnable intelligence.* New York, NY: The Free Press.

Petrulis, R. (2002). Olivet College: Portfolio assessment of college-wide learning outcomes. In A. Doherty, T. Riordan, & J. Roth (Eds.), *Student learning: A central focus for institutitons of higher education* (pp. 93–96). Milwaukee, WI: Alverno College Institute.

Polanyi, M. (1958). *Personal knowledge: Towards a post-critical philosophy.* Chicago, IL: University of Chicago.

Portfolio program user's manual. (1997). Olivet, MI: Olivet College.

Portland State University. (2000). *Progress report: University Studies.* Retrieved June 3, 2002, from http://www.ous.pdx.edu/ assess/title.html

Portland State University. (2001). *University studies.* Retrieved June 3, 2002, from http://www.ous.pdx.edu/

Portland State University. (2002). *Senior capstones.* Retrieved June 3, 2002, from http://portfolio.pdx.edu/Portfolio/Community_Global_Connections/Senior_Capstones/

Portland State University, University Studies. (2001). *Freshman inquiry themes.* Retrieved June 3, 2002, from http://www. ous.pdx.edu/frinq/describe.html

President's Commission on the Undergraduate Experience. (2001). *The second chapter of change: Renewing undergraduate education at the University of Michigan.* Ann Arbor, MI: University of Michigan.

Quehl, G. H., Bergquist, W. H., & Subbiondo, J. L. (1999). *Fifty years of innovations in undergraduate education: Change and stasis in the pursuit of quality.* Indianapolis, IN: USAGroup Foundation.

Ramsden, P. (1992). *Learning to teach in higher education.* New York, NY: Routledge.

Ramsden, P., Beswick, D. G., & Bowden, J. A. (1986). Effects of learning skills interventions on first-year university students' learning. *Human Learning, 5,* 151–164.

The Reinvention Center, SUNY Stony Brook. (2002). *Spotlight: Undergraduate research.* Retrieved April 3, 2002, from http://www.sunysb. edu/Reinventioncenter/Research%20spotlight.html

Riordan, T. (1994). *Beyond the debate: The nature of teaching.* Milwaukee, WI: Alverno College Institute.

Schaefer, W. D. (1990). *Education without compromise: From chaos to coherence in higher education.* San Francisco, CA: Jossey-Bass.

Schilling, K. M., & Schilling, K. L. (1999). Increasing expectations for student effort. *About Campus, 4* (2). Retrieved July 18, 2000, from http://www.josseybass.com/JBJournals/tocs/abv4-2art.htm

Schneider, C. G., & Shoenberg, R. (1998). *Contemporary understandings of liberal education.* Washington, DC: Association of American Colleges and Universities.

Schön, D. A. (1983). *The reflective practitioner: How professionals think in action.* New York, NY: Basic Books.

Schön, D. A. (1987). *Educating the reflective practitioner: Toward a new design for teaching and learning in the professions.* San Francisco, CA: Jossey-Bass.

Schrage, M. (1989). *No more teams! Mastering the dynamics of creative collaboration.* New York, NY: Doubleday.

Seanor, D. (2001). *Graphic communication technologies: Barrier free update.* Wausau, WI: Northcentral Technical College.

Senge, P. M. (1990). *The fifth discipline: The art and practice of the learning organization.* New York, NY: Doubleday.

Shoenberg, R. (2001). *General education in an age of student mobility: An invitation to discuss systemic curricular planning.* Washington, DC: Association of American Colleges and Universities.

Shupe, D. (2001a). *A systemic approach to the assessment of student learning outcomes.* Unpublished manuscript.

Shupe, D. (2001b, September-October). Re-assessing assessment. *Assessment Update,* 6–7.

Shupe, D. (2002). *Envisioning a thoroughly academic accountability and a thoroughly accountable academy.* Unpublished manuscript.

Silverman, S., & Casazza, M. E. (2000). *Learning and development: Making connections to enhance teaching.* San Francisco, CA: Jossey-Bass.

Smith, B. L. (2001). Evergreen at twenty-five: Sustaining long-term innovation. In B. L. Smith & J. McCann (Eds.), *Reinventing ourselves: Interdisciplinary education, collaborative learning, and experimentation in higher education* (pp. 65–90). Bolton, MA: Anker.

Smith, B. L. (in press). *Learning community history: Education for what? Education for whom?*

Steinberg, L. (with Brown, B. B. & Dornbusch, S. M.). (1996). *Beyond the classroom: Why school reform has failed and what parents need to do.* New York, NY: Simon & Schuster.

Stevenson, H. W., & Stigler, J. W. (1992). *The learning gap: Why our schools are failing and what we can learn from Japanese and Chinese education.* New York, NY: Simon & Schuster.

Study Group on the Conditions of Excellence in American Higher Education. (1984). *Involvement in learning: Realizing the potential of American higher education.* Washington, DC: National Institute of Education. (ERIC Document Reproduction Service No. ED 246 833)

Sylwester, R. (1995). *A celebration of neurons: An educator's guide to the human brain.* Alexandria, VA: Association for Supervision and Curriculum Development.

Tagg, J. (1998, June). The decline of the knowledge factory: Why our colleges must change. *The World & I, 13,* 293–305.

Tinto, V. (1997). Classrooms as communities: Exploring the educational character of student persistence. *Journal of Higher Education, 68* (6), 599–623.

Tinto, V. (1998). Colleges as communities: Taking research on student persistence seriously. *The Review of Higher Education, 21* (2), 167–177.

Tinto, V., Goodsell-Love, A., & Russo, P. (1994*). Building learning communities for new college students: A summary of research findings of the Collaborative Learning Project.* University Park, PA: National Center on Postsecondary Teaching, Learning, and Assessment.

Transforming undergraduate education: An interview with Richard Guarasci. (2001). *Peer Review,* Summer/Fall 2001. Retrieved May 3, 2002, from http://www.wagner.edu/wagcom/provost/peerreview01.html

Traverso, E. (1996, December). 'Learning': Buzz word or new insight. *FACCCTS: The Journal of the Faculty Association of the California Community Colleges, 3,* 2.

Trow, K. B. (1998). *Habits of mind: The Experimental College Program at Berkeley.* Berkeley, CA: Institute of Governmental Studies Press, University of California.

Truchan, L. C., & Gurria, G. M. (2000). Self assessment as practiced in the sciences. In G. Loacker (Ed.), *Self assessment at Alverno College* (pp. 41–56). Milwaukee, WI: Alverno College Institute.

Tussman, J. (1997). *The beleaguered college: Essays on educational reform.* Berkeley, CA: Institute of Governmental Studies Press, University of California.

University of Delaware. (1997). *Institutional vision for the integration of research and education in science and engineering.* Retrieved April 9, 2002, from http://www.udel.edu/RAIRE/proposal.html

University of Maryland, Gemstone Program. (2000). *Gemstone: Be a part of the solution—2000 annual report..* Retrieved May 7, 2002, from http://www.gemstone.umd.edu/gemstone/info/annual2000.doc

University of Michigan. (1996). *Integrating research and education: Diversity through engagement in research.* Retrieved April 10, 2002, from http://www.undergraduate.research.umich.edu/RAIREapp.pdf

University of Michigan. (1999–2000). *UROP faculty handbook.* Retrieved April 10, 2002, from http://www.umich.edu/~urop/facres/faculty HB.htm

University of Michigan. (2002). *Undergraduate research opportunity program.* Retrieved April 10, 2002, from http://www.umich.edu/~urop/

University of Missouri-Kansas City, Center for Academic Development. (2000). *Review of research concerning the effectiveness of SI from the University of Missouri-Kansas City and other institutions from across the United States.* Retrieved April 17, 2002, from http://www.umkc.edu/cad/si/Sidocs/sidata97.htm

Vaill, P. B. (1996). *Learning as a way of being: Strategies for survival in a world of permanent white water.* San Francisco, CA: Jossey-Bass.

Valencia Community College. (2000). *LifeMap: A learning-centered system for student success.* Retrieved July 2, 2002, from http://valencia.cc.fl. us/lifemap/pbs/

Valencia Community College Strategic Learning Plan. (2001). Orlando, FL: Valencia Community College.

Vygotsky, L. S. (1978). M. Cole, V. John-Steiner, S. Scribner, & E. Souberman (Eds.). *Mind in society: The development of higher psychological processes.* Cambridge, MA: Harvard University Press.

WASC 2001 handbook of accreditation. (2001). Alameda, CA: Accrediting Commission for Senior Colleges and Universities, Western Association of Schools and Colleges.

Watson, G. H., & Groh, S. E. (2001). Faculty mentoring faculty: The institute for transforming undergraduate education. In B. J. Duch, S. E. Groh, & D. E. Allen (Eds.), *The power of problem-based learning: A practical "how to" for teaching undergraduate courses in any discipline* (pp. 13–22). Sterling, VA: Stylus.

Wellman, J., & Ehrlich, T. (2001). *Progress report on the study of uses and alternatives to the student credit hour.* Washington, DC: Institute for Higher Education Policy.

Wenger, E. (1998). *Communities of practice: Learning, meaning, and identity.* New York, NY: Cambridge University Press.

Western Association of Schools and Colleges. (2002). *A guide to using evidence in the accreditation process: A resource to support institutions and evaluation teams.* Alameda, CA: Accrediting Commission for Senior Colleges and Universities, Western Association of Schools and Colleges.

Whitehead, A. N. (1929). *The aims of education and other essays.* New York, NY: The Free Press.

Whitmore, R., & Doberneck, D. (2000). *Bailey at year two: Evolution of the Liberty Hyde Bailey Scholars Program.* East Lansing, MI: University of Michigan, Liberty Hyde Bailey Scholars Program.

Wiggins, G. (1998). *Educative assessment: Designing assessments to inform and improve student performance.* San Francisco, CA: Jossey-Bass.

Wiggins, G. P. (1993). *Assessing student performance: Exploring the purpose and limits of testing.* San Francisco, CA: Jossey-Bass.

Willimon, W. H., & Naylor, T. H. (1995). *The abandoned generation: Rethinking higher education.* Grand Rapids, MI: William B. Eerdmans.

Wilson, C. D., Miles, C. L., Baker, R. L., & Schoenberger, R. L. (2000). *Learning outcomes for the 21st century: Report of a community college study.* Mission Viejo, CA: League for Innovation in the Community College.

Wingspread Group on Higher Education. (1993). *An American imperative: Higher expectations for higher education.* Racine, WI: The Johnson Foundation.

Zydney, A. L., Bennett, J. S., Shahid, A., & Bauer, K. W. (2002). Faculty perspective regarding the undergraduate research experience in science and engineering. *Journal of Engineering Education, 91* (3), 291–297.

Index